KV-421-438

TEN YEARS: TEN CITIES

THE WORK OF TERRY FARRELL & PARTNERS 1991–2001

for Milly: with all my love . Dad . 17.1.02. X

TEN YEARS: TEN CITIES

THE WORK OF TERRY FARRELL & PARTNERS 1991–2001

LAURENCE KING PUBLISHING

Published 2002 by Laurence King Publishing Ltd
71 Great Russell Street
London WC1B 3BP
tel: +44 (0)20 7430 8850
fax: +44 (0)20 7430 8880
e-mail: enquiries@laurenceking.co.uk
www.laurenceking.co.uk

A catalogue record for this book is available from the British Library.

UK ISBN 1 85669 275 2
US ISBN 3-8238-5564-6

Distributed in the United States and Canada by
te Neues Publishing Company
16 West 22nd Street
New York, New York 10010
tel: 212 627 9090
fax: 212 627 9511
www.teneues.com

Design by Sandra Grubic, Wordsearch

Printed in Hong Kong

ACKNOWLEDGEMENTS

At Terry Farrell & Partners the project manager for this book was Jane Tobin. General text was written by Jane Tobin based on Terry Farrell's notes. The images were selected and compiled together with Eugene Dreyer, with general assistance from Beth Thompson. Steven Smith contributed to the city introductions.

Thanks are due to Hugh Pearman for the care and consideration he put into the introduction, setting the practice's work in context, to Ideias do Futuro for their help with the Lisbon chapter, and to TFP Hong Kong and Edinburgh for sourcing illustrations.

The practice is especially grateful for the guidance supplied by the publisher, Laurence King – particularly to Philip Cooper, Liz Faber and Felicity Awdry – and our special thanks go to Diane Hutchinson and Sandra Grubic at Wordsearch for their tolerance and invaluable creative input.

CONTENTS

FOREWORD 7

INTRODUCTION 12

CHAPTER 1: PEARL DELTA SUPERCITY 32

Pearl Island, Cultural Plaza for Guangzhou Daily, Government Headquarters, Kowloon Station + Masterplan, Kowloon Ventilation Building, Peak Tower

CHAPTER 2: BEIJING 88

National Opera House

CHAPTER 3: SEOUL 100

Transportation Centre, 'Y' Building, 'C' Building, 'H' Buildings

CHAPTER 4: SYDNEY 124

Parramatta Rail Link

CHAPTER 5: SEATTLE 136

South Seattle Masterplan, Aquarium + Masterplan for Pacific North-West

CHAPTER 6: LISBON 152

Port of Lisbon Masterplan, EXPO 98 Masterplan, Gare do Oriente, Do Rosso Station + Masterplan, Barreiro Ferry Station + Masterplan

CHAPTER 7: EDINBURGH 174

International Conference Centre + Masterplan, Health Club + Spa, Dean Art Gallery + Masterplan, The Mound

CHAPTER 8: NEWCASTLE 208

East Quayside Masterplan, International Centre for Life

CHAPTER 9: HULL 238

The Deep

CHAPTER 10: LONDON 252

Docklands/Thames Gateway, National Aquarium, Greenwich Promenade, Royal Parks Study, Lots Road, Home Office Headquarters, Three Quays Hotel, Paddington Basin + Orange Headquarters, Swiss Cottage Mixed-Use Development, Samsung Europe Headquarters

APPENDIX 308

List of works 1991–2001, Credits

PLACES + FACES

FOREWORD BY SIR TERRY FARRELL

The work in this book covers ten years from 1991 to 2001. Before 1991 the practice had not worked outside the United Kingdom and virtually all work was based in London. At the end of the 1980s, three large London projects were commissioned, which led to 15 years of reforming, regrouping and restructuring the office – firstly to staff these large projects (the office grew from 15 to more than 100 staff in 12 months), and then to regroup as the projects were completed and new work began in Hong Kong, where we won three competitions in 12 months, between 1991 and 1992. The Hong Kong projects finished at the end of the 1990s, and the staff who had gone there returned to London, ushering in another new period of re-organizing and restructuring. The lead people have stayed constant during the entire period and all are now well used to treating change and adaptation as a normal consequence of exploring cities and places around the world.

The ten cities have been arranged here as much geographically as chronologically. Pearl Delta is the obvious starting point as we have kept an office in Hong Kong since July 1991, when we won the Peak competition. The Hong Kong office energetically links up with work in China, Korea, Singapore and Australia, and staff there have also on occasion visited Seattle. While design leadership has always been maintained in London, it is possible with today's communication to lead and link up from any distance at any time. The Seoul airport building, for example, was designed firstly from our London office, secondly from the engineer's Los Angeles office and thirdly from the Seoul client and local architects' office. The eight-hour time difference between these three cities allowed a continuous 24-hour relay, with each party receiving work at the beginning of the working day and passing on the 'baton' at the close, eight hours later.

The book's journey goes on to Europe via Lisbon and then travels down the British Isles from Edinburgh through Hull and Newcastle, arriving back in London. London has evolved over time, as has our work, and our response to it now is different to what it was during the 1980s. The central concern has always been the relationship between urban design and built architecture; between creating first a place and then evolving an architectural face, which grows out of this deliberate sequencing of the design process. Architecture is grounded; it is fixed firmly to a location, be it town, city or village. There is never a contextual vacuum: the people, culture, history and physical character of a place are always the starting and ending points as the act of creating a new building adds to, and changes in some way, the very place it has grown out of.

Each chapter of this book begins with 'place' and then moves on in sequence to describe the evolution of the built project, to realize the 'face'. Exploring and understanding the world's towns and cities is a passionate commitment here at Terry Farrell & Partners and we have had the privilege to study and work in some wonderful places over the past ten years. Buildings, towns and cities are the most powerful and moving elements of our existence, as powerful as religion, music, art or politics. Yet cities are, and always have been, more than these: they are permanent, public and shared in both expression and achievement. Architecture, and particularly urbanism, I have no doubt, are mankind's greatest achievements.

10 CITIES: 10 LESSONS

It is interesting to speculate on the lessons in city-making that each of the ten cities have provided. Of course, urban issues – including density and transport; the new age of the railway; and pollution and sustainability – repeat from city to city. But from each city there has invariably been a focus for our thoughts and from these I have speculated ten 'lessons' learnt from our work in ten cities over ten years:

1. PEARL DELTA

Good cities, good urban districts and good masterplans are the result of the work of many hands, only achieved as a result of including those who inhabit and adapt them as well as all those who plan and build them.

In Hong Kong, the balance between control and order in infrastructure planning is contrasted with a visual freedom of expression. The city is truly seen as the work of many hands, a collective expression, exaggerated by its very rapid growth. The outcome is a city of extraordinary diversity and liveliness.

2. BEIJING

In our world of increasing global standardization, the good masterplan is physically fixed to its site, and its foundation is the shape, history and general context of the location. Place is often the best and most enduring 'client', and the best source of a 'brief'.

Beijing is an interesting city in which to explore the issue of context. Identity, in the case of Beijing, begins with the Forbidden City, which is made up of an extraordinary repetition of units based on vernacular buildings. One of the challenges of urbanism, as we showed in our Beijing National Opera proposal, is to adjust large-scale city components – buildings and infrastructure – by infusing a sense of identity and place, continuity and conservation, as the very foundations of the project.

3. SEOUL

Culture does not merely take a place within the city – but the city itself and its districts are cultural phenomena. Urbanism is a culture – the culture of place.

Seoul illustrates the way that urbanism depends for its very identity on the culture of place and how in the modern world it can be a considerable challenge to create identity in the face of globalized culture and rapid change and growth. Starting again after the Korean war from Ground Zero, what is the uniqueness of Seoul and how can it develop itself? One distinguishing characteristic is that it has many clearly defined sub-centres that reflect the workings of Korean society. With much of Korean life centred around business empires, or *choebals,* such as Daiwoo, Samsung and Hyundai, each physical centre is a city within a city and each *choebal* is a complete organizational world in itself. TFP's Seoul-based projects respond to the dispersed characteristics of each concept of 'centre', and are self-contained 'centred' worlds within the bigger picture.

4. SYDNEY

Urban design is not the same as big architecture, nor the same as small planning. It has its own professional and skills territory and its own scale and methodology.

The Parramatta railway station in Sydney is a place first – the heart of the town linking to all parts – and a building second. The station as city complex contains a town square, meeting and eating places, and pedestrian linkages re-connecting the city. It is urban design first and building second.

5. SEATTLE

The electronic information age can accelerate change in urban design and its benefits by, for example, increasing democratic participation, explaining, presenting and studying options and choices, and by freeing lifestyles from fixed preconceptions of place and time.

Experience gained from our work on Seattle's new aquarium has shown that the ability to ask questions and get answers from a variety of parties is beginning to shift the way that cities work, as well as the way we react to them. The connected society allows interchange to build new urban concepts. The 'e-place' versus the physical place and mobility versus remoteness are as much key issues for the urban designer as they are for the architect. Seattle represents many of the contradictions inherent in contemporary urban living: the placeless workplace versus the central business district, e-commerce versus the high street and virtual experience versus the real. The home of Microsoft could lead the way in truly creative management of the urban realm.

6. LISBON

The public realm, including infrastructure, is the heartland territory of a masterplan: the use and architecture of individual buildings follow the dictates of the public realm.

I feel particularly strongly about the creation of a tangible public realm, the vital spaces in between buildings. The great European tradition of the 'civic' is exemplified by Lisbon, with its open space of squares, streets and boulevards. These places are the city's living rooms, places where we are able to commune, communicate and be our public selves. The public realm is where the pedestrian is king, where infrastructure (of all kinds) is the glue, the very structure of the city itself.

7. EDINBURGH

A good masterplan should contain nothing less than the entire universe (after architect Luis Barragán, who wrote that 'a perfect garden should contain nothing less than the entire universe').

Edinburgh brings to mind this degree of inclusivity, of diversity: our Dean Art Gallery and masterplan creates a backdrop for the display of Dada and surrealist art that is followed through in all aspects of the design – from the smallest interior fittings to the larger encompassing masterplan. All styles, all opinions, all possibilities – it is this inclusivity that makes great urbanism, where there is inclusivity, tolerance, freedom and variety of choice, and maximization rather than minimalism.

8. NEWCASTLE

A good masterplan energetically reacts to (and receives from) a wide area outside its red line boundary, and a criterion for judging its quality is the breadth of change and improvement it effects beyond its boundaries.

One of the great things about urban regeneration now is the knock-on effect that one successful development – be it architecture or urban design – can have on a whole city, and we look to Newcastle as the example here. No urban site can ever be an island 'entire unto itself'. The success of a masterplan is judged as much by its effect outside its time/space boundary as within its 'red line'. The boundaries of a masterplan are not clear-cut like those for architecture. Newcastle's East Quayside regeneration has had considerable impact in the transformation of Tyneside, which includes such adjacent projects as our International Centre for Life, Wilkinson Eyre's Millennium Bridge, Norman Foster's music centre and Dominic Williams's Baltic Mills, and the regeneration of the railway station lands and Ouseburn Valley.

9. HULL

When done thoroughly and with full follow-through, masterplanning and urban design are today's best vehicles for adapting and changing our cities and towns for the better.

The transformation of Hull from a run-down city to a flourishing urban centre addresses the long-term aspects of urban design and regeneration through a series of masterplans and architectural projects such as The Deep – a public aquarium millennium project designed to act as the iconic 'face' for the regenerated city. Masterplanning is affecting the urban renaissance in this depressed northern city. Long-term commitment is characterized by continuously revisiting and re-evaluating social, economic and environmental sustainability, the basic criteria for effectiveness.

10. LONDON

Masterplanning is process driven: unless this is recognized and accepted virtually no progress can be made.

There are various cynical approaches to masterplanning, such as that of the client, who will procure a masterplan in order to obtain a planning consent but will evidence no follow-through, or of the architect, who will agree to provide a masterplan for free in order to get a building out of the process. This is not masterplanning as it could and should be. During the last 200 years, London has had very little proper masterplanning and urban design input. It is a city that has grown from being a collection of villages to a great world metropolis, without the intervening stages of a coherent civic life, of being a city, an urban unit, bypassing the familiar traditions of European urbanism. The most critical factor is much-needed civic leadership, continuity and sustainability. It is management and leadership that really make the long-term difference. Good civic leadership has made a radical difference in places as diverse as Hong Kong, Barcelona, Portland, Oregon, and Bilbao. Poor civic leadership (or none at all) has led to London's ill-maintained, under-invested public transport system and appalling public realm deficit. While it is masterplanning and urban design that are today's most effective vehicles for achieving change in our cities, it is the misunderstanding of the processes involved in revitalizing and successfully managing cities (not money or any other factor) which is the biggest single impediment to change.

INTRODUCTION

INTRODUCTION
BY HUGH PEARMAN

Terry Farrell used to be easy for us critics to pigeonhole. He was the apostate, the one who had renounced the faith of cool orthodox modernism in favour of something altogether gamier, more pagan. So the pigeonhole we selected was the one marked postmodernism. And this was true, up to a point. But the question should not have been: is Farrell post-modern? The question might have been turned around. Given that Farrell was post-modern, then who else was, from that period? Jim Stirling? Jeremy Dixon and Edward Jones? Aldo Rossi? Frank Gehry? Even Richard Rogers? Select your own list: your *pigionnier* will quickly become full to bursting with architects, most of whom always vehemently denied they were post-modern, or anything like it.

Now, time has passed and the aesthetics and politics of architecture have moved on. There is no style war in progress today. It is not a question of us and them. It is not necessary to take sides. It is becoming rapidly apparent that both sides borrowed heavily from each other during that experimental period. There is now virtually no disagreement between the key figures in contemporary architecture over the necessary steps to take to re-civilize our cities. Many of these steps were outlined by Farrell in some early urbanistic studies. The difference, then, is increasingly one of detail, of personal expression in a continuum. Without wishing to second-guess the immediate future, we would not appear to be operating in a time of manifesto statements and architectural divergence. It is, instead, a time of architectural synthesis and convergence. All architects have heroes and, in the case of Farrell, what can be traced throughout his work is the influence of Frank Lloyd Wright, Louis Kahn and Robert Venturi: three architects with such different approaches tending to colour his work at different periods of his professional life, but all with a taste for the monumental.

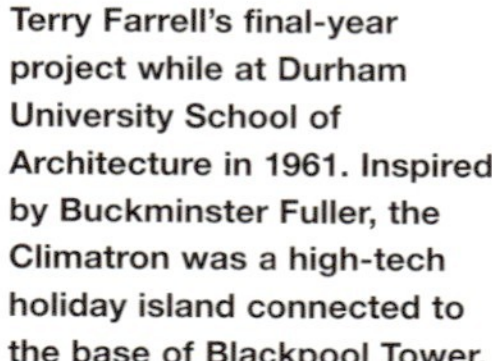

Terry Farrell's final-year project while at Durham University School of Architecture in 1961. Inspired by Buckminster Fuller, the Climatron was a high-tech holiday island connected to the base of Blackpool Tower.

The northern Blackwall Tunnel ventilation shaft, 1961–64, with Richard Rogers' Reuters Building (right), public housing by Erno Goldfinger (behind) and Robin Hood Gardens by Peter and Alison Smithson (left).

The southern Blackwall Tunnel ventilation shaft within the Millennium Dome, 2000.

Farrell is an architect who, like all architects, has continued to evolve his own personal style. Moreover, he has expanded his horizons significantly. He used to be a London architect. He used to do small buildings. Now, he is an international architect, and does some very large buildings and building complexes indeed. Moreover, his particular strength – that of architect-planner, or, if you prefer, urbanist – has been given full rein. This is why this book adopts the form it does: being primarily about the particular characteristics of certain world cities and megalopolises, and secondarily about the Farrell interventions within those areas. In that sense it is to do less with architecture, and more with spirit of place. Which prospect brings a smile to the lips because context is one thing, but response to context is quite another. The one thing you never normally expect a Farrell building to be is a built understatement.

True, there are some buildings, such as the Dean Gallery in Edinburgh or the Lots Road power station-into-apartments project in London's Chelsea, which are essentially re-orderings of existing historic buildings – and this has always been a Farrell strength because he has always relished working work with, and around, existing structures. It is part and parcel of dealing with the difficult, rewarding, city. But there are other places, such as Kowloon in Hong Kong, where you are effectively at a city's Year Zero. You might find yourself, as Farrell and sundry other architects have done in both the Far East and Europe, building on newly-made land. Land which was even previously sea. In that context, you have to make your own context. Thus the diametric opposite of the Dean Gallery would be the Kowloon Station Interchange of 1992–8, a great hall that breaks the tyranny of the pure arch: or its more biomorphic successor in Korea, the integrated transportation centre for Inchon International Airport. For all that these are self-contained worlds, in both of these you see some evidence of Asian influence. It is a world away from the crude iconography employed by some Western architects upon winning commissions in Eastern regions, but it is nonetheless the case that Farrell employs different abstract imagery in Europe or America.

But let us go back right to the beginning. From September 1961 to April 1962, Farrell worked in the architects' department of the London County Council – his first job in his early twenties on returning from the University of Pennsylvania where, as a Harkness Fellow, he had studied under Kahn and Venturi at what was a crucial time of their development as well as his. The LCC, a noted public office, was the first job for so many architects of the day, particularly those who, like Farrell, were gaining practical experience prior to official qualification. There, for instance, he met his future partner Nicholas Grimshaw. At the end of 2000, an identical pair of buildings he designed in the LCC's Special Works Division at that time was officially 'listed' by the government as being of historic and architectural importance. The twin buildings are the ventilation shafts of the Blackwall Tunnel, a duplicate road tunnel in East London built to relieve pressure on the late Victorian original alongside and form an under-river link in what was intended to be part of an inner London motorway 'box'. Only fragments of the motorway box were ever built, but the eastern section including the new tunnel was one of them.

Early influences, from left to right: Pier Luigi Nervi's Palazzo dello Sport, Rome, of 1960, Frank Lloyd Wright's Falling Water, Pennsylvania, of 1935 and Buckminster Fuller's New York dome of 1965–66.

Farrell also worked on such mundane but vital matters as the tunnel linings and the maintenance yard, but it is the ventilation shafts that received their due acknowledgment 40 years later. Some see them as influenced by Oscar Niemeyer's work in Brasilia, but according to Farrell this is not so: he refers instead to Felix Candela and Pier Luigi Nervi, prime exponents of advanced concrete structure. The funnels are beautiful white sculpted curvilinear objects, each designed both to vent exhaust fumes, draw in fresh air and monitor pollution. They are therefore a precursor to the exhaust/inlet stacks of many an eco-friendly, naturally ventilated building of today. They exploited the then-new technique of sprayed concrete on stressed cables to achieve their fluidity of form. One can perhaps detect certain influences such as the rooftop ventilator stacks on Le Corbusier's Unité d'Habitation in Marseilles, but Farrell's are at once more 'modern' and older. They fit the mood of the early space age, yet they betray a certain nostalgia for the ocean-liner architectural symbolism of the 1930s.

They had sat in this forgotten district of East London for decades, surrounded first by old-fashioned industrial processing complexes, latterly by urban wasteland as the area became ripe for redevelopment. You had to be a pretty serious architecture buff to take the trouble to find them. What helped to bring them to official attention after so many years of virtual invisibility was the building of Richard Rogers and Mike Davies' Millennium Dome on the cleared North Greenwich peninsula – the southern landfall of the tunnel. The Dome virtually filled the site and had to make allowances for the tunnel rising beneath and its ventilation shaft. Davies' solution was simply to punch a tubular aperture through one side of the Dome for the stack to sit in: thus it could absorb it, like an amoeba. Ideas were batted to and fro between Farrell and Davies over ways to display the stack to the Dome-going public, perhaps linking the visual display with a televisual one showing the rushing traffic in the tunnel beneath. Unfortunately the idea was squashed by safety concerns: the powers that be did not want the presence of the tunnel to be manifested. The section of Dome enclosing the stack was not made transparent, and very few visitors were ever aware of the reason for the strange tensioned-fabric intrusion into the otherwise perfectly symmetrical space.

No matter: Farrell's first built public work had become associated with the Dome and with the regeneration of both North Greenwich and – on the other side of the river – Poplar, where the organic aesthetic of the tower is in marked contrast to both the 1960s exposed-concrete aesthetic of housing blocks by the Smithsons and Erno Goldfinger, and the later machine aesthetic of Nicholas Grimshaw's *Financial Times* printworks and Richard Rogers' Reuters data centre. Interested architects sought out the designer of the vent shafts: it was architect Ian Ritchie whose researches first revealed the hand of Farrell. With wholesale redevelopment now well under way on both sides of the river, the towers were perhaps becoming vulnerable. Hence their subsequent listing. It is interesting to note that, in the mid-1990s, Farrell returned to this overlooked building type with his Kowloon Ventilation building. This serves the rail link from Hong Kong out to Norman Foster's new Chek Lap Kok airport. Containing floodgates and power transformers as well as ventilation plant, it is sited in Kowloon Point Park overlooking Victoria Harbour, so required a greater than usual public presence. Its powerfully angled and brightly coloured towers – one thinks again of funnels or ventilator horns on ships – make an important mediation between the busy waterfront and the towers of the city behind – including, on the skyline, the raised hull of Farrell's Peak building.

The listing of the Blackwall vent towers was important because of the way they reminded everyone that there was a great deal more to Farrell's architecture than his high-profile London commissions of the 1980s. In this context one might, for instance, also consider his 'Climatron' student thesis project, much influenced by the thinking of Richard Buckminster Fuller at a time when Fuller was not the household name he is today. The American influence on the young Farrell was significant, as it was on so many other architects training in the 1950s and early 1960s, from Richard Rogers and Norman Foster to John Winter. Each extracted what he wanted from the experience. For some, it was Eames and the Californian Case Study Houses. For others, the inspired Brutalism of Paul Rudolph. Farrell appears to have cast his net wider than most.

Then came the years of the Farrell Grimshaw partnership, from 1965 to 1980. Sitting in the same room, working often on the same projects, Farrell and Grimshaw carved out a niche for themselves in the then very English field known as high-tech. Equally English was the very low-cost nature of many of the projects – factory units, warehouses and so forth. But again, a significant building from that time has recently been listed: the 1970 Park Road apartment tower, which took advantage of new legislation allowing housing co-operatives to be set up. Farrell worked mainly on the planning and overall form of the building, Grimshaw the detail design. Among those who lived in the tower in the early years was John Young, later to be crucial to the success of the Richard Rogers Partnership. Given the often short-life nature of many early high-tech projects, with some iconic buildings by various hands now demolished, the official recognition of Park Road is timely.

With Farrell Grimshaw, Farrell worked on such projects as the spiral student hostel 'service tower' of 1967 in London, the 1972 Citroën warehouse in Runnymede, Thames Water Authority building, and Wood Green industrial units. Then the two architects went their separate ways, but it is a mistake to assume that Farrell immediately plunged into post-modernism. What he did, working at various times with architects Jan Kaplicky and Eva Jiricna and the structural engineer Peter Rice, was to start to hybridize high-tech into something else. Fascinated by the possibilities of lightweight structures, he produced in 1981 what was then the largest architectural use of Teflon-coated fabric in the UK, a temporary exhibition hall at the fire-damaged Alexandra Palace in north London.

Classical references started to appear in his Clifton Nurseries projects in Bayswater and Covent Garden, but what set the mood for the Farrell of the later 1980s, however, was the cheap and cheerful TV-AM headquarters in Camden Town of 1981–2, complete with fibreglass eggcups on top. Something else, clearly, was going on. The image boost that TV-AM – Britain's first independent breakfast TV channel – gave Farrell was out of all proportion to the size or cost of this relatively basic renovation job. It led to a sequence of projects culminating in the three landmark London projects commenced later in the decade.

These require some examination before we return to the most recent projects: firstly because of their prominence, secondly because of what they tell us about the political and commercial imperatives of the times, and finally because they fixed an image of Farrell in the British mind which is only now beginning to change in view of both the earlier and the later work.

These three projects were what first catapulted Farrell's practice from the fringe to the mainstream. Ever since he had split with Grimshaw in 1980, Farrell had been in the news for breezy, low-budget projects such as TV-AM in Camden Town or Limehouse Studios in the West India Docks: both adaptations of existing industrial buildings, both essentially decorated sheds. These were regeneration stormtroopers, anticipating what turned out to be a massive revival of their respective inner-city and docklands areas. Limehouse Studios, a former banana warehouse, vanished to make way for the Canary Wharf office city, London's equivalent of New York's Battery Park City, Paris's La Défense, or Kuala Lumpur's new commercial district.

40 co-ownership flats, Park Road, London, 1970.

Water Treatment Centre, Reading, 1982.

Top left: Alexandra Pavilion, Haringey, London, 1981.

Centre left: Clifton Nurseries, Bayswater, London, 1979.

Centre right: Clifton Nurseries, Covent Garden, London, 1980.

Bottom left: Interior of TV-AM, Camden, London, 1982.

Bottom centre: TV-AM on the cover of *Architectural Design*'s British Architecture special issue, 1982.

Top right: Charles Jencks's house, London 1981.

Top left: Interior of Terry Farrell's house, Maida Vale, London, mid-1980s.

Top right: Limehouse Television Studios, West India Docks, London, 1983.

Bottom: Comyn Ching Triangle, Covent Garden, London, 1985.

Arguably more typical of Farrell's approach at this time was the painstaking repair and reinterpretation of a venerable block of buildings in London's western Covent Garden/theatreland area: the Comyn Ching Triangle, named after a firm of architectural ironmongers of that name which inhabited the decaying block. This too anticipated and to a large extent instigated the subsequent revival of what had become a dead zone, such that by the end of the 20th century the immediate area was home to some of London's most fashionable hotels and restaurants. It is often the case that Farrell's projects are catalysts for regeneration, bridgeheads into previously run-down or even derelict areas. His Tobacco Dock project of the late 1980s is a further example: the enlightened conversion of a remarkable surviving Georgian warehouse complex into a speciality shopping centre. The economic recession of the early 1990s meant that it had to wait some years for London to catch up with it. One must remember that he is an example of what, in Britain, is an increasingly rare breed: the qualified architect-planner, a member of two ideally congruent professions that had, towards the close of the 20th century, become increasingly separate, to the point of confrontation.

The scale of Farrell's projects – and of his office – then expanded rapidly and irrevocably in the economic boom of the late 1980s. From such creative make-do-and-mend exercises, he found himself suddenly commissioned for three new London buildings that were large and prominent enough to be complete urban landmarks and which, in a sense, summed up the feel of an era: politically, the Thatcher era. These were Embankment Place, an office and retail development which clasps within itself the Charing Cross railway terminus; Alban Gate, similarly commercial, the first big piece in the redevelopment of the 1960s slab-and-podium office district of London Wall; and the Mayan fortress of Vauxhall Cross, facing Tate Britain, the original Tate Gallery, across the Thames. Add to these Farrell's unbuilt masterplans for the South Bank cultural centre and the slightly later commercial-classical Paternoster Square office district north of St. Paul's Cathedral, and you have a body of work of which it can be said: ah yes, that was the 1980s. Even if much of it spilled over into the 1990s. Decades, after all, have a habit of starting and ending late.

Again, this analysis is true up to a point. It would be difficult to imagine such a trio of giant calling cards being built today, even by Farrell. At the time they were controversial, providing as they did fuel for the modern-postmodern debate. But time and familiarity have done their work, neighbouring blocks have been built subsequently, the city has proved as absorptive as ever, a certain amount of reassessment has taken place. Of the three, the one with the most prominent site and most glamorous associations – Vauxhall Cross, which happens to be the headquarter of MI6, the British secret service – has even (along with Tobacco Dock) received the blessing of a starring role in a James Bond movie's opening action sequence. It also happens to be the oldest design of the three, since it was modified from an earlier competition-winning scheme for housing: first as a speculative office building, and finally as a very bespoke HQ for an organization with very particular security needs. Again, given that the riverside in Vauxhall was one of the bleakest, most blighted, most hostile areas in London, this turned out to be the first piece in a jigsaw of regenerative schemes that is only now coming to completion. Perhaps it is the very massiveness of the MI6 building, with its honey-coloured concrete panelling and thick green glass, which has given it the edge over the other two – which are commercial buildings, built to a market price.

Farrell's undoubted monumentalism is often achieved by sleight-of-hand – hence the early decorated sheds – but at Vauxhall Cross you get the real thing. Farrell, however, was already moving decisively away from that particular aesthetic.

Opposite: Embankment Place, London, 1990.

Villiers Street redevelopment, Embankment Place, London, 1990.

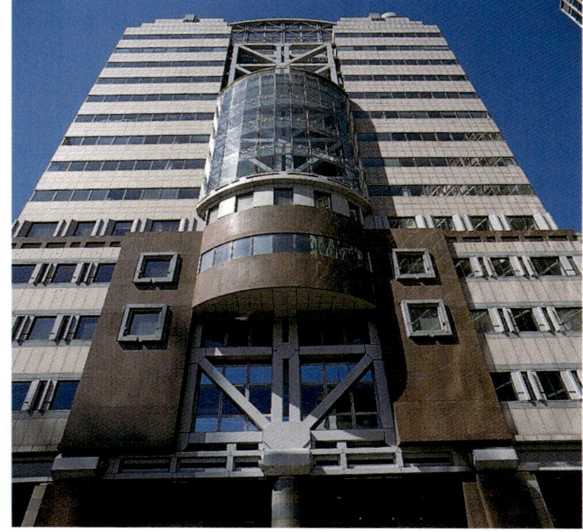

Alban Gate, London Wall, 1992.

Vauxhall Cross
(MI6 headquarters),
London, 1992.

Alban Gate, designed later but completed contemporaneously, is certainly bulky – it consists of two large-floorplate office blocks, hinged where they touch at one corner, with one block spanning a road junction on the four-lane highway of London Wall. But it is far lighter than the Vauxhall building in its elevational details and incorporates a four-storey all-glass curved curtain wall which shows Farrell can do the high-tech thing with perfect aplomb if he so chooses. This is, however, only a detail. Farrell was not concerned with the kind of transparency achieved a decade later by Richard Rogers' Daewoo building, built opposite. He was consciously making a landmark – the building was intended as a gateway to the City of London's financial district, an equivalent of the old barbican fortified city entrances. In this, it does not wholly succeed, not least because of the bulk engendered by the large-floorplate obsession of the time – there was a huge cult of the City 'dealing floor', which became a developers' obsession and which has now largely vanished as working methods have changed. Typically, he was also concerned with making a fragment of mixed-use city rather than a monocultural pile – as happened also at Embankment Place but not, because of its high-security demands, at Vauxhall Cross. It tends to be forgotten that Alban Gate incorporates housing: and that this is not housing within the towers, on the American model, but low-rise housing around a sheltered square at the building's base. This was the first new housing development within the boundaries of the City of London since the immediately adjacent Barbican area was laid out in the post-war years.

So what do we mean when we talk about Farrell in the post-modern context of this time? To add buildings to some of the names cited at the start of this introduction, the 1980s in London were also about the completion of Richard Rogers' baroque-tech Lloyd's of London building, of Stirling's freestyle-classical Tate Gallery extension and the first designs of his Number One Poultry office/retail complex. They are about the first, classically-tinged design for Jeremy Dixon and Ed Jones's Royal Opera House redevelopment, which survives virtually unchanged in the reinstated arcade of the north-eastern corner of the Covent Garden piazza. (By one of those fine London coincidences of which writer Peter Ackroyd is so sensible, this element of the Opera House was built on the site of an earlier, temporary Farrell building, the tongue-in-cheek classical temple of Clifton Nurseries which combined Venturian irony with advanced tensile-fabric technology.)

The 1980s were also about Nicholas Grimshaw's *Financial Times* printworks, famously described as 'an inlaid jewel box' by Jean Muir, in the glass and metal façade of which you can, if you are so minded, trace the ghostly, perhaps subconscious, outline of classical columns, cornice and frieze. This approach is to be found much more overtly in Norman Foster's Carré d'Art in Nîmes, designed in 1985 but not completed until 1993. The impact of a neo-classical revival on the ultra-modern architects of the 1980s is worthy of a study in itself. But the decade also bore differently interesting fruit in the form of John Outram's cosmological, highly symbolic architecture – mostly denied its full expression in Britain, though it finally reached a logical, explosively polychromatic conclusion in his Computational Engineering Faculty of 1993–7 at Rice University, Texas. Earlier, Will Alsop and John Lyall had gone through what may loosely be described as their post-modern phase with the unbuilt Riverside Studios project. Nigel Coates, with Doug Branson, was putting flesh on the bones of his 'narrative architecture', Zaha

Hadid was splintering and skewing, designing, coincidentally, the first competition-winning design for Hong Kong's Peak Club. All this just relates to the British contingent, because Britain at that time was undergoing an architectural step-change more sudden than that of many countries. But the questioning was of course global, and related questions, yielding different answers, were being asked by Rossi, Mario Botta, the Krier brothers, Frank Gehry, Eric Owen Moss, Arata Isosaki, Makoto Sei Watanabe, Jean Nouvel, Bernard Tschumi, Renzo Piano, Daniel Libeskind, Rem Koolhaas, Wes Jones, Edmond and Corrigan, Coop Himmelb(l)au, Michael Graves, Philip Johnson... again, compile your own list. The Memphis collective of designers and architects, to take just one example, was hot in the early 1980s. For the true Memphis building, however, we had to wait until the Groningen Museum of

Above: Terry Farrell (right), and his brother, visit the Festival of Britain, South Bank, London, 1951.

Opposite: Southbank Masterplan, London, 1984–92.

1990–94, masterminded by Alessandro Mendini: building as designer tea set, a compact urban masterplan, with architects lifted out or dropped in at will. This is the context in which one must judge Farrell's work of the time.

So it all depends on what filters you wish to use when scrutinizing the architecture of the 1980s, what symbols you wish to seek. Summing up all these incredibly disparate approaches, we can say now, with an obviousness verging on bathos, that the mood amongst all the leading architects of the time was for a return to richness, a greater expressiveness. What that richness might consist of was the matter in hand. All of the buildings mentioned above are questioning buildings. They are what-if buildings, where-do-we-go-from-here buildings. From that period of inquiry, of self-examination, all were setting off in their own new directions. Farrell's outlook was evolving as rapidly as that of any of his colleagues, at home or abroad.

At this point, Farrell changed abruptly from being a London architect to an international one as the market collapsed at home and a string of large new commissions, many in the Far East, came his way. This meant that the experimentation continued overseas: which meant in turn that perceptions in Britain of where Farrell stood tended to remain rooted in the 1980s. The pictures from overseas did not show much sign of a return to conventional modernism: on the other hand they were very different from the earlier work, taking on – in such projects as the Peak Club in Hong Kong, or the Kowloon transport interchange – an almost Futurist feel. Farrell was still a problem architect for the pigeonholers. If he were a Shakespeare play, he would be *Measure for Measure*.

You can look at Farrell in two interlinked ways: as an architect of buildings, and as a planner of urban districts. Because his indicative masterplans often, in the past, involved sketch buildings of his own devising, this sometimes suggested that a particular architecture would dominate the composition. This was certainly a widespread misunderstanding of his South Bank Centre masterplan in London, 1988. The first of many by successive hands, it is still regarded, when it is thought about at all, as being all about Farrell architecture. In fact – as is normal with masterplans – a variety of architects was always going to take part as the various elements of the cultural quarter were built out. Such was the case with the Paternoster Square masterplan, which got a lot further down the road before the economic doldrums took their toll. In both cases, it is instructive to look at the spaces between and through the buildings rather than at the indicated façade treatments: immediately what you find is an

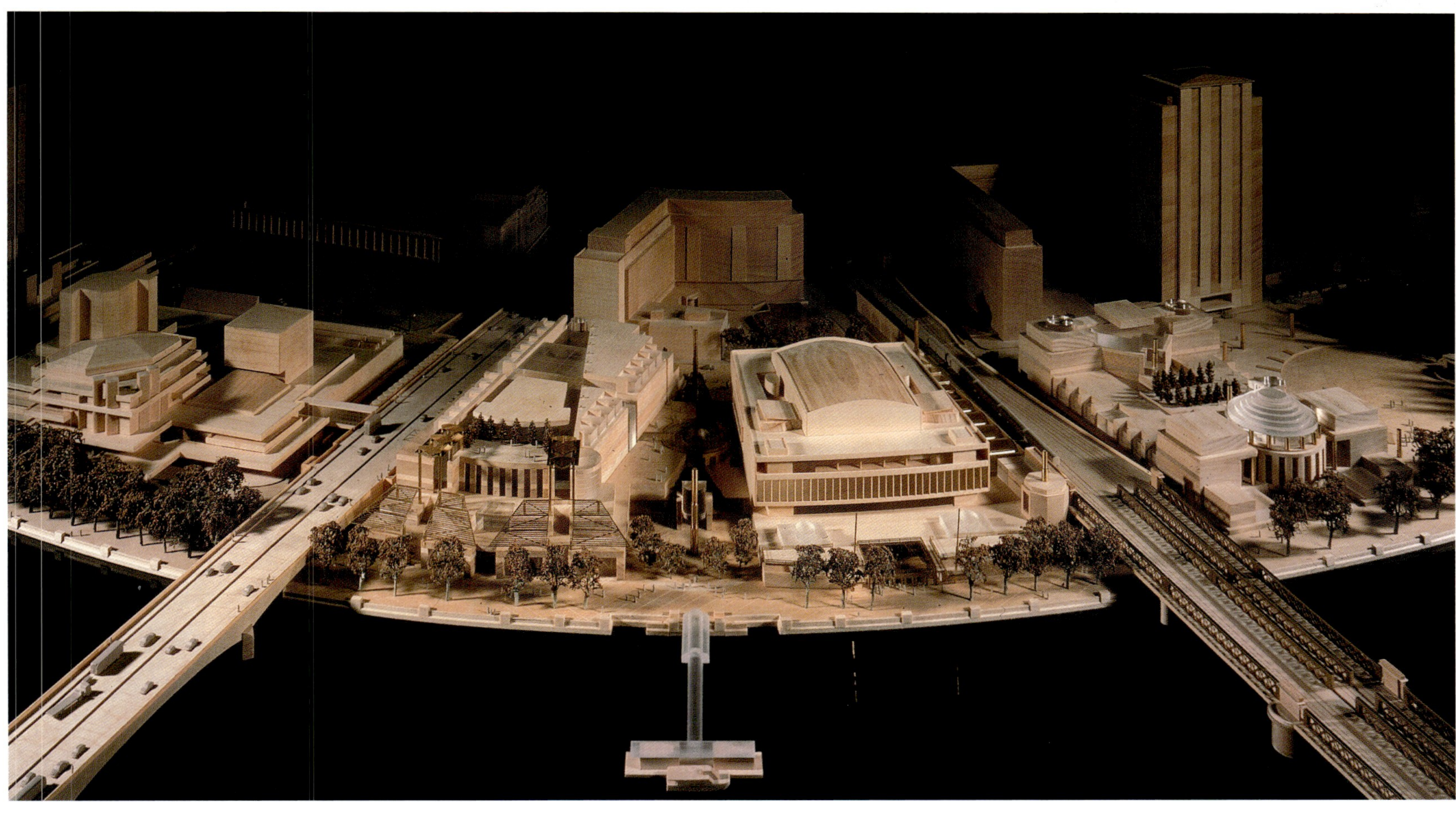

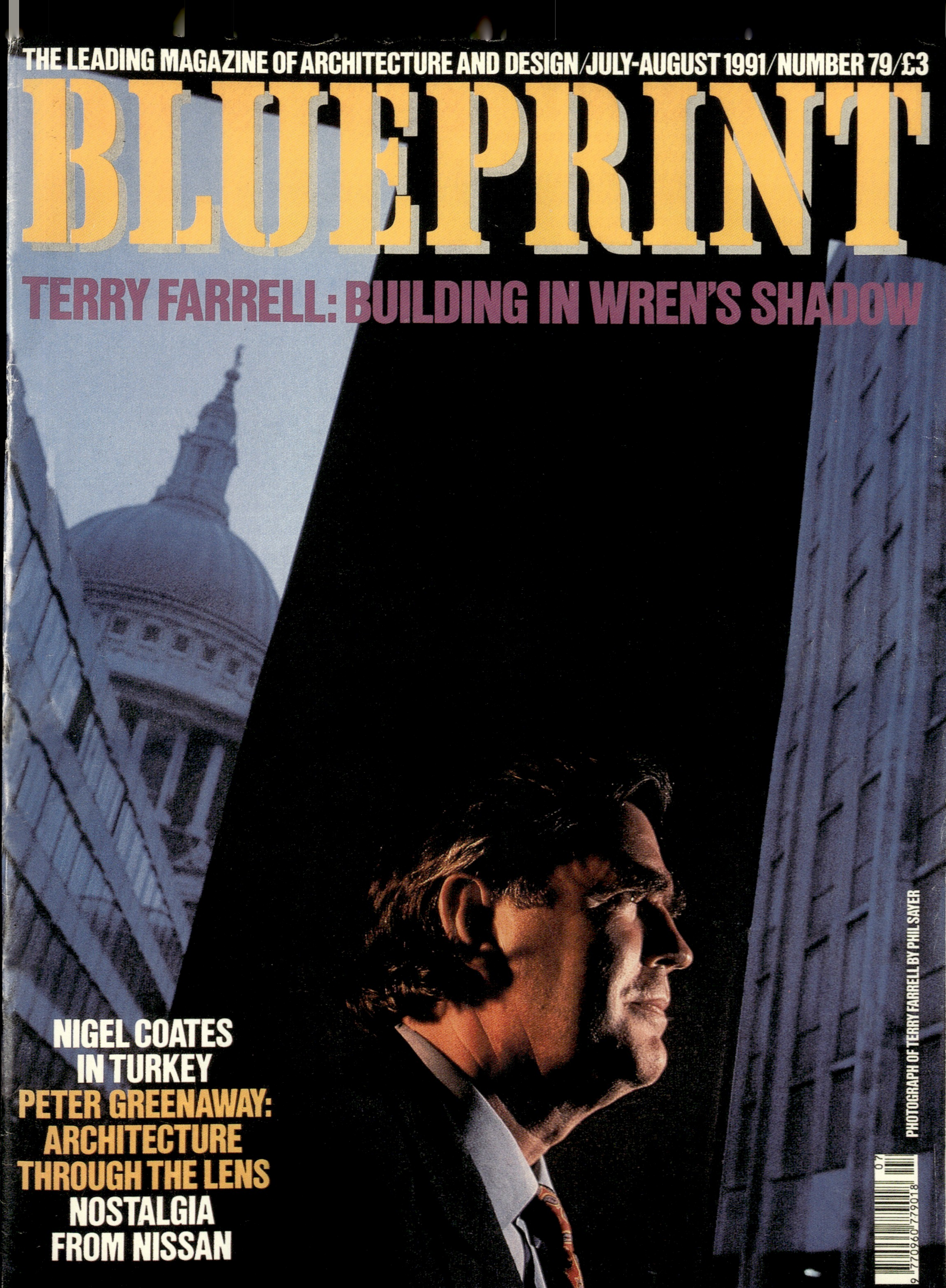
THE LEADING MAGAZINE OF ARCHITECTURE AND DESIGN/JULY-AUGUST 1991/NUMBER 79/£3
BLUEPRINT
TERRY FARRELL: BUILDING IN WREN'S SHADOW
NIGEL COATES IN TURKEY
PETER GREENAWAY: ARCHITECTURE THROUGH THE LENS
NOSTALGIA FROM NISSAN
PHOTOGRAPH OF TERRY FARRELL BY PHIL SAYER

Cover of *Blueprint* magazine, July-August 1991.

understanding of the wider urban grain. Farrell was always a masterly 'invisible mender' of streetscapes, from his earliest projects. That predilection has survived, and is what has informed his approach to this book: it is not a question of taking the building and working outwards from there, rather the reverse. Start with the city: what does it tell you?

Farrell has found himself working in areas as diverse as Britain's post-industrial northern cities – the city of Newcastle where he first attended university, for instance, and Hull – and simultaneously in the almost frighteningly expansionist area of the Pearl River Delta in China, where the unfettered commerce of tiny British-controlled Hong Kong was giving way to the tiger economy of its enormous neighbour. The International Centre for Life in Newcastle is as much a planning diagram as it is a building – this largely abandoned area close to one of the great Victorian railway stations has an urban job to do which goes far beyond genetic research and a visitor attraction associated with it. It forms part and parcel of the continuing large-scale revitalization of the Newcastle/Gateshead area, and provides a scientific balance, on the north bank, to the arts campus developing on the south. Its architecture is also nothing remotely like the Farrell architecture of the 1980s, which arguably worked itself out in the imposing rotunda of the Edinburgh International Conference and Exhibition centre, designed in 1989 and completed in 1995, which follows a sequence of linked cylindrical forms, old and new, and balances the oval dome of the Usher concert hall nearby. His later adjacent Sheraton Hotel health club (1996–9) with its rectilinear blue glass elevation interrupted by a scooped-out curving terrace and balcony, is a total contrast and shows once again the enduring influence of Niemeyer and Brasilia: modern romanticism.

At Newcastle, the built area is broken down according to the patterns of movement and usage within it: it is a new form of campus within the city, on an irregular site, where the three main elements (Life Centre, Bioscience Centre, and genetics research building) adopt different forms and perform a frozen dance around the public space. Paradoxically, this very large project is a great deal less monumental than some of Farrell's smaller, earlier schemes. The Life Centre, a curving copper-clad form rising from the ground, is reminiscent of some of the work of Renzo Piano at this period, and engages with contemporary debate about the relationship of buildings to ground plane. It is, essentially, about the creation of public space in the convivial city. But elsewhere, more visible landmarks are called for: hence the maritime museum in Hull known as 'The Deep'. The aesthetics of this project – striated, angular – derive to some extent from an earlier design for an aquarium in London's docklands but are tailored specifically to the point of land, projecting into the Humber Estuary, on which it is sited: its situation is like a Sydney Opera House, only without the enclosing harbour: this is where earth and sky meet. Perhaps more directly comparable to Sydney – in location, but by no means in form – is the Pacific Northwest Aquarium in Seattle, due for completion in 2005. There, the building rises directly out of the waters of Puget Sound. Like Hull, however, the waterfront had become run-down, with abandoned piers nearby and a moribund park. The Seattle Aquarium also shares characteristics with earlier Farrell projects in that it is a redevelopment of an existing building, also an aquarium. It will double it in size, while making a place that sets out to be not so much a building as an elevated demonstration section of Pacific coastline.

Hull and Seattle are both projects that are about making connections between the city and the sea. In Hull, a separate study for the River Hull Corridor reveals that The Deep, while being an ambitious Millennium project in its own right, is part of a greater masterplan for a city that is reinventing itself as a technological and cultural centre, following the decline of its traditional maritime industries. The Hull – a small river running south to meet the Humber – had effectively been a private kingdom of industrial wharves, and is now envisaged as a cultural precinct by 2020, linked to the centre by bridges across the river, and with The Deep as its southerly riparian conclusion. In Seattle, similarly, the destination building is part of an urban redesign that helps to connect the centre with Puget Sound.

Similarly in Portugal, Farrell's masterplan studies for the Port of Lisbon as long ago as 1994 indicated a way of connecting the city to the water along 14 kilometres of the River Tejo or Tagus, in anticipation of Expo 98 in the city and the completion of the Tagus river crossing. What Farrell noted in particular was the continuing, almost Venetian, strength of commuter ferry traffic in this historic waterway: this led to one of his lesser-known commissions, the Barreiro Ferry Station complete with a masterplan for surrounding housing and retail. Later Farrell was to work with the same local practice – Ideias do Futuro – on the redesign of Lisbon's famous Do Rossio Station.

The Pearl River Delta, as you would expect in a part of the world that is expanding as explosively as Farrell's native Manchester did in the 19th century, offers some fascinating projects. Some have been built, such as the projects in Hong Kong and Kowloon: others are as yet masterplanning studies, such as ‘Pearl Island’, a 520-hectare city suburb of Shenzen that is a 21st-century take on the ‘Metabolist’ Tokyo Harbour projects of the early 1960s: land reclaimed from the sea to save the sprawling metropolis. Its circular form makes you expect the obvious Radburn-influenced radial plan: instead you get something more like Manhattan, where the island city is laid out on a grid plan sliced through by roads and waterways. By expanding the city as a new island community, a beneficial by-product is a greatly increased waterfront: here fully exploited with a waterfront park.

As we have seen, such masterplanning studies are one of Farrell’s great strengths: we find him in Sydney, for instance, dealing not with the famous waterfront, but a typical urban condition: part of the city long divided by a railway route. The Parramatta station and transport interchange project is, typically, more than the creation of a building. Instead, Farrell uses it as a generative force, allowing the development of new urban townships served by a new rail link to relieve an existing, over-congested route. In some of these masterplans there are Farrell buildings, in others, not. And in some cases – particularly on the Pacific Rim – the scale is such that the building begins to assume characteristics of the city itself.

The transport projects in Kowloon and Seoul are as all-encompassing as you would expect such massive interchanges in such a fast-growing area to be. The competition entry for Beijing’s National Grand Theatre, with its floating, shallow-domed roofs and immense flanking staircases, begins to give you a feel for the scale of buildings now being routinely commissioned in that part of the world: the indicated human figures are ant-sized. But even with that preparation, the scale of the Guangzhou Daily and Cultural Plaza project still catches you unawares. Here, the idea is not so very dissimilar

The Peak Tower and Kowloon Ventilation Building, Hong Kong, 1995.

to Hugh Stubbins' 1977 Citicorp Center in New York, but on a scale to compare with Johann Otto van Spreckelsen's Grande Arche at La Défense in Paris, or Rafael Vinoly's Tokyo International Forum building as macro-scale urban event. Two buildings are elevated high in the air at right angles to each other, outlining and enclosing a one-hectare public space. The buildings might seem huge, but by Guangzhou standards they are not, being a mere 34 storeys, reaching 134 metres. The square, described as a 'city room' is made by pulling out the lower parts of the towers as separately expressed cubes. Farrell is revisiting his groundscraper ideas of the 1980s in London, but doing it on a site that allows the creation of a far more complete civic realm. You would get much the same floorspace – 234,000 square metres – in a conventional landmark tower, but with little or none of the civic trade-off. In contrast, when buildings and public space are conceived as being interdependent, more interesting urban forms start to emerge.

The Guangzhou project should perhaps be set on a scale against the Blackwall ventilator shafts of 40 years earlier as a graphic representation of how far Terry Farrell has come, in every sense. But the same urban concerns can be traced all the way through his career. Why should a functionalist bit of semi-industrial kit be either ugly or dull? Could it not instead be intriguing and uplifting? And why should floorspace not be rearranged in a way that will benefit, rather than isolate, the life of the city, so allowing a richness of uses and experiences rather than a succession of monocultural activities? Never mind Guangzhou: in London, Farrell is replacing three early 1960s fortress tower blocks, universally loathed, previously home to (irony of ironies) the British government's Department of Environment, with a low-rise, high density, urban-scaled replacement. All cities are different: but a shared approach to the problems of scale can yield similar rewards on the Pearl River or the Thames.

Farrell sees cities in the round. For him, the buildings are visible manifestations of an underlying organism that advances and retreats, is damaged, mends itself, finds new possibilities within itself. The architecture that results from this is wholly distinctive, usually somewhat apart from whatever we might conceive to be the prevailing ideology of the given period: be that a transport interchange in Korea or a boat-shaped office building in London's Paddington. This independence of spirit adds diversity and richness to our cities. A slightly mischievous ability to provoke, by offering a non-standard solution, is undoubtedly part of the Farrell technique. Style is not quite the issue. It comes down to personality.

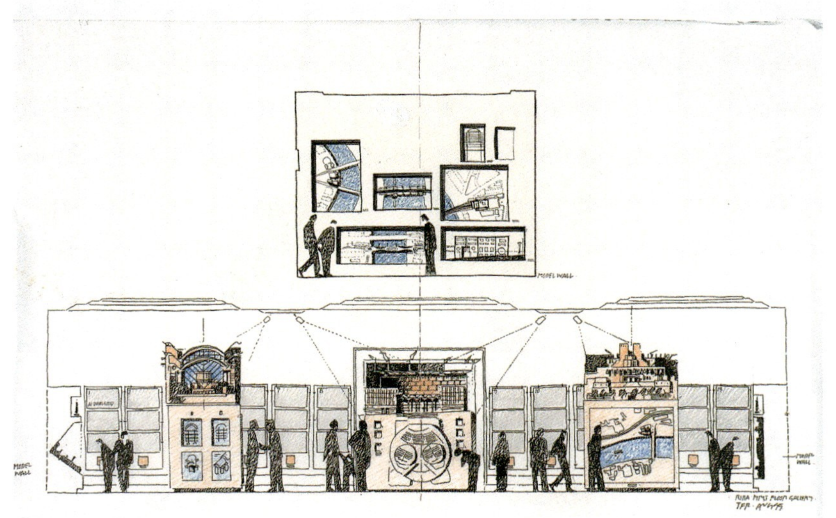

Sketches by Aidan Potter for the layout of 'Terry Farrell: A Retrospective and Current Projects', held at the RIBA Architecture Centre, 1995.

PEARL DELTA SUPERCITY

PEARL DELTA SUPERCITY

Air travellers circling above the estuary and islands of the Pearl Delta Supercity look down on an urban civilization without parallel on earth. Separated from the rest of the People's Republic of China by well-maintained borders, the megalopolis comprises four principal cities – Hong Kong, Guangzhou, Shenzen and Zhuhai – designed to promote a thriving mixed economy. To support a projected population of 40 million people, motorways, railways, airports, power stations and other infrastructure works have been constructed on a huge scale and at an astonishing speed. The region presents to us a new urban phenomenon: a complete structural form that embraces visual chaos through its scale, speed of transformation, methods and outlook. Western in inspiration but with eastern ideas of implementation, the Pearl Delta cocktail is a giant landscape of car-based planning, commercial and residential complexes and shopping malls.

Guangzhou (formerly Canton) was once the historic trade gateway to China, but was latterly eclipsed by Hong Kong. A British possession from the mid-19th century until it was returned to China in 1997, Hong Kong was transformed, for trading and defence reasons, from a diverse land of steep mountains and waterways into a flourishing harbour. The technological supports on which modern Hong Kong depends include air-conditioning to overcome humidity, lifts to enable high-density living, and trams to reach mountainous peaks. Key to all this people-movement is the escalator, which has enabled the city's characteristic multi-level, three-dimensional planning. The two historic centres of Guangzhou and Hong Kong are being consumed by the Pearl Delta phenomenon, and subsumed within the new urban mega-city.

Terry Farrell & Partners' work developed in direct response to the Pearl Delta phenomenon. The Peak Tower acknowledges the city's potential for quickly identified iconic forms. The design for the British Consulate makes an emblem of memory and the low-rise, integrated layout of old Hong Kong. The Kowloon masterplan marks the new urbanism of infrastructure while the West Rail project views the region as a linear landfill transportation network. The Pearl Island masterplan finds inspiration in the global branded corporate community, while the Guangzhou Daily News Headquarters reflects a particularly Chinese brand of corporate gigantism.

Satellite view of Pearl Delta, where the Pearl River estuary meets the South China Sea.

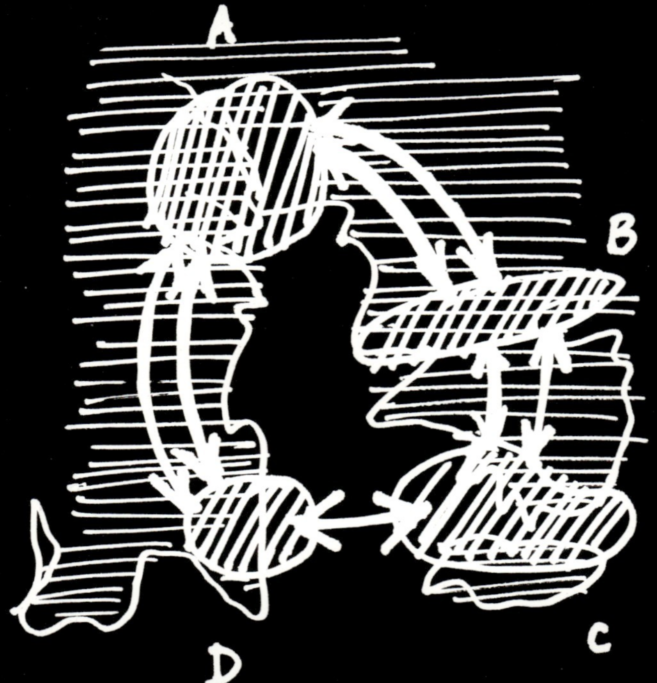

Concept drawing by Terry Farrell. The four mega-growth centres connect up to make a world supercity.
A. Guangzhou
B. Shenzen
C. Hong Kong
D. Zhuhai

Top: Satellite view of Hong Kong.

Centre: Historical view of Hong Kong.

Above: Shenzen panorama.

Top: The banks of the Pearl River.

Centre: Contemporary view of Hong Kong.

same scale, the plans of London and Hong Kong show the same population (in excess of 6 million) distributed in totally different ways. Compared with

concentrated along limited high density areas (top right), leaving vast areas of natural landscape and water. The result, assisted by the steep granite mountains, is a highly

comparisons. London's parks (left) are about the same size as Hong Kong's built up areas, while Hong Kong's parks (right) are the size of London's inhabited areas.

each place.

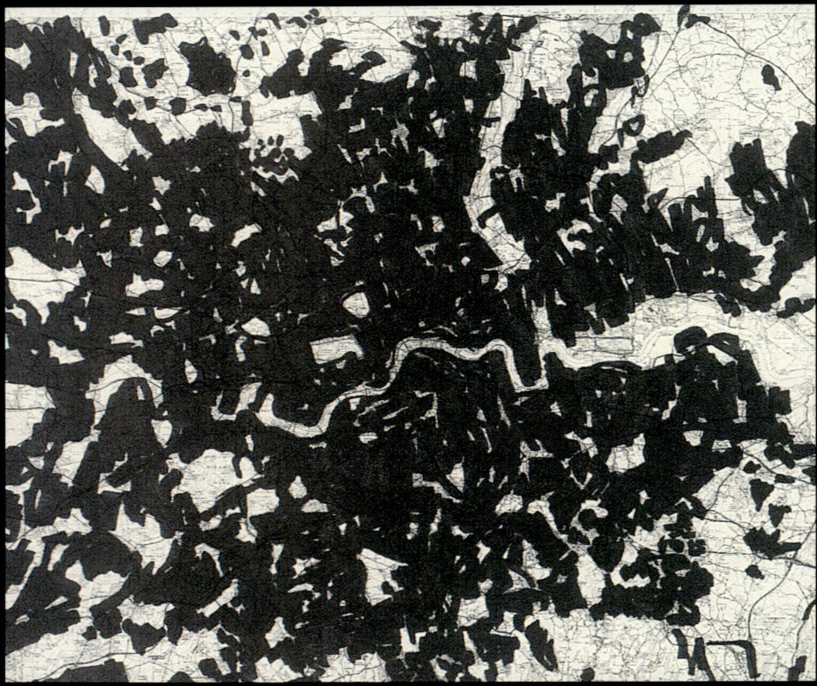

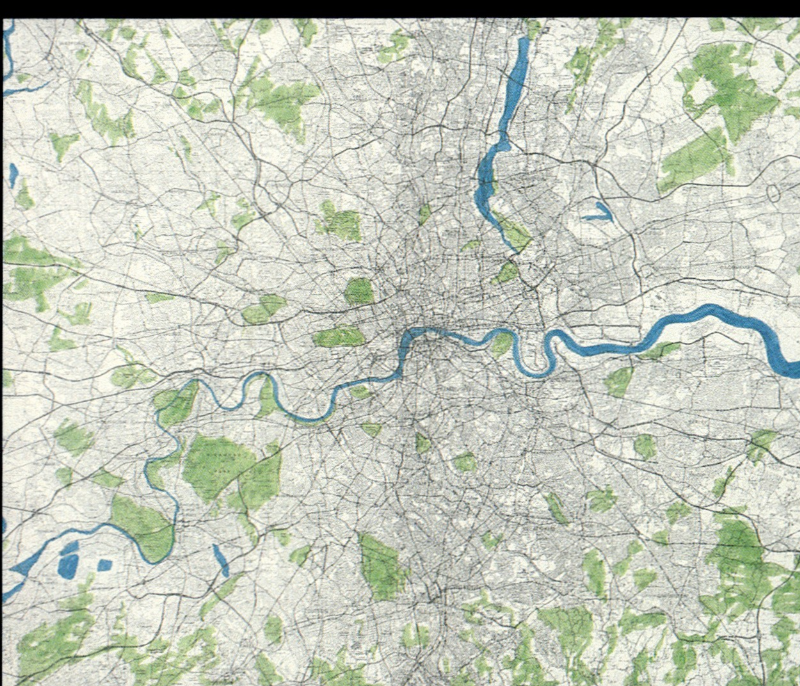

Top left and right: Concept drawing by Terry Farrell and Hong Kong view with TFP's Kowloon Ventilation Building in the foreground and the Peak on the horizon. TFP has identified four areas and four typologies that characterize Hong Kong.
1. The 'sky building', such as the Peak, is silhouetted on mountain tops, accessible by winding steep roads or, in this case, the funicular rail.
2. Because of the limited land area to build on, high rise high density is the norm, especially on the landfilled harbour edge (see pages 36–37).
3. Along the contours are linear 'mid-level' building types, such as the Consulate, which runs between the harbour edge and the sky buildings.
4. There are many examples of the 'floor' or 'lid' type. These are free-standing objects on the harbour's edge, such as TFP's Kowloon Ventilation building.

Bottom: Night view of Hong Kong from the Peak.

TFP's Hong Kong projects continued to follow the four typologies that occupied the office during the 1990s.

TFP undertook the station scheme design for the Kowloon Canton Railway Corporation's West Rail project – a through-train service between China and Hong Kong and a mass transit service connecting the north west New Territories with the urban centre of Kowloon.

Top left: Model for Tseun Wan West station.
Centre: Sketch for Lok Ma Chau station.
Bottom: The West Rail project.

Mini stations were designed on wide pavements to give direct access from the street to the existing MTR stations below ground. The facility has resulted in easy station access – particularly for wheelchair users.

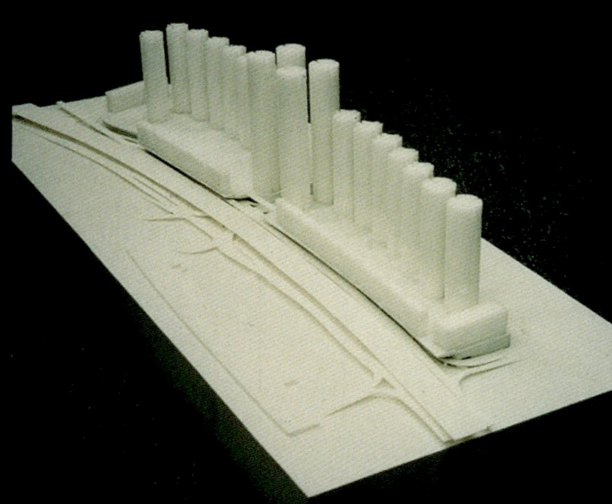

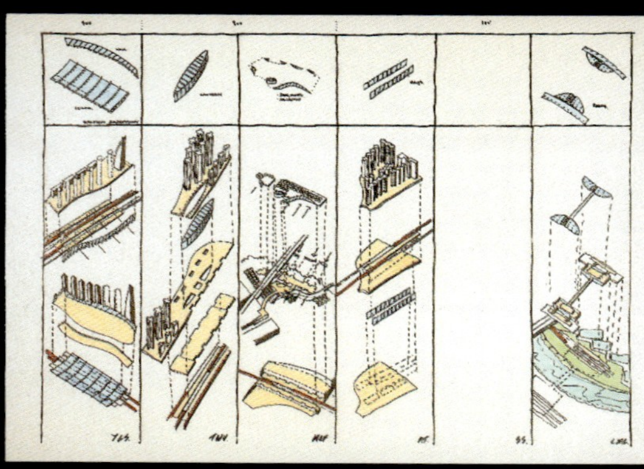

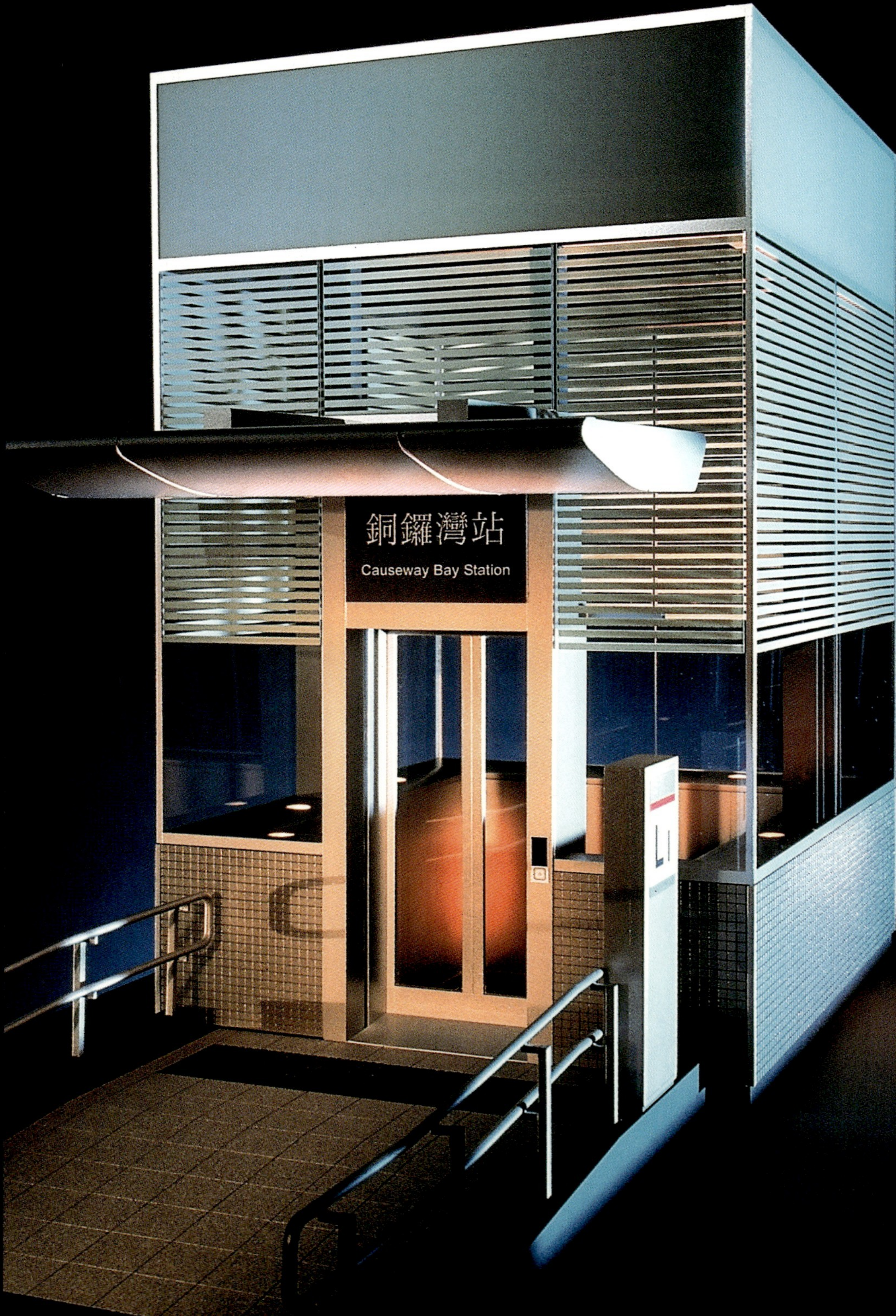

Series of tower studies for Hong Kong (see page 35). Top left: Sincere Building. Bottom: Nathan Road Tower. Top right: Concept sketch by Doug Streeter showing the Landmark Tower for Kowloon Station masterplan.

Model of the Landmark Tower.

PEARL ISLAND

Although 20 years ago little more than a fishing village, Shenzen has grown to a city of 6 million inhabitants. Its unprecedented growth is due to its designation as a Special Economic Zone bordering the Hong Kong territories, together with the synergy it has established with Hong Kong itself. Terry Farrell & Partners' masterplan at the western end of the city – its gateway to the Pearl Delta – forms part of this phenomenal growth.

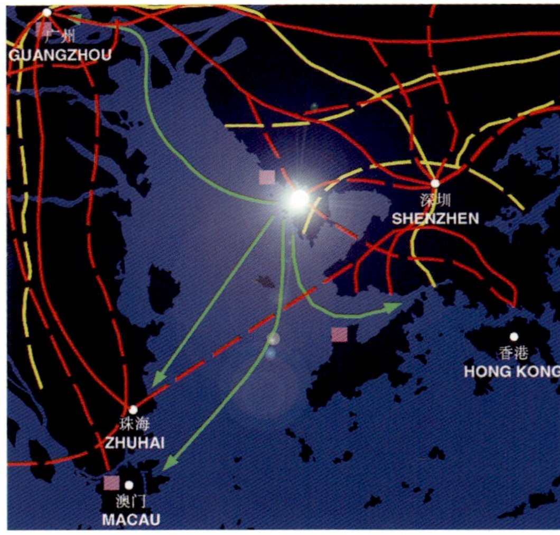

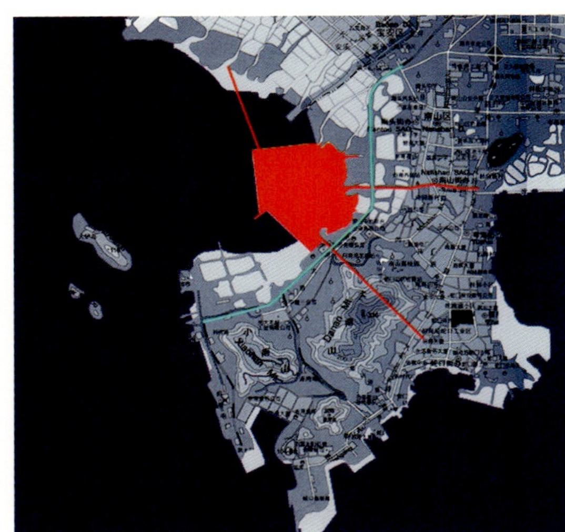

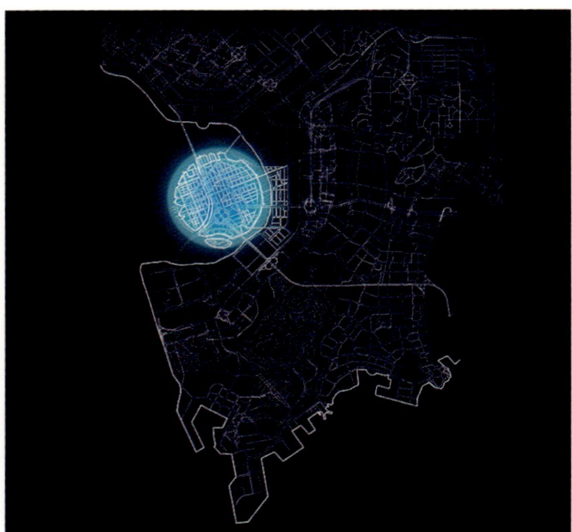

Concept design sketch.

Top left: Location plan.

Top right: Site plan showing proposed landfill.

Centre left: Local topography and coastal edge.

Centre right: Local context plan.

Above: Panorama of Qianhai Bay.

Plan view of model. The planned highway system was a 'given', and the new city had to adapt to it as though it already existed.

In September 2000, TFP submitted a competitive proposal for the design of the 520 hectare coastal city. The brief was to create a conceptual masterplan for a high-quality city for 85,000 inhabitants, including commuters to Hong Kong and Shenzen by train and ferry. In order to emphasize its symbolic significance as a gateway, and also as a rational response to the delta's hydrodynamics and the industrial character of the area, an island form was chosen as the basic urban idea. Connections to Shenzen have been carefully considered so that the island is a fully integrated piece of city fabric. This is expressed by the many proposed bridges and ferry connections. The island form also makes the new city a focal point on the route between Guangzhou and Hong Kong. In a coupling of Asian and European principles of city planning, TFP aims to bring to Shenzen the best elements of the world's great maritime cities.

The city grid is oriented to maximize the site's natural assets. The north-south grid is aligned to benefit from views towards the Baoan Hills to the north and the Nanshan Hills to the south. The east-west axis aligns with views of off-shore islands in the Pearl River, while the eastern edge of the site is formed by an ecological park along the edge of the bay. The city is divided into a matrix of neighbourhoods, each with a distinct character and a set of amenities. A network of sinuous cycle and pedestrian routes superimposed on the grid contrast with the linear geometry of the urban block structure, bringing an element of the unexpected to the city and contributing to its formal diversity. Boulevards, vistas and public spaces create a series of outdoor 'rooms', the centre of which is Pearl Island Square, which provides a focus for civic activities. Contrasting with this in scale are the neighbourhood spaces consisting of small parks, water gardens and pavilions.

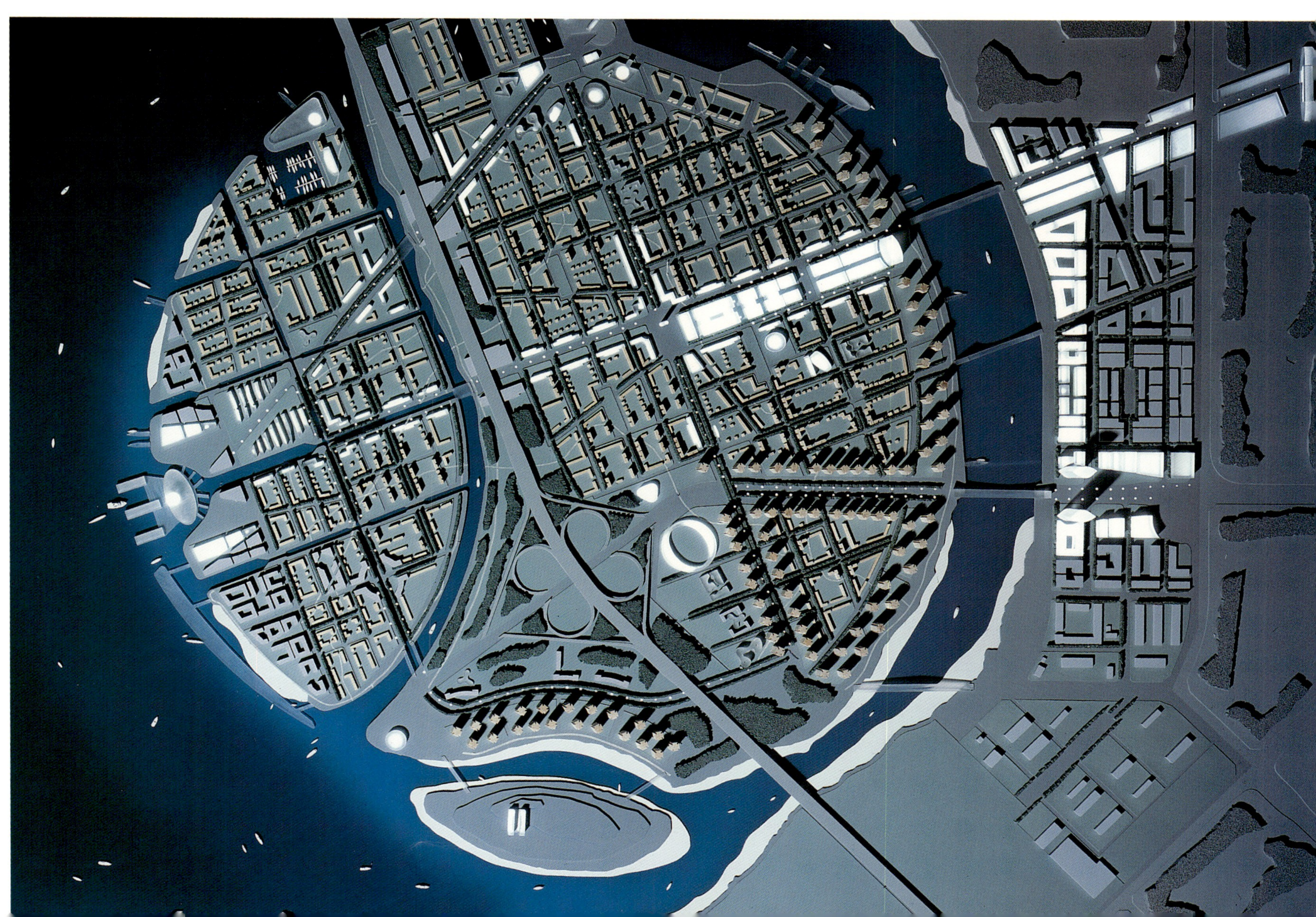

Aerial view of model.

Top: Marine structures and connections.
Centre: Urban blocks and precincts.
Bottom: Figure ground.

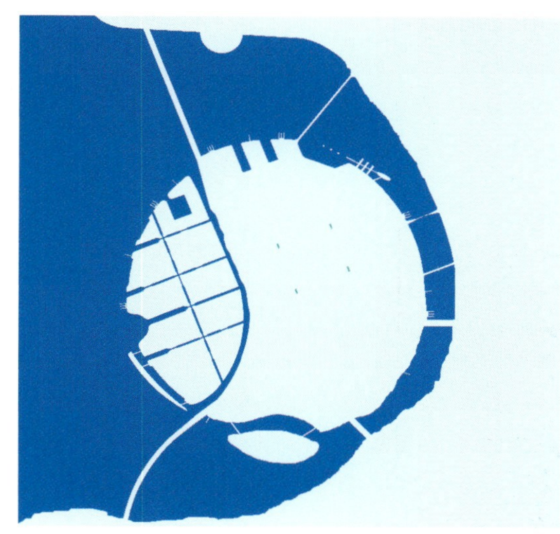

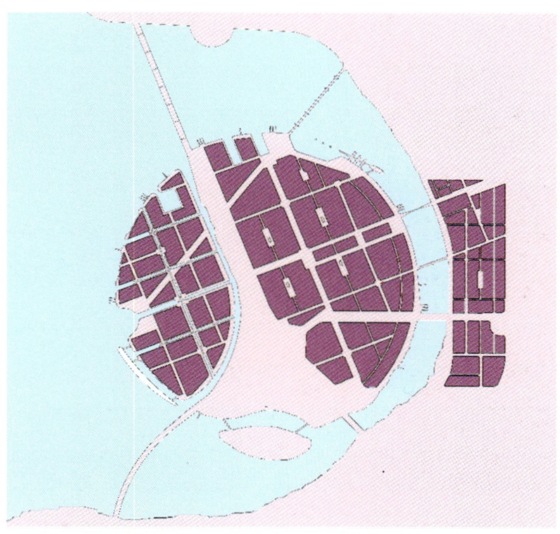

CULTURAL PLAZA FOR GUANGZHOU DAILY

Guangzhou, formerly the ancient city of Canton, is now one of China's most dynamic and fastest growing urban centres. The large-scale scheme involves a 250,000 square metre public arts complex that integrates the headquarters building of China's largest newspaper publisher, the Guangzhou Daily News, with a 1 hectare public plaza, a library, an exhibition hall, an arts centre, a five-star hotel with banqueting facilities, and retail space. It will also include the world's largest bookshop, an ice-skating rink, a conference centre and an IMAX cinema complex. The diversity of uses – cultural, touristic, commercial and retail – ensures that the site will attract a good cross-section of visitors both during the day and at night. It is conceived as a cultural magnet that will add vibrancy and heterogeneity to the city.

A

C

B

D

100m

100m

E

View of Tianhe, Guangzhou's new financial district.

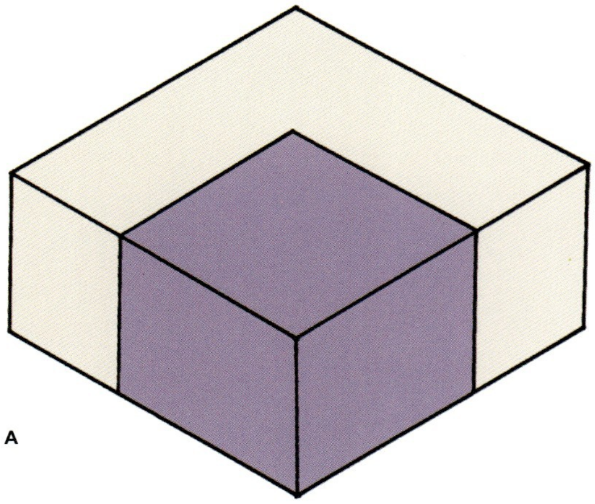

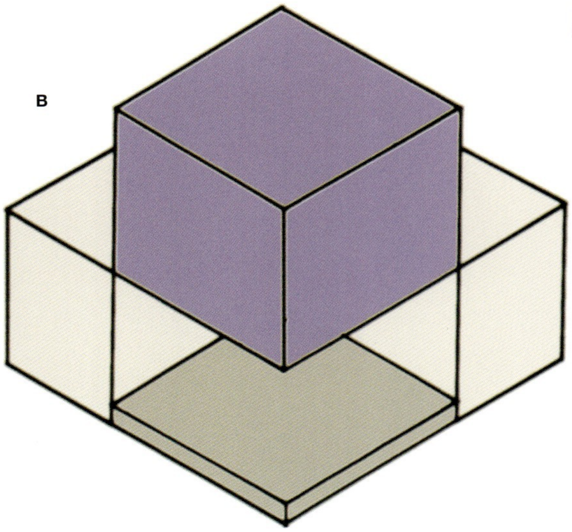

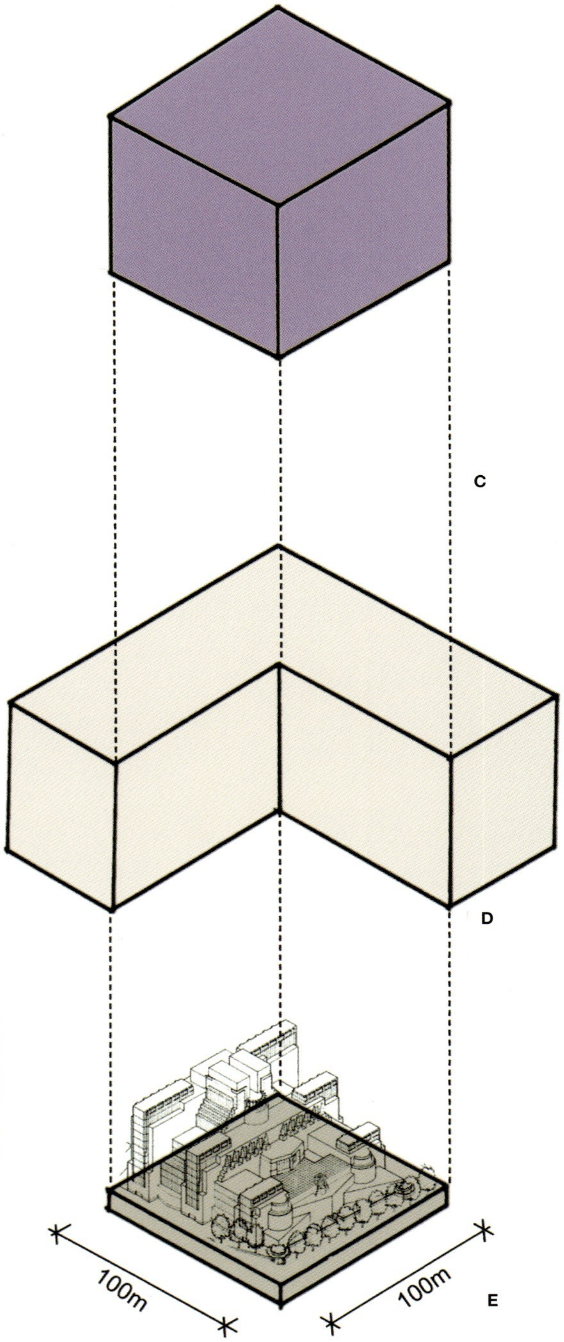

Concept of the big urban room.
A and B: The city room is created by displacing accommodation vertically to create a void.
C, D and E: The Guangzhou Daily Cultural Plaza's great public space or 'city room' has parallels with Western ideas of public space, but has a totally different Chinese scale. The diagram (right) shows TFP's MI6 building in London fitting within Guangzhou's great room. This is enclosed at the lower levels by civic and cultural buildings, with the private hotel and office buildings on top.

Below: Plan of Guangzhou. The site is to the east of the city, in its developing financial district.

Matching the scale of a building to its setting is an essential part of the architectural process for Terry Farrell & Partners. The practice has no fear of a challenging site, whether it is a mountain peak, the banks of a river or a venerable historical location. Additionally, it has a tradition, stretching back to its work at London's Embankment Place, of creating landmark buildings that rejoice in place-making. Terry Farrell has called these buildings 'groundscrapers': iconic structures that are horizontally integrated into their environment. While the isolated, object-fixated tower block was emblematic of the 20th century, it is urban design and place-making – creating buildings that interact with their context – that are becoming the mantras of 21st-century architecture. TFP's recent commission in Guangzhou, southern China, embraces on a grand scale the practice of place-making.

The overriding aim was to define a new district for Guangzhou that was imbued with a sense of place. Rather than providing a vertiginous, skyscraping totem – a familiar site in China – it was decided to create an iconic landmark from a lower-rise, 34-storey structure (the average height of buildings in Guangzhou is 40 storeys) that embraced its location and was permeable to its surroundings. The 134-metre-high building is positioned on the eastern side of the site, next to the road edge, in order to emphasize the sense of a gateway to the city. A large open public plaza is located to the west of the site. This plaza filters people as they arrive from or move to the city centre, and its vast open nature offers a startling contrast to the drama of the adjacent building.

The design concept is simple. Two interlocking geometric shapes are the basis of the building's three main components: a raised cube formed by two angled towers, and an L-shaped block and a podium at ground level. The distinctive form grew out of manipulating the blocks in such a way that a corner was extracted from the cube and lifted vertically, creating below a grand public square, described as the 'city room'. The city room, square in plan, represents the Chinese symbol for earth. On either side, in a dramatic gesture, two blocks are raised in the air. A circular void – a Chinese symbol for the 'floating' heavens – is carved out of the centre of this volume, allowing daylight to flood the plaza below, as well as connecting upper and lower (public) spaces. At the top of the raised cube is a sky-lobby 33 storeys above ground, with panoramic views and its own microclimate. A rooftop landscape, comparable in size to London's Jubilee Gardens, provides sky-high parkland for hotel residents. Glazed, transparent elevations make a vibrant background for the public city room and western plaza, which are linked and freely accessed by two gateways. These spaces are intended to provide a stage for public performances, exhibitions and events. The conjunction of cube, sphere and void creates a sequence of fluid environments – public, private, internal, external, closed and open – as rich and varied as a city experience, yet intensified.

The Guangzhou Daily Cultural Plaza is designed to be experienced within the context of a long-established city. It is not an isolated icon but a structure that will both symbolize and act out its connectedness with old Guangzhou.

Model showing site location.

Bottom: Concept drawings by Doug Streeter of the Guangzhou building.

Floor levels drawing.

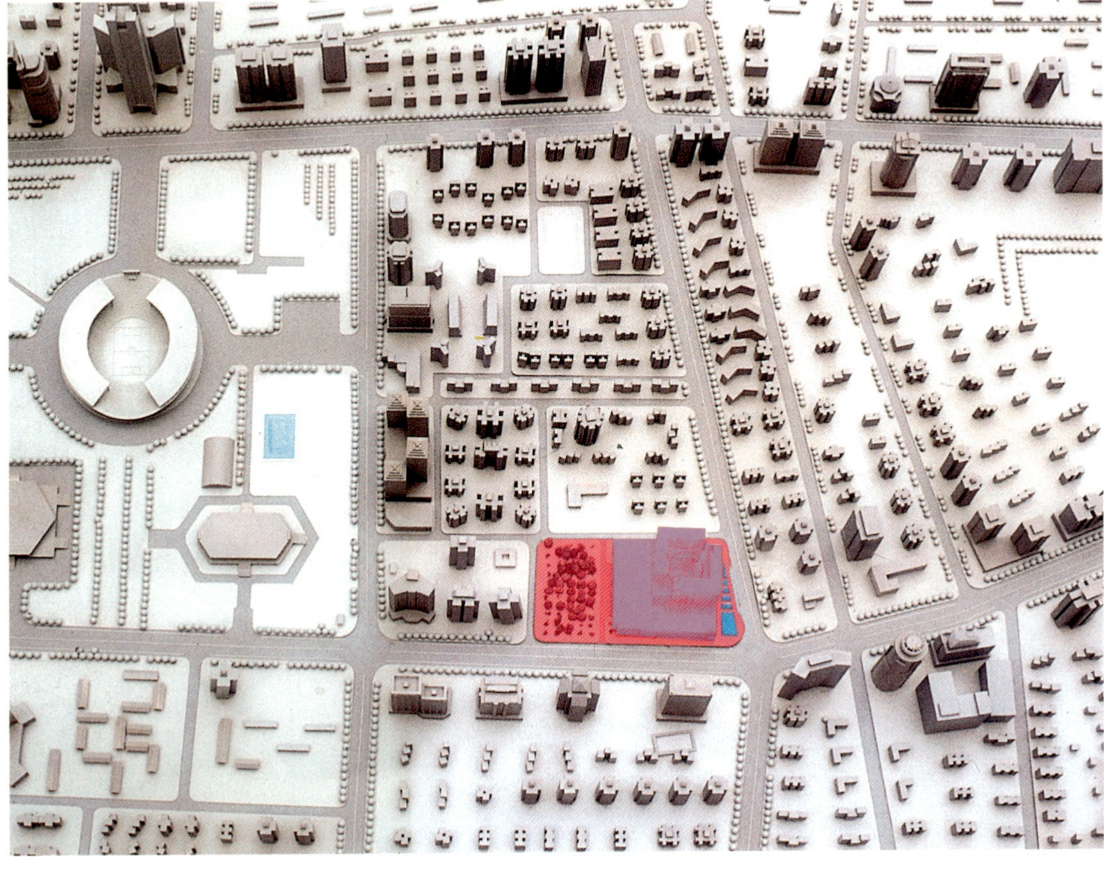

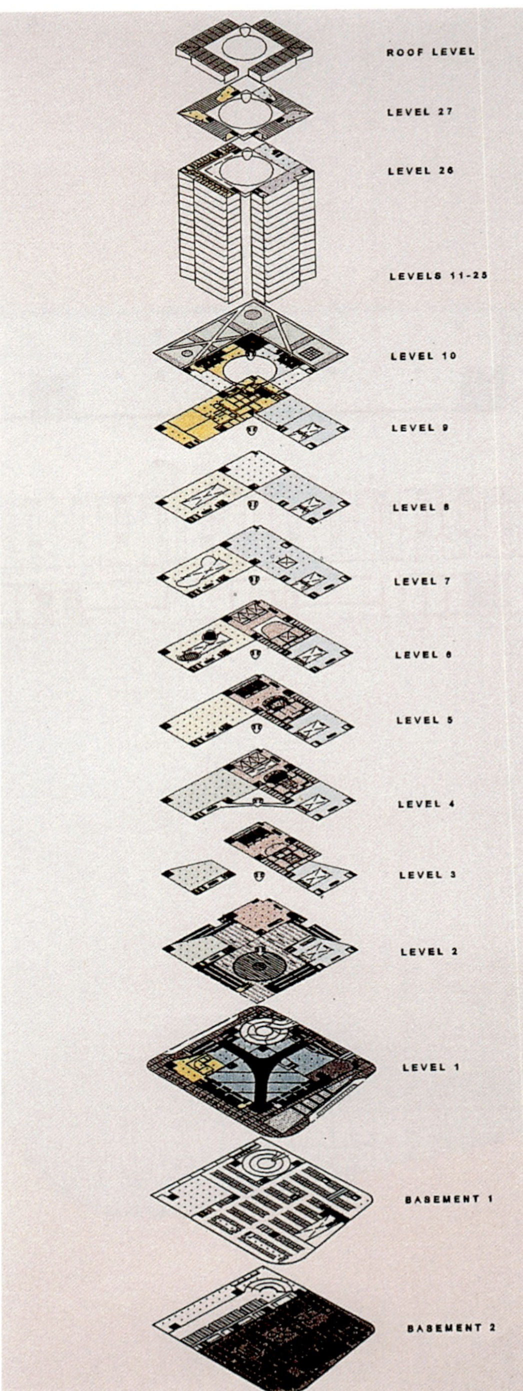

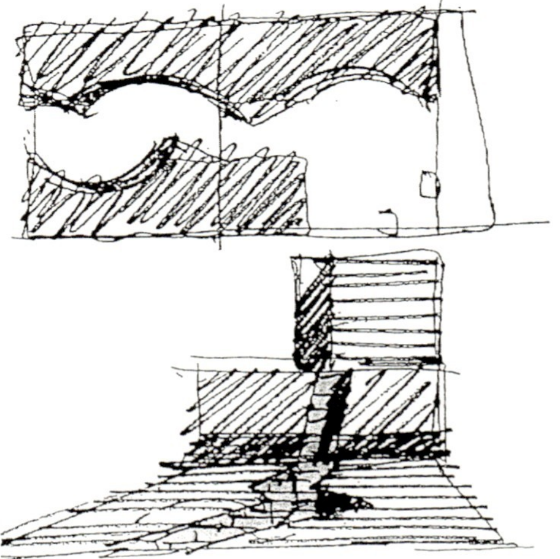

Competition stage scheme showing the great public space with the surrounding civic and cultural buildings at low level, and the office and hotel buildings rising above.

Inset below: Concept sketch by Terry Farrell.

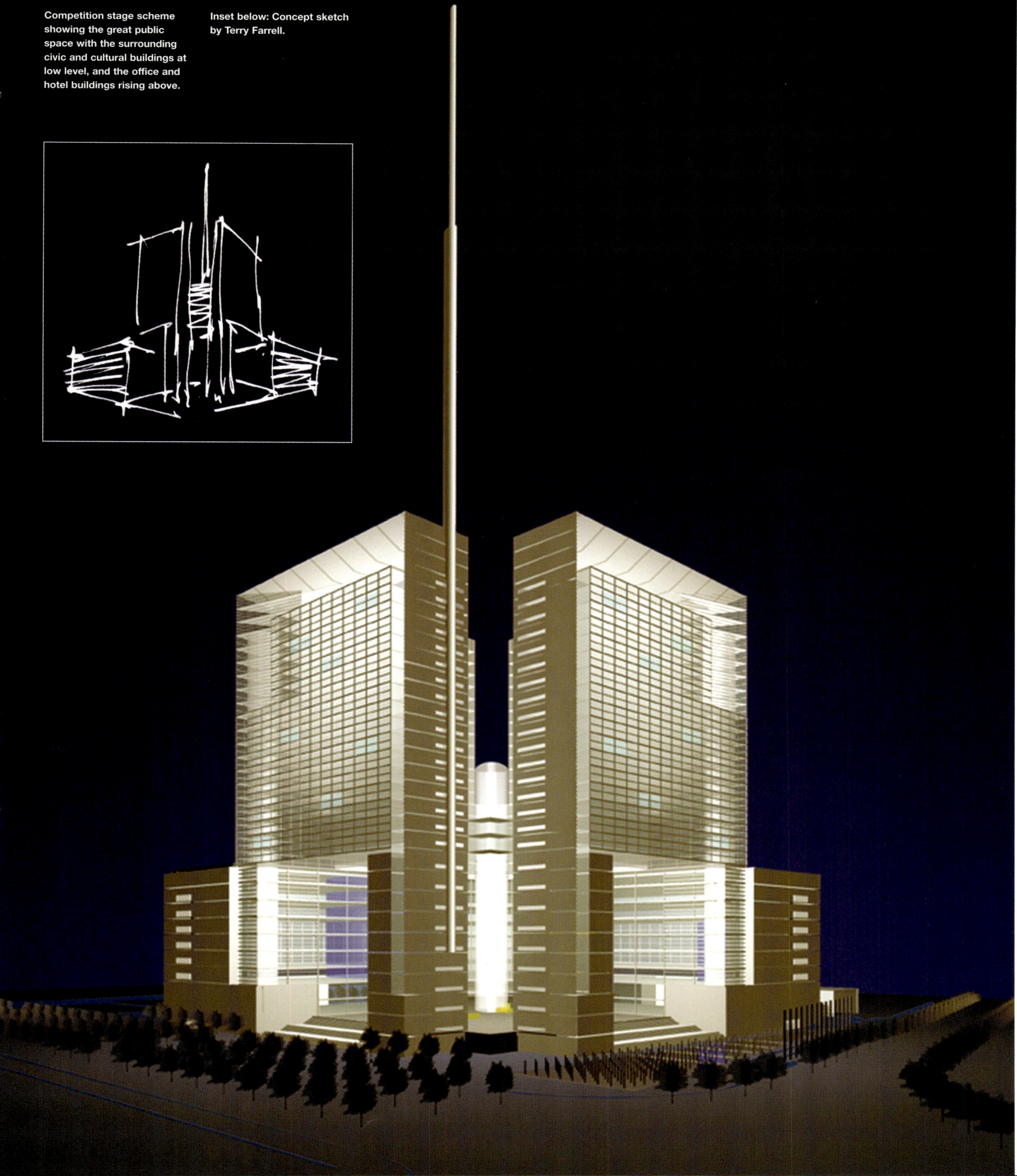

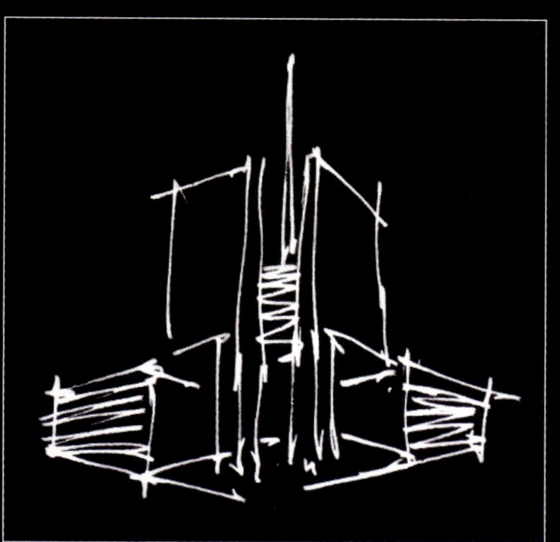

GOVERNMENT HEADQUARTERS

FOR BRITISH CONSULATE + BRITISH COUNCIL

Set on steeply sloping land next to Hong Kong Park in the Admiralty District, the headquarters of the British Consulate and British Council is intended to carve out a strong street presence. Terry Farrell & Partners felt that, while Hong Kong's vertiginous streetscape gave the city drama and vigour, particularly when seen from afar, the dissipated streets and ill-defined spaces had resulted in a neglect of spaces between buildings. In their approach to the project, the practice gave as much thought to urban design as to architectural design. Ever mindful of weaving tradition and continuity into the urban scene, TFP looked to the city's precedent of dignified, low-rise public buildings.

To maintain separate identities, the Consulate and British Council offices are each housed in their own distinct headquarters building. The two buildings are set at right angles to each other and linked by a shared entrance pavilion. The site is laid out to exploit to the maximum the views up and down the two main approach roads of Supreme Court Road and Justice Drive. The three building elements (the two headquarters buildings and a residential block) create a long and continuously changing public street front to the north. Its curved form means that the composition of the complex cannot be appreciated in its entirety from any one angle. From street level, it appears to consist of independent buildings, although its unity is maintained by the roof and the consistency of materials. To the south, juxtaposed with the street elevation, lies a beautifully landscaped private garden. Low by Hong Kong's standards, the 10-storey building presents a welcoming face to visitors, in contrast with the aloofness of the surrounding tower blocks.

The steeply sloping site was utilized to create a

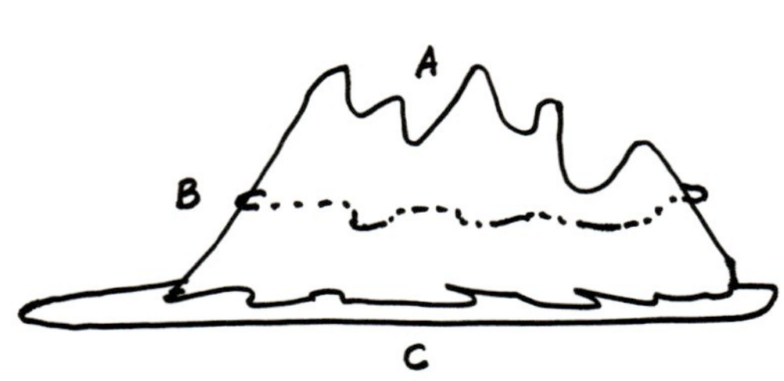

Concept sketch by Terry Farrell showing building typologies and land form.
A. The Peak
B. Mid levels
C. Harbour landfill

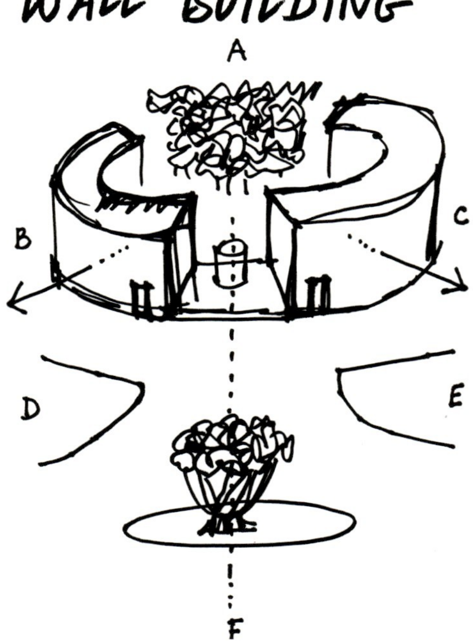

Concept sketch of the Consulate.
A. Internal private garden
B. British Consulate
C. British Council
D + E. Hotel
F. Public garden and Banyan tree

Top: View of the British Consulate at the mid-levels.

processional route from the ground-floor entrance of each building that leads through the security area to reception and waiting areas. Internal public spaces of generous height and plan depth demonstrate another way in which the multi-level site has been used to advantage. While the same circulation diagram from entrance to lifts applies to all three buildings, the experience of the route is dramatically different in each building, exemplifying Terry Farrell's belief in the need for richness and diversity in architecture.

The raison d'être of this government building is to replace the architecture of inaccessible officialdom with a place that generates activity and contributes to the liveliness of the city. At the British Consulate and British Council, the idea was to give the home of Britain's representation in China an amenable face that would meld with and enhance its surroundings.

The complex was completed in 1996 – a year before Hong Kong's reversion from British to Chinese sovereignty. It was commissioned and designed in the early 1990s against a highly public and political backdrop that ensured the building international prominence. In 1988, the British prime minister, Margaret Thatcher, deemed that, following the handover, Britain's official representation should be housed in a single landmark building whose stature would symbolize Britain's continuing interest in Hong Kong. It would bring together in the same complex the British Trade Commission, the offices of the Sino-British Joint Liaison Group, the British Council and the Passport Office, which was previously maintained by the Hong Kong government.

TFP was selected in 1992 from a shortlist of six architectural practices drawn up by the Foreign and Commonwealth Office (FCO). TFP's outline designs interpreted the FCO's brief in a 8500 square metre British Consulate headquarters, a 2000 square metre residential building and a 6600 square metre British Council headquarters. John Partridge, advisor to the FCO throughout the selection process, said the practice's submission was 'a coherent architectural statement responding to a complex urban context. The design sets its own style and artistic integrity and has the conviction of presence to hold its own with the neighbouring tower buildings.' In Terry Farrell's words, the building was to be 'well dressed': fine in appearance, welcoming, overtly British and geared towards projecting British interests. The client envisaged that the new British Consulate building, which in the final design provided a gross floor area of 17,000 square metres, would surpass many embassies in size and prestige.

Topped by a simple thin-edged flat-roof

Competition-stage drawing showing how the Consulate and British Council buildings have a long linear form that runs along the contour line. Front doors and pavement-edge events change the nature and character of the building as it unfolds around the site.

Exploded isometric.

View between the British Consulate and British Council towards the gardens beyond.

overhang, the elevations are composed of geometric forms rising from solid masonry bases that become lighter and more open as they rise – an effect achieved by increased areas of glazing. The palette of materials for the external elevations consists of Kirkstone slate, white and dark-grey granite, natural anodized aluminium and green-tinted glass on the front elevations, with render substituting the stonework to the garden elevations and residential block. While firmly part of the overall composition, the residential building next to the Consulate at the south-eastern, most secluded part of the site offers a playful contrast to the formality of the headquarters buildings through its large, sweeping balconies and denser window grids. The interior public spaces are characterized by planes of white plaster and simple detailing, while the British Council building is distinguished by the use of strong primary colours.

The Consulate and British Council building resolves itself through a complex interplay of opposites: open and closed spaces, solid and void, flat and sloping, public and private, urban bustle and natural tranquillity. This is not an architecture that attempts to over-simplify life by paring down reality. Like the city itself, it is a building constantly in flux, providing a different face for each situation.

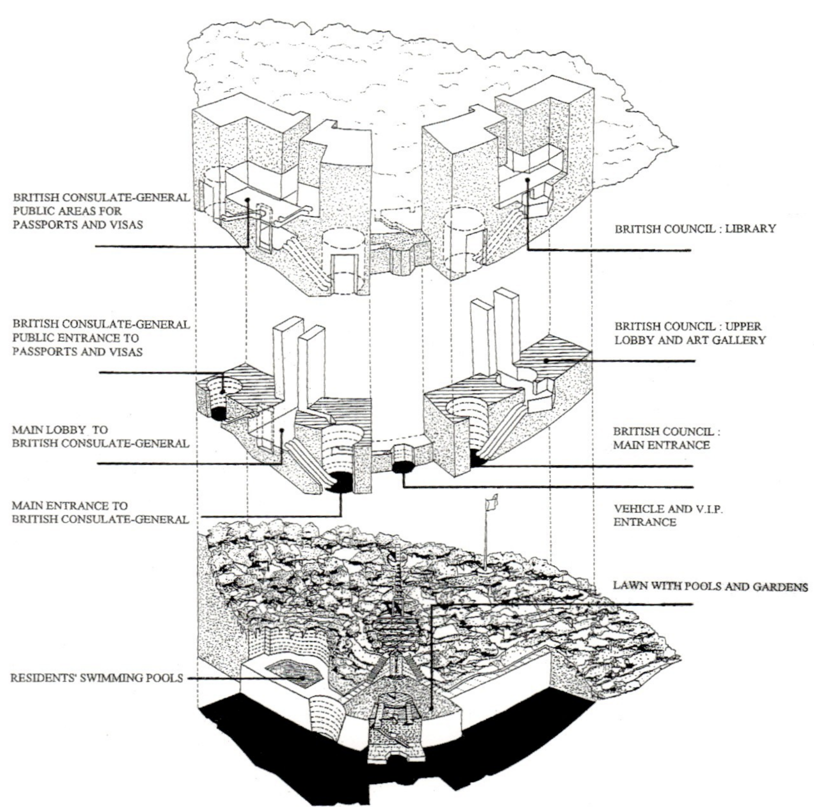

Concept sketches at competition stage.

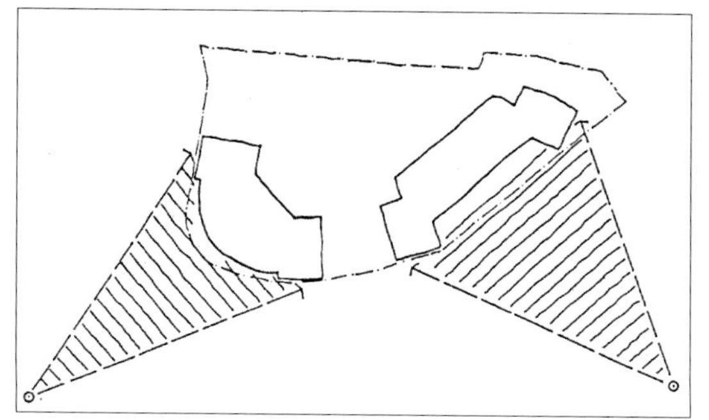

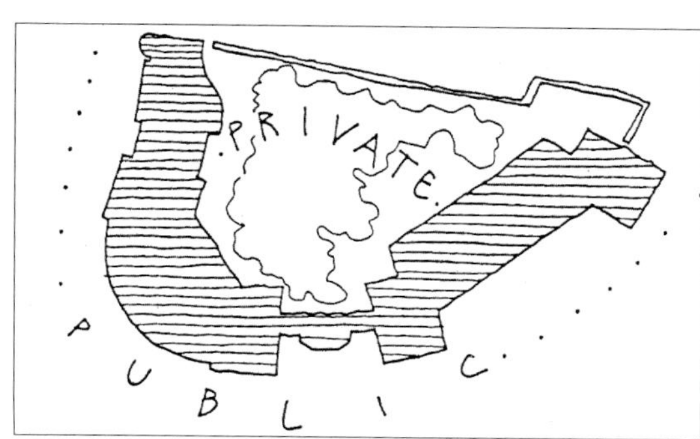

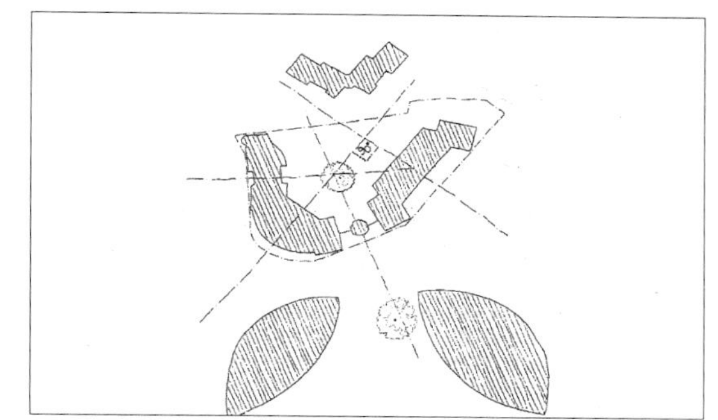

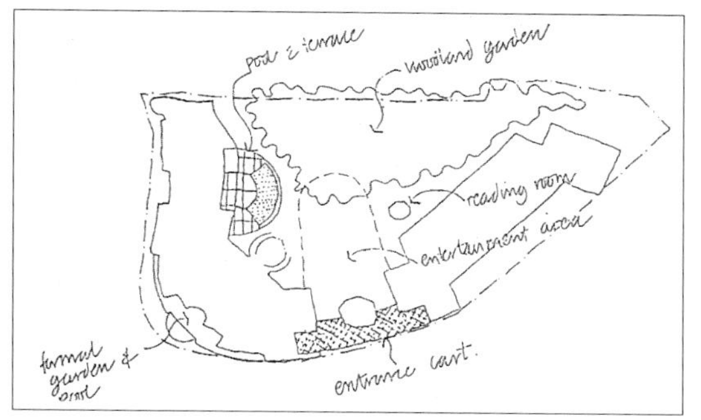

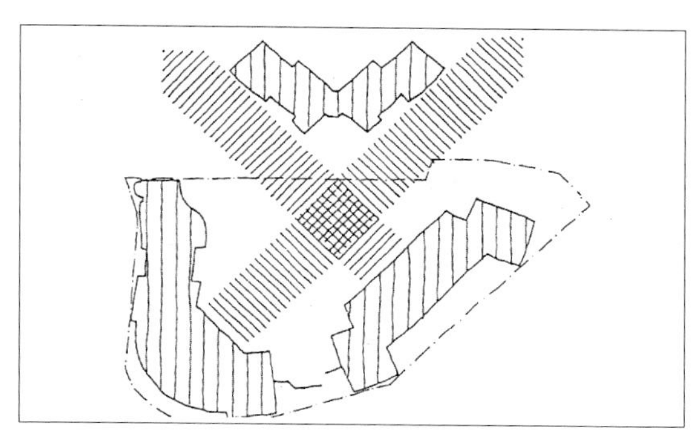

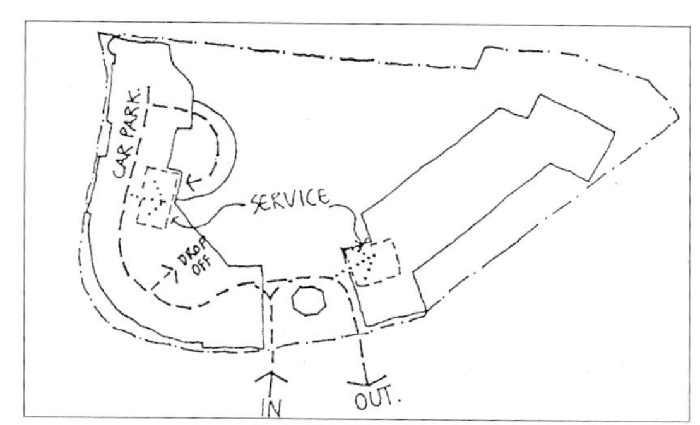

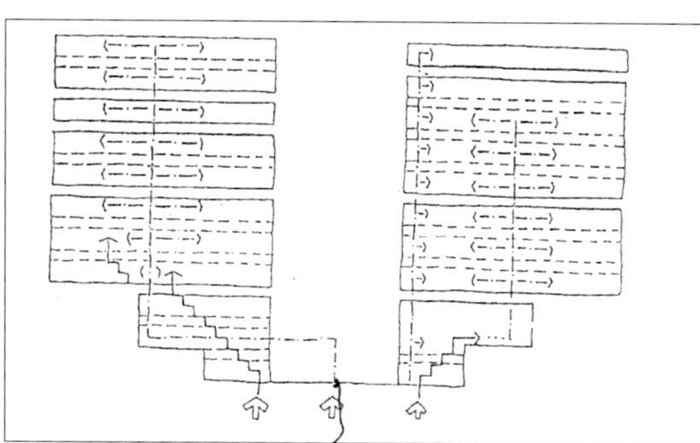

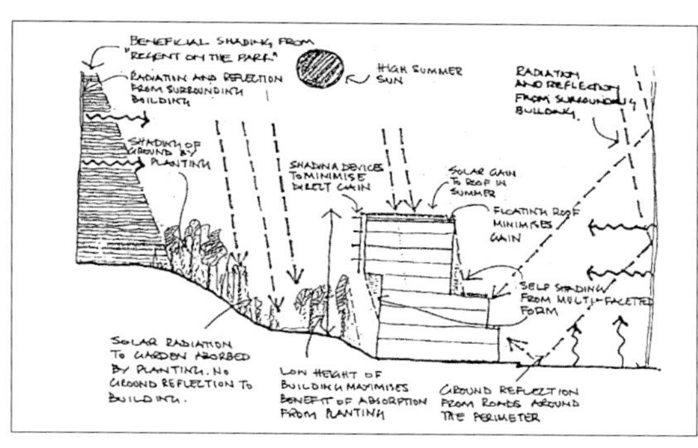

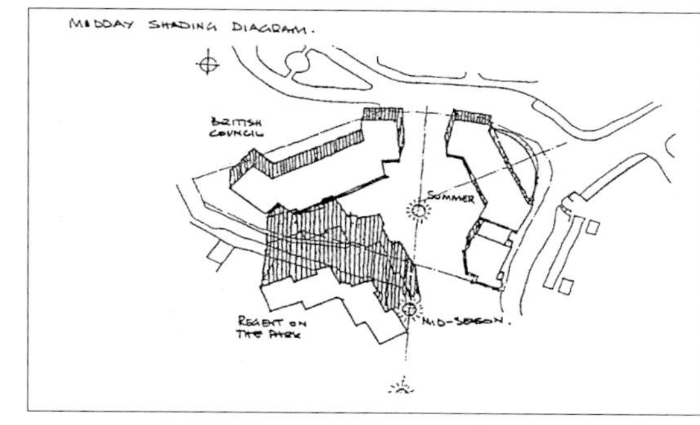

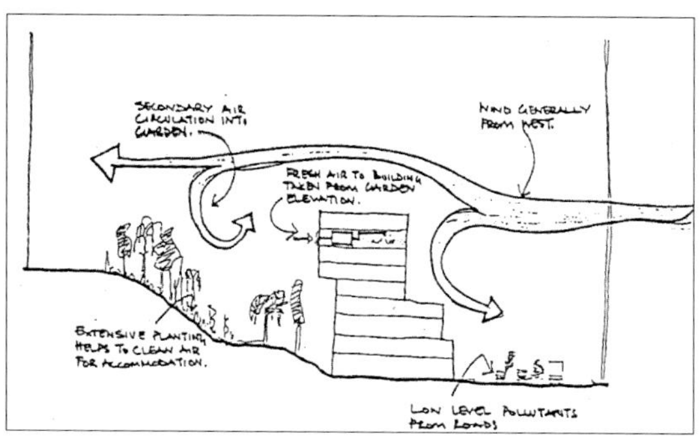

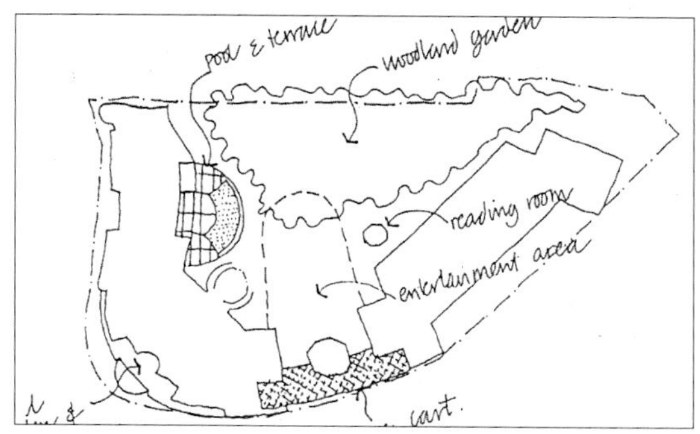

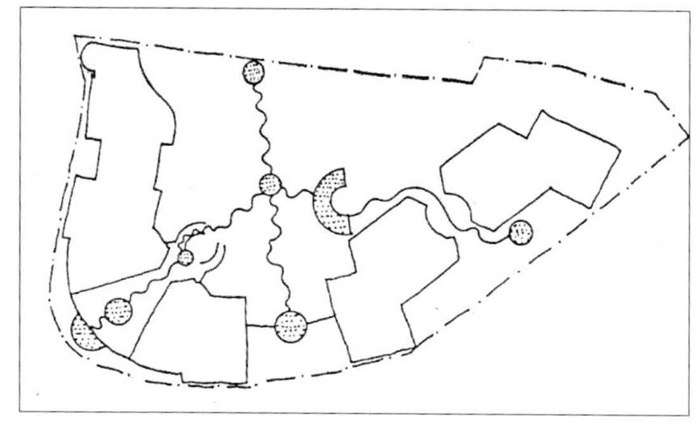

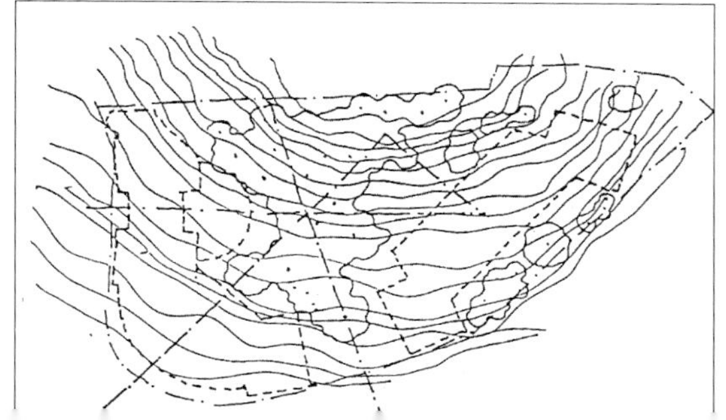

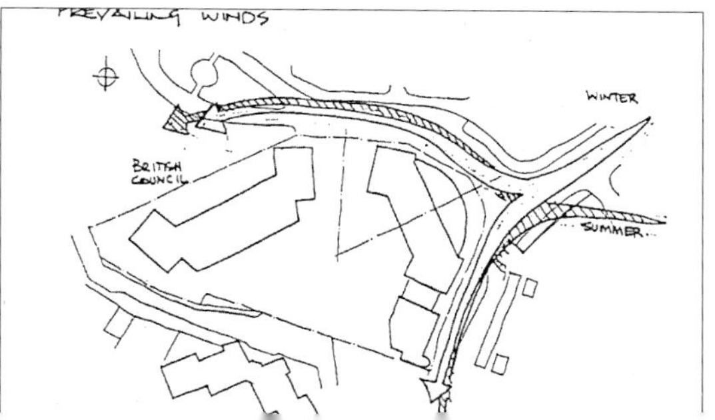

View of main elevation from Supreme Court Road.

Bottom: Views of study model.
Left: North elevation showing British Consulate to left, the entrance court to the centre, and British Council building to the right.

Centre: North-east elevation of Consulate building.
Right: North-west high-level view of whole complex.

Top: Elevation detail.

Centre: The ground-scraping form of the Consulate creates a street presence such as that found in older but vibrant Hong Kong districts.

Elevation of British Consulate.

Bottom: Ground-floor plan and section.

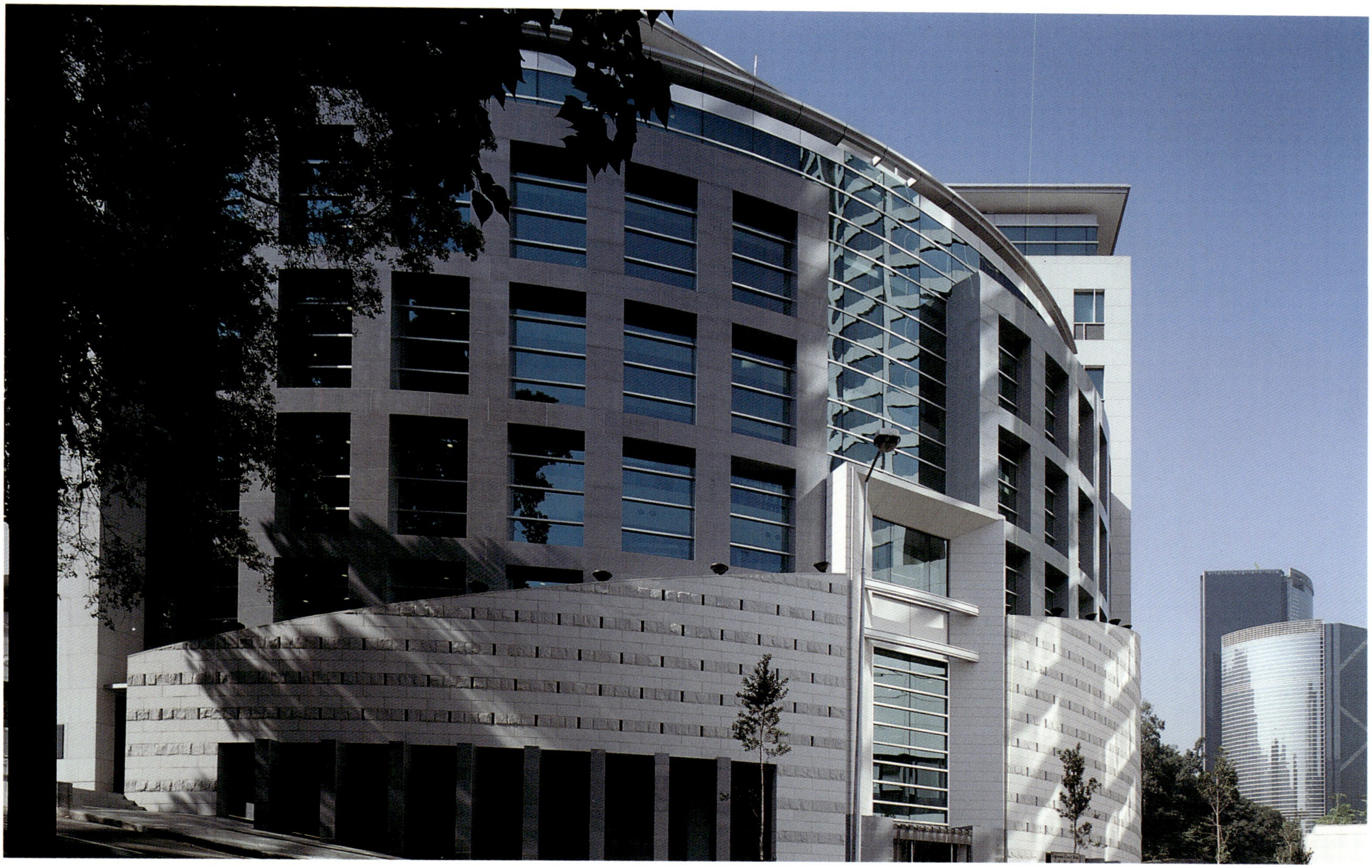

GROUND FLOOR

SECTION THROUGH CONSULATE

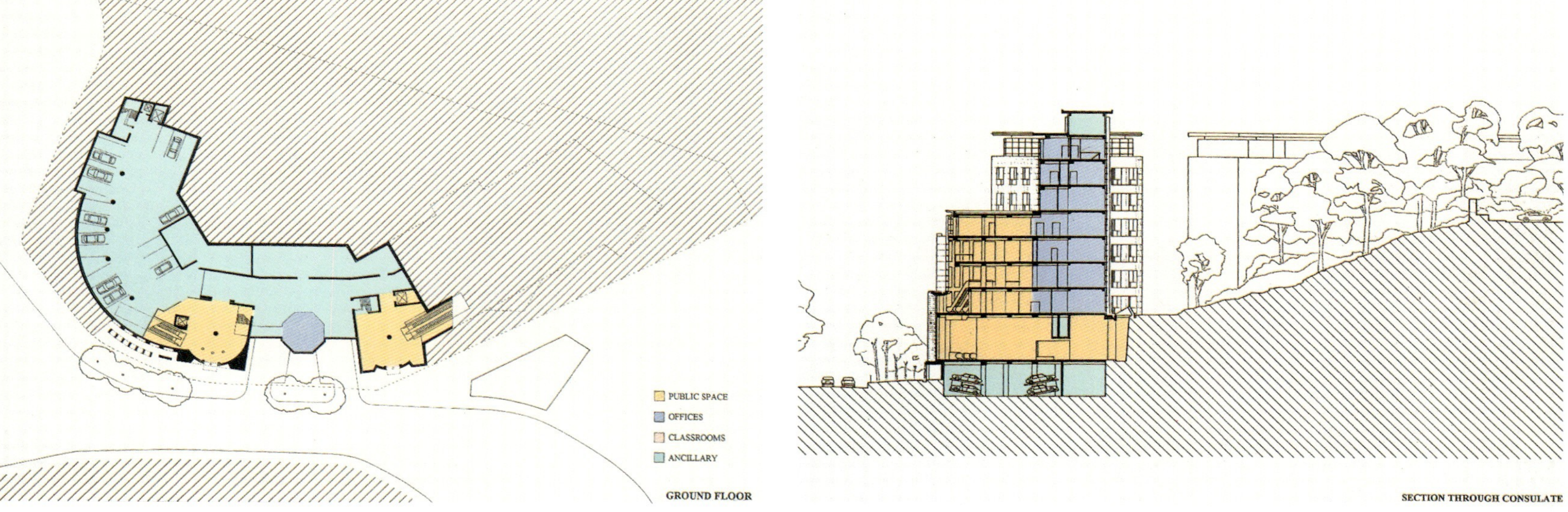

The British Council Building
from Hong Kong Park.

Left: Consulate reception hall.
Centre: Detail of British Council.
Right: Visa and passport section of the Consulate.
Bottom: British Council library.

Right: The British Council looking towards the adjacent residential block.

KOWLOON STATION + MASTERPLAN

The concept behind Kowloon Station and its air-rights development – a project that incorporates all urban systems in one giant web – is the supremacy in the modern world of urban connectivity. On a global level, the transport system provides a high-speed link to Chek Lap Kok airport and the world beyond. On a micro level, the urban plan, driven initially by route planning within the station, ensures that this quarter of the city has superb internal connections.

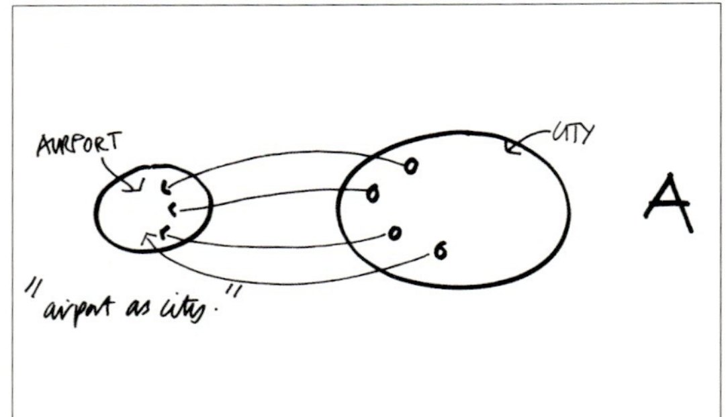

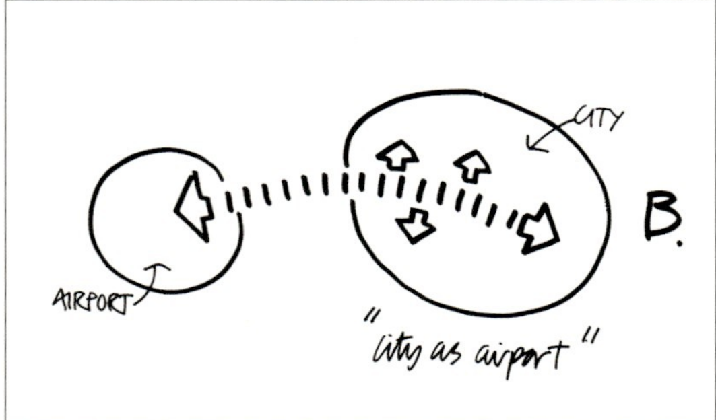

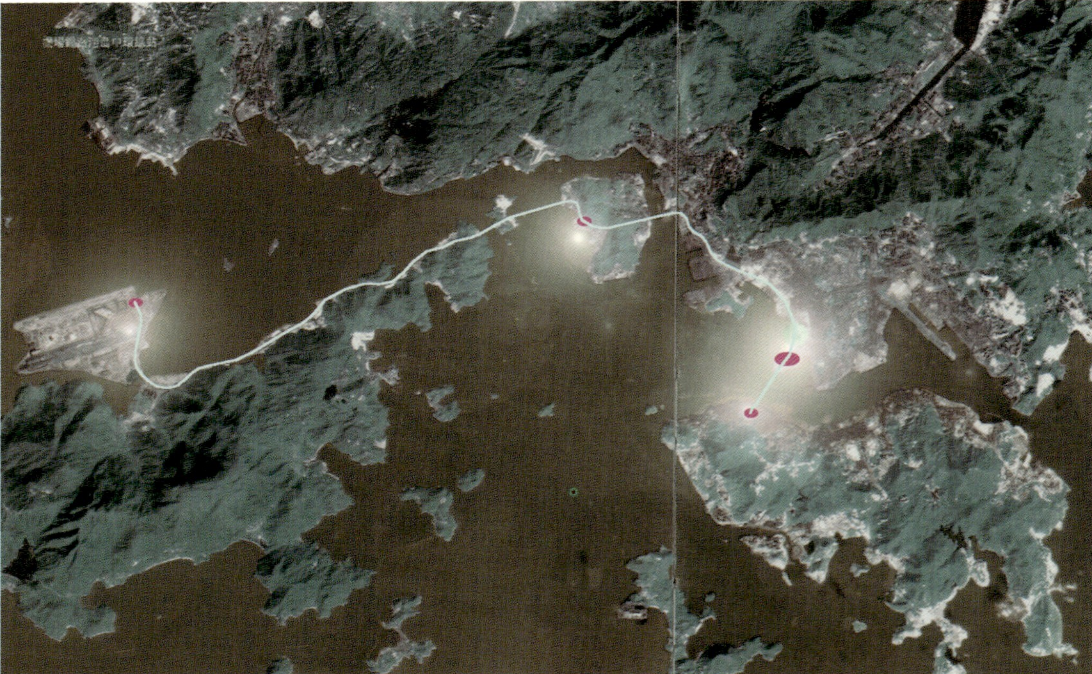

Diagram 'A' shows the traditional relationship of an airport to a city where the airport is a self-contained object with independent transport links back to the city. 'B' shows the new concept of the airport with fast rail link into the city, which thereby has a presence in the city, which in turn contains a piece of the airport. Kowloon Station and masterplan is this kind of airport city within the city.

Top: Station and masterplan under construction with the Kowloon Ventilation Building in the foreground.

Photomontage showing the new airport at Chek Lap Kok and its rail link to the city and the landfill.

The Kowloon Station development represents the convergence of large-scale trends in architecture and urban design. Sustainability, people movement, city planning in three dimensions and public space are key themes of the scheme. The project offers a model for dense urban living, including land conservation, and for the development of an architecture that is in tune with modern technology and mass transit. Key to the station design is the conceptual shift towards passengers' needs and away from the train shed, traditionally a bustling place where people took second place to trains.

The project had its roots in the London transport interchange and air-rights development at Embankment Place, Charing Cross. Together with Alban Gate in London Wall and the MI6 headquarters at Vauxhall Cross, this was one of the three most challenging building schemes – formally, technically and politically – in London at the time. All three involved the reconfiguration of large swathes of land on high-profile sites involving considerable teams of experts. In the early 1990s, with the UK enmeshed in economic recession – and the consequent dearth of comparable projects in the country – the Kowloon commission gave Terry Farrell & Partners the option of expanding in Hong Kong, where the practice had set up an office in 1991 after winning commissions to design the Peak Tower and the British Consulate-General and British Council.

Kowloon Station is a part of a plan instigated in 1989 by the Hong Kong government to replace its congested airport at Kai Tak with a new £12 billion airport on the man-made island of Chek Lap Kok. The airport is linked to Hong Kong Central, the city's business core, by a sophisticated road and high-speed-rail corridor, called the Lantau Area Line and the Airport Express Line. The railway stations, which also include Central, Olympic, Lai King, Tsing Yi, Tung Chung and Chek Lap Kok, are envisaged as much more than transport hubs. They are intended to become platforms for compact city districts linked by rail lines that will eventually form a 193 kilometre integrated linear city sweeping north as far as the mainland city of Guangzhou.

In contrast with most airport transport systems, which are developed incrementally in an ad hoc fashion, direct links to the city had to form part of the plan for the new airport. This requirement inspired a full-scale development of integrated rail and road access, with facilities for in-town check-in and baggage-handling facilities. Even for Hong Kong, a city accustomed to bold and grandiose gestures, this was a remarkable undertaking. Symbolizing the city's political and economic significance, the airport attracts ever-expanding air traffic, while the rail infrastructure

Concept sketches by Doug Streeter for the new station roof.

services the needs of commerce and tourism, as well as supporting the projected expansion of the city.

The transport corridor was built on newly reclaimed land along the west coast of Kowloon and the north coast of Lantau Island to Chek Lap Kok. Kowloon Station, the largest station on the Airport Express Line and a focal point for development, borders the water on a 13.4 hectare site at the southern edge of the West Kowloon reclamation. The brief for Kowloon Station presented by the Mass Transit Railway Corporation (MTRC) included access to the Airport Express; parking lots and bays for buses and taxis; 5126 residential units; a shopping mall; offices, hotels and recreation facilities to be located within a multi-floor podium; and 22 towers (18 residential, two office, one mixed-use and one hotel). The design concept was to provide a landmark structure with an identity befitting its position at the core of the development.

Therefore, when TFP were appointed architects in October 1992, after a competitive tender, their task was a lot more challenging than designing a stop on the Underground. Neither was it a case of turning to the precedent of the traditional Victorian lightweight train shed. If anything, the design of the station looked to the grand scale of modern airports, with their distinct transport, retail and office zones – although the urban setting required a more complex three-dimensional architectural solution than is required in the open spaces of an airport terminal.

The brief was to create a complex transport interchange with a footprint of 75,000 square metres and a gross floor area of 220,000 square metres that would, by 2010, be contained within a new town built to sustain a population of 50,000. The three-dimensional plan comprises six layers – two below ground level, two above and one podium rising to 18 metres above street level and supporting the masterplan towers. Such dense

1999

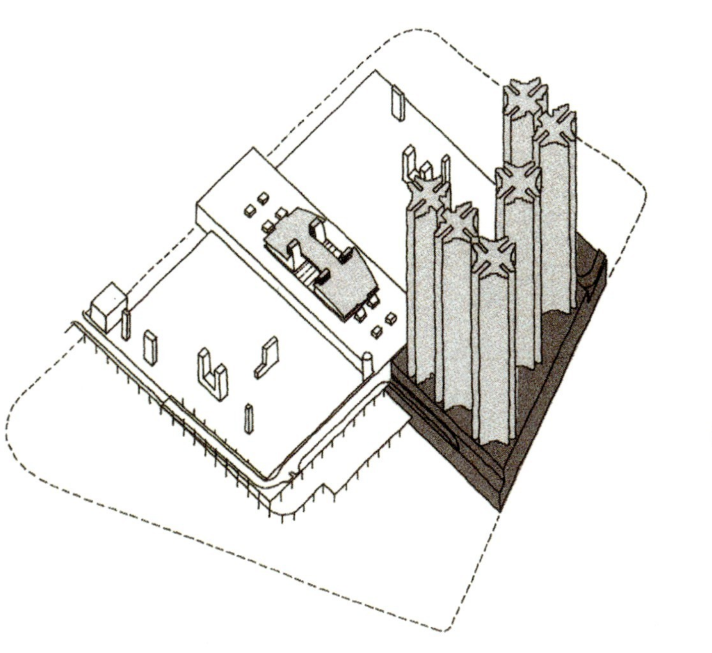

2002

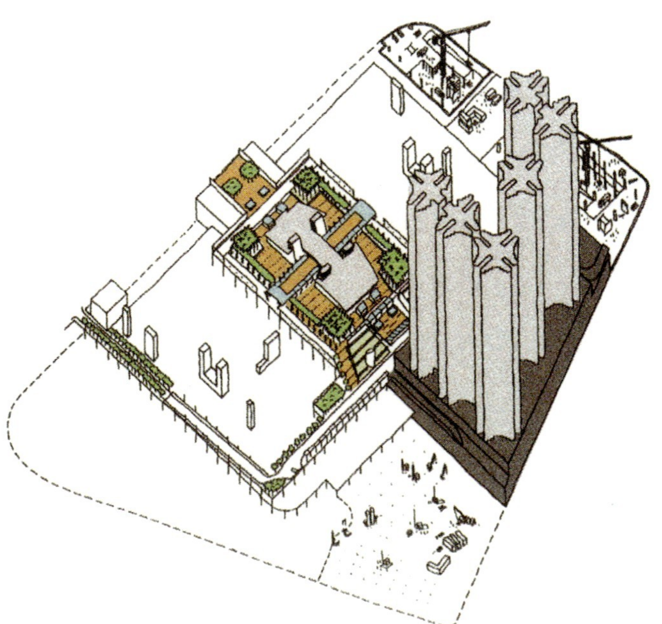

Diagrams illustrating the phasing of the masterplan. Each phase had to be independent, able to exist in spite of delays in each phase, and self-contained and workable in its own right.

Bottom: The two Kowloon stations. On the left is the main line and on the right is the Hong Kong mass transit line, which TFP designed during the 1990s. Had the main line been built, the complex would have been the world's largest transport interchange.

layering is one way to overcome the scarcity of land in Hong Kong.

In response to this – by European standards – almost surreal brief, the practice learned to look at architecture and city design in new ways. Within the context of Hong Kong Island, the dictates of such influential British masterplans as Poundbury and Milton Keynes were meaningless. Hong Kong's complex blanket of high-rise towers draws on European and American precedents but the city also has its own brand of urbanism in which land, buildings and economic order are seen as inextricably linked. The city's influence on the art of modern-day city-making is to be found in the density and diversity of its infrastructure, the layering of circulation systems and the grand air-conditioned interiors. It was these principles that were to be expanded and vibrantly expressed in the design of Kowloon Station.

The station city has three principal levels: ground level is zoned for road and public transport; level one is dedicated to shopping and pedestrian circulation; and the podium level is given over to access and open spaces. The six-layer station is the first part of the project to be completely realized. Seven development and infrastructure construction phases have been planned to follow; phase one is completed and phase two is now on site. Public transport, shopping circulation, pedestrian movement and podium gardens form part of the plan for a complete urban system.

On a functional level, Kowloon Station caters for multiple uses, and this is reflected in its final design. Rather than taking the form of a pared-down architectural statement, a 'one-liner' in the tradition of so much 20th-century architecture, the exterior is a highly graphic structure that works as an iconic focus for the development but is also richly varied, referencing the excitement and heightened awareness that comes through travel and city life. In the words of design partner Doug Streeter, 'There was certainly the idea of a big

2004

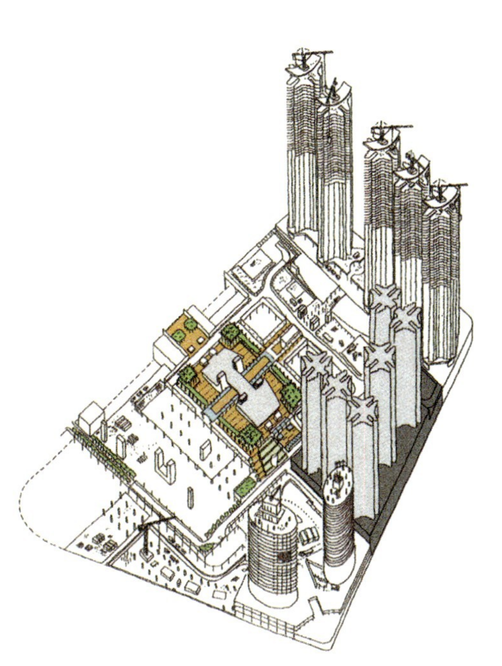

2006

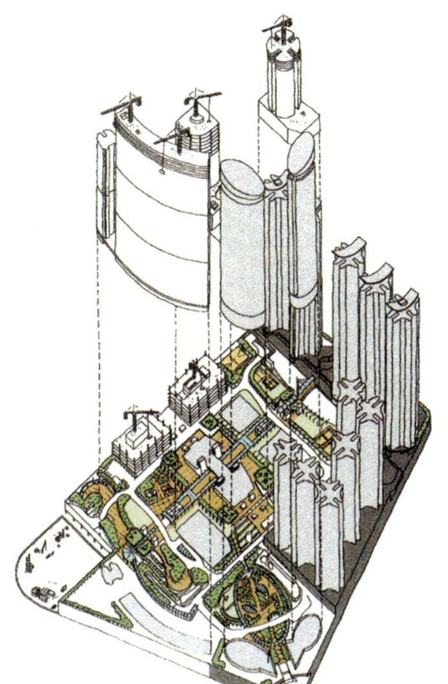

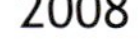

2008

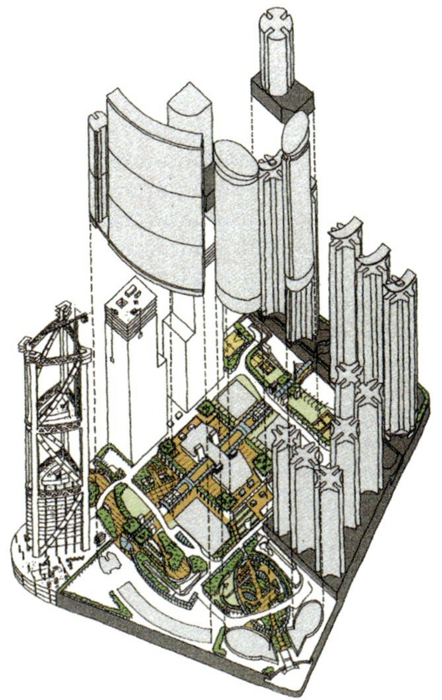

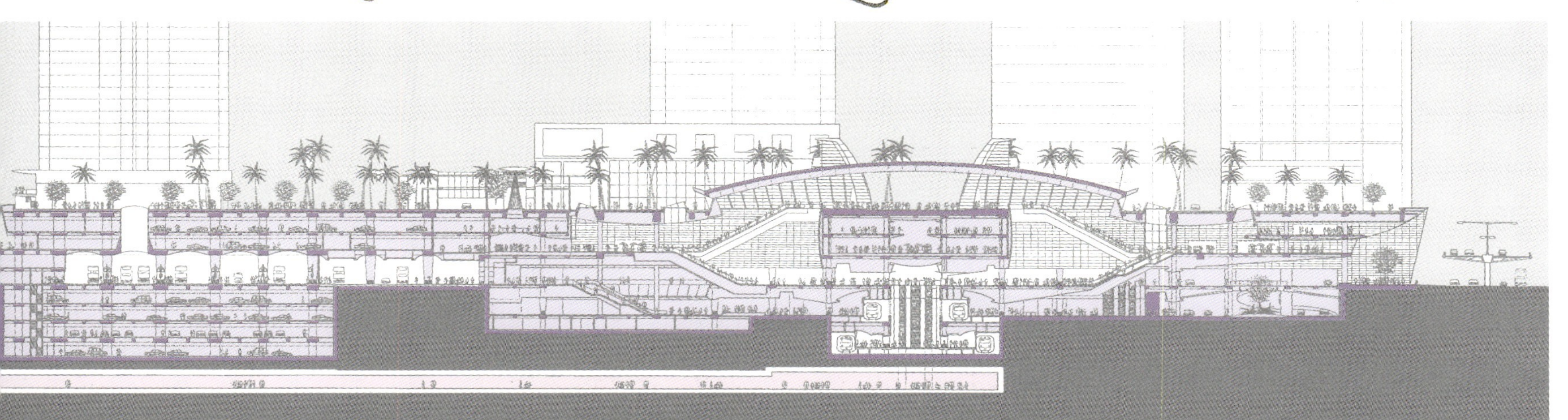

Kowloon MTR Station

space, the big cohesive idea, a major urban focus.' The ground-hugging station's distinctive roof form provides a much needed visual contrast with the homogenous tower blocks beyond. For a building so compact, the design makes use of surprisingly diverse architectural forms: horizontal and vertical, solid and void, sharply angular and softly curved. This is not a static or serene building but one that flows to represent movement, using dynamic form to respond to context and function.

TFP's design for the station represents a union between the dense urban context of Hong Kong and the traditions of Europe. In European fashion, the station square forms the core of the project and is the gateway between the Airport Express Line and the city. Rising from the station square is the Asian-style 'super city': an urban state where growth is upward and compact rather than sprawling. The idea of this landscaped central public space takes the concept of the historic square onto a more futuristic plane. The traditional station concourse has evolved to provide a dramatic volume to hold the station's vertical circulation, as well as giving access to the surrounding cityscape above. The single space makes it simple for people to find their way around. It incorporates a void extending up to the station roof, where natural light is admitted through skylights. This lessens the passengers' sense of being underground and makes orientation easier.

Clad in 3280 square metres of stainless steel, the roof of the station concourse rises east-west from its podium in a low-slung vault that, Eastern-style, turns softly upwards at each end. Four columns spring up from level one, two storeys below, to make a covered open square. The two main entrances are placed on either side of this square. Below the station roof are six public levels and one service level, 10 metres below sea level. Along the north-south rail axis, escalators and stairs descend 14 metres through a glazed escalator hall from ground level to the Tung Chung MTR line platforms at the station's lowest level. Seven glass-encased elevators operate between these levels, complementing the 34 escalators and 71 staircases. The station is planned to encourage visual connections and permeability between different levels, as well as to provide maximum convenience for the maximum number of passengers. While most passengers pass through the station without changing levels, others use escalators bordered by windows with views to neighbouring platforms and trains. From the Airport Express departure area, openings through the walls of the in-town check-in hall allow views through to the arrivals side. In this way, the movements of departing and arriving passengers are visible across the full expanse of the station.

In 1992, when TFP were appointed to the project, Kowloon Station's future site was submerged below Victoria Harbour. Constructed in just 44 months (between November 1994 and June 1998), the station now forms the seed of an 'instant' new city. It clearly demonstrated that the essence of new-city making today is infrastructure. It is roads, transit systems and public space that provide a framework for the evolution of urban life.

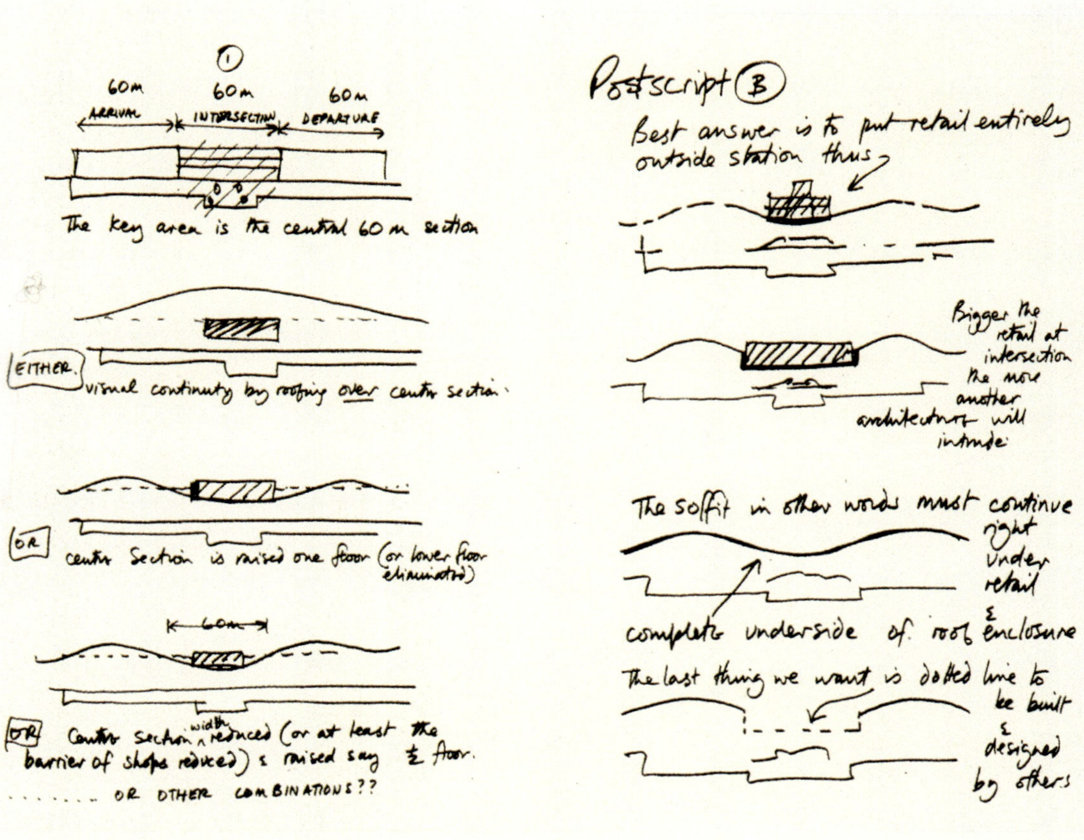

Typical concept drawings by Terry Farrell sent by fax to Hong Kong during the 1990s. Shown here are broad strategy ideas for handling the relationship of the station roof to the station itself.

The concept sketches were finally realized in three-dimensional form.

Masterplan strategy diagram.

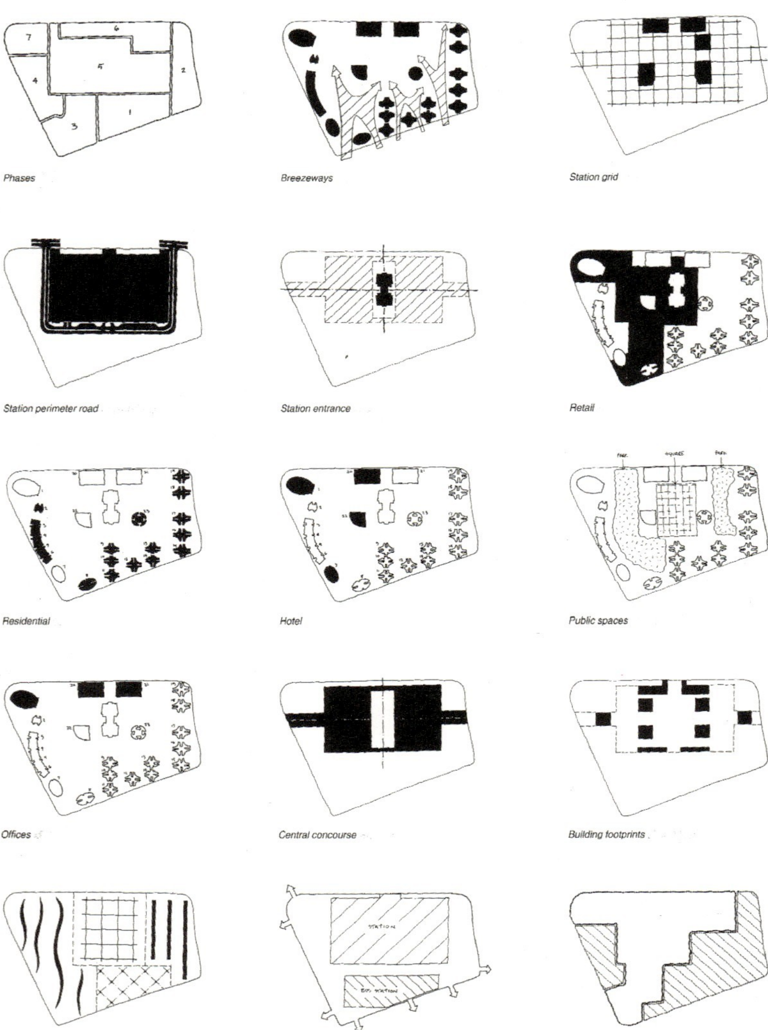

Top right: Model of the masterplan.

Bottom: Ground-level plan of station and development above.

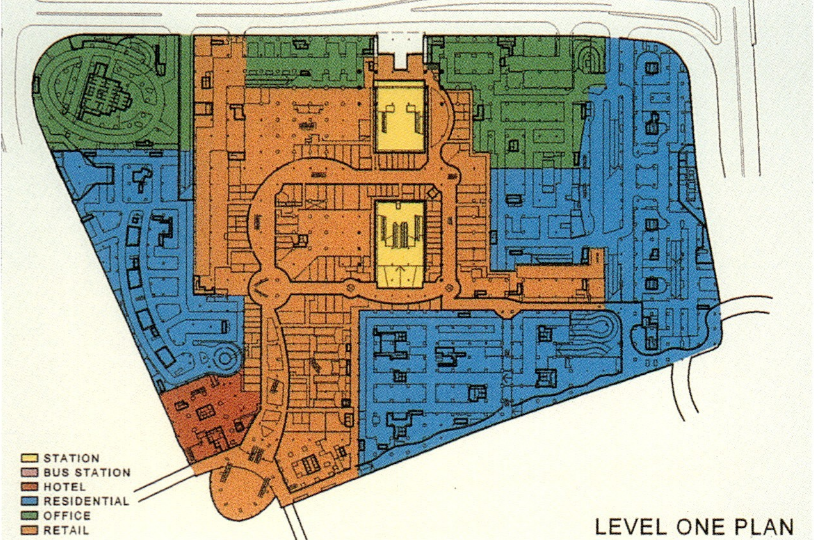

Bottom: Level one plan.

Miniature diagrams showing the various combinations of pedestrian connection and routes of arrival and departure throughout the station.

Bottom: Model showing section through scheme and (right) the iconic gateway roof that covers the station.

Computer drawing showing the station's great halls.

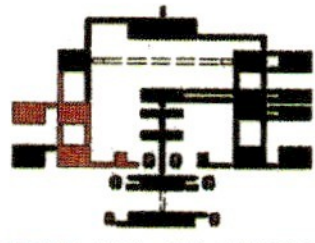
DROP OFF ITCI - AEL DEPARTUI

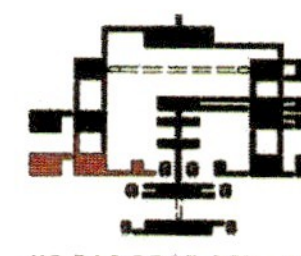
NO BAG DROP OFF - AEL DEPARTURE

CITY - ITCL / AEL DEPARTURE

BUS - ITCI / AEL DEPARTURE

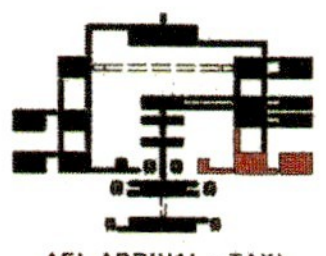
AEL ARRIVAL - TAXI

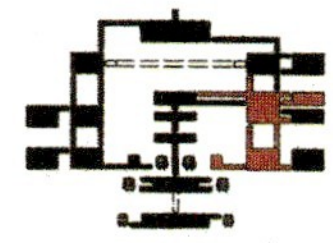
AEL ARRIVAL TO LFB

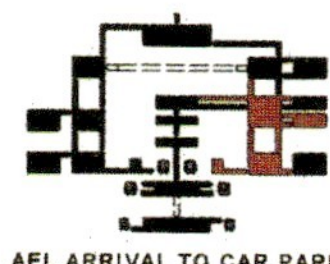
AEL ARRIVAL TO CAR PARK

CAR PARK TO AEL DEPARTURE

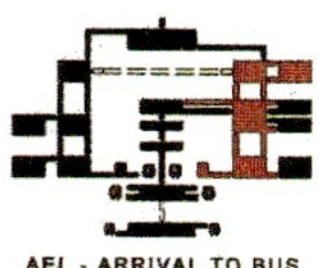
AEL - ARRIVAL TO BUS

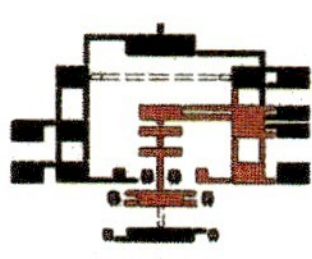
AEL ARRIVAL TO LAL

LAL TO ITC & AEL DEPARTURE

AEL ARRIVAL TO CITY

SHOPPING TO ITCI / AEL DEPARTURE

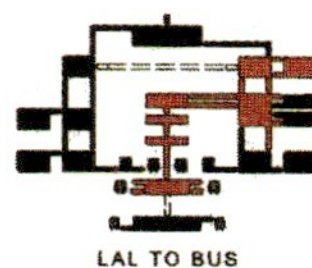
LAL TO BUS

LAL TO CITY

LAL TO SHOP

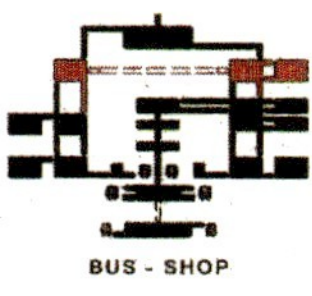
BUS - SHOP

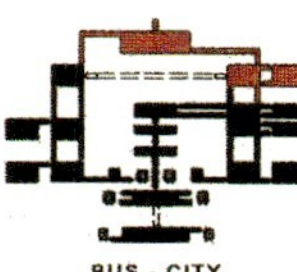
BUS - CITY

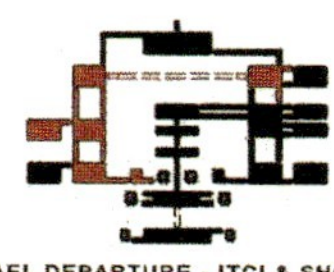
AEL DEPARTURE - ITCI & SHOP

CITY & SHOP

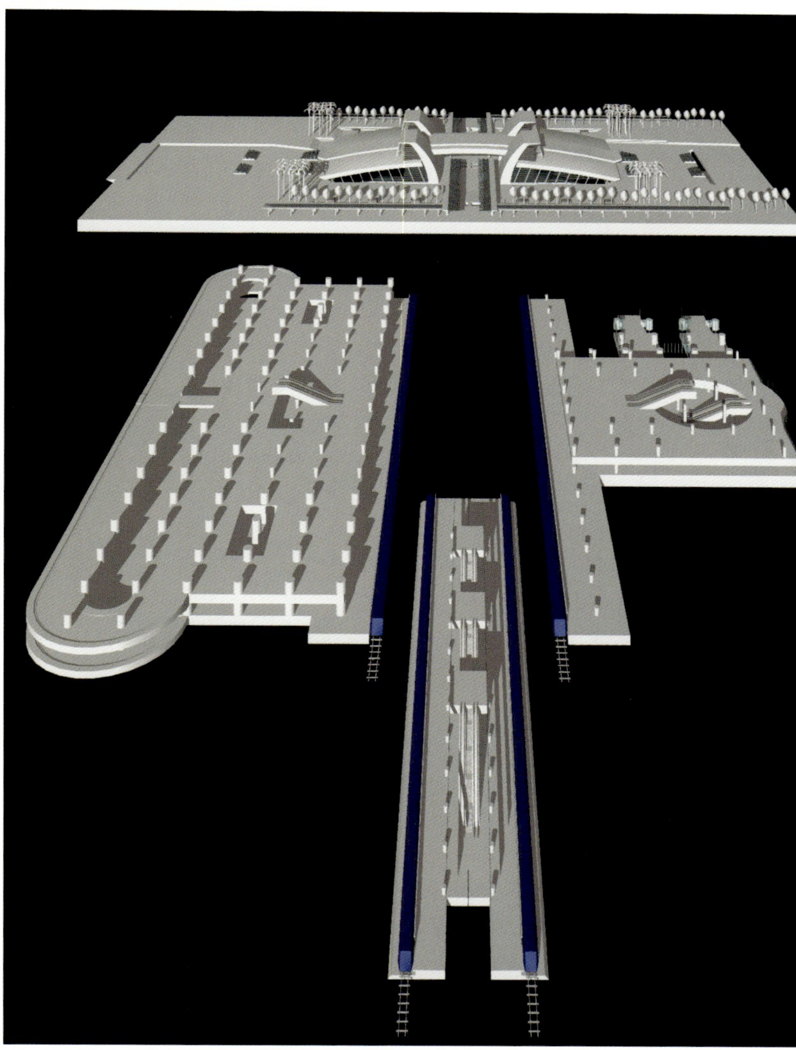

Station interiors.

Over time, the station – shown here in grand isolation – will gradually become part of a major new urban district, with 4000 dwellings, several office and hotel buildings, over a million square feet of retail space, bus stations, large garages and car parks, which will fill in around the station's arched roof.

View of station entrance with new square being built around it.

The main station entrance.

地鐵
MTR

KOWLOON VENTILATION BUILDING

Kowloon Ventilation Building (KVB) is sited in what will be the West Kowloon Regional Park, by Victoria Harbour, strategically located above the railway at the point where the cross-harbour rail tunnel crosses the Kowloon shoreline. KVB faces the world's most imposing urban waterfront – an unusually prominent location for such a utilitarian building. The building is a visual celebration of the landfill and harbour frontages that characterize the new man-made Hong Kong.

FLOOR "LID" BUILDING

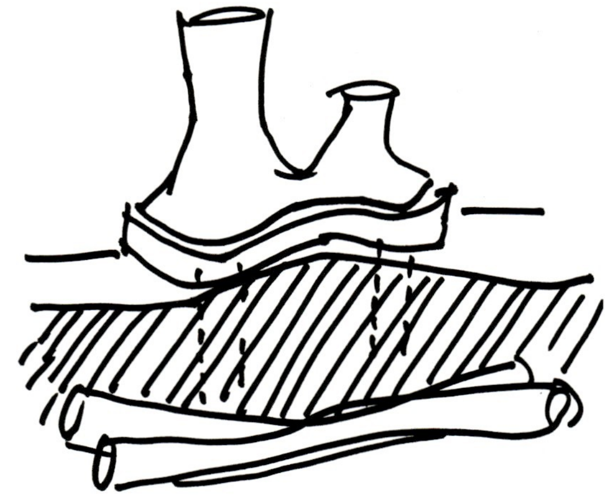

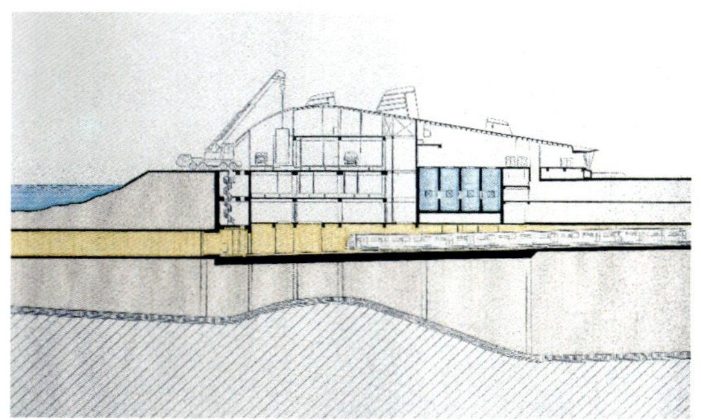

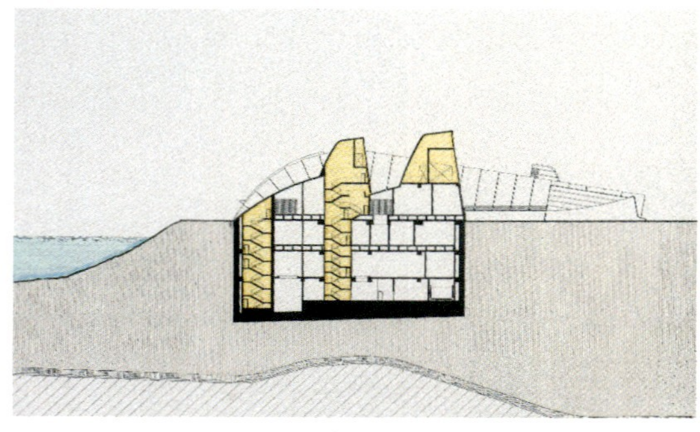

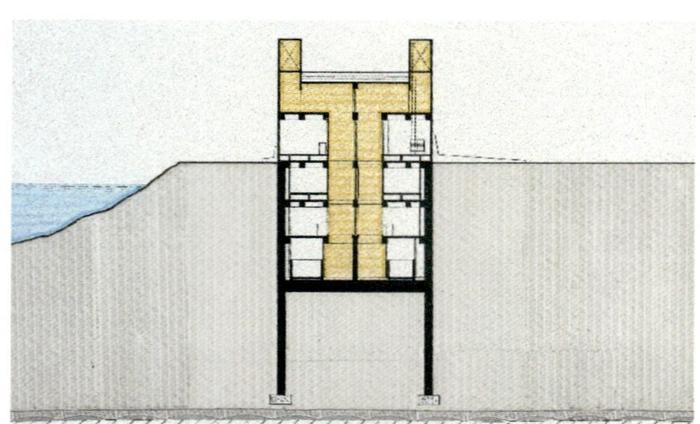

Sections.

View of the building under construction.

Top: Concept sketch by Terry Farrell showing the Blackwall Tunnel Ventilation buildings from 1961 (right) compared with the Kowloon Ventilation Building (left): industrial Buildings as sculptural form.

Concept drawings done in collaboration with Richard Portchmouth.

Linked to the Kowloon Station commission, the Kowloon Ventilation Building provides technical support for the station and approach tunnels. The building is 90 metres long by 27 metres wide and its primary function is to disperse the build-up of heat from trains, plant and passengers. This is achieved by pumping sea water from the harbour to the station, where it is passed through a heat-exchange system before being filtered, electro-chlorinated and returned to the harbour for disposal. The cooling process relies on the daily pumping of 650 cubic metres of water through two pipes 1.5 metres in diameter, which are located in the KVB's cavernous chambers. Ventilation of the underground railway lines and the pressure release caused by the piston effect of trains passing along the tunnels are also handled by the KVB. Two huge shafts resembling sculptural louvred towers suck air into and vent air from the railway tunnels below. The KVB also houses two sets of gates to protect the cross-harbour or approach tunnel against flooding, escape shafts, line maintenance access and power generation supply and back up.

Once the operational functions had been dealt with, the architects were faced with the challenge of how to integrate such a utilitarian structure into a public park. In the event, only a third of the building is visible; the remainder is buried in a vast excavation that extends 20 metres down to the rail tunnels. Above ground is a low-cost reinforced-concrete building finished in simple materials – grey metal cladding and yellow and grey tiles – but designed as a dynamic, swooping form that allows it to masquerade as sculpture, with much popular appeal. The form is so dynamic that the building profile changes from different vantage points: from some views it appears to be an animal emitting air and sucking up water, while from others it appears as a passive, landscaped hill. Terry Farrell empathizes with the way the Chinese use stories and metaphors. Kowloon means 'nine dragons', a name derived from the nine hills surrounding the island. The ventilation building, with its dragon-like features, can therefore be seen as a gently humourous reference to its location.

The design of the ventilation building mirrors the graphic typology of the Kowloon Station concourse roof so that the two buildings together form a physical and visual relationship. The commission strangely mirrors Terry Farrell's first built scheme, the now-listed Blackwall Tunnel Ventilation Towers of 1964, which stand on the north and south bank of the River Thames.

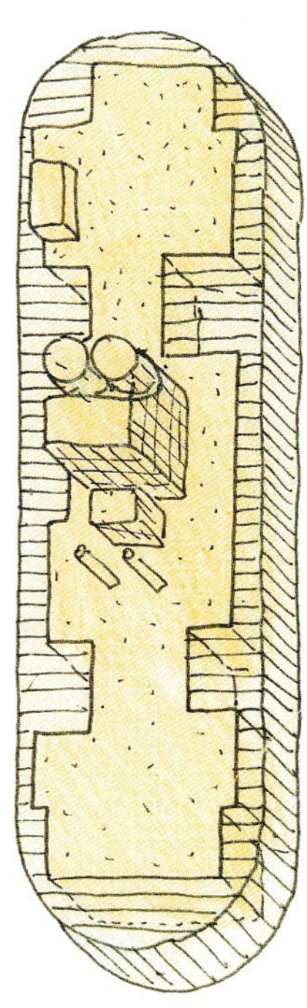

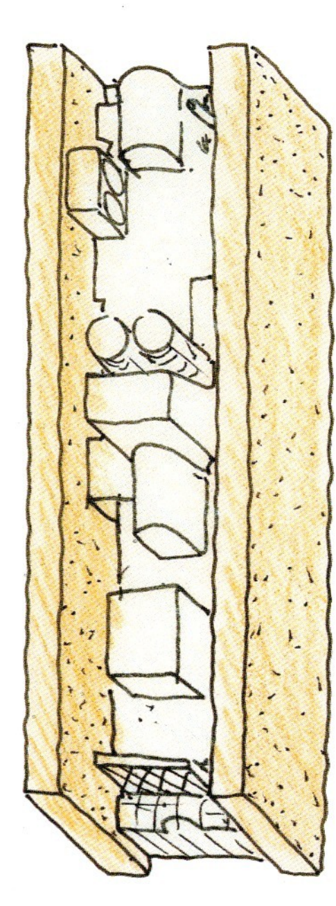

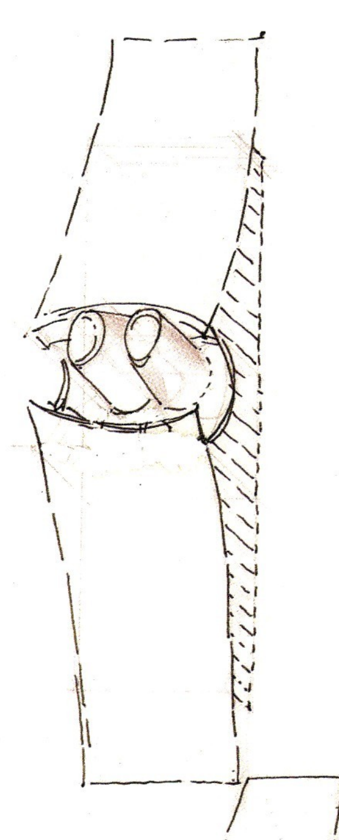

Top left: The Blackwall Tunnel Ventilation Building was an early precursor of the Kowloon Ventilation Building. Similar in function, the building was given its own expressive sculptural form in the belief that an engineering building is also a piece of sculpture.

Views of the Kowloon Ventilation Building.

Series of early model studies exploring colour.

Bottom: Views of early computer model.

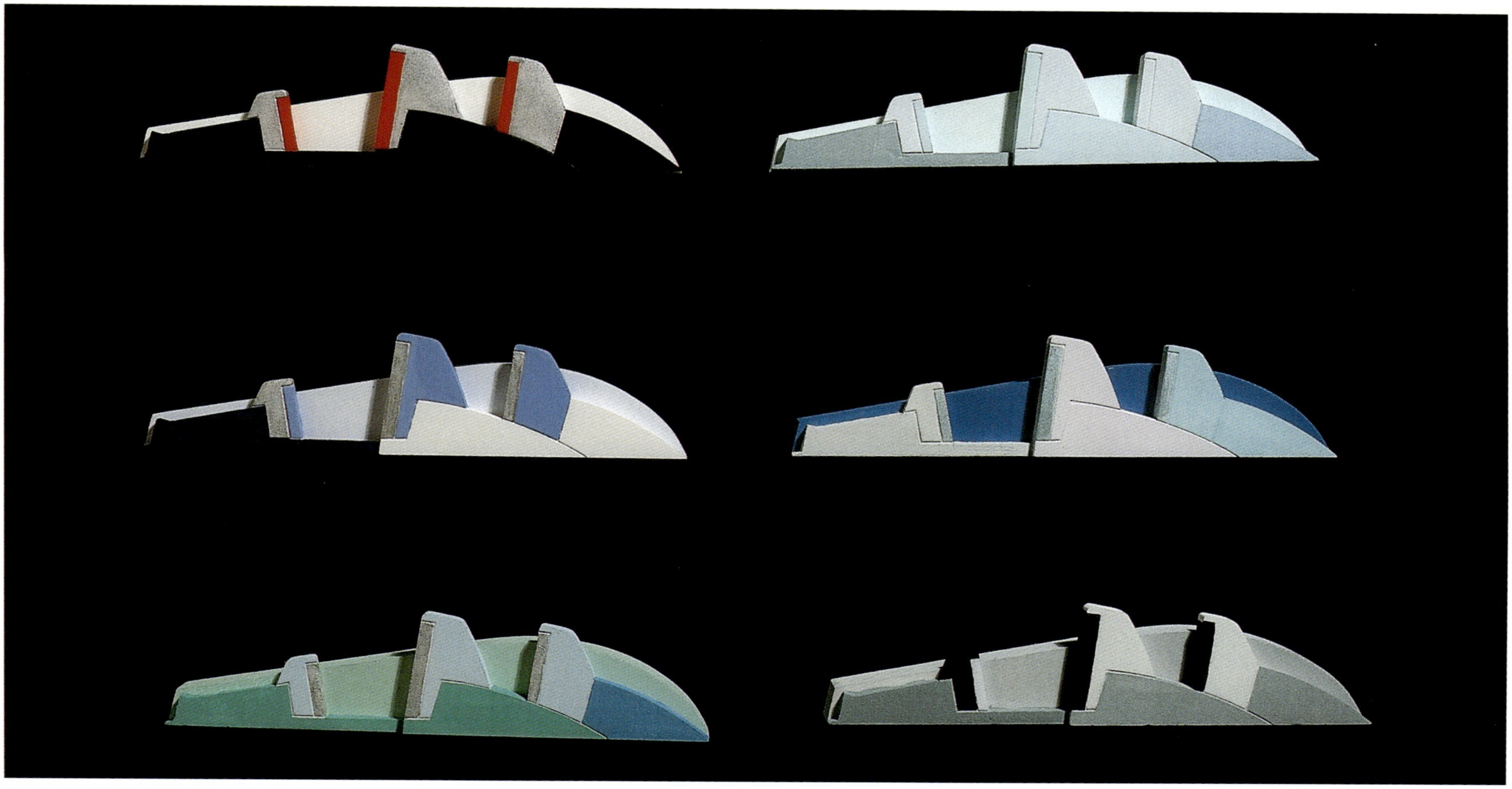

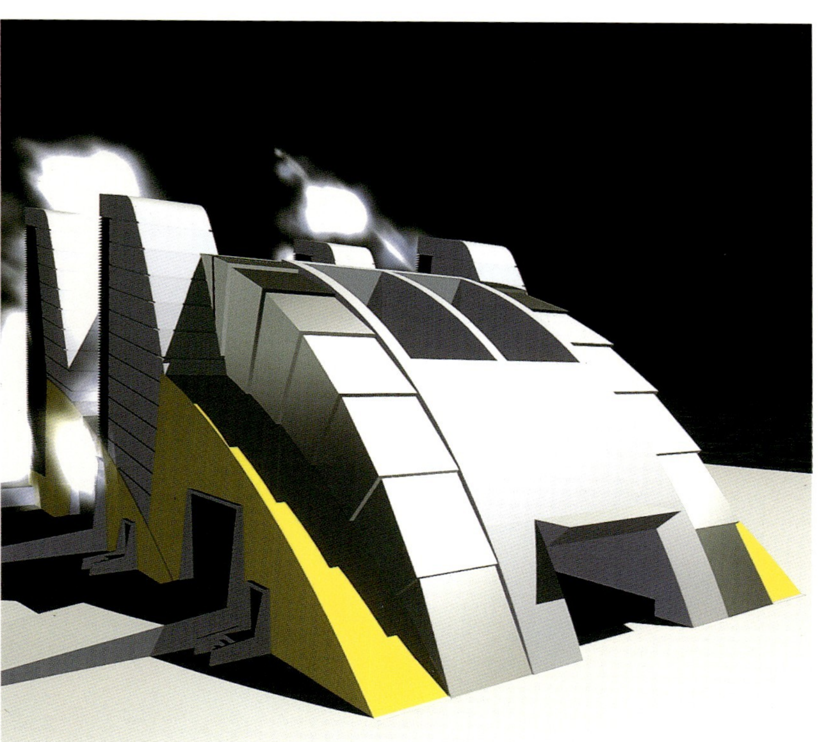

Photographs of the
completed building.

The Ventilation building shown before the completion of its park setting. In the distance, the 'sky' building of the Peak, a form that is pressed up against the sky, contrasts with the ventilation building, which is its inversion. The result is the 'grounded' bowl and the 'flying' bowl.

PEAK TOWER

The Peak Tower was the first project undertaken in China by Terry Farrell & Partners. Indeed, before 1990 the practice had never built out of London. Perhaps surprisingly for a ground-breaking commission, the Peak is a building that confidently lays aside European precedents and wholeheartedly engages with the Hong Kong spirit. Hong Kong was, in Terry Farrell's words, 'the first step into the unfamiliar', and for the practice, freed from the British tendency towards mild-mannered architecture, the Peak represented previously unimagined possibilities.

Victoria Peak, the site that was to be built on, had been inspiring spectators with its views over Hong Kong to the north for more than a century. The Peak tramway, a funicular railway, was Hong Kong's most popular tourist attraction. Before the railway opened in 1888, pampered colonials had been transported by sedan chair up the 400 metre

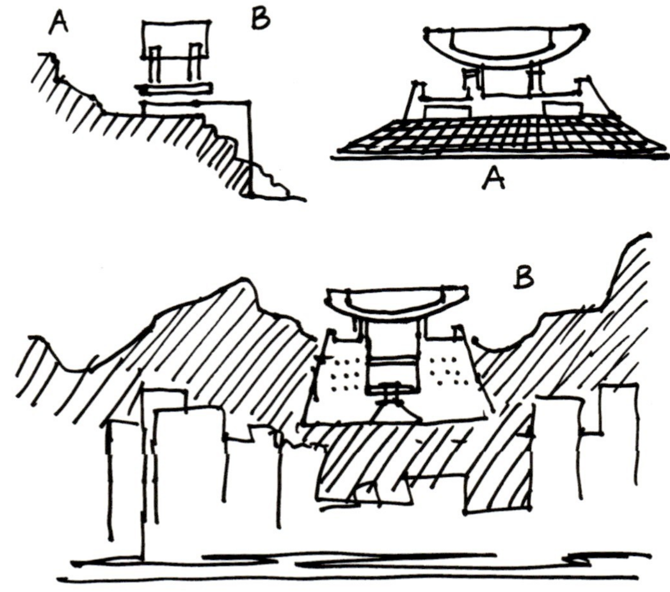

The funicular tram arriving as it has done for over 100 years, now underneath the new Peak bowl.

The Peak viewed from a long distance across the harbour.

Top: Concept drawings by Terry Farrell showing the two faces of the Peak.
A. Five-storey building on the local urban public square.
B. Twelve-storey building in hill-top city-wide context.

Top: Tourist memento of the Peak and other recognizable Hong Kong buildings.

View of the funicular from the 1930s.

View from the early 1960s before the building of a visitor attraction.

Top: North elevation.

Conceptual ideas behind the Peak at competition stage.

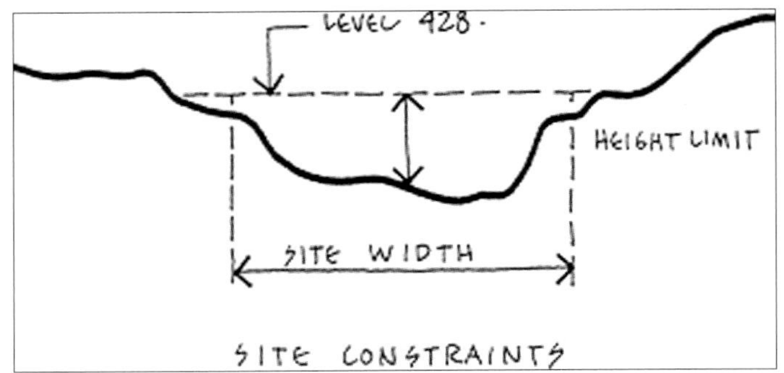

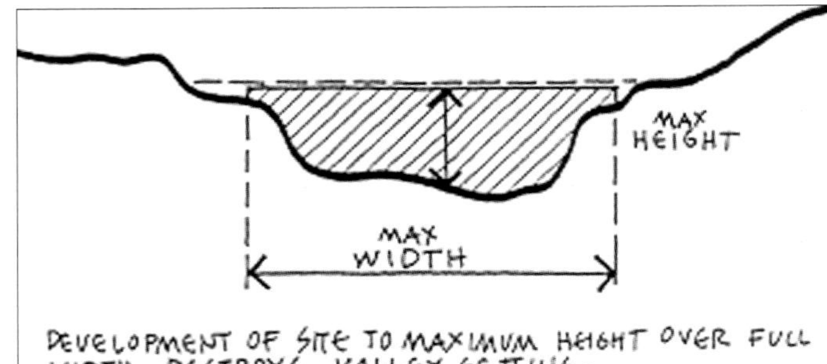

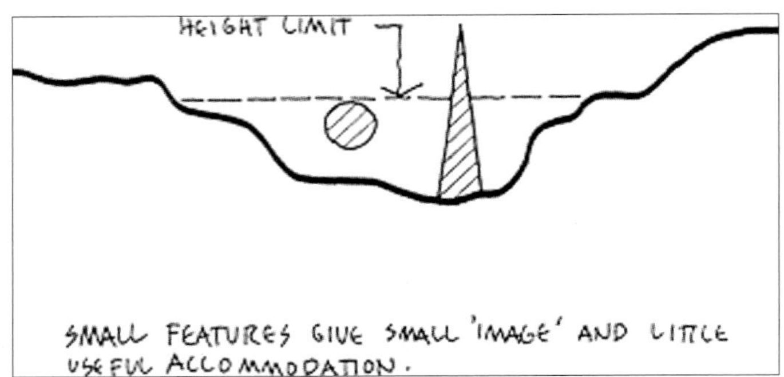

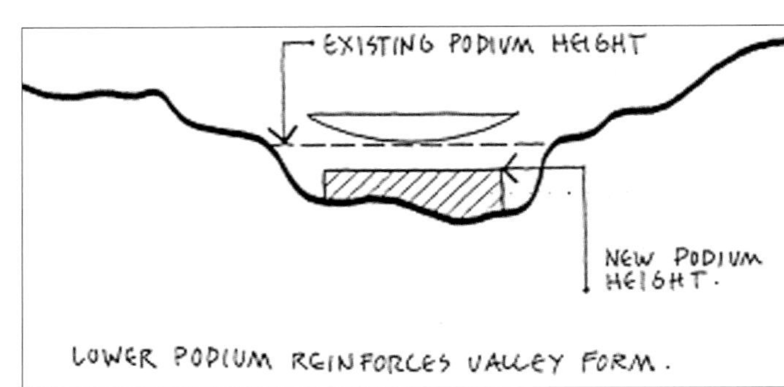

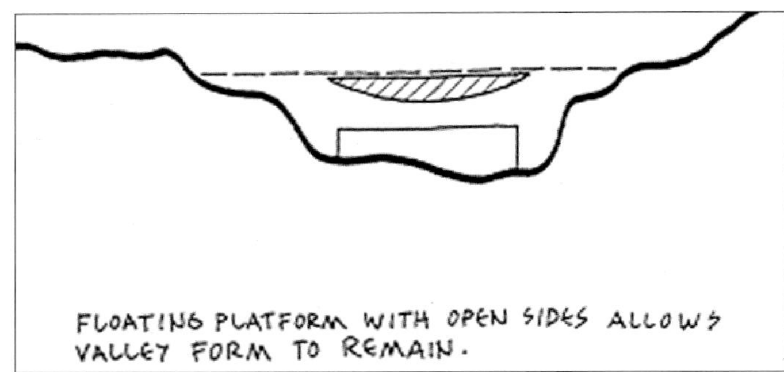

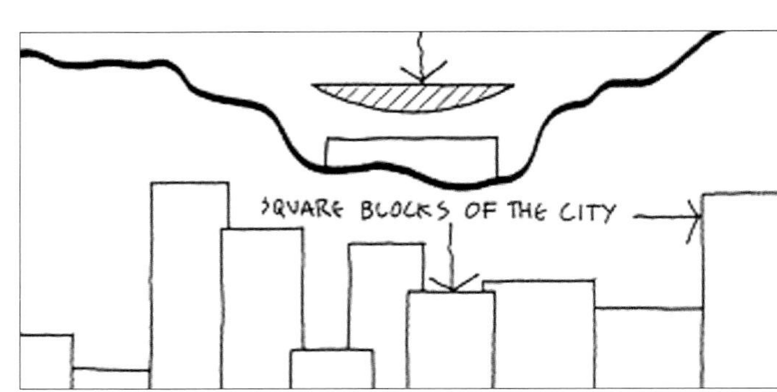

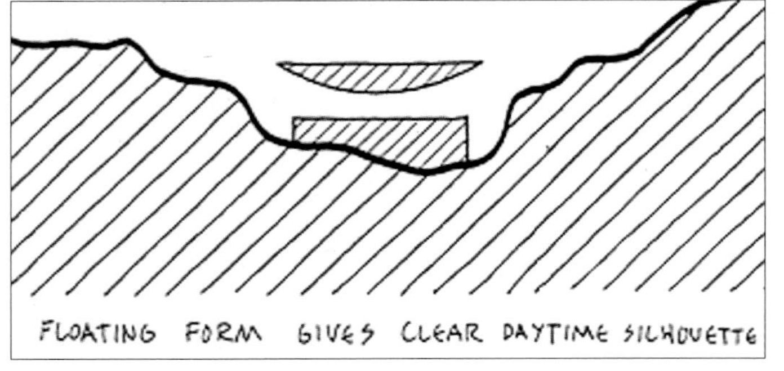

peak to marvel at the spectacular panoramas of mainland China and Macau, as well as to experience the cooler air.

Terry Farrell first went to Hong Kong in 1964, but it was only in 1972 that the potential for a Victoria Peak visitor centre was realized, and a small tram-station building was constructed in a valley by Palmer & Turner, albeit without shops or a restaurant. By the end of the 1980s, the client, Hong Kong and Shanghai Hotels Ltd, had realized that the existing building was too small for the growing number of visitors. When, in June 1991, TFP was invited to enter a competition with Aldo Rossi, Tadao Ando and three Hong Kong architects, the practice recognized the need for a landmark visitor attraction that exploited its location and advertised its presence. While some fanciful responses to the brief, such as a Ferris wheel, were submitted, TFP put forward a design package that simply built on what was already there. The practice saw the benefits of providing a heroic silhouette that could be recognized from a great distance and would create a startling backdrop to Hong Kong's spectacular cityscape.

The width of the site was limited to take account of the natural line of the surrounding hills, and the tower's height was restricted to 428 metres above sea level. As its cross section shows, the building would stand on dramatically sloping land. These site conditions resulted in the need for an unusual proportion of 3-1, which eventually resulted in a floor plate 75 metres long and 25 metres deep.

TFP's design wove elements of traditional Chinese architecture into a forward-looking building. The separation between the pagoda base and its series of floating tile roofs – a familiar motif – was utilized to conjure up an elevated bowl-like form that seems to hang in space above the mountain skyline. In contrast with the floating quality of the bowl, the lower part of the building is rooted to the mountain and takes its cue from the grandeur of the steeply sloping fortified walls of traditional Chinese and Tibetan ceremonial buildings. Heroic in intent, the building's combination of solid base, open podium and floating roof with upswept eaves recalls, yet softens, the order and authority found in imperial Chinese architecture. The Peak rejoices in this continuity between old and new, past and future.

Terry Farrell embraced the symbolism inherent in the Chinese architectural tradition, and the result has been likened to a pair of hands, a bird in flight and a boat. Whichever simile is most accurate, the curved bowl makes a startling impact when seen against the tightly packed angular tower blocks that make up Hong Kong's harbour, as well as creating a silhouette that is unmistakable both during the day and at night.

The design process had to take account of a number of pragmatic considerations. For example, the building would be exposed to high wind velocities, particularly during typhoons, so a wind tunnel had to be used to produce accurate designs for the large areas of glazing and aluminium. The construction phase also raised logistical problems. The demolition of the existing building on the site required careful planning because the weight of the elevated structure had helped the original retaining walls to hold back the site's ground pressures. To compensate, an extensive, continuous caisson wall of over 40 caissons, anchored with pieces of steel 20 metres long, was inserted into the rock before demolition began. The discovery of a number of unexploded shells from the Second World War presented the contractor with an unexpected challenge. The principal construction issue for the superstructure was erecting the reinforced concrete frame of the bowl in its elevated position. Access was difficult along the remote and narrow Old Peak Road, so a temporary steel platform was installed from which to place the formwork for casting more than 1000 tonnes of reinforced concrete.

After arriving at the tram terminal, visitors cross a public square and enter the Peak Tower from the south. The north elevation, facing the city and harbour beyond, drops over the cliff edge, diving down four storeys below the entrance level. Seen

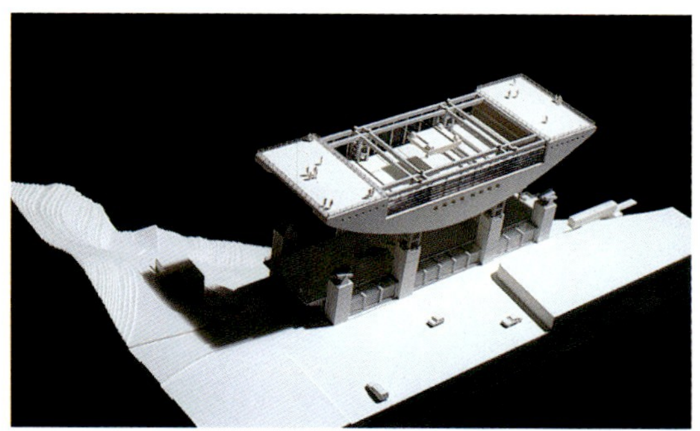

Model at competition stage.

Final plans and sections.

from the harbour side, this elevation presents what looks like a heroic 12-storey frontage. The architects conceived of grand events for the basement and the top storey of the tower to encourage visitors to explore all levels. For example, the double-height basement includes a themed ride, which ends at the lowest level; from there, visitors proceed upwards towards the bowl, which contains the viewing platforms, restaurants and shops. Escalators and high-speed lifts, as well as building services, are contained within the building's four 'legs'. The remodelled upper tram terminus is incorporated in the design, and the tram machine room is housed in the centre of the building.

The building offers new perspectives on two very different scenes: to the south are the mountains, and to the north are the harbour, waterways and city – it is the latter that attracts observers. People love watching building sites, traffic interchanges, aircraft taking off and the movement of traffic. Away from the city, the peaceful environs of the Peak Tower provide a vantage point from which to understand and think about Hong Kong.

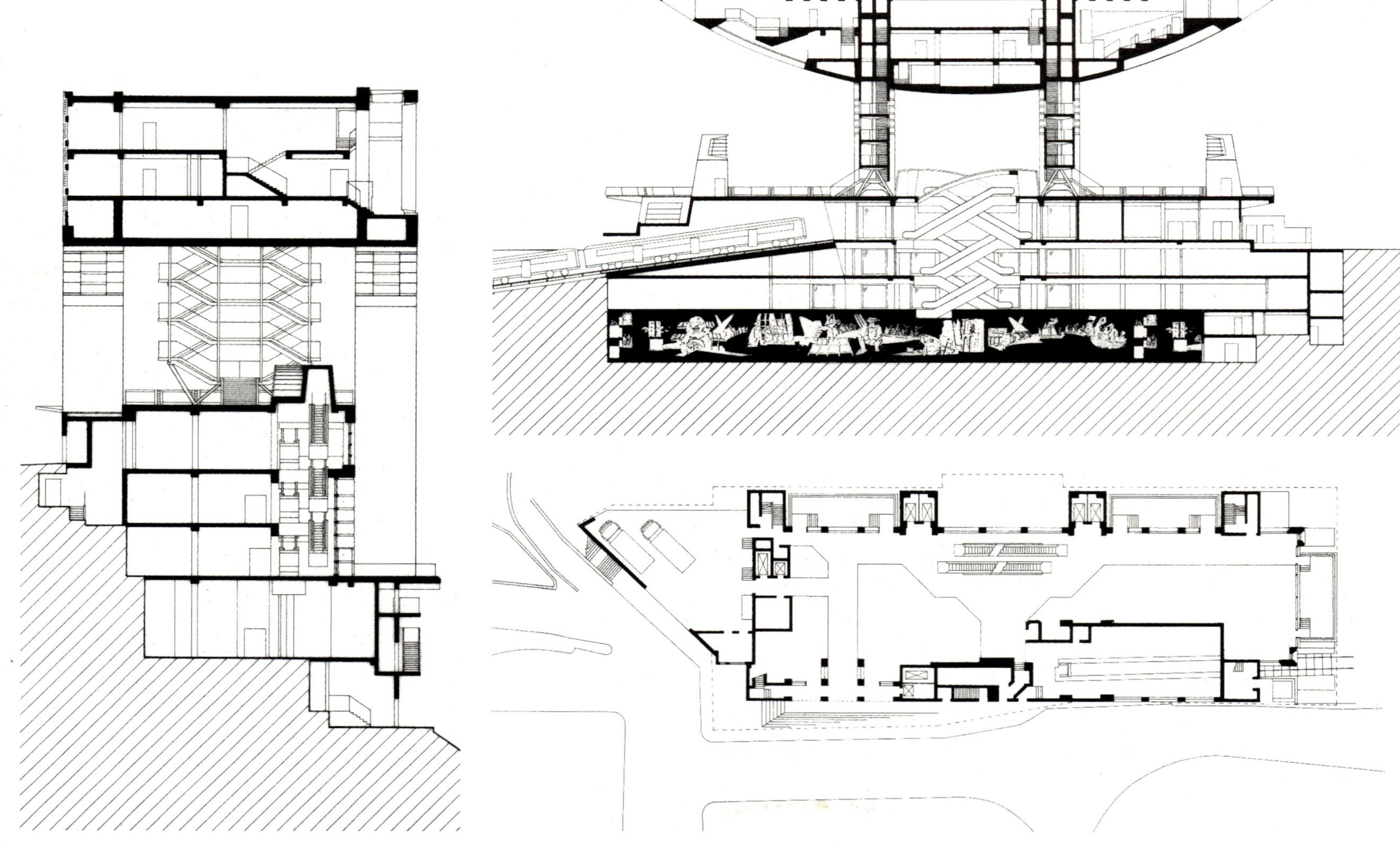

The Peak at night.
The Hong Kong Shanghai bank is illuminated in the mid-ground.

East elevation.

Bottom: View from south side of the new square where the Peak sits as a building in a group of buildings.

Detail.

Detail of south elevation.

BEIJING

BEIJING

Top left: Satellite view. Beijing is at the centre with a light grey rectangle in the middle of the city. Tian'anmen Square is a light-grey rectangle in the centre, with the Forbidden City located above.

Bottom left: Aerial view of the Forbidden City. The geometry is continuously repeated down to its smallest forms.

Below: Plan of Beijing showing its great axes and outer ring.

One of the world's oldest cities, Beijing has been the capital of China for more than 700 years. It was laid out to repel the threat of invaders coming across continents, and its enormous scale matches that of the steppes of the great Eurasian plain. The city is planned as a series of cities within a city – each protected, Russian-doll-like, by a walled enclosure – with the emperor's quarter, called the Forbidden City, at the hub. Beijing is the physical embodiment of heaven, the emperor, the government and the people, gathered together in a single structure and expressed in the form of a city.

Beijing's meticulous regularity reflects a strictly hierarchical society. Its rationale is the explicit order of systems and form where micro and macro are one. Based on a microcosm, the city takes as its model the vernacular village dwelling that faces north–south. The city plan is derived from this infinitely repeated cell, which is based on a great east–west axis with a powerful north–south cross artery. The overriding geometry of the city comprises south-facing entrances and main spaces tempered by a controlled and protected enclosure to north winds. The combination of the giant-scale planning imposed by a succession of emperors and the tiny but obsessively repetitive unit of the east–west building form – like a DNA code or fractal geometry – makes the plan of the city unique. As Edmund Bacon wrote ir *Cities*, Beijing is 'possibly the great man on the face of the earth'. Refle of rule that no longer exists, the fo City differs from the central meetin other major metropolitan centres. A inflexibility of such a highly structu Beijing's modern developments ha occurred along its outer concentric problem is how to incorporate cha In what was probably the greatest vandalism in our time, the great cit 10 kilometres from the centre, was in the 1960s to make way for a me

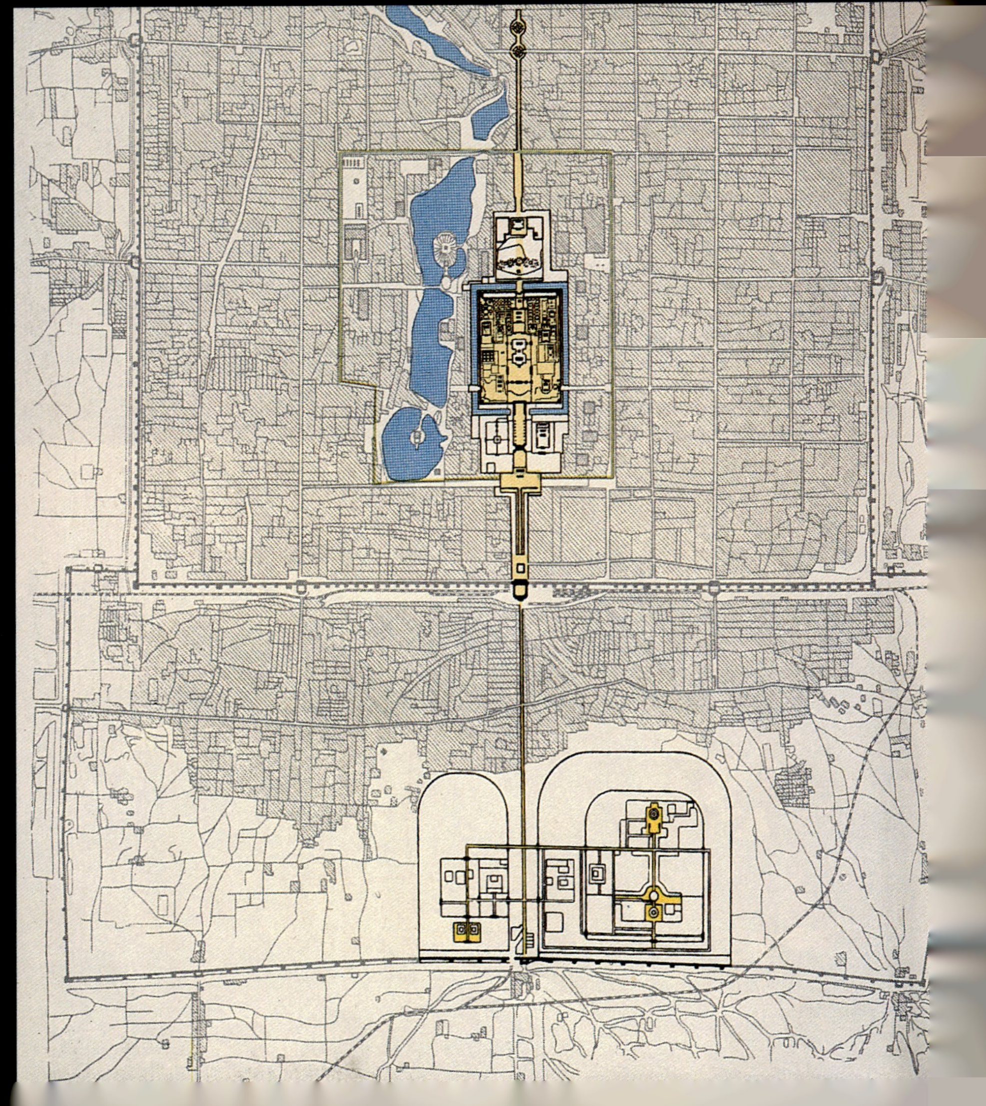

Below: Detailed plans of the Forbidden City showing Russian-doll style organization of main buildings.

Bottom left: Beijing's continuous repetition of micro and macro forms recall fractal geometries.

Bottom right: Aerial photograph of the Forbidden City.

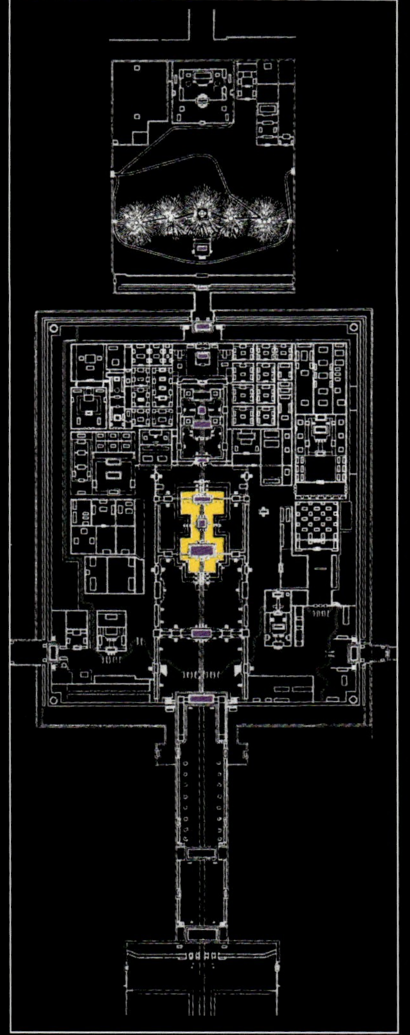

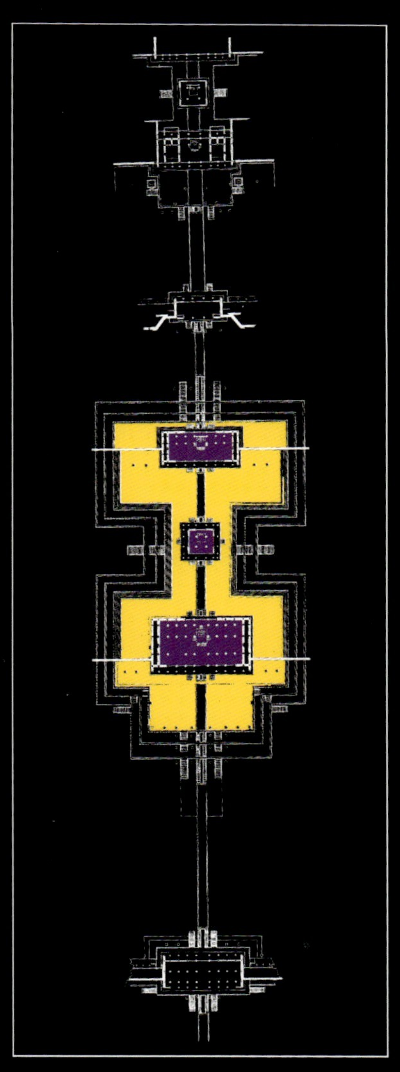

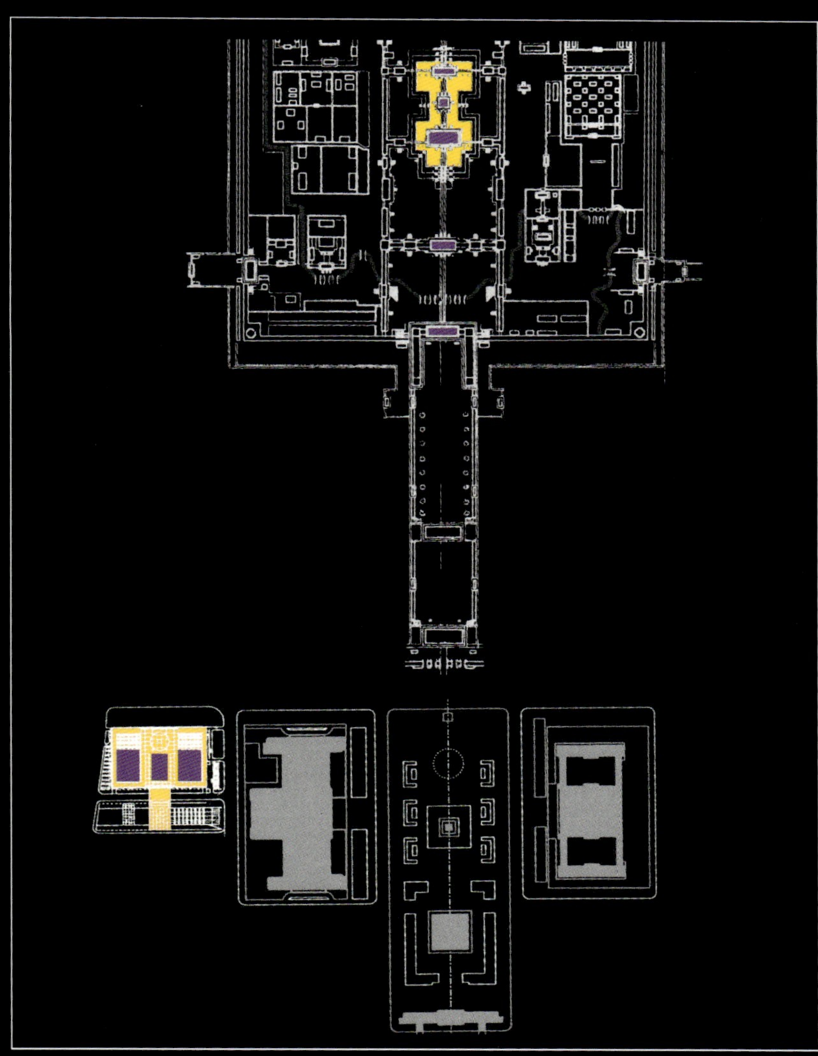

NATIONAL OPERA HOUSE

Terry Farrell & Partners' approach to the Beijing Opera House project was based on Colin Rowe's ideas of 'space positive' building (illustrated in his book *Collage City*), where the spaces between buildings are as lively and useful as the spaces inside. TFP sought to knit the opera house into the traditional fabric of the city. In Terry Farrell's words, 'I believe the building is critically part of the very tissue of Beijing, with its arteries and veins integrated into the larger body. This integration of structure and fabric is vital for any new part of the Tian'anmen complex, as other geometries would be foreign, alien and not part of the whole.' Responding to the city's scale and perspective, the opera house reflects Beijing's *hutongs*, or fractal-like city grid.

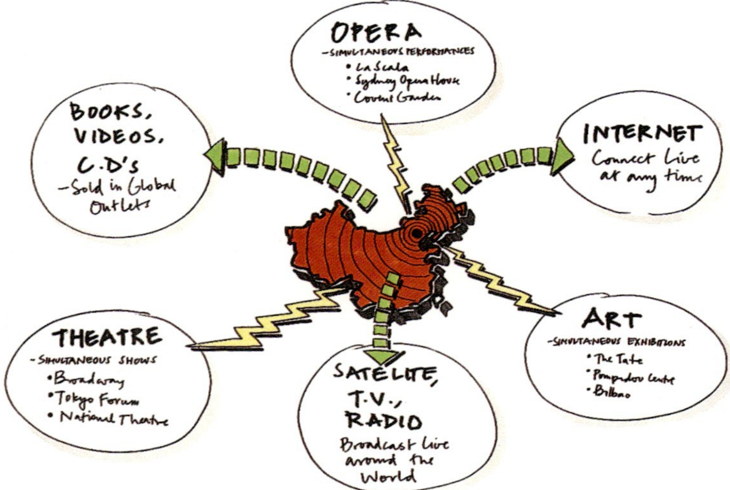

Above: Outward connectivity. The opera house connects China outwardly to global cultural events.

Top right and centre: CAD elevation and model from the north illustrating TFP's first-stage sketch scheme submission.

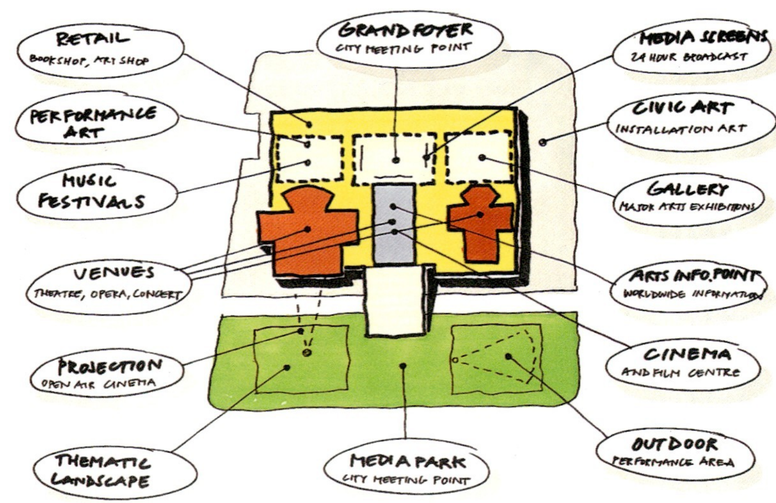

Above: Inward connectivity. The cultural campus showing events within the complex.

The great foyer. TFP's first-stage sketch scheme submission.

Beijing's international architectural competition was a highly politicized series of events involving many changes of direction. As Terry Farrell stated at the time, 'It is not architectural models or drawings that win these things alone. It is the sheer investment of the nation in trying to achieve it.' In the final analysis, Chinese government support ensured the success of this unprecedented opportunity to market and export architectural skills to China. The project – a public statement about 'openness', Chinese identity and common cultural purpose – is of great significance to China. For TFP, the competition was Britain's chance to build the 21st-century equivalent of Paris's Pompidou Centre.

The story begins in April 1998, when an open competition was announced by the Chinese government to design 'one of the best arts palaces in the world'. The proposed development incorporated a 2200-seat opera house, a concert hall, a national theatre and mini-theatre (altogether seating 6500) and a public park. The 3.89 hectare site was opposite the Forbidden City and next to the Great Hall of the People in Tian'anmen Square. The scheme draws on – and, in true Chinese style, magnifies – the increasingly popular phenomenon of the cultural district, as exemplified by developments in Sydney and Bilbao. At 120,000 square metres, and with a budget of £300 million, the project will be the world's largest cultural complex. It is equivalent to having London's National Theatre, Royal Festival Hall and Covent Garden Opera House planned as one complex and situated beside Parliament Square.

The selection process consisted of five different briefs in five stages over an agonizing 16-month period. In June 1998, TFP was one of 40 international practices to be shortlisted. The results of this first stage were exhibited in the Great Hall of the People. TFP, in collaboration with the Beijing Institute of Architectural Design & Research, produced a vast, colourful, low-rise box 250 metres long, 30 metres high and 150 metres deep,

First-stage sketch scheme submission. View from north-east corner facing Tian'anmen Gate.

Below: Figure ground (left). The TFP scheme is space positive, enclosing squares and spaces between orthogonal north–south buildings in an arrangement traditional in Beijing.

Figure ground (right). Paul Andreu's winning scheme places object-positive buildings within a prairie of open space.

Bottom: Terry Farrell's concept sketches of the Opera House in various stages of design.

distinctive for its incorporation of technology and apparent weightlessness. The design responded to China's scale and, through its transparency, expressed the country's desire for connection and openness with the rest of the world. The complex was organized within a nine-square grid, each section of which was dedicated to a separate but linked function.

The three sections facing the main, north elevation were connected to form an entrance and foyer space where ordinary citizens would meet the fantasy world of the theatre. The three central sections – each a different colour – housed the theatre (red), concert hall (blue) and opera house (gold), emphatically arranged on one axis. The three southern sections were given over to back-of-house facilities, which were grouped around a central atrium. Inside, enormous foyers responded to the huge scale of the place and helped to accommodate the 10,000 people who were expected to be in the complex at any one time. Their walls were clad with totemic screens beaming out performances from the main auditoria that could be broadcast around the world. The foyers were also envisaged as animated social spaces in the tradition of Beijing's great public squares. TFP sought to promote the idea of using communications technology to relay performances from other international cultural venues, such as La Scala opera house in Milan, which could be broadcast within the building's grand foyer.

A major consideration in the TFP scheme was the internal relationship between the 16 venues on the site itself, which also needed to interact with the city as a whole. The nine-square grid plan responded to the formality and symmetry of Beijing's urban grid. The result was a microcosm of the city plan of Beijing, where omnipresent accommodation blocks are oriented north–south and bounded by circulation routes and public spaces.

For the second stage, in September 1998, a list of 15 architects was reduced to six, with TFP representing Britain. The other contenders were Paul Andreu (France), HPP International (Germany), Arata Isozaki (Japan), Carlos Ott (Canada) and the Chinese Architectural Design Institute. In the revised scheme, the permeability of the north elevation was enhanced by a transparent crystal wall designed to bring the performance spaces into the street and vice versa; the wall's juxtaposition with the solidity of the neighbouring buildings in Tian'anmen Square emphasized the effect. Movable screens between the two glass layers in the wall allowed the elevation to act as a filtering screen, producing an ever-changing vision of light and colour.

The third stage, in January 1999, was a refining process, in which TFP was told to inject into the scheme more references to Chinese tradition. In response, the practice set the fly towers of the opera house and theatre beneath two saucer-like roofs that reflected the weightlessness of traditional Chinese roofs. The concert hall was raised to incorporate a central gateway motif, which allowed the public to walk straight through the complex within a Chinese landscape that extended over the whole site. At this point, the indication was that TFP's scheme was strongly favoured.

However, the brief was again amended in January 1999, when the Chinese prime minister, Zhu Rongji, moved the site from Tian'anmen Square to a larger but less prominent area 70 metres behind the Great Hall of the People. Along with the change of site came the removal of an earlier height restriction and less emphasis on Chinese tradition. In May 1999 TFP submitted its refined fourth-stage scheme. The design retained the transparency of the original concept, but exhibited a greater solidity and a dramatic roofline. By the time of the fifth-stage entry in July 1999, TFP was one of only two architects remaining in the competition. The other was Paul Andreu, who responded with a completely different design – a grandiose titanium-clad dome – and emerged the victor. For TFP, the Beijing brief had focused on exploiting the potential of urban design to create an enduring and sublime setting for a major cultural complex. The antithesis of Farrell's interpretation of the site, Andreu's architecture is composed to sit as an isolated object that contrasts rather than harmonizes with the rest of the city.

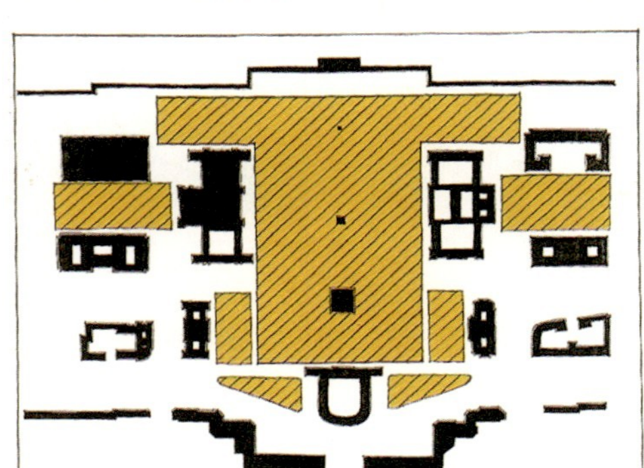

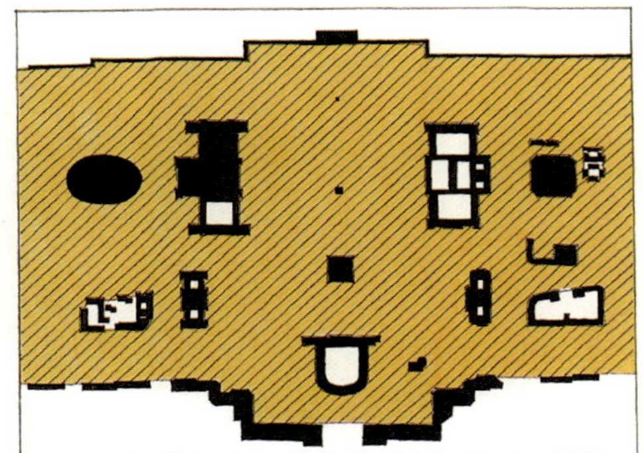

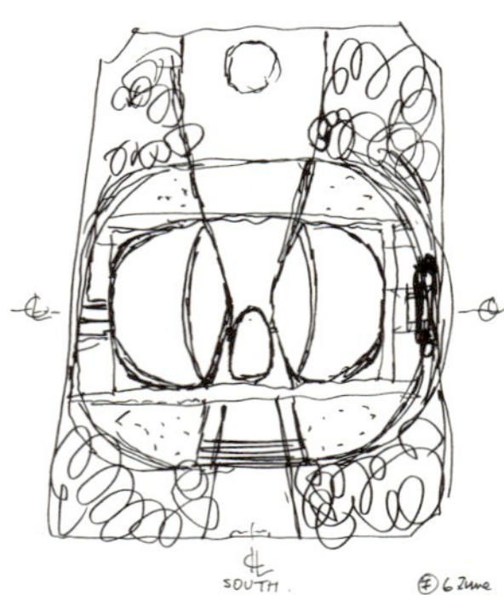

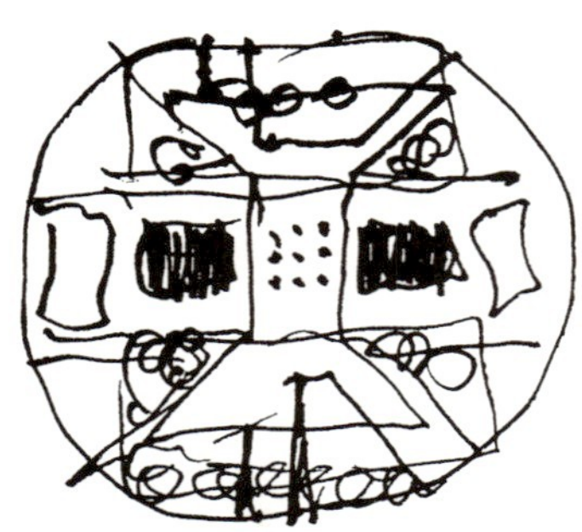

Below: The grand foyer as a highly flexible and responsive cultural events space.

Bottom: Cross section and ground floor plan of the final scheme.

劇院
Theatre

演奏會
Concert

歌劇
Opera

國劇大堂內觀 - 選用節目
Grand Hall Interior Views - Alternative Events

FARRELL PARTNERS

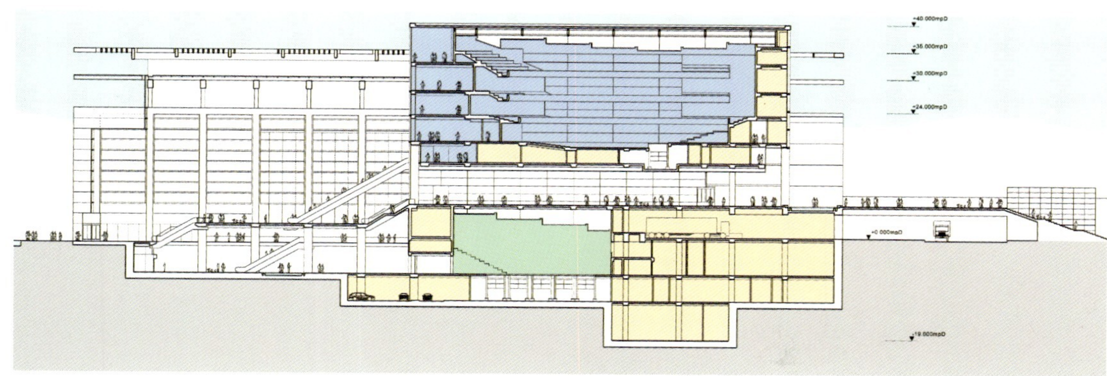

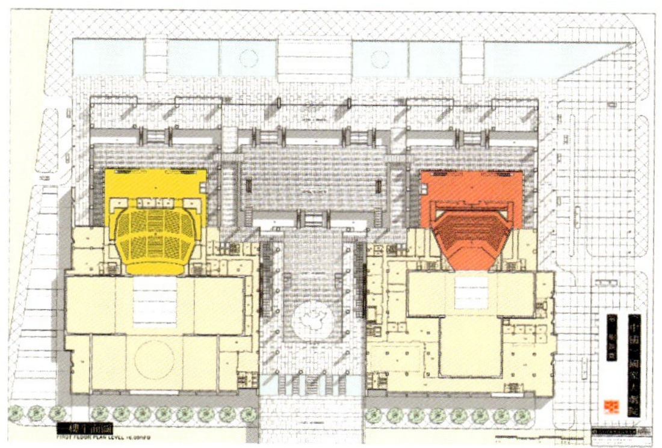

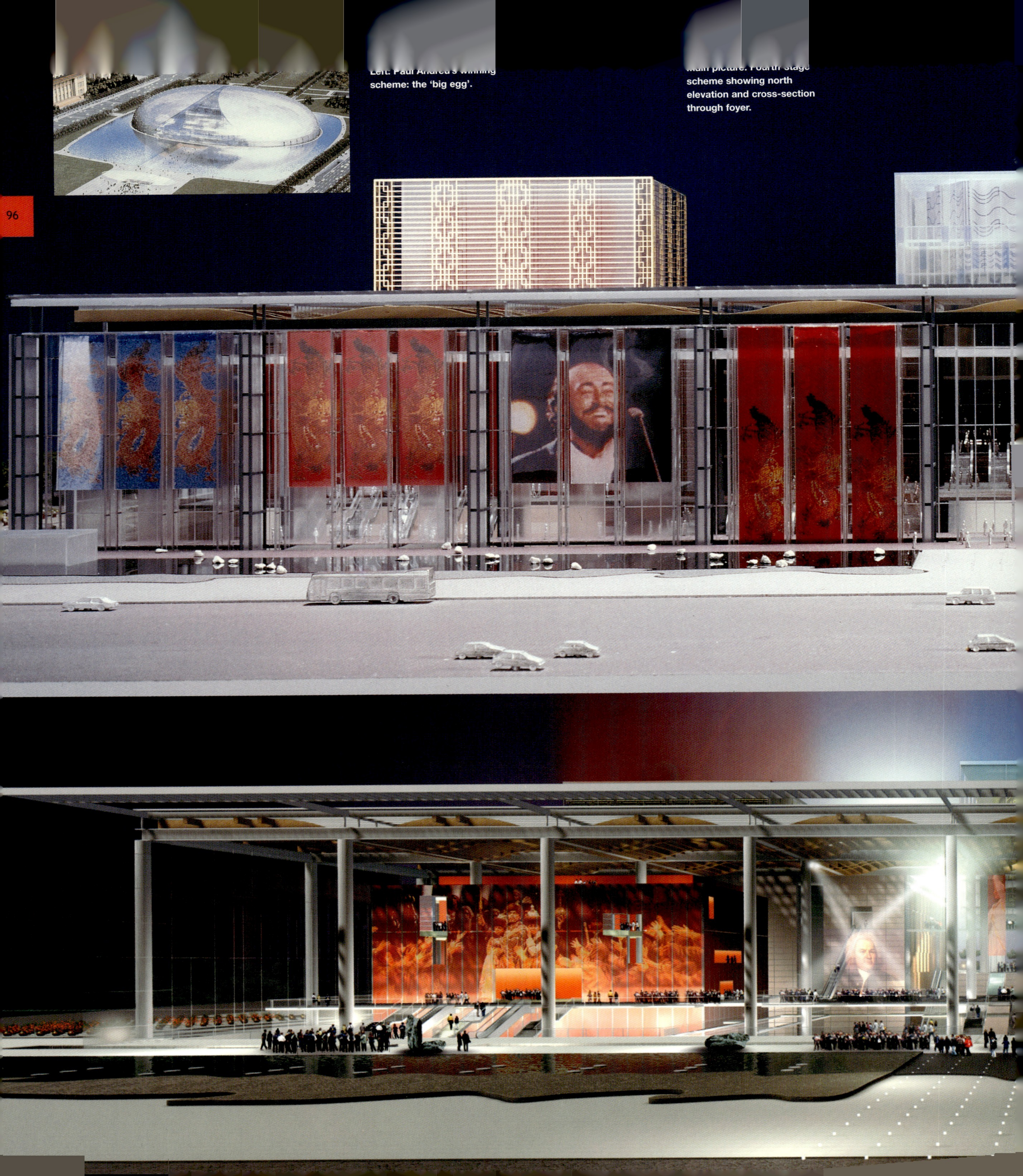

Left: Paul Andreu's winning scheme: the 'big egg'.

Main picture: Fourth stage scheme showing north elevation and cross-section through foyer.

Right: TFP's fifth and final scheme responds to a request to provide a study based on Andreu's suggested new location.

SEOUL

SEOUL

Seoul is a city that has imposed a new order on a great ancient heritage. The image of the historic city gate subsumed by traffic is a continual reminder of the new overwhelming the old. Recovering from war-time destruction, a pattern of world corporations has grown up, dividing the city into brand-owned plots. The city is an outward expression of corporate power, in the form of its cars, buildings, signs and products. The result is a muddled, poly-centred place expressed as corporate process: signs and brands (Samsung, Hyundai and Lucky Goldstar) rather than urban structure.

Terry Farrell & Partners' ground transportation centre at Seoul's new international airport is to be the nation's most recent brand image, expressed in the form of iconic architecture.

The River Han (top right) flows through the centre of Seoul to the Yellow Sea (left). Inchon, a major port on the Yellow Sea, is centre right in this satellite image, and the new Inchon International Airport can be seen top left.

Top: Panorama taken from Seoul Tower on Mt Namsan.

Above: View from Namdaemun Gate, downtown Seoul.

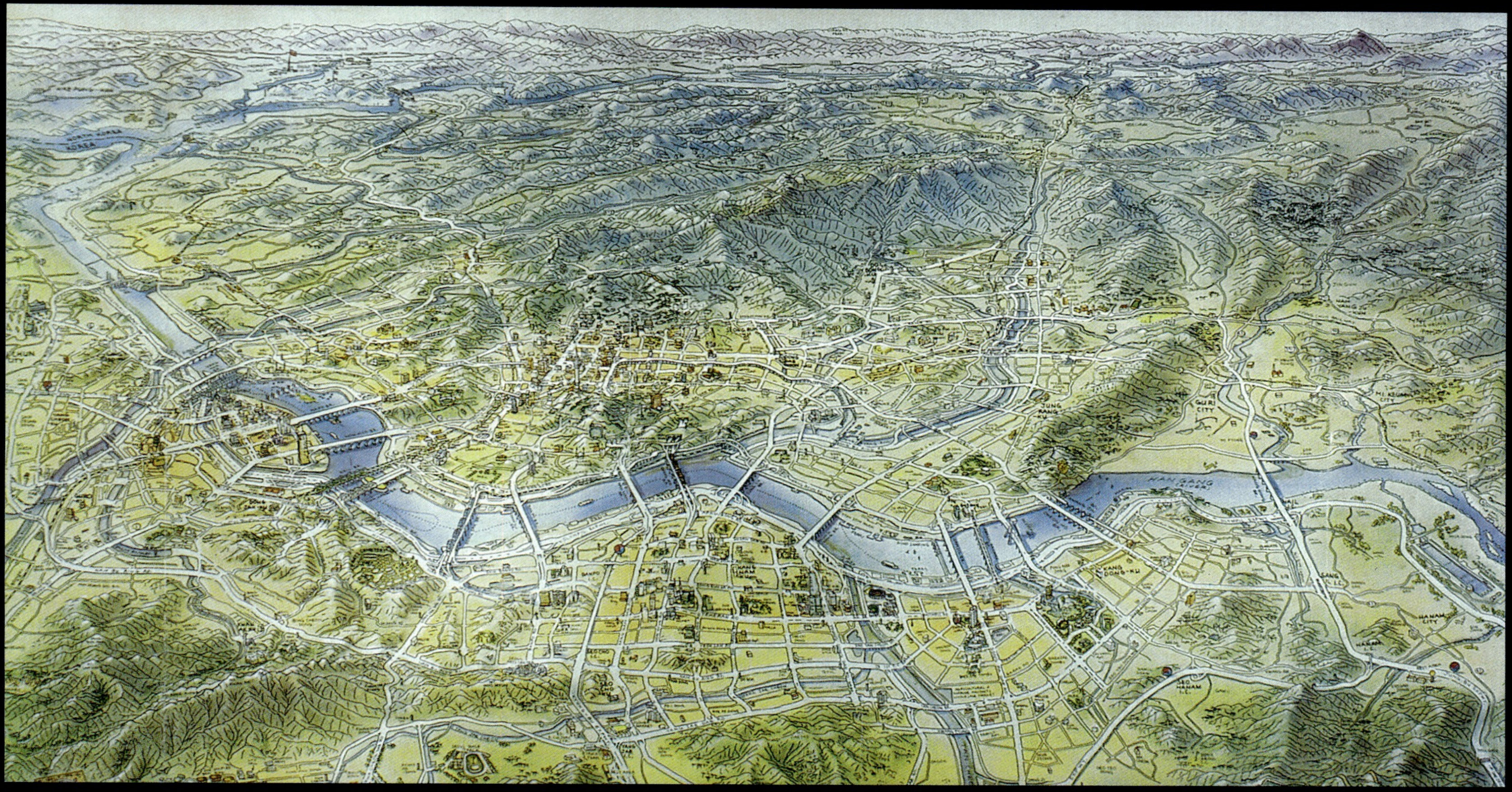

Top: Seoul has many clearly defined sub-centres that reflect the workings of Korean society, which is centred around business empires, or *choebals*, such as Daiwoo, Samsung and Hyundai. Each of these centres is a city within a city, and each *choebal* is a complete organizational world in itself. TFP's Seoul-based projects respond to the dispersed character of each centre and are self contained 'centred' worlds within a world.

Above: Seoul sits on the River Han, which flows through the central part of the Korean peninsula and bisects the city into northern and southern Seoul. The city's character originates from its poly-centred organization – rather like London, it comprises a multitude of districts, each with its own centre.

TRANSPORTATION CENTRE

INCHON INTERNATIONAL AIRPORT

Korea's second largest port, Inchon is the commercial centre for Seoul. Created from 5617 hectares of tidal landmass, the airport site sits between what were once two islands (Yong-Jong and Yong-Yu) separated by ocean. At the start of construction in 1992, land was dredged from the sea floor and excavated out of the surrounding mountains. The completed area, which covers eight kilometres from north to south and six kilometres from east to west, is 52 kilometres from western Seoul. The new gateway to and from East Asia, Inchon is, for Terry Farrell & Partners, a fitting successor to Kowloon's integrated transportation node. Kowloon Station is at the city end of the railway to Chek Lap Kok airport – where the airport arrives in town – while Inchon, its town planning partner, is at the airport end of the city.

Top: The airport site.

Above: Inchon and Kowloon: the complete airport rail link system. The Seoul interchange at Inchon and the Hong Kong interchange at Kowloon are the two ends of the airport rail link system: uniquely, TFP have completed the system at the largest of scales, albeit in two different cities.

Above: Aerial view showing the complete airport city.

Top right: Kowloon Station is the city end of the airport complex, while Inchon's ground transportation centre is the airport end of the city. Both projects together symbolize the twin ends of transportation connection.

One of the world's largest construction projects, Inchon International Airport will serve as the focus for transatlantic and inter-Asia trade and commercial activity. Reflecting the dynamic changes taking place within East Asia, air-traffic demand in the Asia Pacific region has increased at a rate double that of the rest of the world. With the population of the Seoul metropolitan area reaching more than 20 million, and with the existing Kimpo Airport reaching saturation point in 1997, Inchon is being designed and built to accommodate future demand for air travel. As a result, it will be read as an uncompromising symbol of the economic strength of Korea. The country's optimism is further reflected in the airport's vast projected capacity of around 50 million passengers: two terminals are currently under construction, but extra land is available to allow for future growth.

To service an airport outside Seoul's city boundary, a high level of transport rationalization was needed. Won in international competition in 1996, TFP's ground transportation centre (GTC), in collaboration with Samoo and DMJM, has been planned to ensure that the facilities and interchange provisions housed there support the smooth-running of the airport – as well as to create a strong physical and psychological gateway in and out of

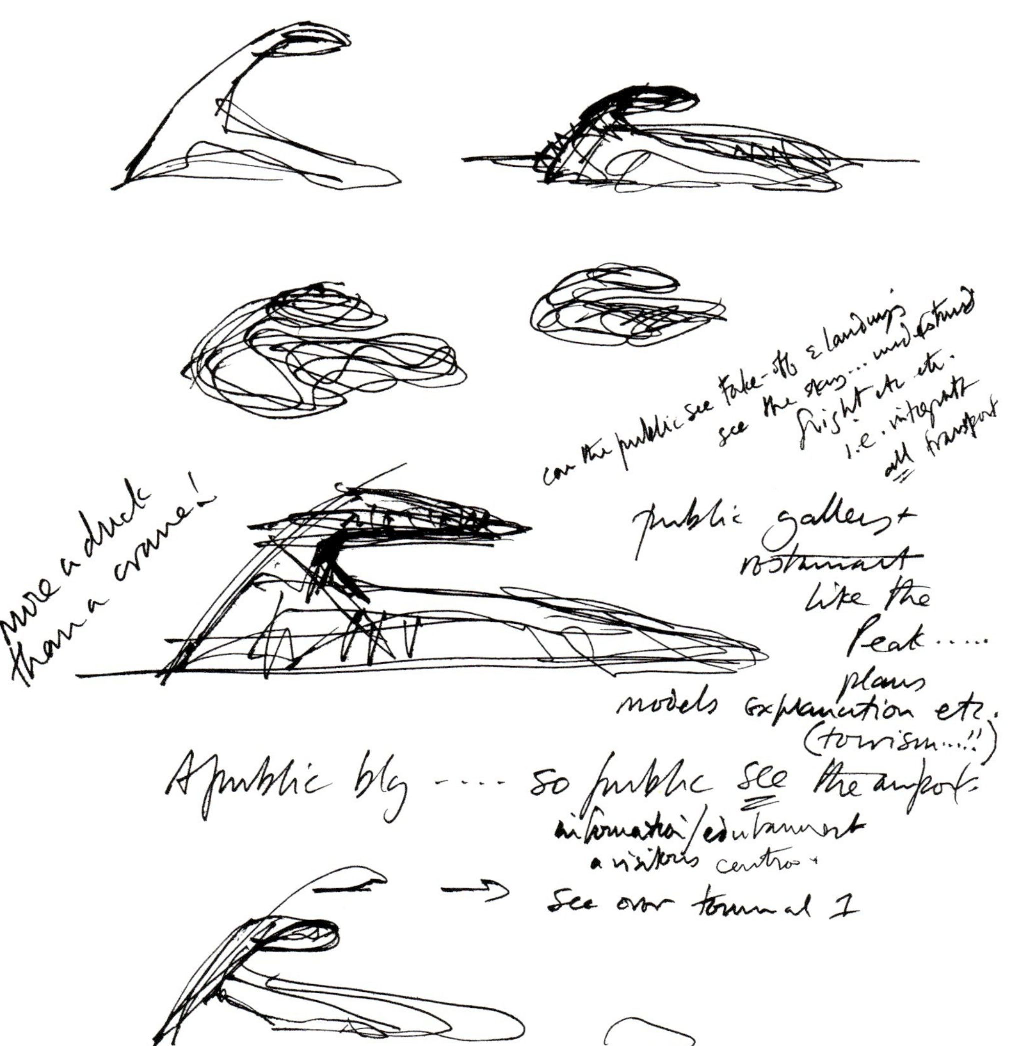

Concept sketches by Terry Farrell.

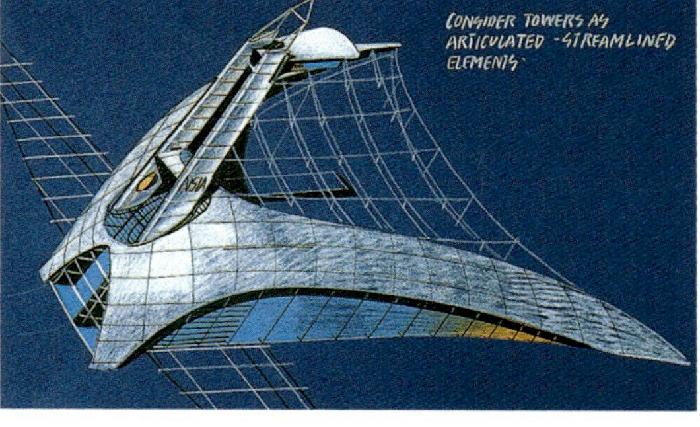

Early development drawings showing the control tower integrated into the scheme – owing to the recession, this structure was later omitted.

the country. The landmark quality of the scheme calls for a dramatic and metaphorical design that celebrates the potential for the reunification of North and South Korea as well as evoking the idea of flight.

Early designs were based on the idea of a bird in flight, represented by a flight-control tower with a slender bird-like neck elevated above the roof of the great hall. During the design process, the Korean airport authority recognized that technological advances meant that the tower facility was no longer required. In order to retain the building's iconic quality, TFP developed a jewel-like aerofoil, constructed from stainless-steel panels and glass, which hovers over the roof of the great hall – a sculptural addition that provides natural ventilation for the great hall underneath. The combination of the aesthetic with the functional continues through other areas of the project, such as the below-ground car park, which provides an opportunity to create a landscaped garden around the great hall. A 200-metre glazed pedestrian gallery, which draws on the Korean tradition of fortified walls, visually and physically links the car park with the great hall while at the same time introducing a powerful new element into the landscape.

A key inspiration for the transportation centre's highly sophisticated form was the great Victorian railway station, where technology was pushed to its limits. Technological challenge was an issue at Inchon, where the construction of the complex curving form was more akin to automobile design than to architecture. As technology for a building of this scale was unavailable, the solution was to sculpt a three-dimensional scale model from foam, which was then sliced into six-metre cross-sections. Coordinates for these sections were digitized to build up a CAD model. From this arose a three-dimensional mesh covering, which provided the basis for the sculptural model of the scheme. This complexity places Inchon within the tradition of dynamic and dramatic architecture for air travel. The building's sculptural form and bold scale echoes landmark structures such as Eero Saarinen's TWA Terminal at New York's JFK airport, which eschews the angular shed form for a more sinuous and visually uplifting architectural language.

The layout of the building is simple in the extreme. A great hall with a spectacular glazed concourse roof and clear spans of 190 metres forms the heart of the project and is the central space through which all passengers will pass. Its large, clear-spanned and naturally lit spaces will be visible from all arrival points, ensuring clarity of organization and helping passengers to find their way around. Positioned symmetrically on the north-south axis of the site, the great hall will be the gateway pavilion between the ground transportation modes and the terminal buildings, which fan out to the north and south of TFP's hub structure. Its location and form respond to the major pedestrian arteries connecting the airport terminals to the GTC.

A freestanding structure between two passenger terminals, the six-storey transportation centre is the airport's primary transport interchange facility. Integrated into the airport's infrastructure, the building will accommodate a predicted six million passenger routes per year. A colossal 250,000 square metres, the transportation centre will house five rail systems (metro, standard train, high-speed train and local passenger-movement trains linked to the airport business centre); a bus and coach station; and taxi, car rental, hotel and tour-bus pick-up points. It will also provide for complex parking requirements (passengers, general public, employees, taxis, rental cars and buses). The building is planned for completion in time for the 2002 World Cup soccer games, which will be co-hosted in Korea.

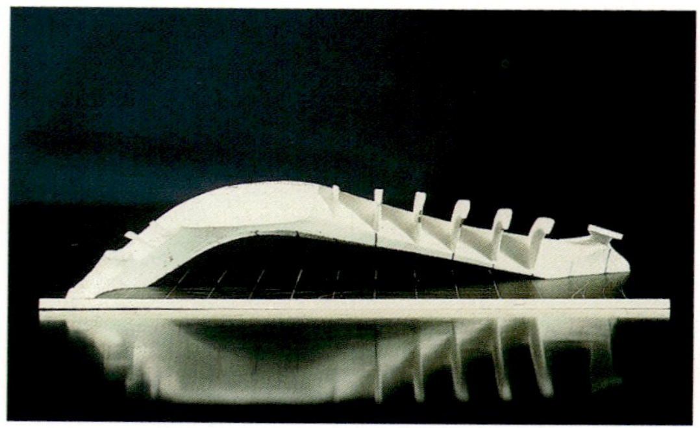

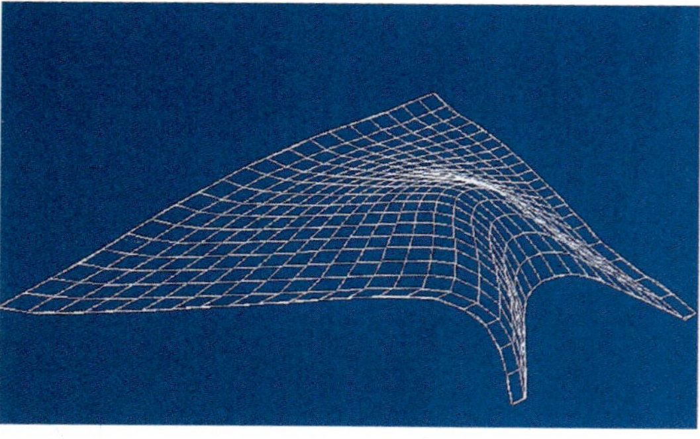

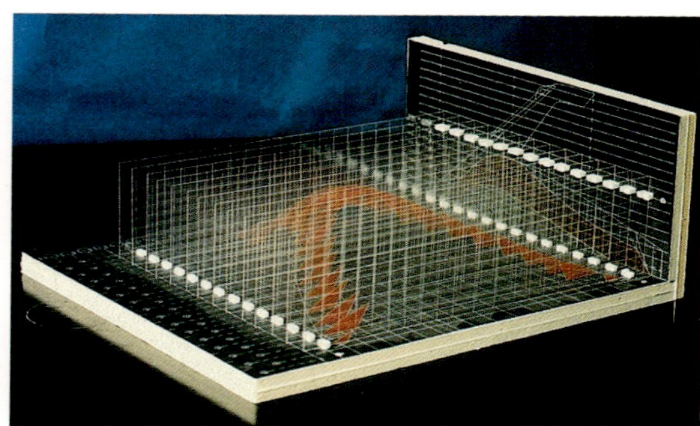

Roof development studies of structure and form.

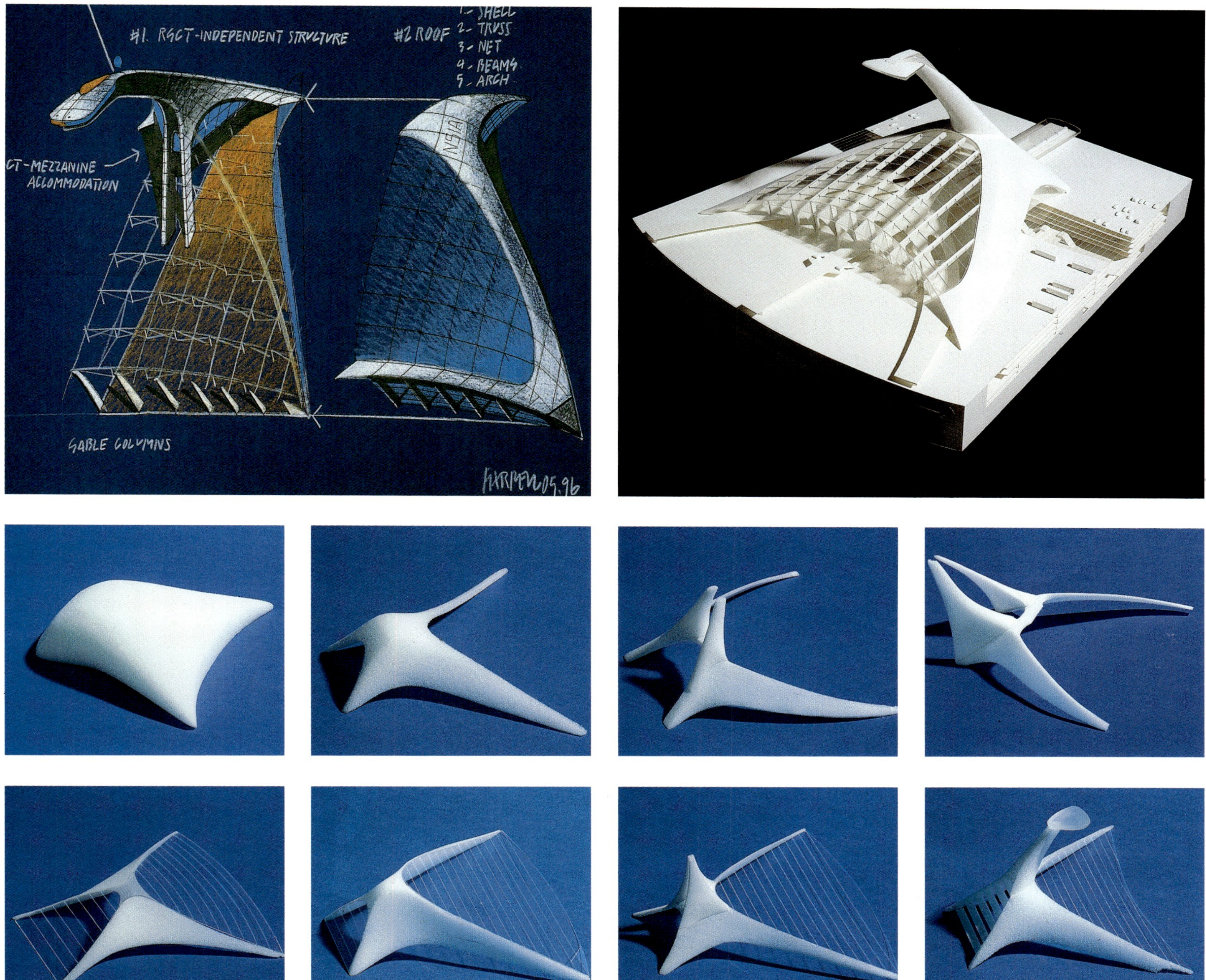

Top: Studies of the first-stage scheme before the elimination of the control tower.

Above: Different option studies show the gradual development of the scheme away from the control tower.

Below: Sketch and model studies of the covered pedestrian access routes that connect the integrated transport centre to the terminal building.

Below: Ground plan and long section.

Bottom: Structural studies and cross section.

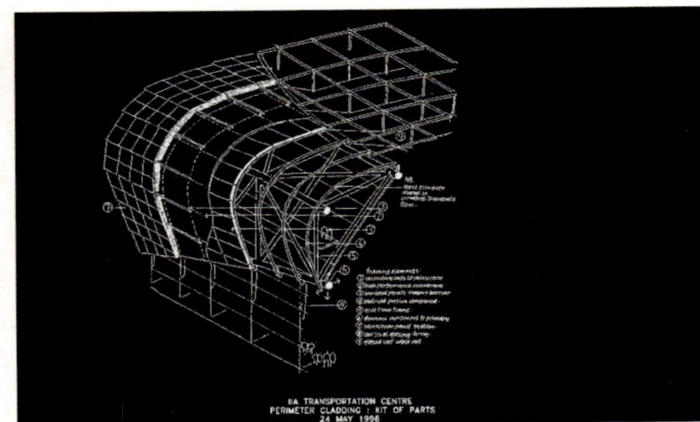

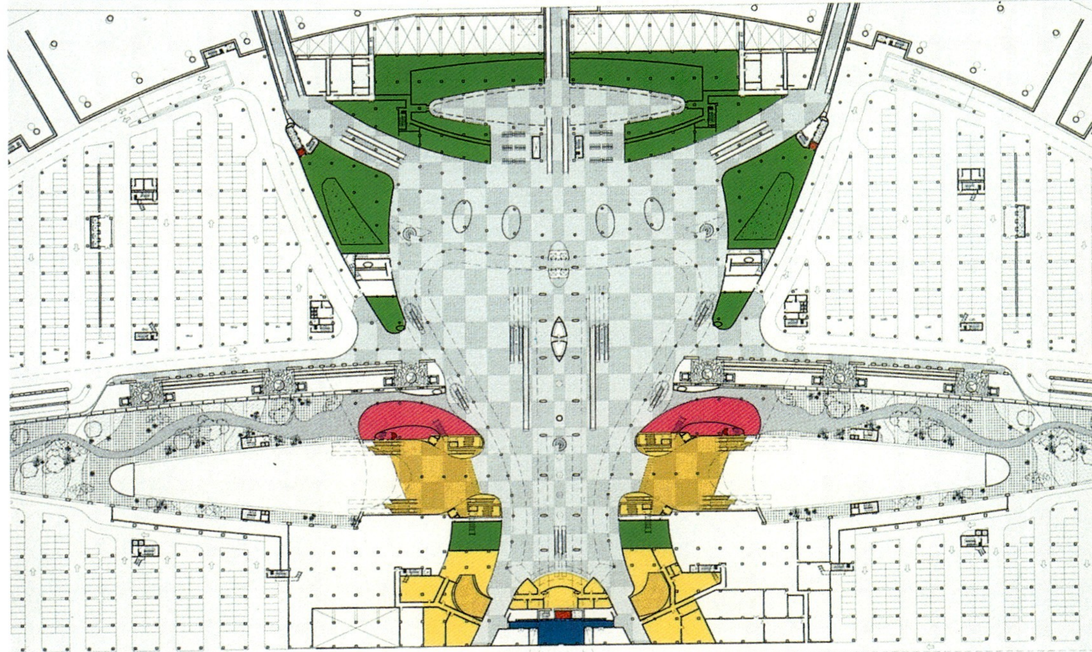

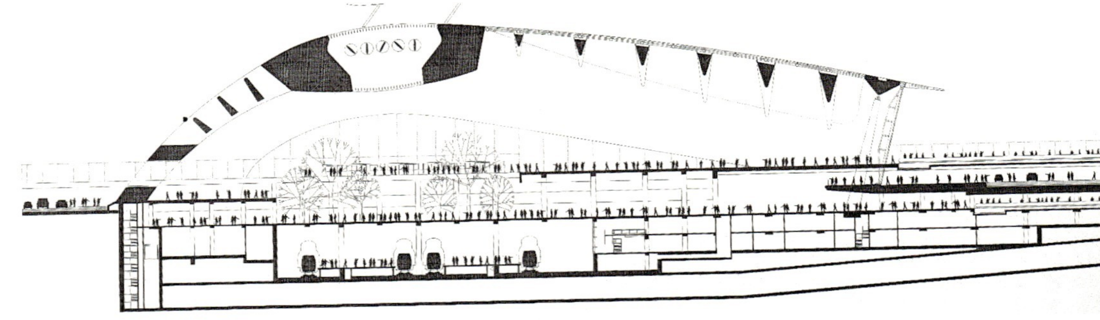

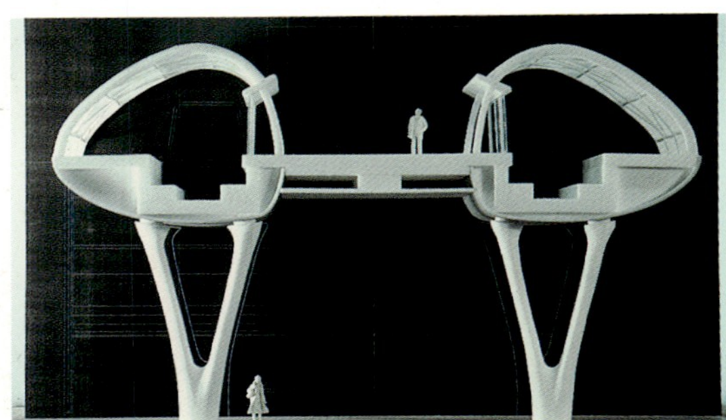

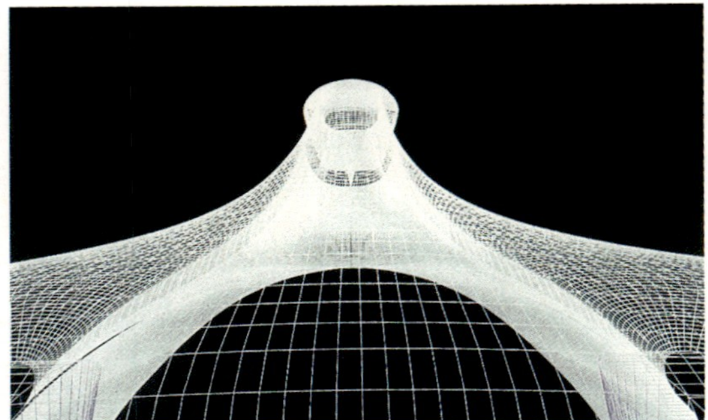

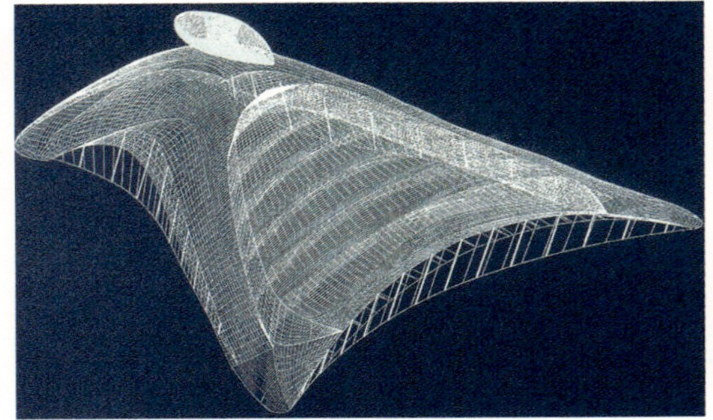

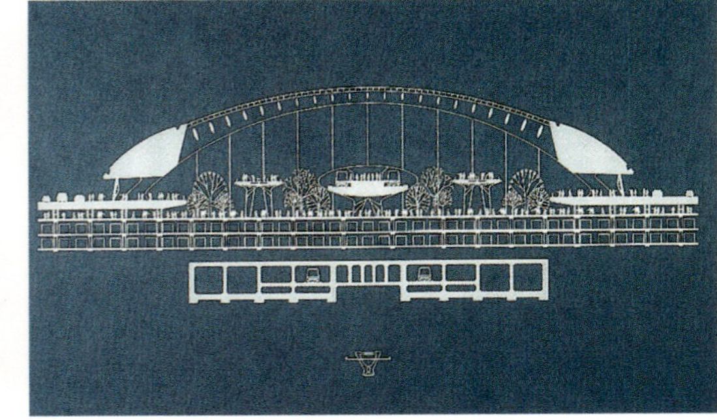

Views of the study model with jewel-like aerofoil.

The final design.

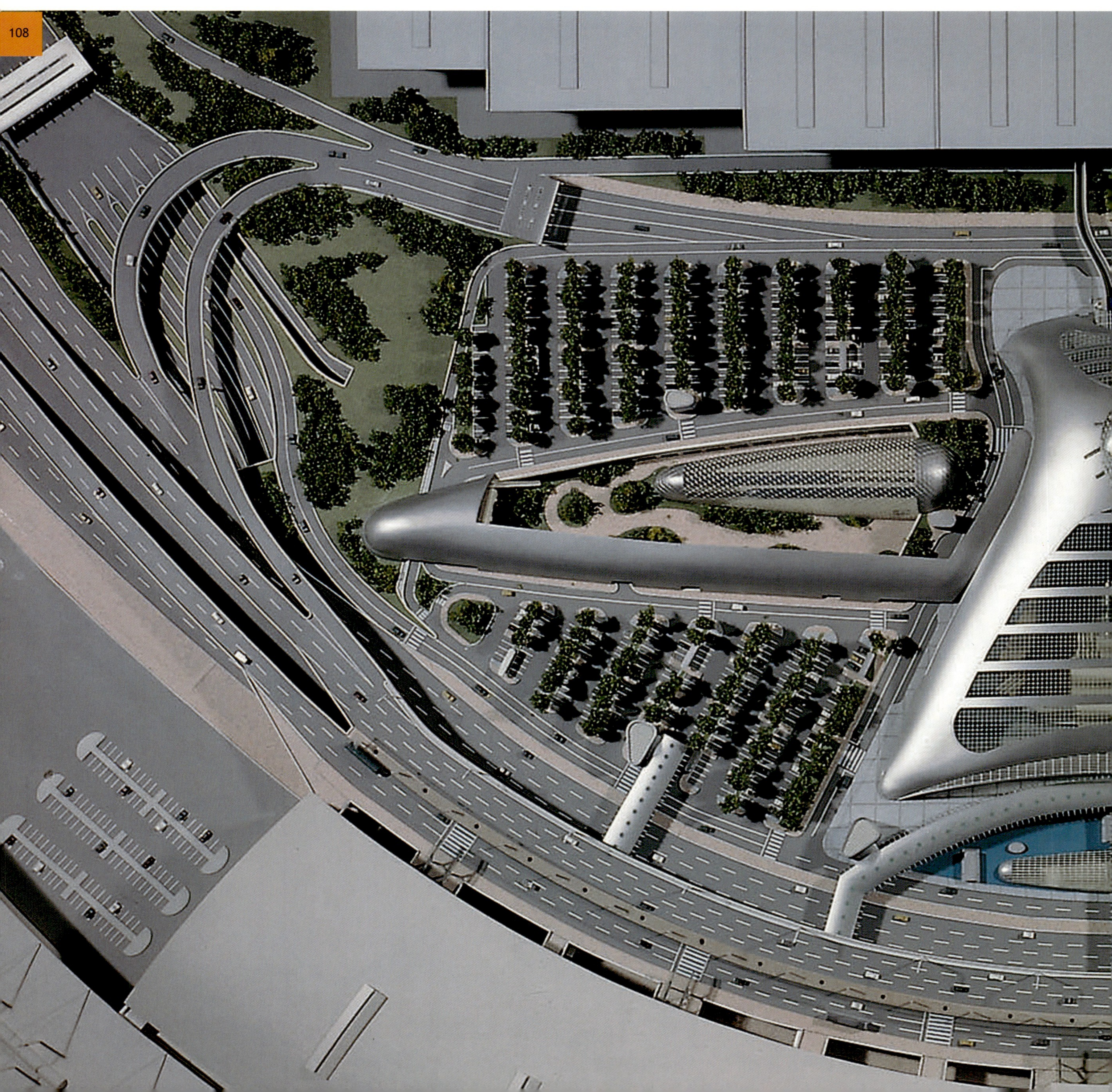

Construction photographs showing the building in spring 2001.

Bottom left: Creation of the landfill site.

'Y' BUILDING

HEADQUARTERS, CHAIRMAN'S APARTMENT, RESTAURANT + SHOWROOMS

A characteristic of Korean urbanism is Seoul's polycentric nature, reflected in the creation of small independent worlds, or *choebals*. TFP's 'Y' headquarters building, housing an exhibition space, café and restaurant, health care facility, secretariat and offices for the corporation's chairman, contains the structure for a self-contained corporate world.

The 'Y' headquarters building sits on a diagonal route within the city grid, and this is reflected within its simple cubic volume. The international competition-winning design comprises a structure of clear, transparent and opaque glazing in front of a skeletal metal frame.

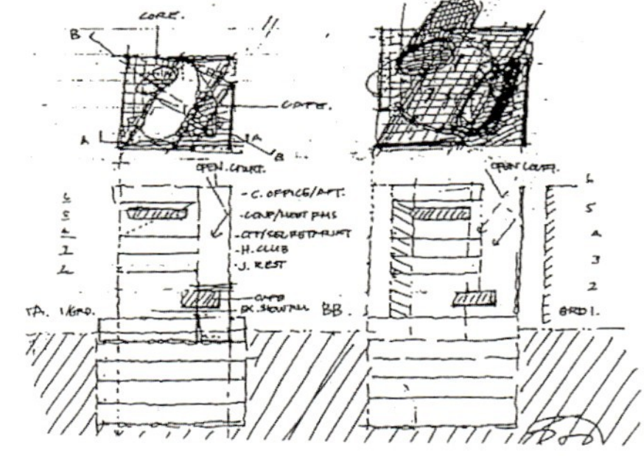

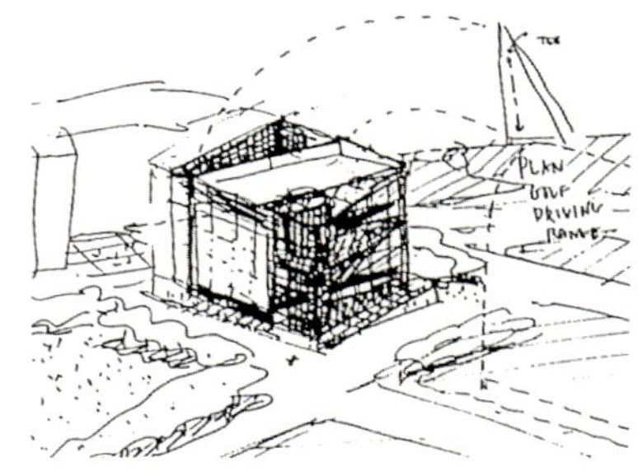

Initial concept sketch by Doug Streeter.

Top: The building set within the urban grain.

Development sketches.

Model of competition-winning scheme.

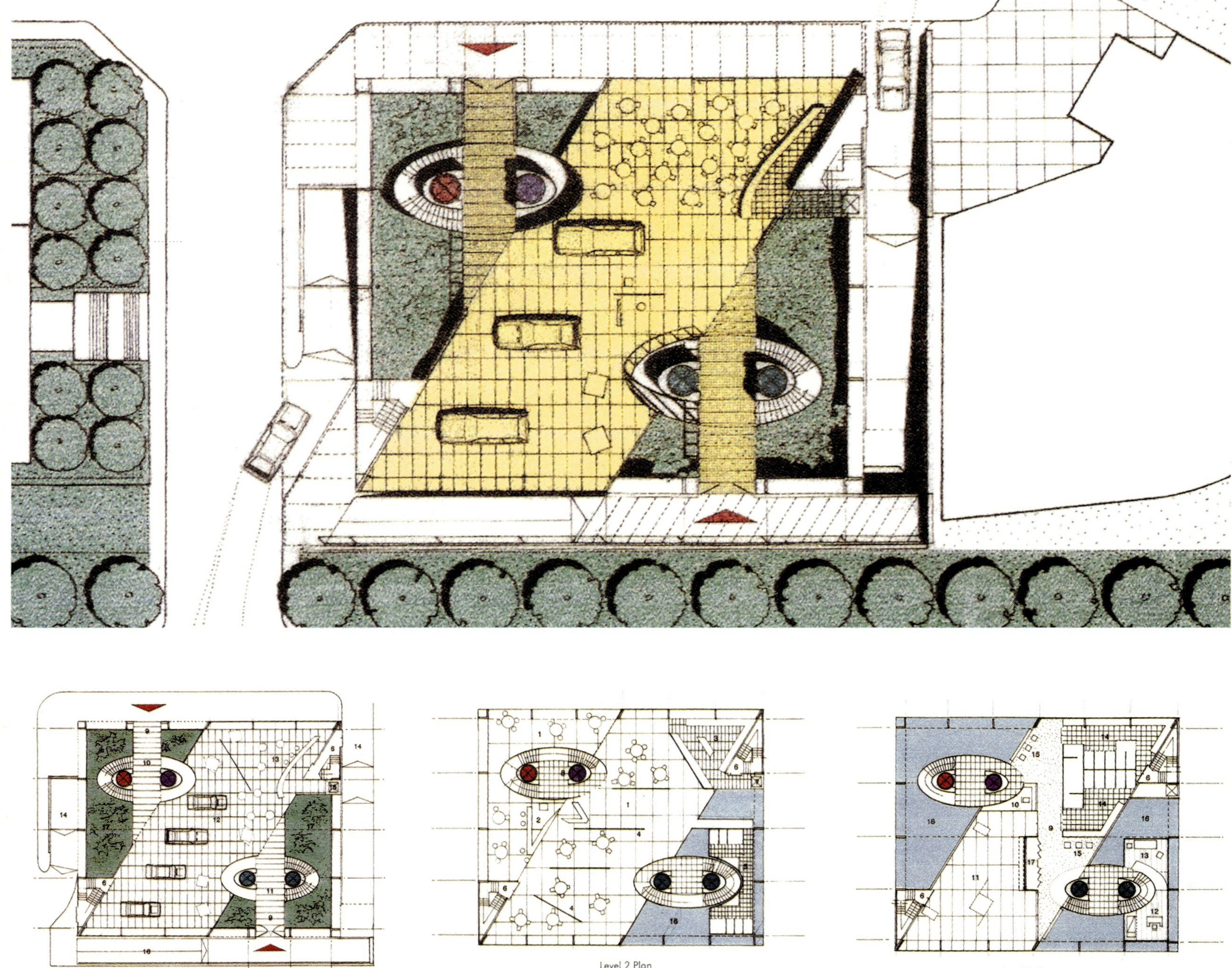

Top: Modified ground plan after competition stage.

Developed plans.

Model of the final scheme.

'C' BUILDING

SHOWROOM, RESTAURANT + CONFERENCE CENTRE

The building is located in Seoul's main business district of Kangnan-gu on an infill site opposite the headquarters of a major Korean company. Its corner plot marks the intersection of a busy four-lane road and secondary road. Commissioned by a Korean industrial organization for their hotel group, the 'C' building exemplifies an urban building type that contains a world within one building.

The eight-storey building accommodates a multi-use exhibition space; Chinese, Korean and Italian restaurants, seating 450 diners; boardrooms; and a banqueting suite. The largest space in the building comprises the showroom of a leading Korean car manufacturer that spotlights latest models and concept cars. Located in Seoul's business district, the building is designed as a landmark to dining, socializing, meeting and corporate entertainment.

The building consists of two cubes. The first, at ground level, houses multi-use exhibition space. On top of this is balanced the second cube, which contains restaurants. These two cubes are pinned together with a vertical cone that allows daylight to filter through the building to the display space at ground level. The ground-level volume is glazed and transparent, while the elevated cube is clad in black marble and granite.

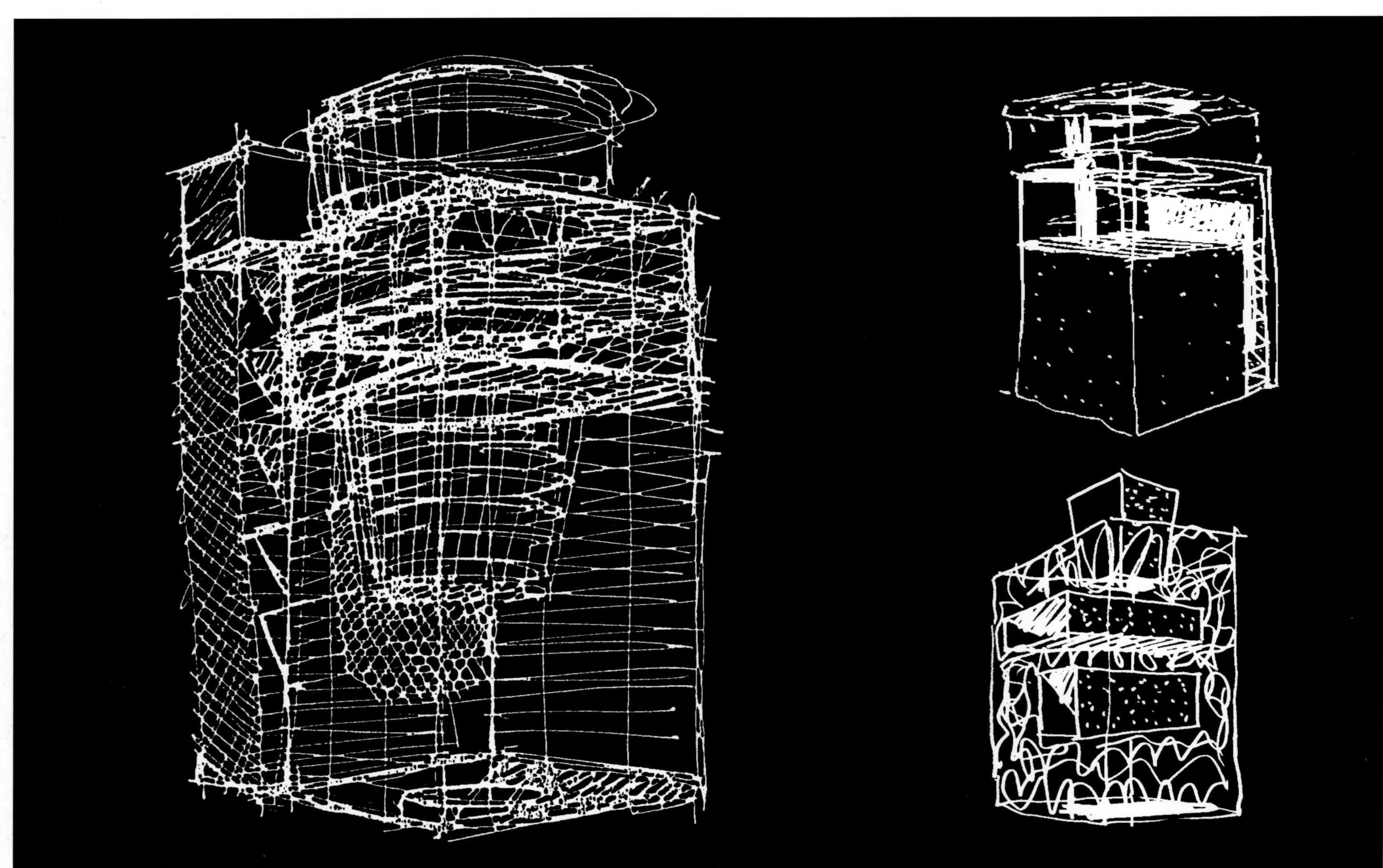

Concept sketches.

Final model of competition entry.

'H' BUILDINGS

GALLERY, RESTAURANT + SHOP, CLINIC

Located on a hill within an existing district in Seoul's Nonhyon-dong, the masterplan is designed to facilitate links and provide unity within a dispersed neighbourhood. Like TFP's other Seoul-based projects, the retail gallery and clinic building reflect the Korean view of a complete world within a world of arts, health, commercial, retail and leisure buildings.

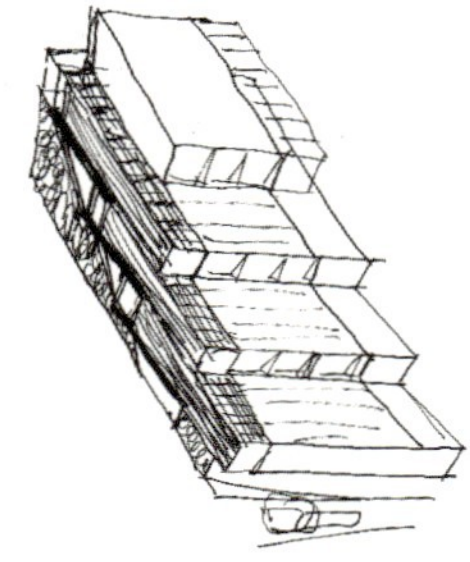

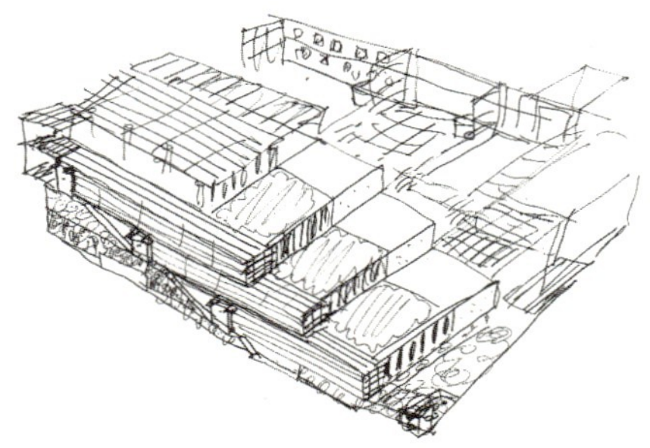

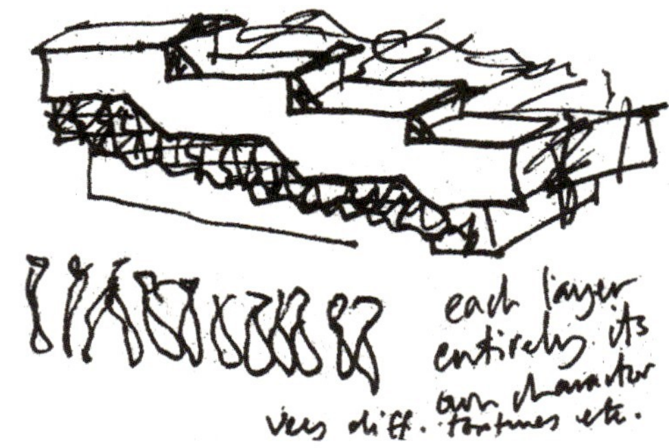

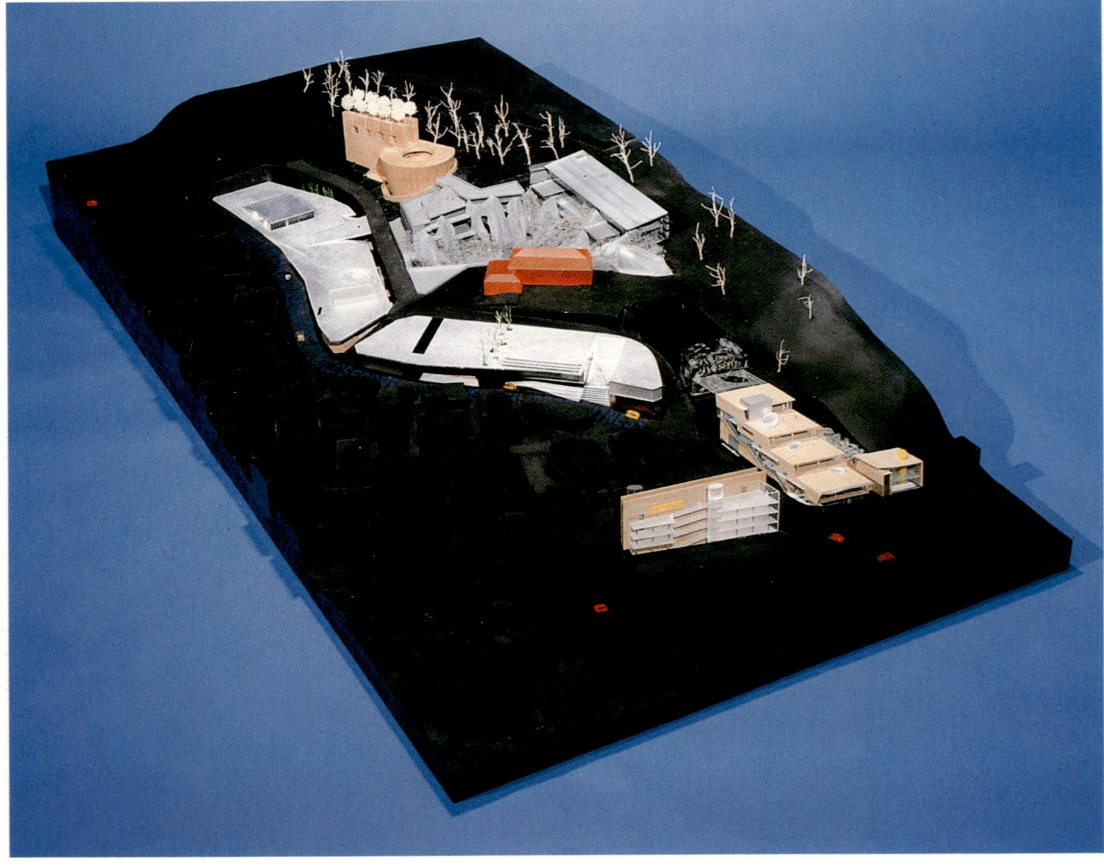

Top: Concept sketches of the clinic building by Doug Streeter and Terry Farrell.

Model prepared by the office of Rem Koolhaas showing all the building components.

Diagrams of the clinic building.

Plan view of the model showing the arts building on the left and the clinic building on the right.

The retail and clinic buildings form part of a collaborative masterplan with Rem Koolhaas, Jean Nouvel and Mario Botta for a mixed-use district, commissioned by a major Korean corporation, incorporating arts, healthcare, commercial, retail and leisure buildings. TFP's contribution comprises a retail gallery and a clinic positioned at the gateway to the complex: the retail gallery is planned at the lowest point of the hill, while the clinic is at its highest, addressing the sloping street. The retail gallery provides the orientation for the whole complex. On arrival the visitor ascends a ramp to a viewing platform, passing galleries and shops. As the ramp descends, it passes either side of a central spine wall displaying objects like a large sculptural assemblage: when seen from the main street, the building itself becomes a giant artwork. The billboard form of the design acts as a display area for themed exhibitions and sales events featuring the work of Korean artists and other specialists. The open exhibition floor and ramped internal circulation are clearly visible through the four-storey glazed wall from the main road adjacent to the complex.

The clinic is planned as a satellite facility to the corporation's medical centre. Pedestrian access is via a stepped communal garden to the building's north, which is also used as an alternative route into the complex as a whole. The building completes the masterplan as it arrives at the bottom of the hill in a series of contour lines or strata, reflecting the rock face of the adjacent retaining wall.

At the heart of the project is a contemporary European response to design, which respects traditional Korean ownership boundaries and the nature of the narrow lanes and high retaining walls. Pedestrian movement through the site is along a sinuous path through the buildings leading to the leisure and theatre studio building at the scheme's hub.

Diagrams of the gallery shop.

Bottom left: Model showing the terraced clinic building.

Below: Visitors circulate via a ramp that passes either side of a central spine display wall.

Bottom right: The shop building: the display wall is a sculptural assemblage.

The gallery is designed to be a one-room-deep glazed rectangular screen.

Bottom: The arts (left) and clinic (right) buildings positioned at the gateway of the complex.

SYDNEY

SYDNEY

In simple terms, the Parramatta link completes the rail connectivity of Sydney around the river and across the harbour. It is a key step towards Sydney's maturity.

Bottom left: Satellite image.

Bottom centre: Sydney panorama.

Bottom right: Aerial view of the sprawling Parramatta suburbs.

Sydney is a great harbour city formed around clearly demarcated river estuaries within a unspoilt landscape. Contained on its eastern edge by the Blue Mountain Ridge, the city is set in the context of endless open space. Surrounded by a vast, low-density suburban grid, Sydney expresses the individualism of the new continent of Australia. Transport forms part of the second wave of the city's regeneration – while air travel has long played an important role in Australian culture, urbanization through railways is a more recent phenomenon.

Parramatta, a suburb 24 kilometres west of Sydney – where Sydney Harbour meets the Parramatta river – is the region's second oldest settlement. Its fertile soil and fresh water has made it an agricultural centre as well as a gateway to the Australian interior. The city's focus is one of density within a dispersed suburban matrix. Terry Farrell & Partners' transportation project for Parramatta looks to the linear transit mode as the infrastructure for future change. The project explores ways to re-urbanize the suburban core through new links and connections in order to support its current population and engender future potential.

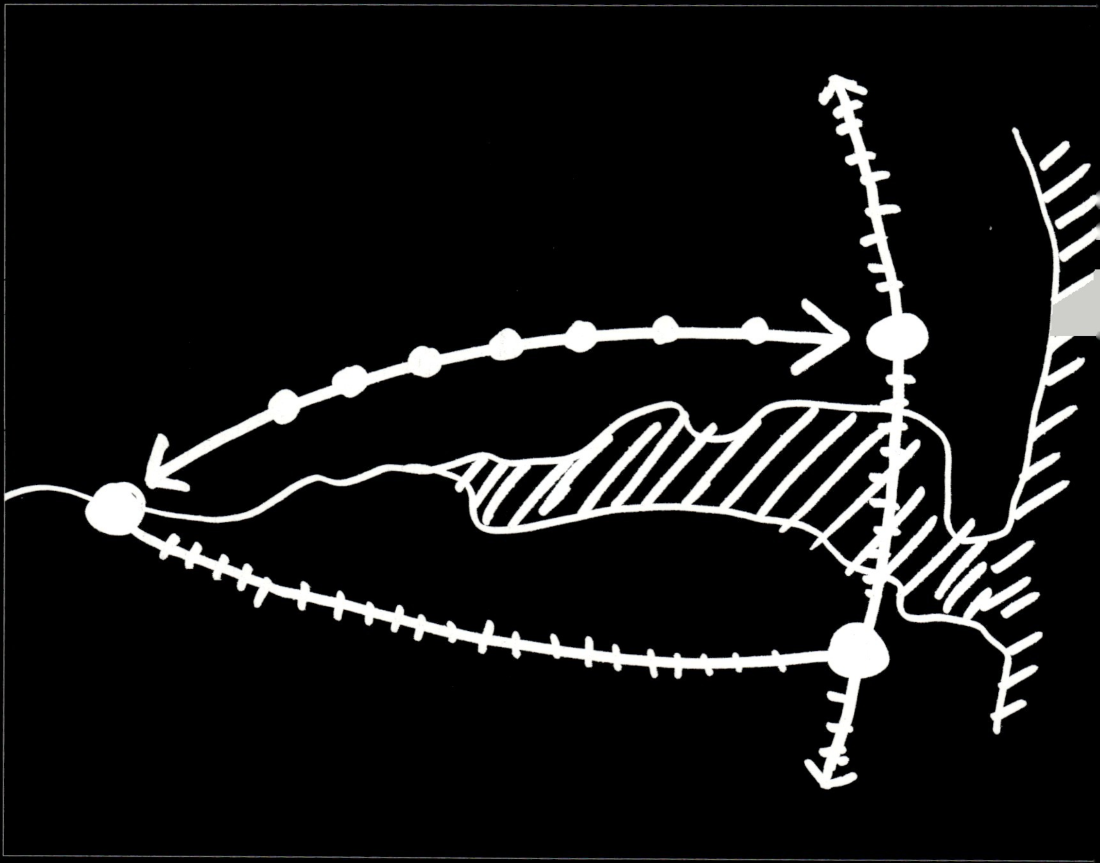

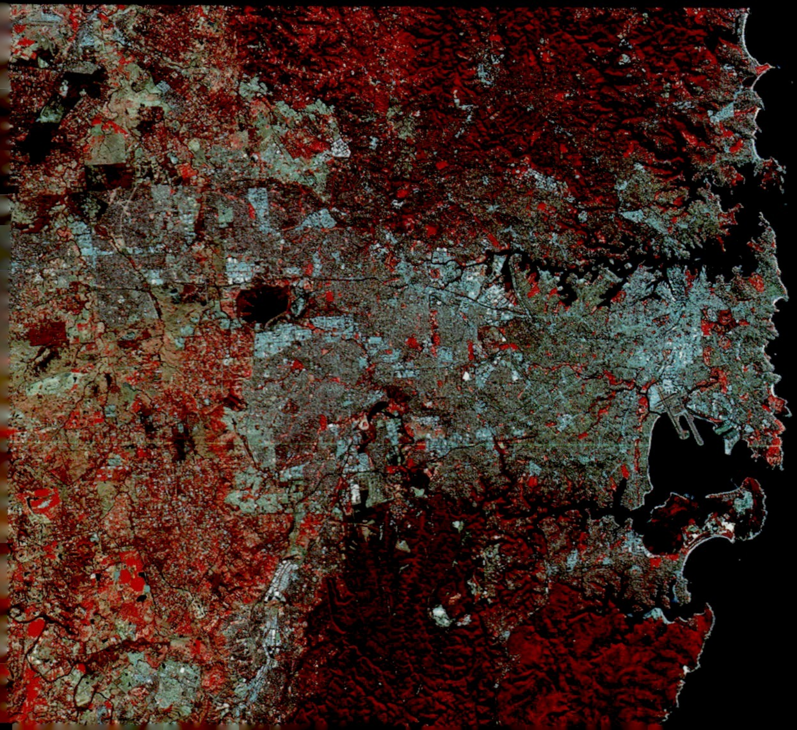

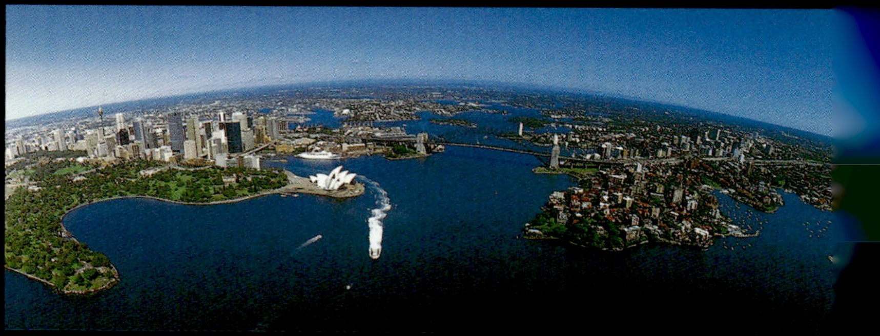

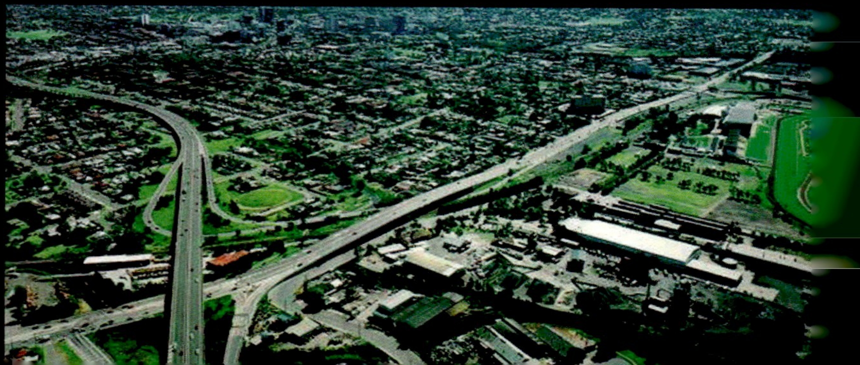

The matrix of different stations. The new stations are classified by typology, which helps to understand the urban design base of individual stations.

Bottom: Plan of the Parramatta rail line.

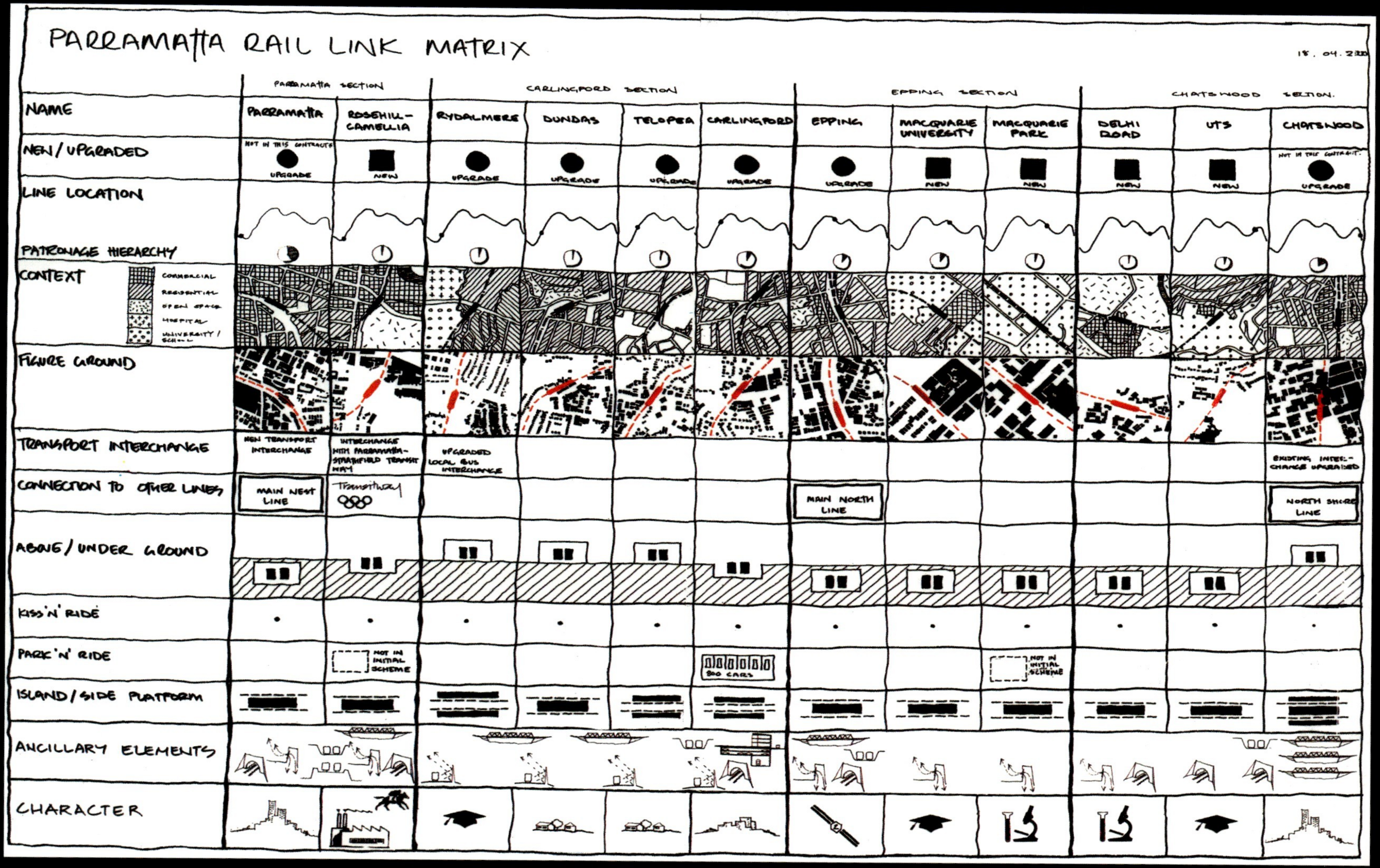

PARRAMATTA RAIL LINK MATRIX

18. 04. 2[illegible]

	PARRAMATTA SECTION		CARLINGFORD SECTION				EPPING SECTION			CHATSWOOD SECTION		
NAME	PARRAMATTA	ROSEHILL-CAMELLIA	RYDALMERE	DUNDAS	TELOPEA	CARLINGFORD	EPPING	MACQUARIE UNIVERSITY	MACQUARIE PARK	DELHI ROAD	UTS	CHATSWOOD
NEW / UPGRADED	NOT IN THIS CONTRACT UPGRADE	NEW	UPGRADE	UPGRADE	UPGRADE	UPGRADE	UPGRADE	NEW	NEW	NEW	NEW	NOT IN THIS CONTRACT. UPGRADE
LINE LOCATION												
PATRONAGE HIERARCHY												
CONTEXT (COMMERCIAL, RESIDENTIAL, OPEN SPACE, HOSPITAL, UNIVERSITY / SCHOOL)												
FIGURE GROUND												
TRANSPORT INTERCHANGE	NEW TRANSPORT INTERCHANGE	INTERCHANGE WITH PARRAMATTA-STRATHFIELD TRANSIT WAY	UPGRADED LOCAL BUS INTERCHANGE									EXISTING INTER-CHANGE UPGRADED
CONNECTION TO OTHER LINES	MAIN WEST LINE	Transitway					MAIN NORTH LINE					NORTH SHORE LINE
ABOVE / UNDER GROUND												
KISS 'N' RIDE	•	•	•	•	•	•	•	•	•	•	•	•
PARK 'N' RIDE		NOT IN INITIAL SCHEME				800 CARS			NOT IN INITIAL SCHEME			
ISLAND / SIDE PLATFORM												
ANCILLARY ELEMENTS												
CHARACTER												

PARRAMATTA RAIL LINK

As a new local railway line, the Parramatta Rail Link will serve the whole of Sydney's north and west side in what is part of a long overdue extension to Australia's railway network. Without a comprehensive railway system, western Sydney has become dislocated from the city centre, resulting in a need for full-scale urban regeneration. The railway project provides the suburb of Parramatta with an opportunity to upgrade its present fragmented centre to an influential central business district that will, in turn, ease pressure on Sydney's city centre.

Instead of creating dividing walls between the northern and southern city districts, the new stations along the railway line are designed to become the central focus of each district. In addition to providing an efficient transport system, the aim of the project is to create a greatly enhanced public realm at street level. This will be achieved by careful urban planning, sensitive architectural treatment and a good balance of development uses.

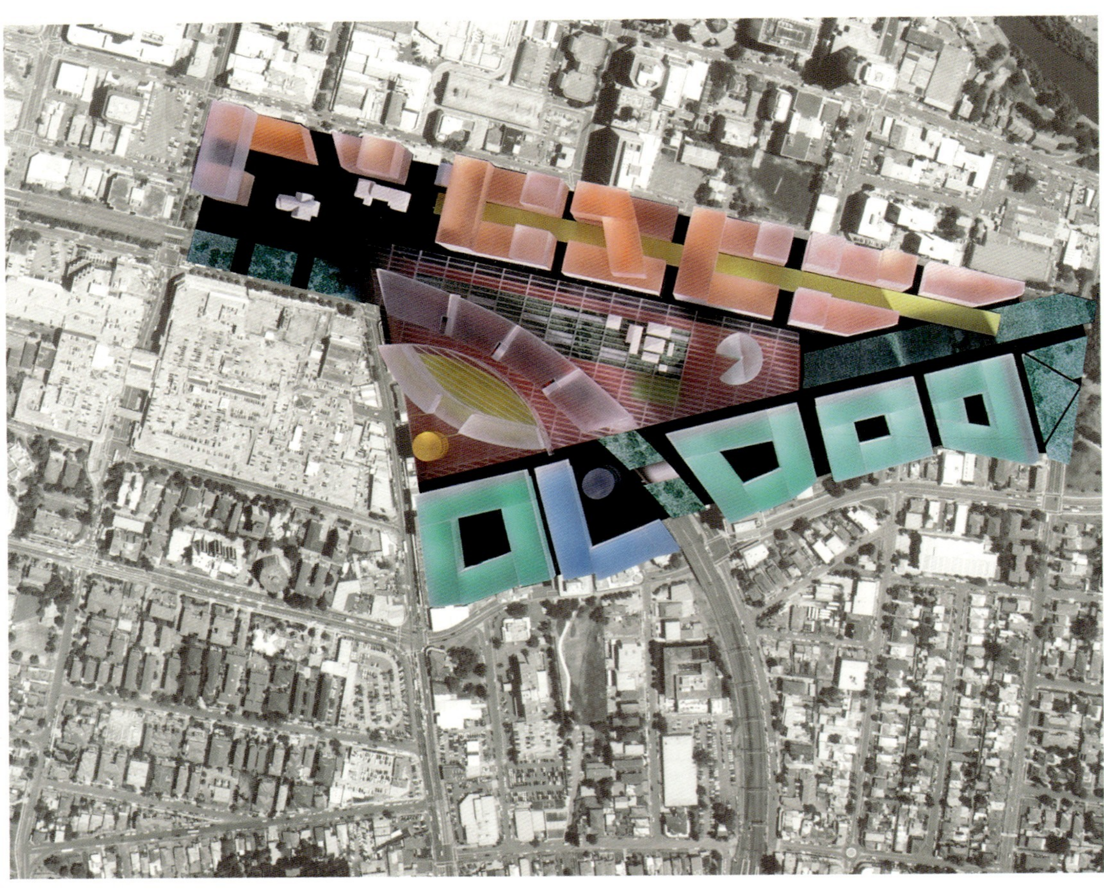

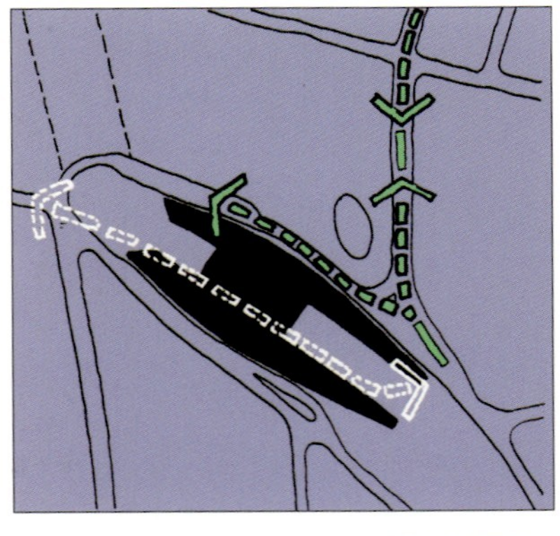

TRANSITWAY

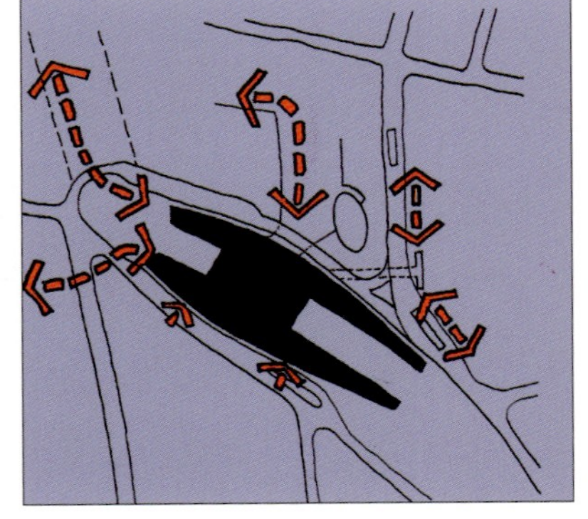

PEDESTRIAN ACCESS

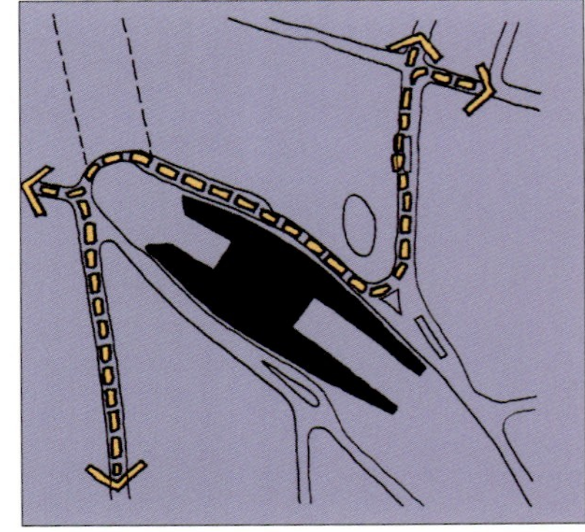

BUSES & COACHES

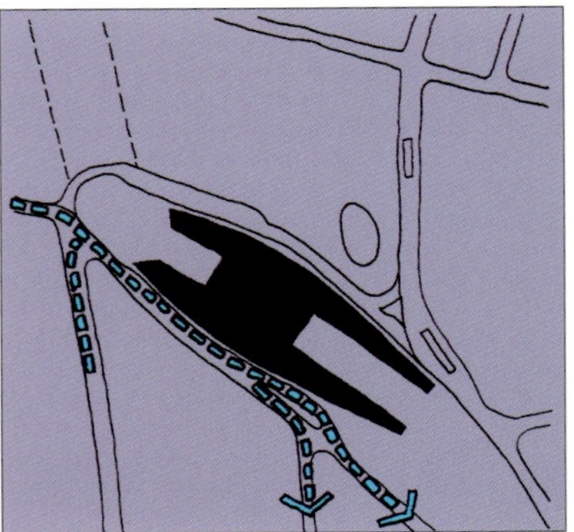

PRIVATE CARS & TAXIS

Sketch studies of the Parramatta station layout. It became clear early on that the design of a station could not proceed without an urban design approach to the town centre. While the existing station generated activity within the town, it also blocked connections across the site. TFP's new design has the potential to connect up the town as well as to deliver a modern, highly efficient state-of-the-art station.

Top: Aerial view of Parramatta station site with initial study model superimposed.

Study for Camellia, one of the smaller stations on the line.

Alternative options for locating light rail, main line, new Parramatta line and their combinations at the top of the hill. The studies investigate the provision of good pedestrian connectivity from one side of the town to the other with easy and efficient access to trains.

Initial studies for the Parramatta town centre plan, which gave more development for the air rights above and around the station.

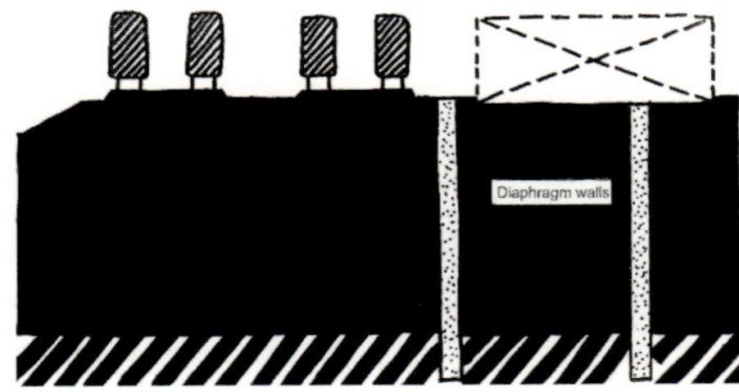

1. Close Argyle Street and divert traffic
2. Install diaphragm walls

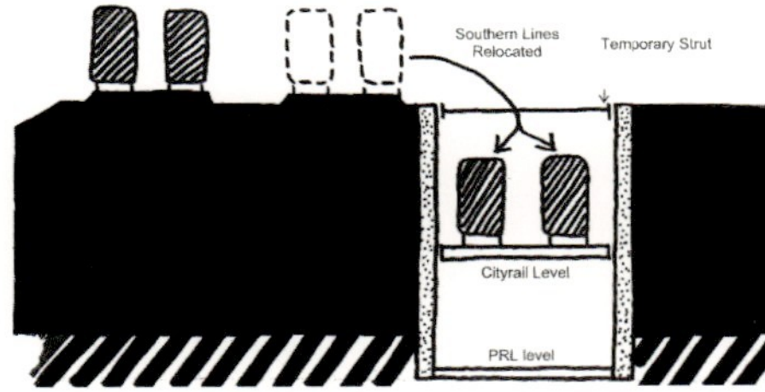

3. Excavate to PRL level 'top down'
4. Relocate southern 'Cityrail' lines

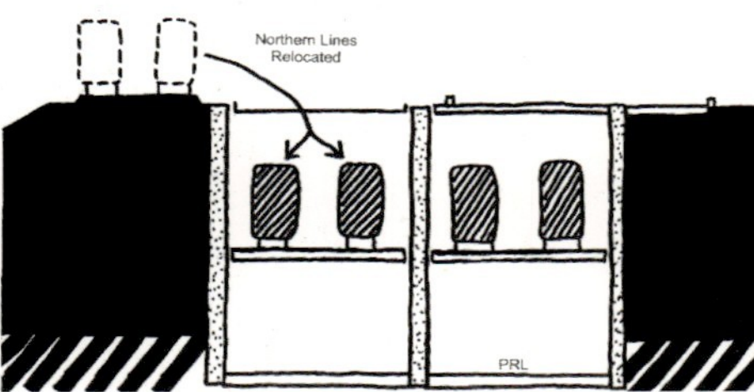

5. Install third diaphragm wall
6. Excavate northern section to PRL level
7. Relocate northern 'Cityrail lines'

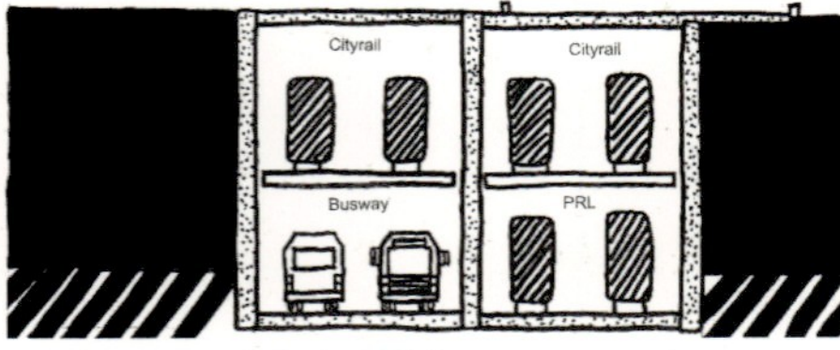

8. Construct PRL lines
9. Construct Busway
10. Develop above

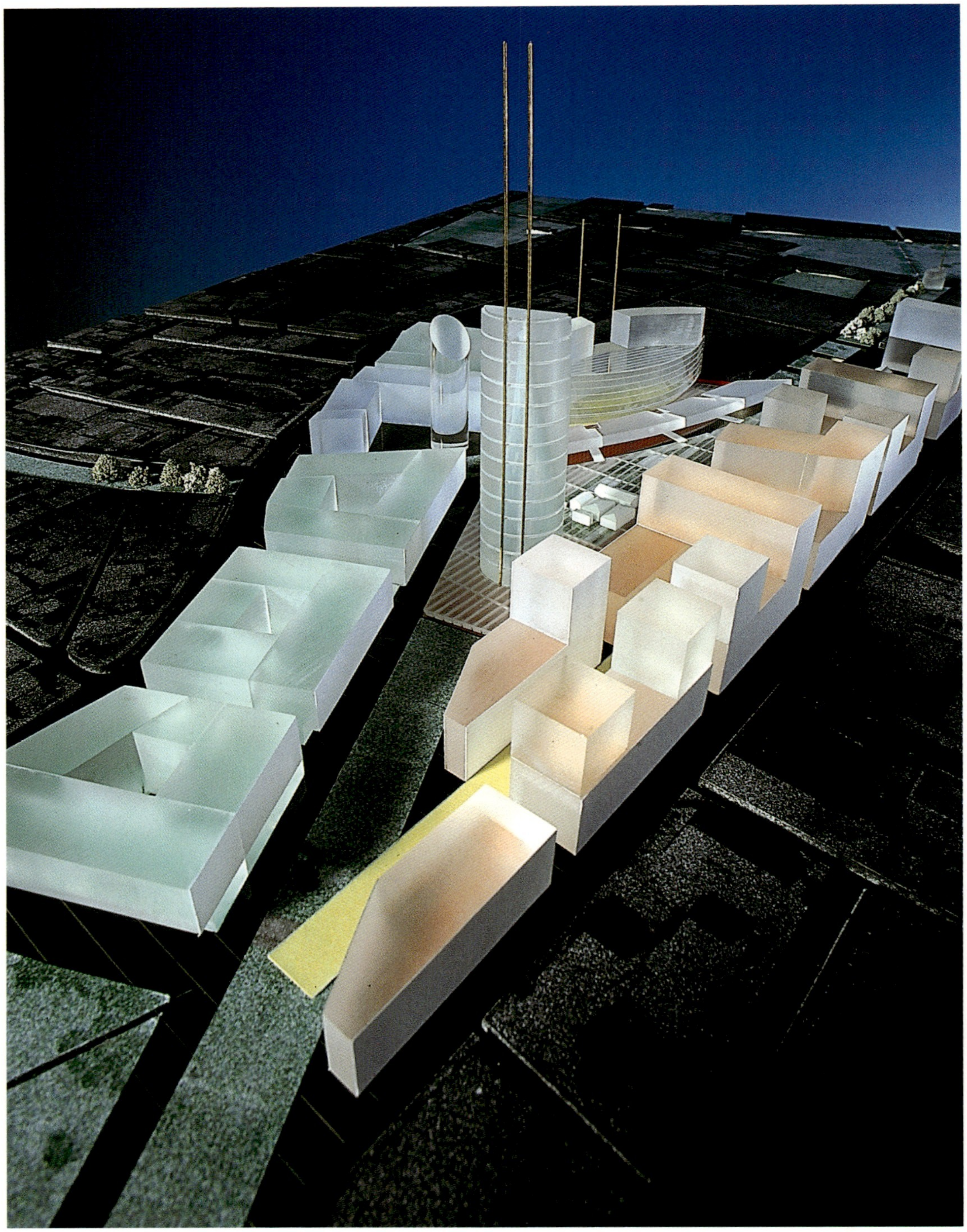

Terry Farrell & Partners, in conjunction with Sydney-based Conybeare Morrison & Partners, submitted an urban design strategy for the Parramatta Rail Link which was shortlisted in competition. The core of the £100 million contract covers 27 kilometres of commuter railway running west of Sydney from Parramatta to Chatswood. The railway is intended to become a catalyst for the growth of new communities in Sydney's otherwise lightly populated suburbs. The project involves the implementation of a new railway link and the design of 12 railway stations, both above and below ground. Several of the stations form part of complex interchanges with existing lines and bus stations. Each station is envisaged as a 'place-maker', enhancing and responding to its context, as well as redefining the character of the urban fabric. Iconic entrances to each station will create a unified identity for the line.

As part of its submission, TFP designed the Parramatta Station Transit Interchange – a point of arrival in the town and a new civic focus. The new interchange offered an opportunity to reconfigure the heart of Parramatta's central business district and put right its current deficiencies. TFP's design removes the barrier effect of the present station and railway line, opening up a large-scale plaza and transit mall at ground level that improves north–south pedestrian and vehicle connections. It re-establishes the importance of the station's hilltop site overlooking the Parramatta river, with the historic railway building and barracks combining to form a heritage precinct towards the eastern end of the plaza. The design consists of an open station, naturally ventilated and admitting sunlight through an apparently floating glass-and-metal roof structure.

The 12 stations have several different functions. They are transport hubs; centres that are well integrated with their surrounding areas, making visible and direct connections through a permeable edge; and mixed-use magnets for pedestrian activity. By integrating transport design with the existing and new urban development, TFP is drawing on its masterplanning and urban design skills in a continuation of the work undertaken at Kowloon Station for MTRC.

Views of initial study model.

Final submitted scheme for Parramatta station.

Below centre: Concept sketch by Aidan Potter. The station roof is a symbol uniting the town visually. Beneath the 'umbrella' is a pedestrian network system that caters for the whole town, not just the station.

Bottom: Concept sketches by Doug Streeter showing the final design with its distinctive roof.

Aerial view of model.

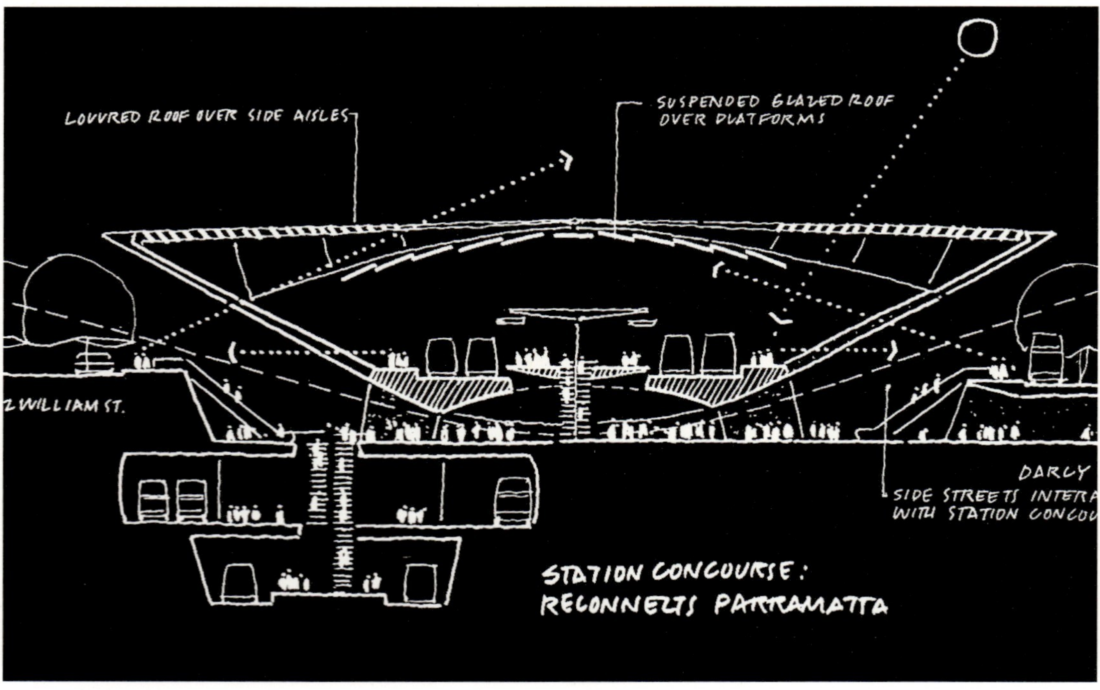

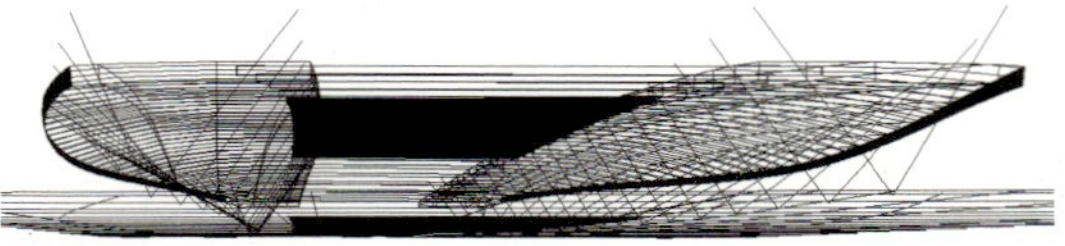

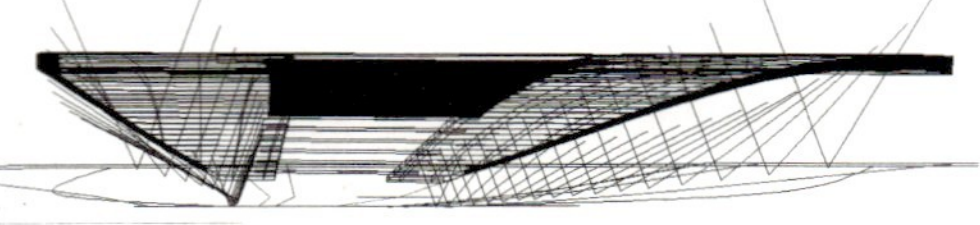

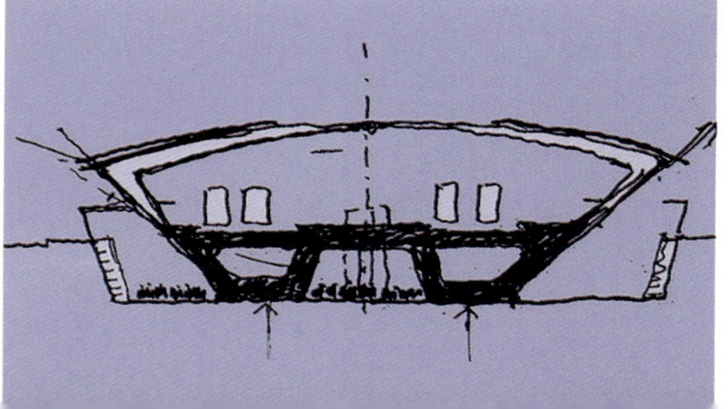

The symbolic roof visually unites the ground floor plane of the station, which, like a town square, is the new heart of the community.

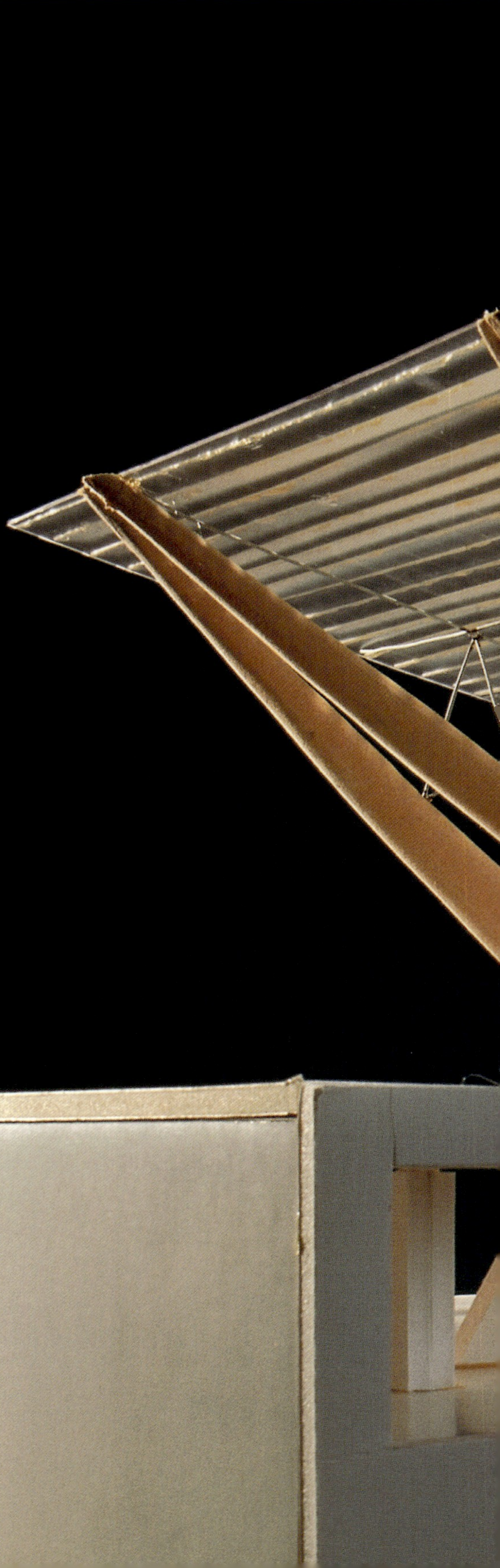

Skeleton structure from the new concourse level, which is the new town square.

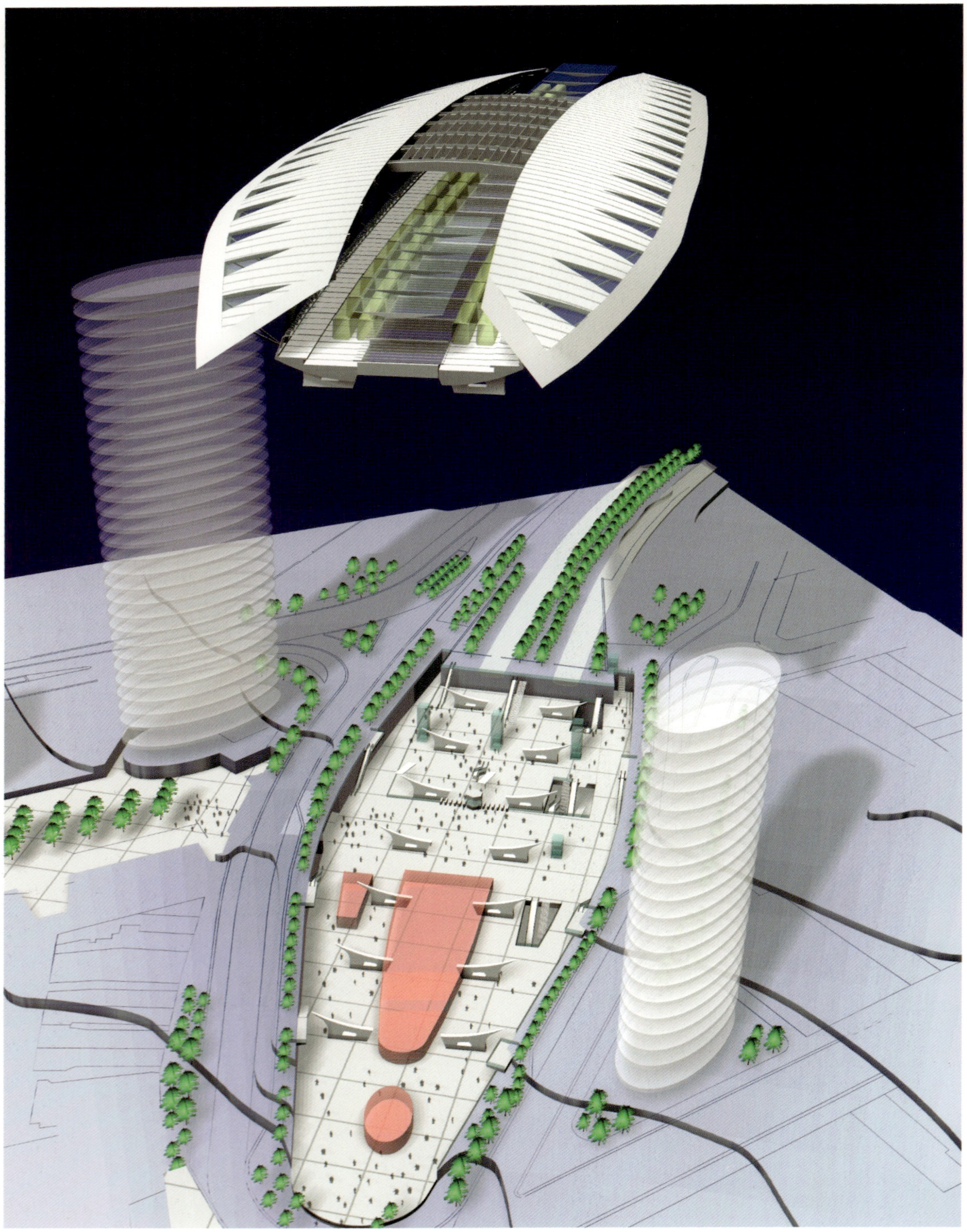

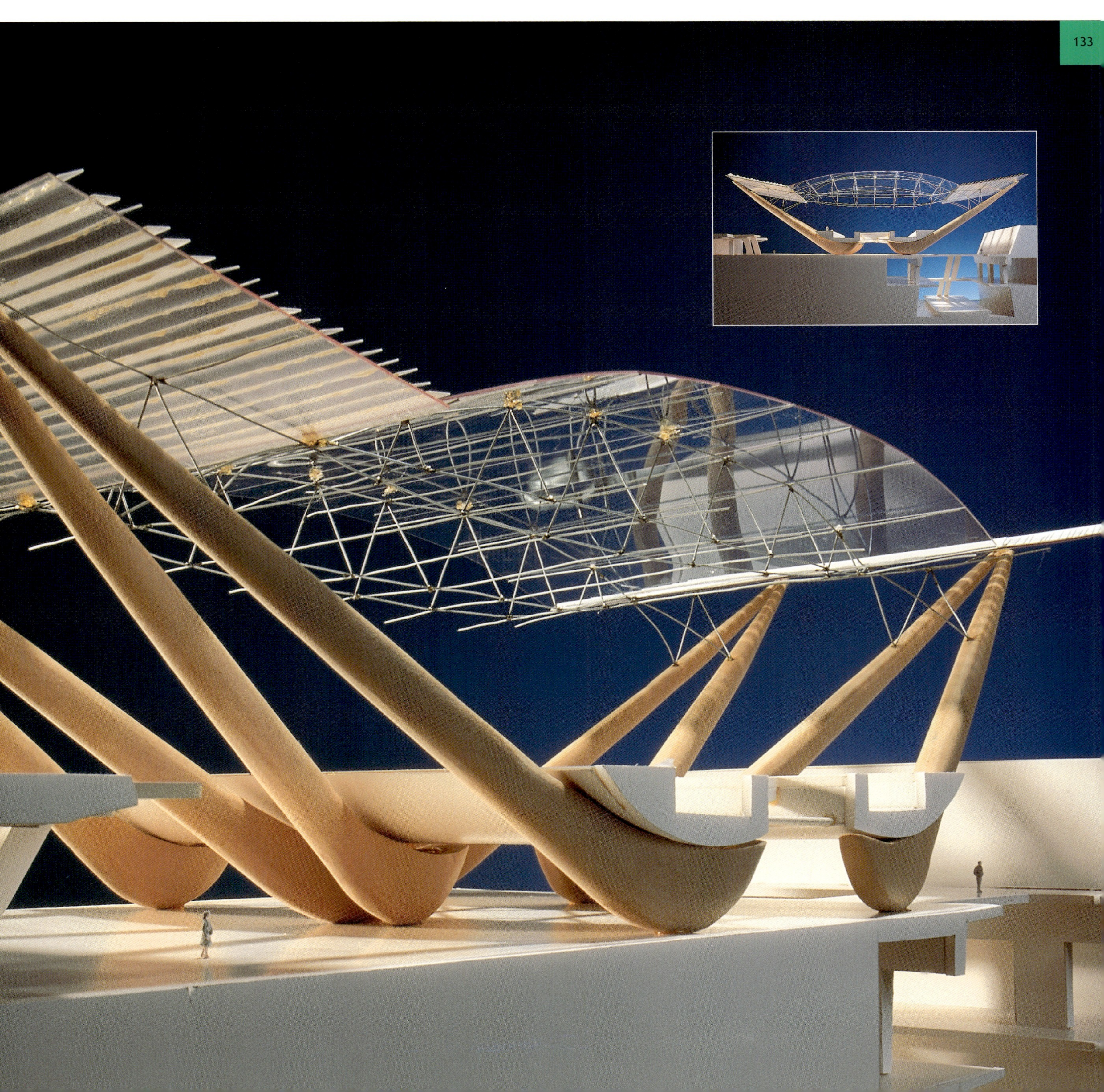

SEATTLE

SEATTLE

Left: Satellite view. Puget Sound, an inlet of the Pacific Ocean, is to the centre.

Centre: Seattle's urban landmarks.

Right: Seattle's regional landmarks.

Bottom: Bird's eye view of the city from 1925. The area comprises thousands of miles of water's edge environment.

Founded as late as 1869, Seattle is now the largest city in Washington state – its economic growth is reflected in the fortunes made by such companies as Microsoft, whose headquarters are in the city.

At its most simple, Seattle comprises a grid laid over a natural landscape and harbour. Within this planning is evidenced a freedom of expression that forms a contrast to the 'order within order' that characterizes a city such as Beijing.

The city is marked by its respect for ecological order, as well as being defined by three systems: the ecology linking mountains to sea; the historic system of real estate that generates Seattle's characteristic grid; and the port and rail processes that underpin the pier configurations along the waterfront. Terry Farrell & Partners' Pacific North-West Aquarium is a response to these three systems. The overall regeneration of the city reflects the global phenomenon of the rediscovery of urban living – reflected in the saving from demolition of Pike Place market in 1971, the growth of the Denny Regrade district to its north and the professional sports venues that came to Seattle in the mid-1970s. TFP's work in Seattle draws on and reflects these histories as being part of the city's modern-day story.

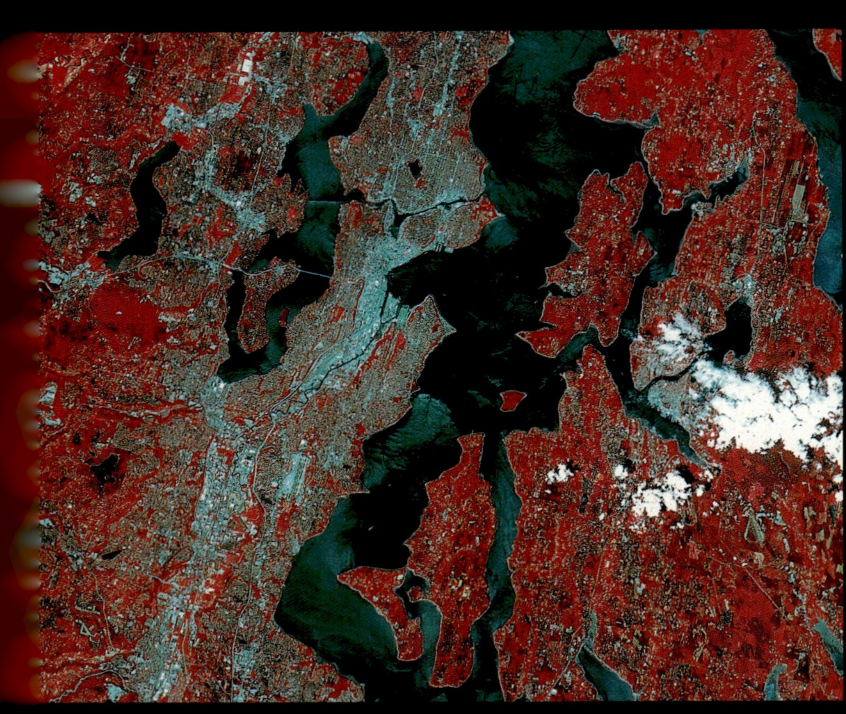

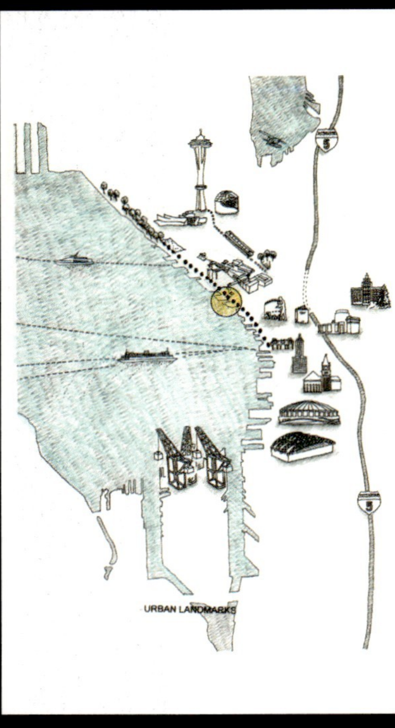

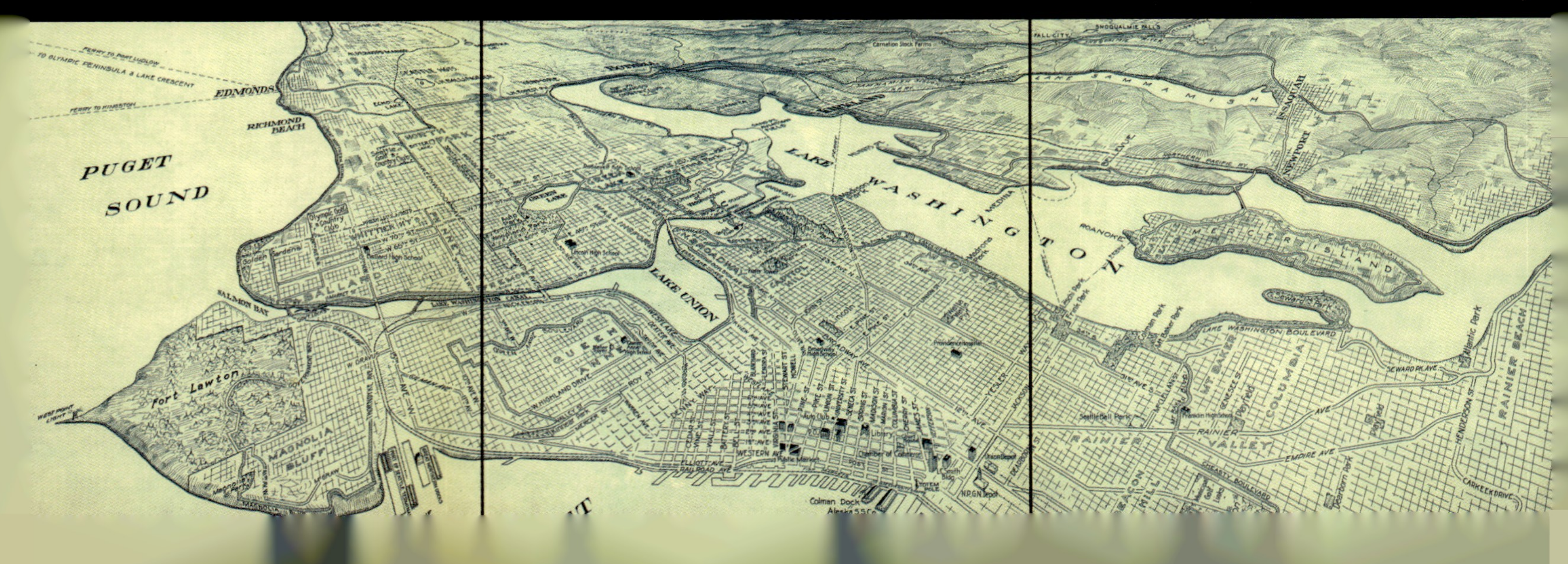

Seattle waterfront on Elliott Bay.

Bottom: Bird's eye view of the burgeoning city from 1884.

SOUTH SEATTLE MASTERPLAN

A study for the regeneration of south Seattle focuses on a site next to Pioneer Square, part of the city's historic core. This quarter is undergoing a massive programme of updating. In addition to the redevelopment of Union Street and King Street railway stations and the building of a new Expo facility, the 1960s' Kingdome sports stadium is being replaced by a new baseball stadium, and a new 72,000-seat football stadium is due for completion in 2002.

Terry Farrell & Partners' study analyzed how the area could be regenerated to create a sustainable mixed-use district comprising residential, office and community facilities. Proposals include implementing an air-rights development over the railway line, providing connections across major highways and extending the pedestrian domain around the railway station.

CAD image showing the new interventions in south Seattle's railway goods yard.

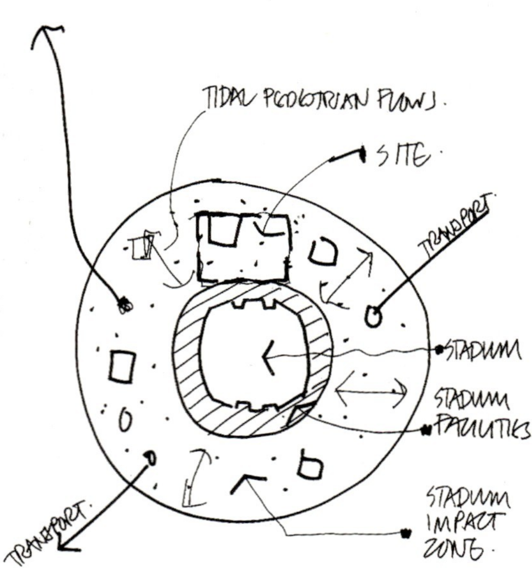

TFP's urban study focuses on a large air-rights site next to three new sports and exhibition facilities. The project involves the creation of a pedestrian link that bridges the railway line and contains mixed-use facilities.

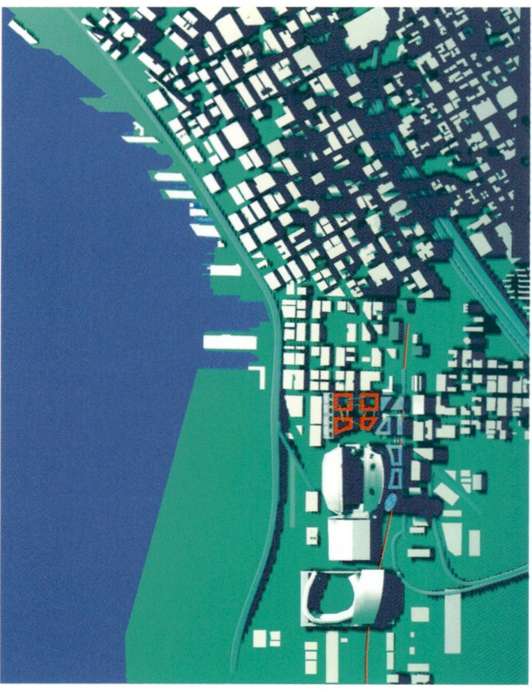

The south Seattle masterplan in context. Compared with the existing urban grain, the site stands out due to its large-scale buildings. The circular building represents the new 72,000-seat football stadium; below is the city's new exhibition centre. The 47,000-seat Safeco baseball stadium, home to the Seattle Mariners, is in the foreground.

AQUARIUM + MASTERPLAN FOR PACIFIC NORTH-WEST

Bounded on the west by Puget Sound's Elliott Bay, downtown Seattle is a strip occupying 945 hectares that slopes east–west towards the seafront. The 40,000 square metre masterplan site is on the coast near the centre point of Elliott Bay with direct access to the city's commercial core to the east. It overlooks an expanse of open waterfront dotted with piers, warehouses, a railway – remnants of the city's industrial past – and a noisy viaduct that has somewhat severed the area from the rest of the city. The piers, built at a tangent to the regular city grid, add an unexpected quirk to the city's topography.

Terry Farrell & Partners' designs for the Pacific Northwest Aquarium, in collaboration with Mithun Partners (affiliate architects), Streeter & Associates (collaborating architects), Weinstein Copeland (urban design consultants) and Robert Murase (landscape architect), were inspired by the natural beauty of Puget Sound and the Olympic Peninsula. The 15,000 square metre 'floating island' responds to its programme and location. Reflecting Seattle's topography, which is half land and half water, the building's form is at once part of the cityscape and of the waterfront.

Top: CAD image of TFP's scheme for the new Seattle aquarium.

Above and right: Aerial views of the existing aquarium site.

The masterplan site includes four historic piers, two of which have already been joined together and renovated. After analyzing new uses for the site as a whole, and seeking to capitalize on the historic nature of the area, TFP, collaborating with local architect Lee Copeland as urban design consultant, recommended an integrated waterfront park with a landmark aquarium building that broke the precedent of the linear pier form.

Seattle's bleacher-like topography has resulted in a city obsessed with views and this impacted very strongly on the design. The principal component of the building is an elevated 'shell' that contains the primary exhibition areas. By cradling the main part of the accommodation within this form, a sense of space is created at ground level, preserving beautiful views of Elliott Bay and the Olympic Mountains. The building's rich roofscape comprises a panoramic environment of tidal pools and water gardens fundamental to the perception of the building as viewed from above, where its watery setting merges with Puget Sound. This landscape is split open, shell-like, to reveal open-air exhibits in rock pools sculpted into a series of terraces that descend to the level of the bay, initiating a dialogue between the natural world and the interpretative world of the exhibits.

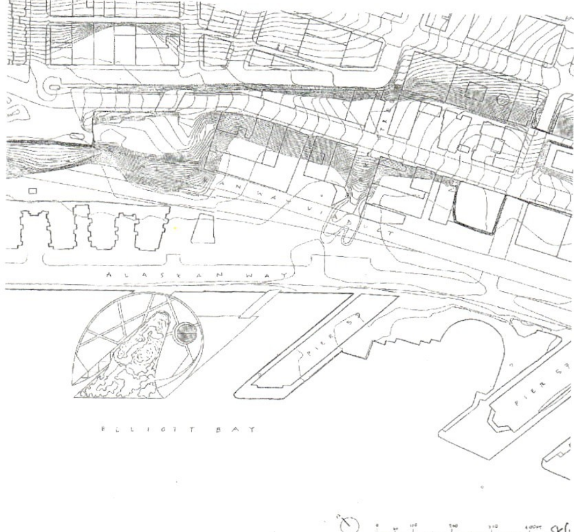

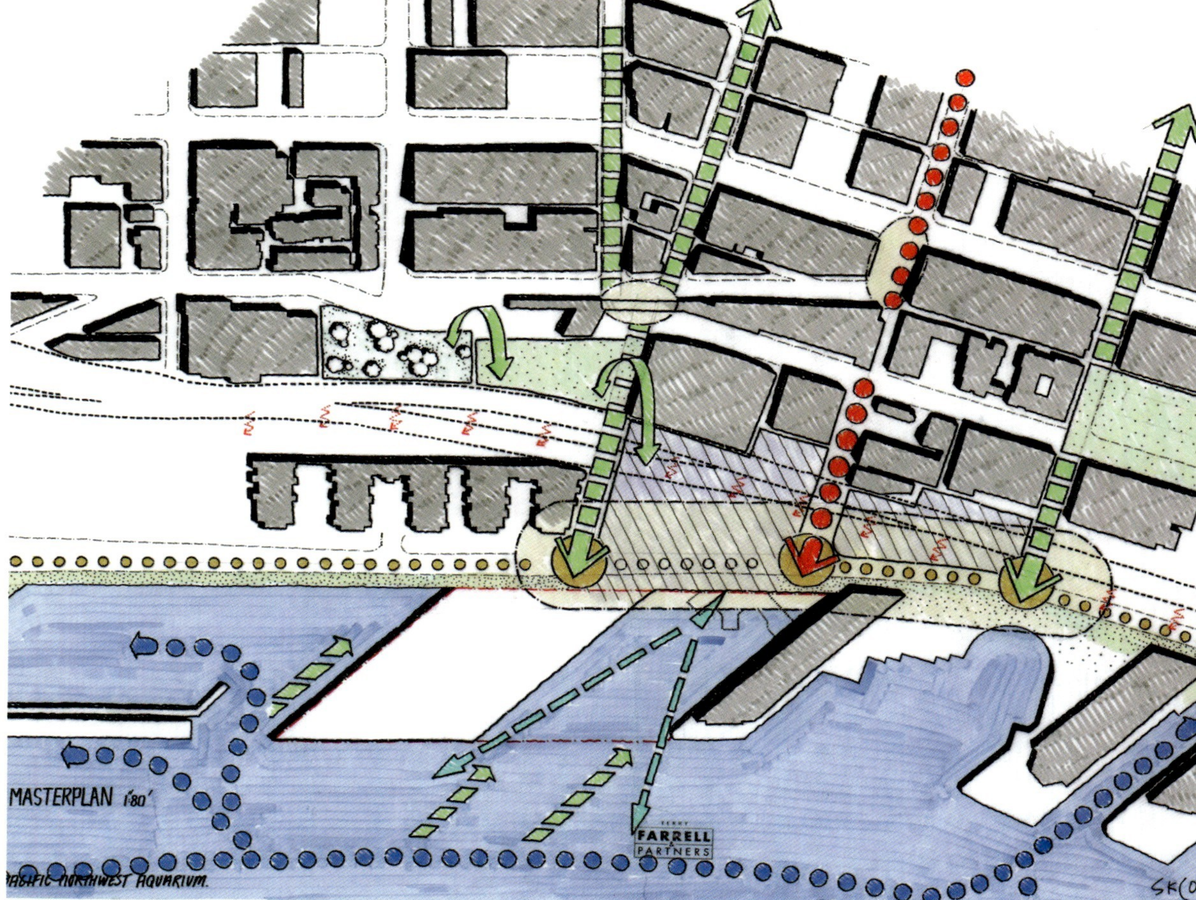

Top: Initial concept proposal for the site.

Above: Concept sketch by Doug Streeter.

Urban analysis diagram showing the principal and secondary routes along the waterfront, culminating in a public space in front of the aquarium site.

Top row, left to right: grids; pier grid; harbour figure ground; city figure ground; city layers; harbour layers.

Centre row, left to right: regional water; harbour water; views to site; views from site; existing tree line; potential tree line.

Bottom row, left to right: connections; viaduct acoustics; existing public open space (top); potential public open space (bottom); existing views (top); potential views (bottom).

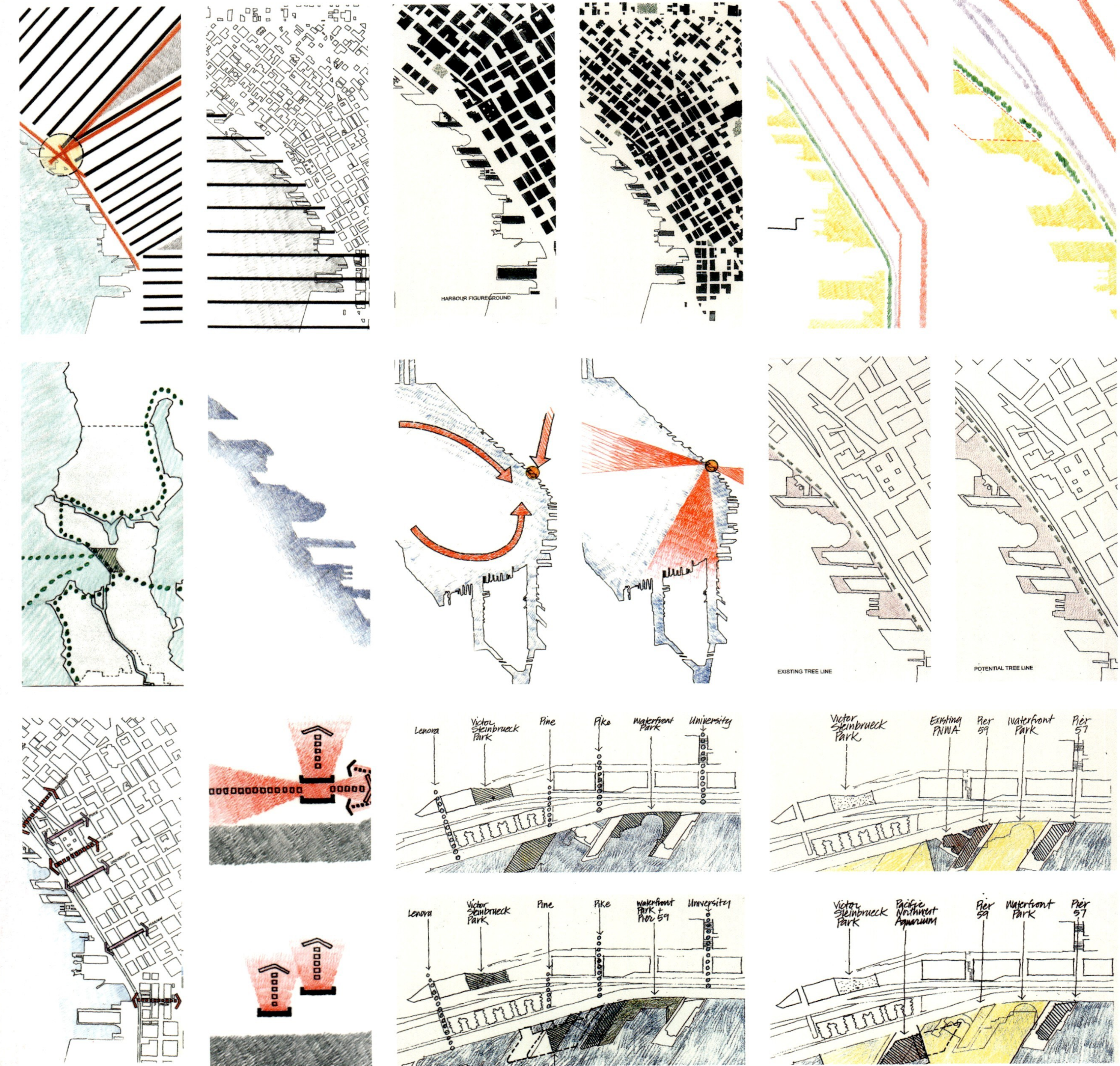

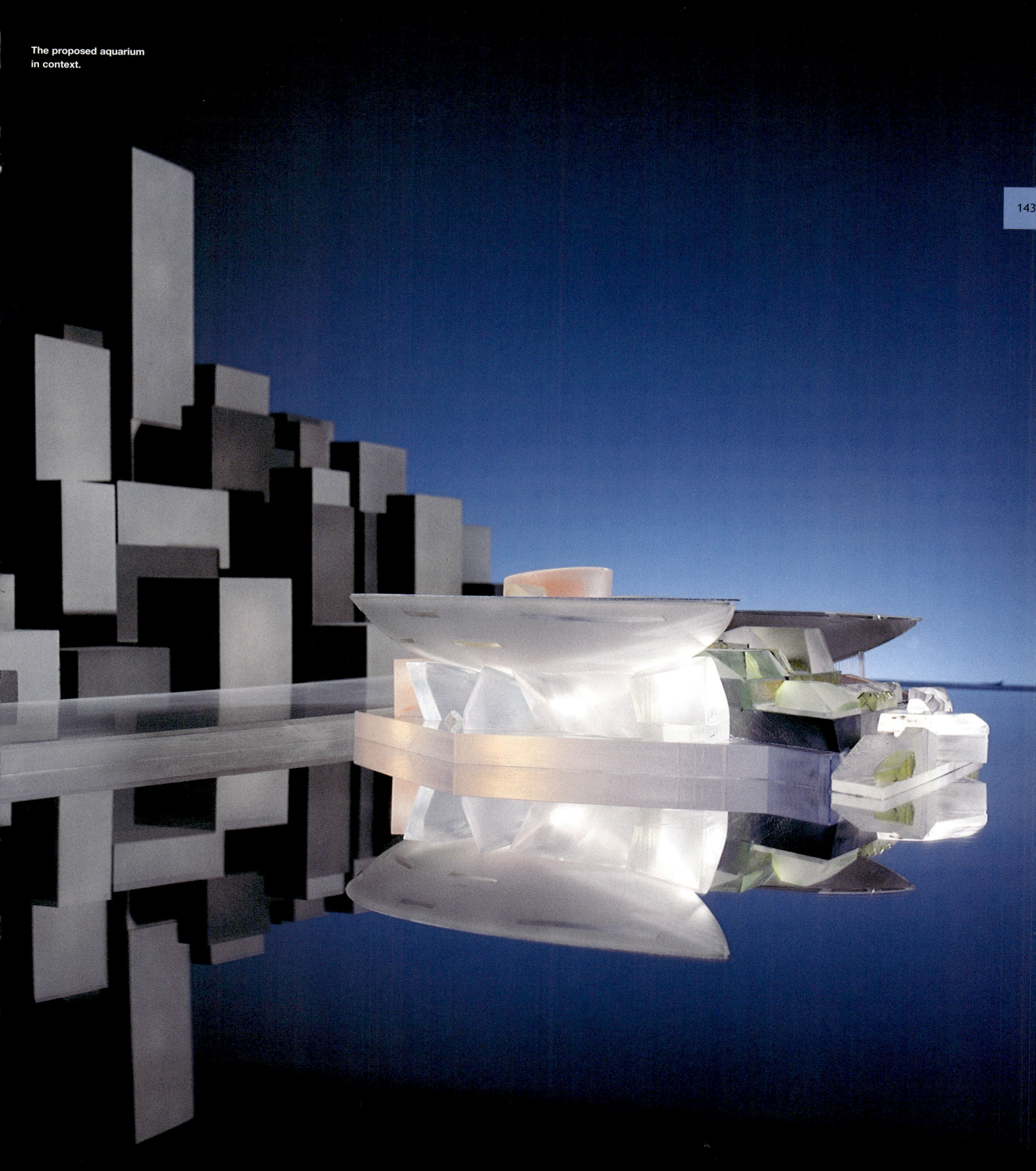
The proposed aquarium in context.

Context section through the new aquarium.

Proposed aquarium model. The elevated form creates a light-filled intertidal zone that sustains the migrating salmon along the shoreline.

The building is reminiscent of a promontory linked to land but forcing its way out to the sea. Its organic form contrasts with the strict geometry of the surrounding urban fabric. From the heights of the city above the waterfront, the roofscape will be seen as a strikingly landscaped habitat. As a place of education, research and entertainment incorporating public open space, promenades, views and access to the water, the $206 million project will significantly contribute to the regeneration of Seattle's central waterfront.

The main entrance to the aquarium is located in a cylindrical transparent hub that rises through the building and forms a feature element on the roof.

Sketch by Terry Farrell.

Seattle's aquarium project provides a good working example of TFP's approach to developing architecture from urban strategies and forms. The initial concept was for a landmark iconic building set in a site free from piers. As discussions with local community groups continued, it became obvious that the retention and consolidation of the historic piers would be much better served if the new aquarium was to utilize part of one of the historic sheds on the pier. This new concept arose from a contextual linear response set between two historic shed piers, based upon the study of urban design principles and the consultation and involvement of Seattle bodies who were active participants in the process.

Different studies for the plots and options.

Organization of original scheme.

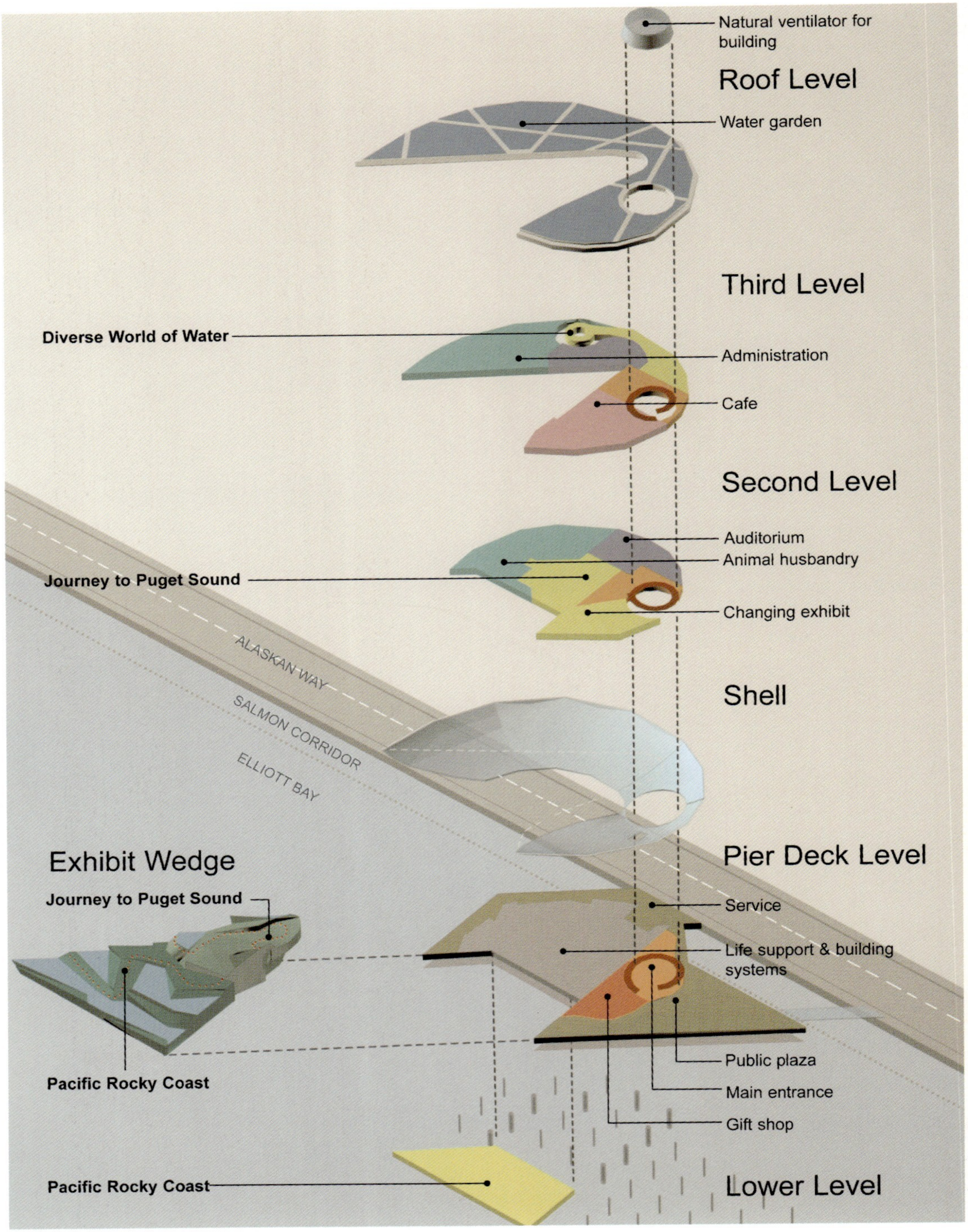

Natural ventilator for building

Roof Level

Water garden

Third Level

Diverse World of Water

Administration

Cafe

Second Level

Auditorium

Animal husbandry

Journey to Puget Sound

Changing exhibit

ALASKAN WAY

SALMON CORRIDOR

ELLIOTT BAY

Shell

Exhibit Wedge

Journey to Puget Sound

Pier Deck Level

Service

Life support & building systems

Pacific Rocky Coast

Public plaza

Main entrance

Gift shop

Pacific Rocky Coast

Lower Level

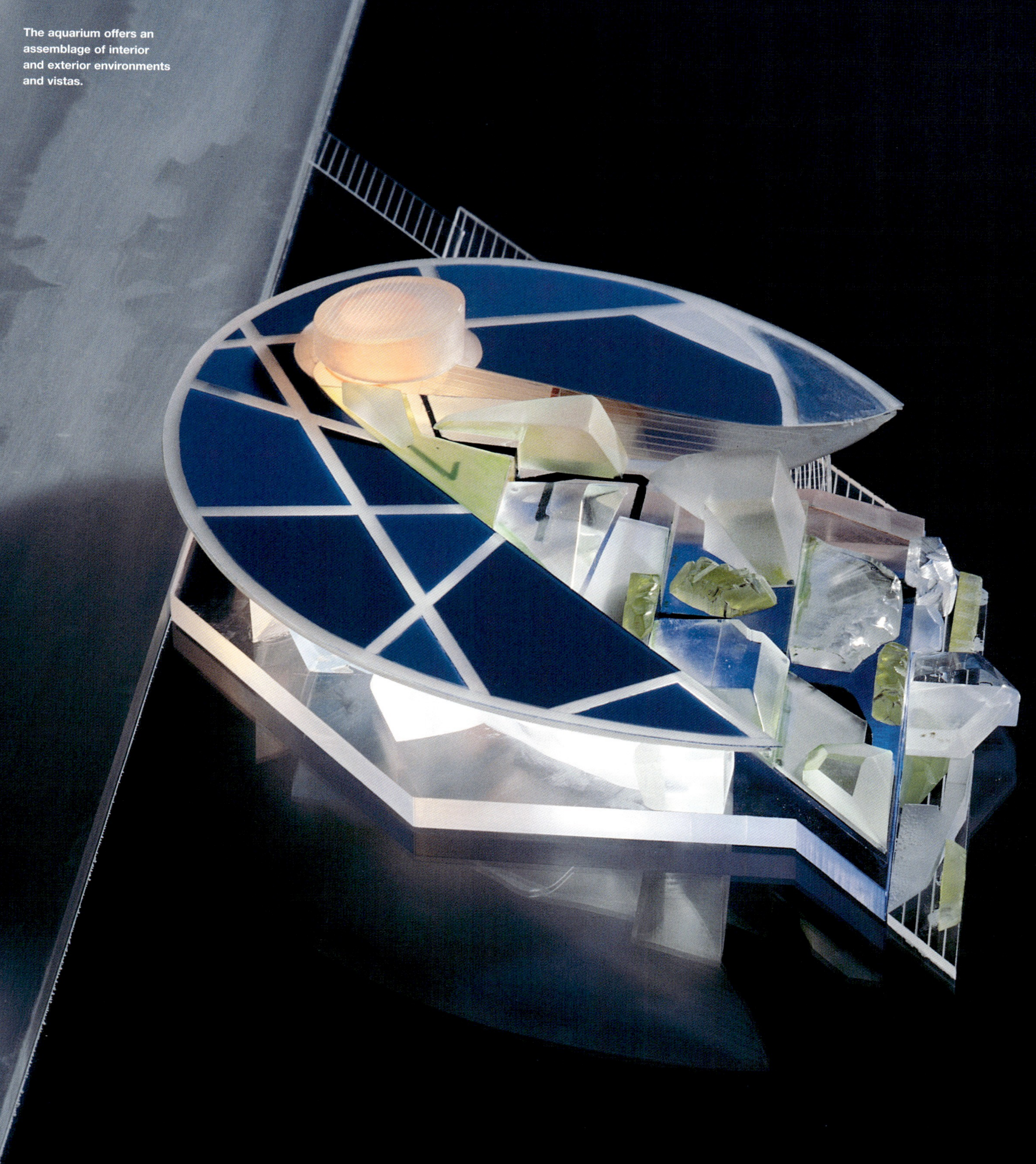

The aquarium offers an assemblage of interior and exterior environments and vistas.

As discussions progressed with Seattle's various interest and civic groups, the scheme evolved following a new urban design basis for the area. The historic pier is to be retained and a new public park integrated into the project, creating a new architectural direction and a wider, richer brief.

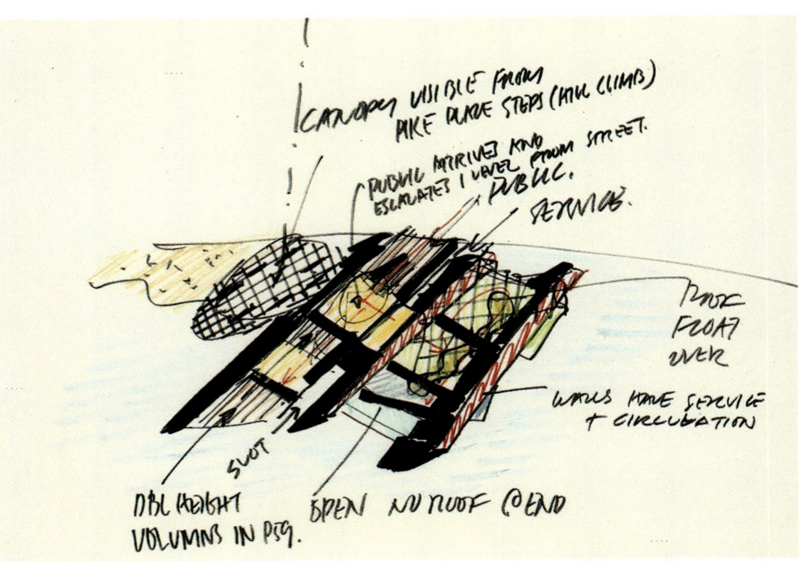

EXHIBIT 'BRIDGES' SPAN BETWEEN WALLS
HIGH TIDE
LOW TIDE
WALL = 'BEAM' ON MIN. STRUCTURE (TRUSS)
READ AS 'WHOLE'
STRUCTURE + SKIN =

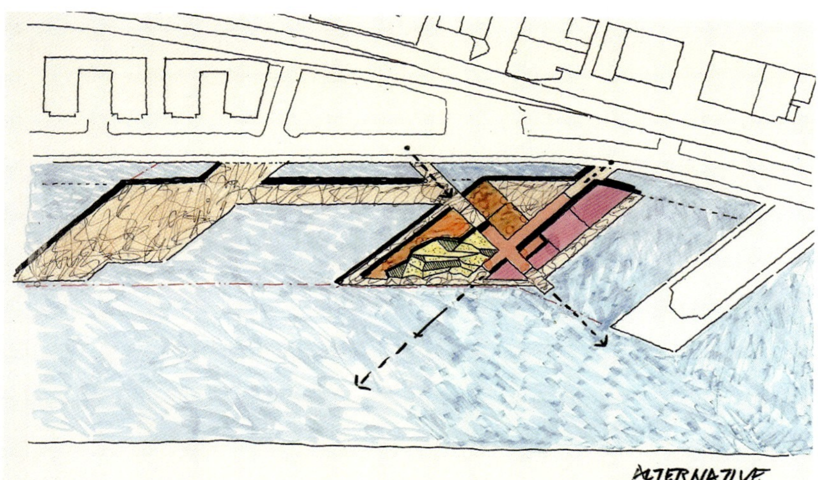
ALTERNATIVE TWO

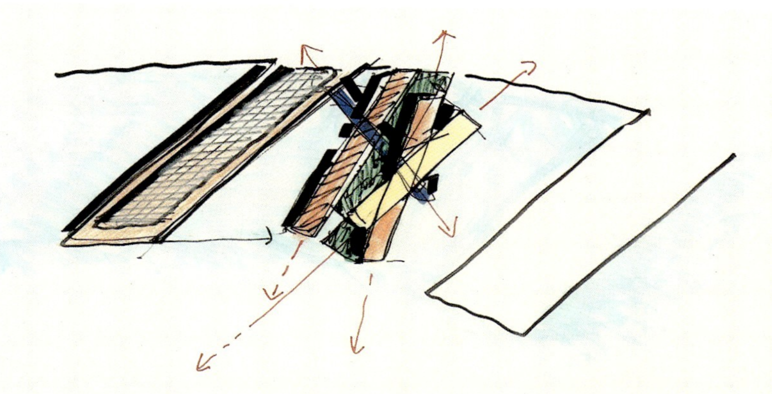
A CLUSTER OF LINEAR VOLUMNS

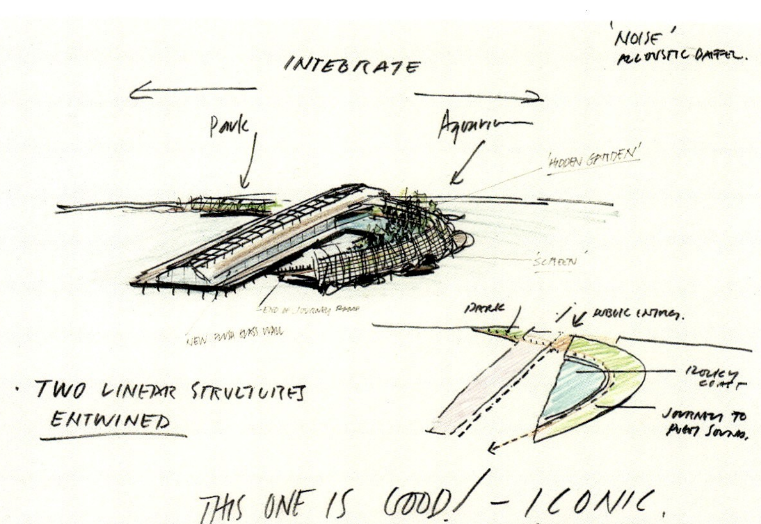
'NOISE' ACOUSTIC DAMPER.
INTEGRATE
Park
Aquarium
'HIDDEN GARDEN'
'SCREEN'
PARK
PUBLIC ENTRY.
· TWO LINEAR STRUCTURES ENTWINED
THIS ONE IS GOOD! – ICONIC. SIMPLE

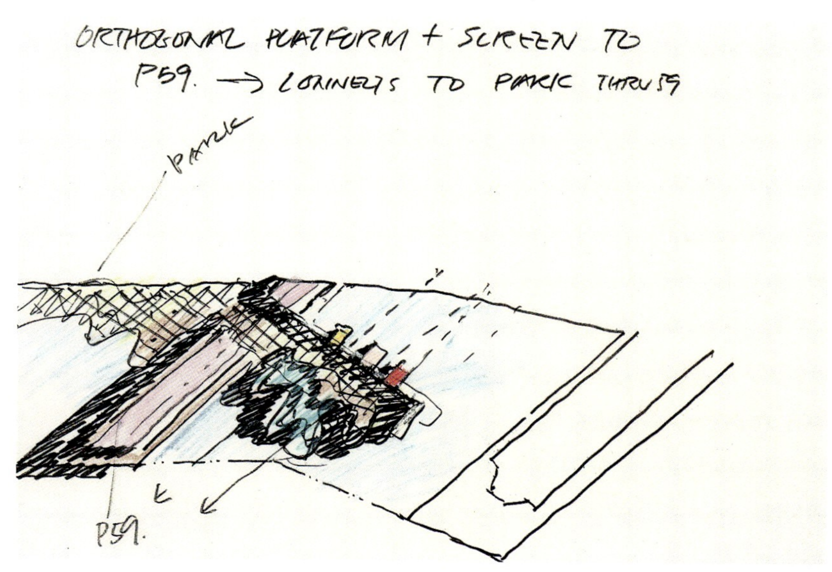
ORTHOGONAL PLATFORM + SCREEN TO P59. → CONNECTS TO PARK THRU 59
PARK
P59.

LISBON

LISBON

Bordered by both river and sea, Lisbon is essentially an estuary city. With its Roman foundations and layered medieval and Renaissance streets and buildings, it closely resembles a great Mediterranean city, but it faces the Atlantic. Lisbon has a great tradition of ocean travel and exploration and it lines the great waterway of the River Tagus with grandeur and confidence. Formerly occupied by Portugal's navy, and previously inaccessible to the general public, the 12 kilometres of publicly owned waterfront comprises an extraordinary public realm. Once separated from the rest of the city through the effects of 20th-century industrialization, the riverfront has recently been revitalised and reconnected to the town by a masterplan implemented by Terry Farrell & Partners and Ideias do Futuro. Expo 98, which was set along the rediscovered water's edge, was one of the city's great triumphs.

The central axis running from Avenida da Liberdade to Rossio and Baixa, through the Arco Monumental and on to the Praça do Comércio is one of the world's finest urban sequences, while the arched gate and the great 'room' facing the river easily rivals St Mark's Square in Venice.

Top: Satellite photo of Lisbon and the Tagus estuary where it meets the Atlantic ocean.

Bottom: Comparative estuary cities: Seattle, Sydney, Lisbon and Hong Kong.

Rossio and the river front.

Monumental and on to the Praça do Comércio.

room', marks the start of the monumental Baixa axis that climbs up the hill to do Rossio station.

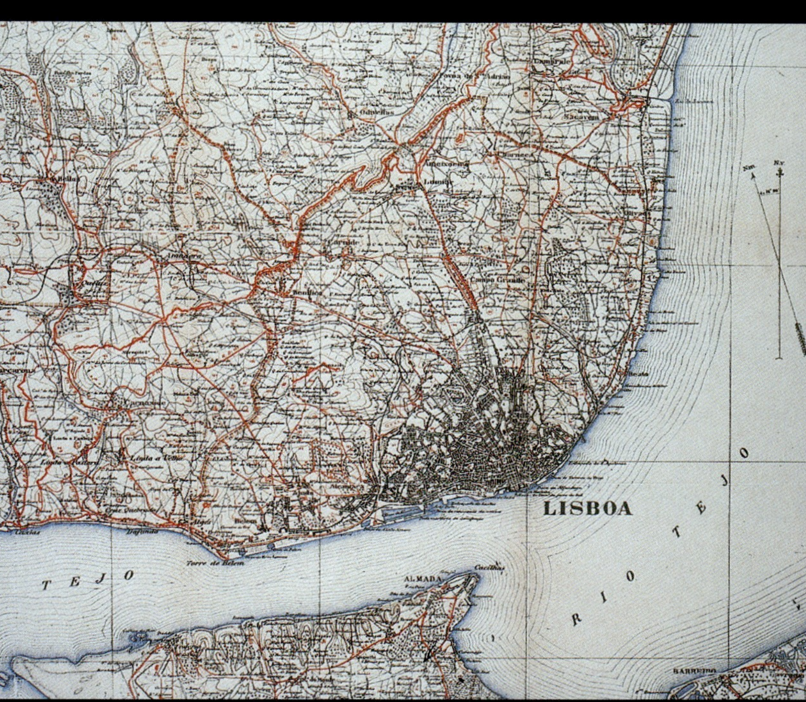

PORT OF LISBON MASTERPLAN

Top strip: Model of the Port of Lisbon masterplan as designed by TFP in conjunction with Ideias do Futuro. The 5-metre model, at 1:500 scale, was put on display at the Gare Marítima de Alcântara in the summer of 1994. The masterplan runs from the Museu da Marinha in the west along the coast past the Praça do Comércio and right up to the area of the Expo 98 site in the city's eastern zone.

Bottom: Drawings of the masterplan study area. From left to right is Doca de Belém, Doca de Santo Amaro, Doca de Alcântara, Praça do Comércio, Santa Apolonia and Doca do Bispo.

The width of the River Tagus as it flows through Lisbon varies from 50 metres to 400 metres. The riverfront includes wet and dry docks, historic buildings and monuments, green spaces, and pedestrian and vehicular links. However, rather than being integrated in the city as a whole, the rundown dockland areas have been cut off from the city centre by roads and rail routes running parallel to the river. The revival of the port's infrastructure and the rationalization and improvement of its activities aims to restore the riverfront as the city's urban boundary.

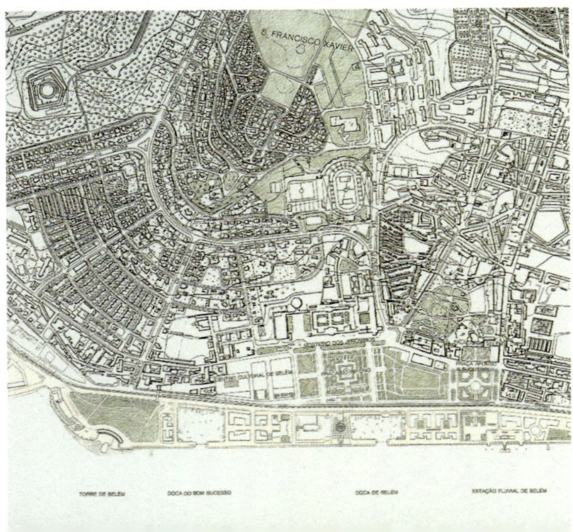

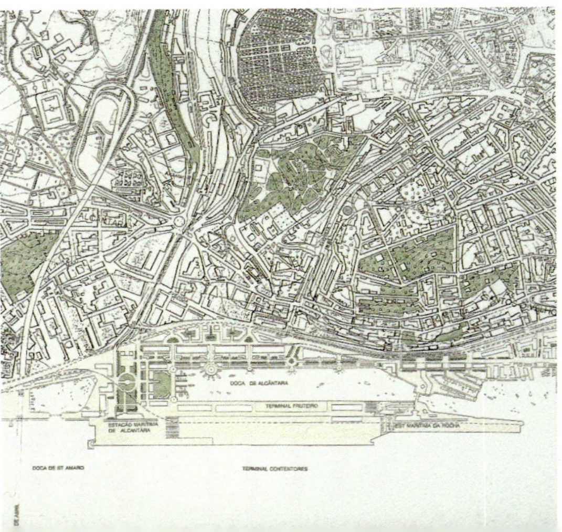

In 1994, following the Lisbon Expo project (see pp.158-159), Terry Farrell & Partners, in conjunction with Lisbon-based Ideias do Futuro, were commissioned by the administration of the Port of Lisbon to undertake a six-month masterplan study into a 14-kilometre stretch along the River Tagus. The aim – as with the Expo site, but on a grander scale – was to reinstate Lisbon's decaying riverside as the city's 'principal façade' while providing connections to the city centre. The commission required TFP to develop an urban regeneration framework in consultation with the Port of Lisbon administration.

In collaboration with Ideias do Futuro, TFP identified a number of separate development zones distinguished by site characteristics and likely land uses. These were analyzed in terms of infrastructure, traffic capacities, pedestrian flows, parking capacities, plot densities and the design of urban forms.

The TFP masterplan addressed ways of overcoming the separation of the port lands from the city centre. Port activities were rationalized and concentrated into defined zones, making other areas available for development. Access, servicing, plot size and phasing were incorporated into the urban design scheme, along with solutions for achieving expansion in sympathy with the scale and grain of the town. Existing buildings and land uses were analyzed and recommendations made about what should be retained and redeveloped. The masterplan advocated transforming the port into a desirable stopover location for international cruise ships as well as a base for new cruise-ship terminals. Existing docks were converted into leisure facilities and mixed-use zones were identified.

In summer 1994 the commission concluded with an exhibition of the proposals in the Gare Marítima de Alcântara , one of the city's principal port buildings, which was opened in June 1994 by the Portuguese minister of sea.

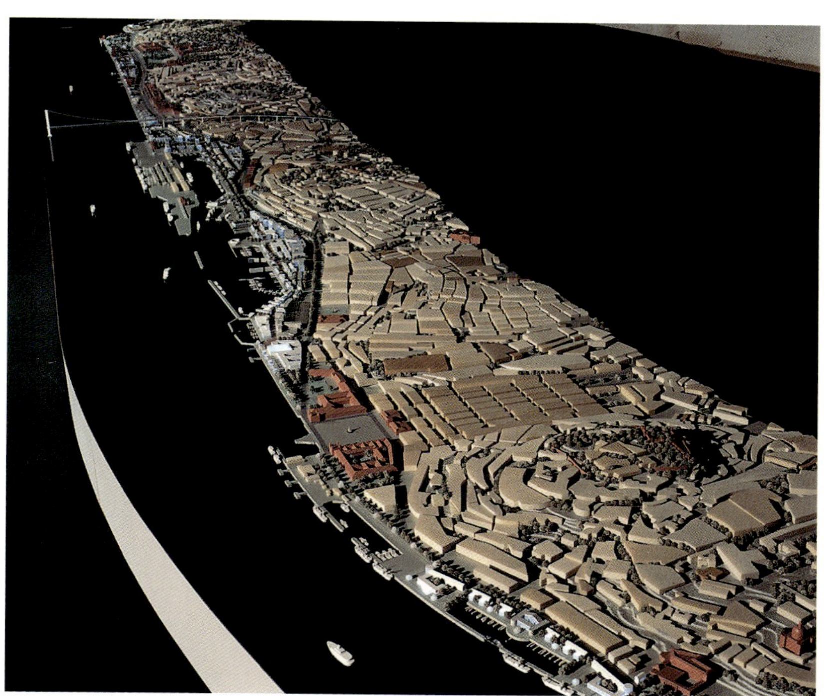

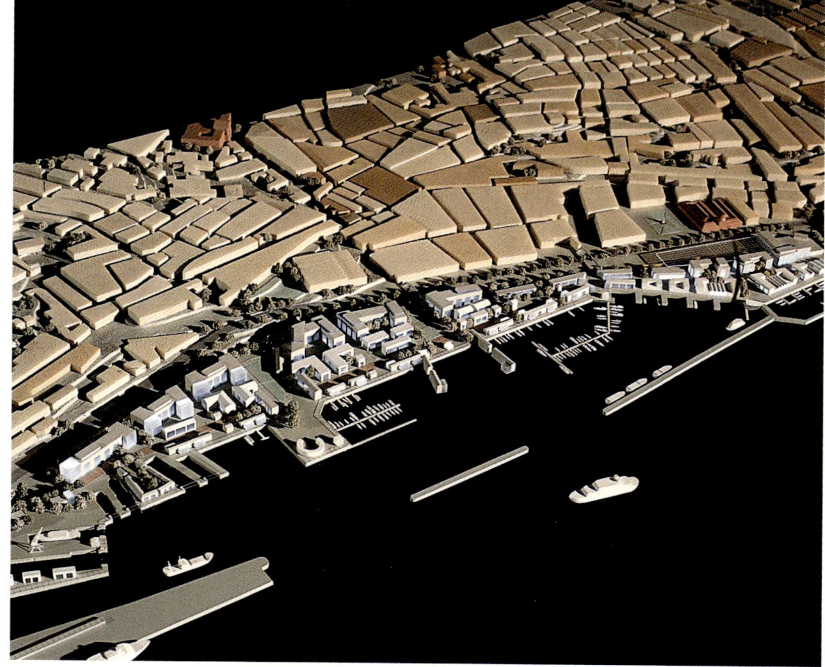

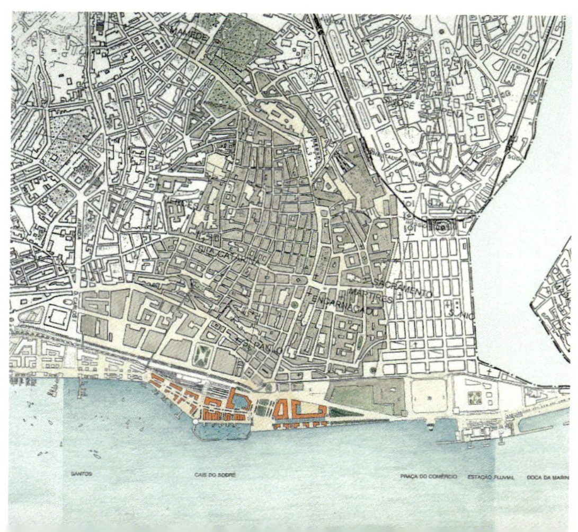

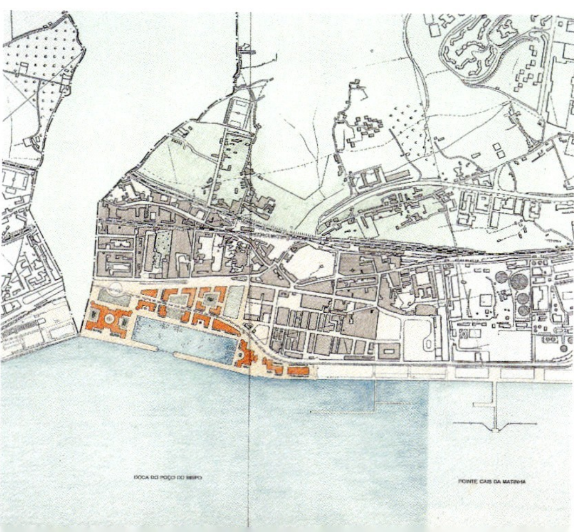

The regenerated Santo Amaro Dock in the Alcântara area.

Bottom: City panorama.

Aerial view of the Expo 98 site.

EXPO 98 MASTERPLAN

Expo 98 was located in Lisbon's Redevelopment Area in the east of the city, enabling an accelerated process of development in a quarter formerly occupied by rundown industrial buildings. The 340-hectare site extended along a five-kilometre stretch of the River Tagus, overlooking the widest part of the estuary around the Olivais Dock, which had been a hydroplane base in the 1930s and 1940s. Terry Farrell & Partners, in conjunction with Ideias

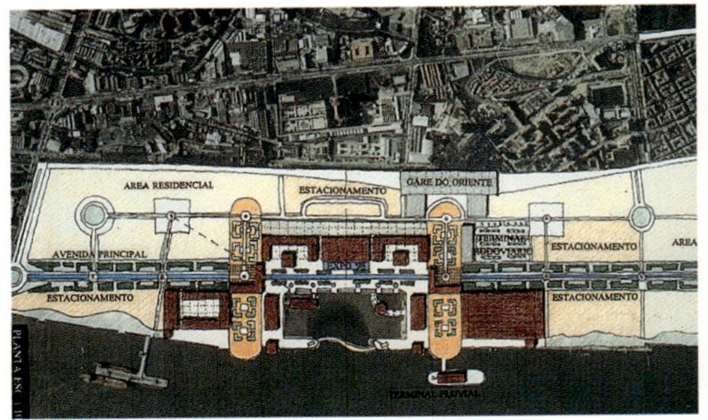

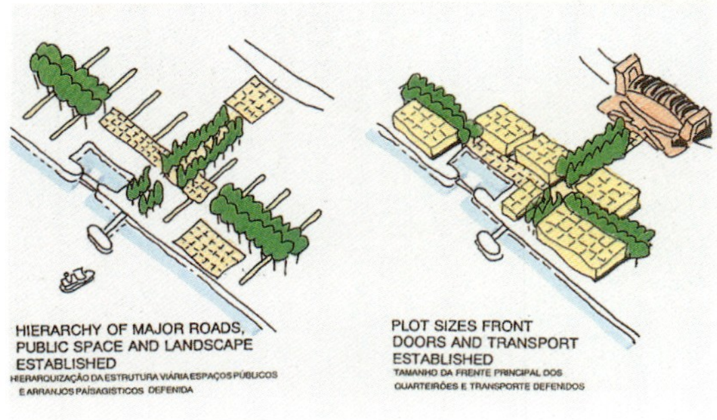

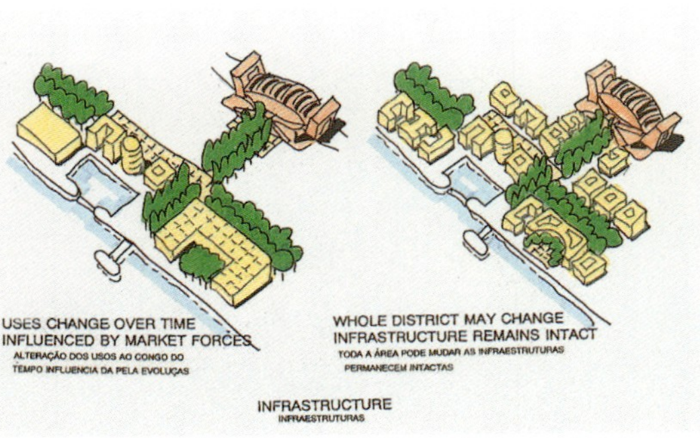

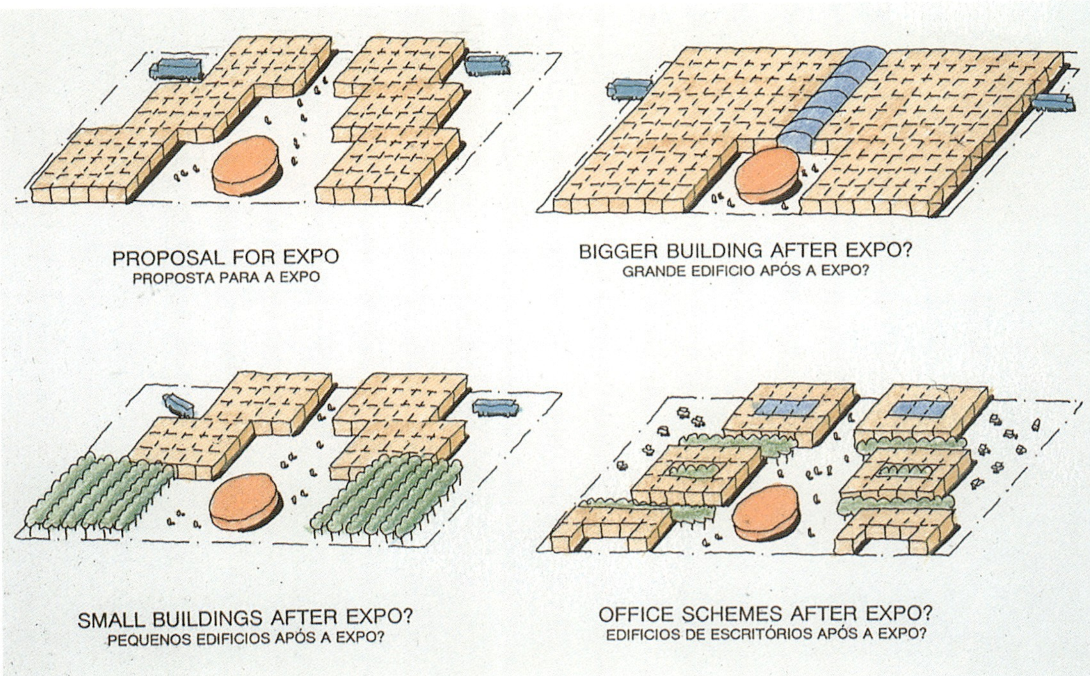

Above: Studies for the organization of buildings on the site showing how they would be planned for the Expo and expanded afterwards. The flexibility of the layout is a central feature of the proposals.

Top left: Outline masterplan for the Expo area by TFP.

Top: Model showing the Expo 98 area.

do Futuro, entered three separate competitions for Expo 98 – for the masterplan, the design of Oriente railway station and the design of the exhibition halls.

Terry Farrell & Partners was one of five practices shortlisted in 1992 by Parque Expo 98 to design the 25 hectare masterplan. The practice concentrated its design strategy on Lisbon's long-term future by using the temporary Expo as an opportunity for planning a full-scale redevelopment of the waterfront. The plan reflected the Expo theme – 'The Oceans: a Heritage for the Future' – by using an inverted representation of the ocean bed as a suspended roof covering. Made of metal netting, this canopy would reflect sunlight but shelter visitors from glare.

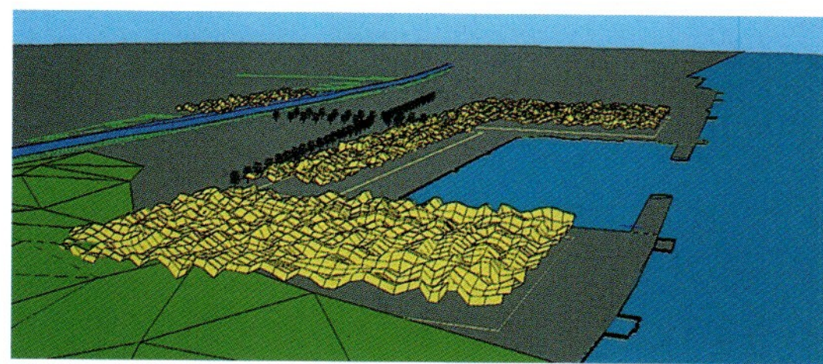

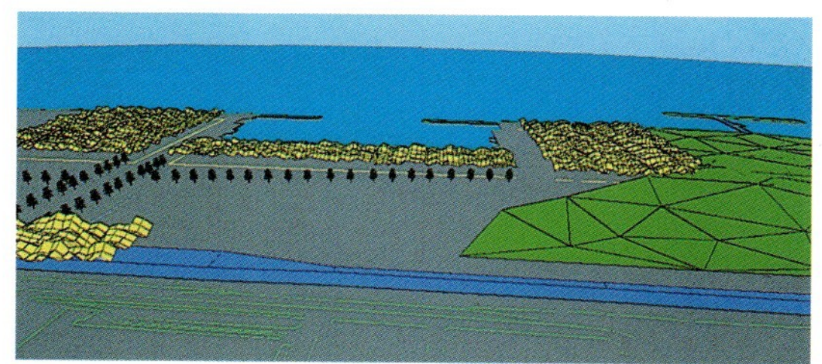

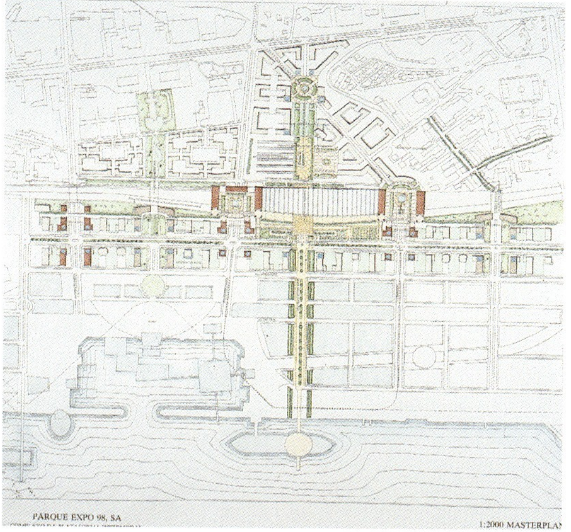

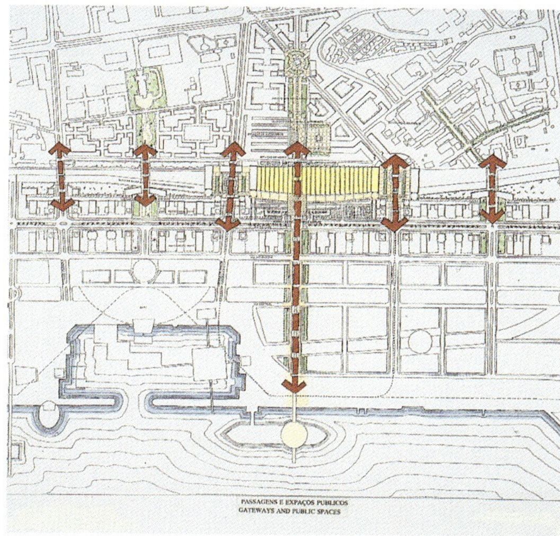

Concept drawings of the Expo 98 pavilions. The roof covering evokes the image of an inverted and suspended ocean bed.

Above: Masterplan of the Expo with the beginnings of the urban design plan for Oriente station (see pp.160–61).

Top: A subsequent proposal for the exhibition buildings.

Centre: After the Expo, the use changed to accommodate offices and workshops.

GARE DO ORIENTE

Competition proposals for the Gare do Oriente with a hotel at one end, an office at the other and a great entrance that leads to a bus station.

TFP was later invited to submit proposals for the Gare do Oriente, a major railway station and transport interchange on a site next to Expo 98's main entrance that offered the potential for a rapid transport link from the heart of Expo to Lisbon airport. The station complex included facilities for the expansion of the railway artery from Lisbon to central Portugal; links to metro, bus and taxi routes; and the integration of retail, office, hotel and leisure facilities.

The design concept is based on a main spine under one roof that provides an axis oriented east–west across the site. Terraced levels linked by ramps, steps and escalators form a plinth that clearly expresses the layout and circulation routes within. Above the plinth rises the gently curving roof. Composed of a series of profiled shell forms reminiscent of a shoal of fish, the roof is oriented to allow northern light to flood the station. The north and south ends of the roof are bounded by blocks accommodating commercial developments.

Together, the plinth, roof and blocks form a simple composition expressing the linear, dynamic characteristic of the railway while providing a link between central Lisbon and the Tagus. Each end of the station complex is fronted by pedestrianized squares that give the scheme a clear identity when approached from neighbouring districts.

TFP's third competition entry was for a 50,000 square metre building containing exhibition halls flexible enough to house not only Expo 98 but also, in future, the Lisbon Trade Fair. The design incorporated communication routes and boundaries that had to link the site with the surrounding area, both during and after the Expo period.

The result was a building that placed minimum restrictions on the future use of space. The essence of the TFP scheme was to provide a neutral framework within which the countries participating in Expo could project their individual identities based on the theme of 'The Oceans: a Heritage for the Future'.

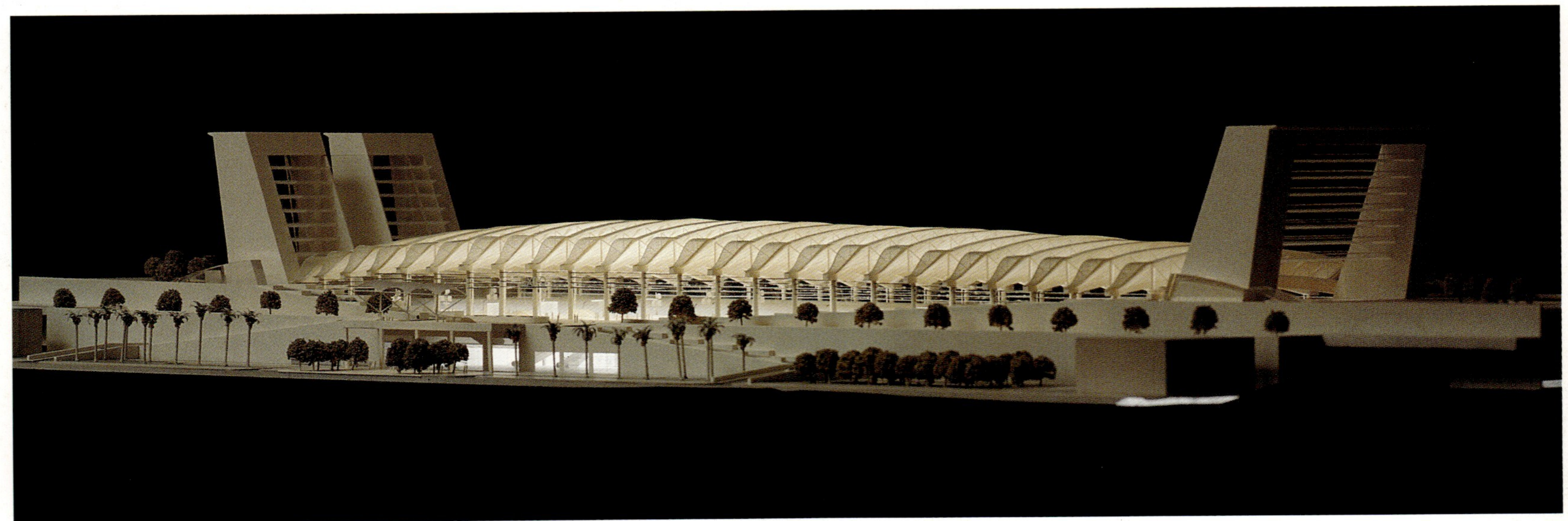

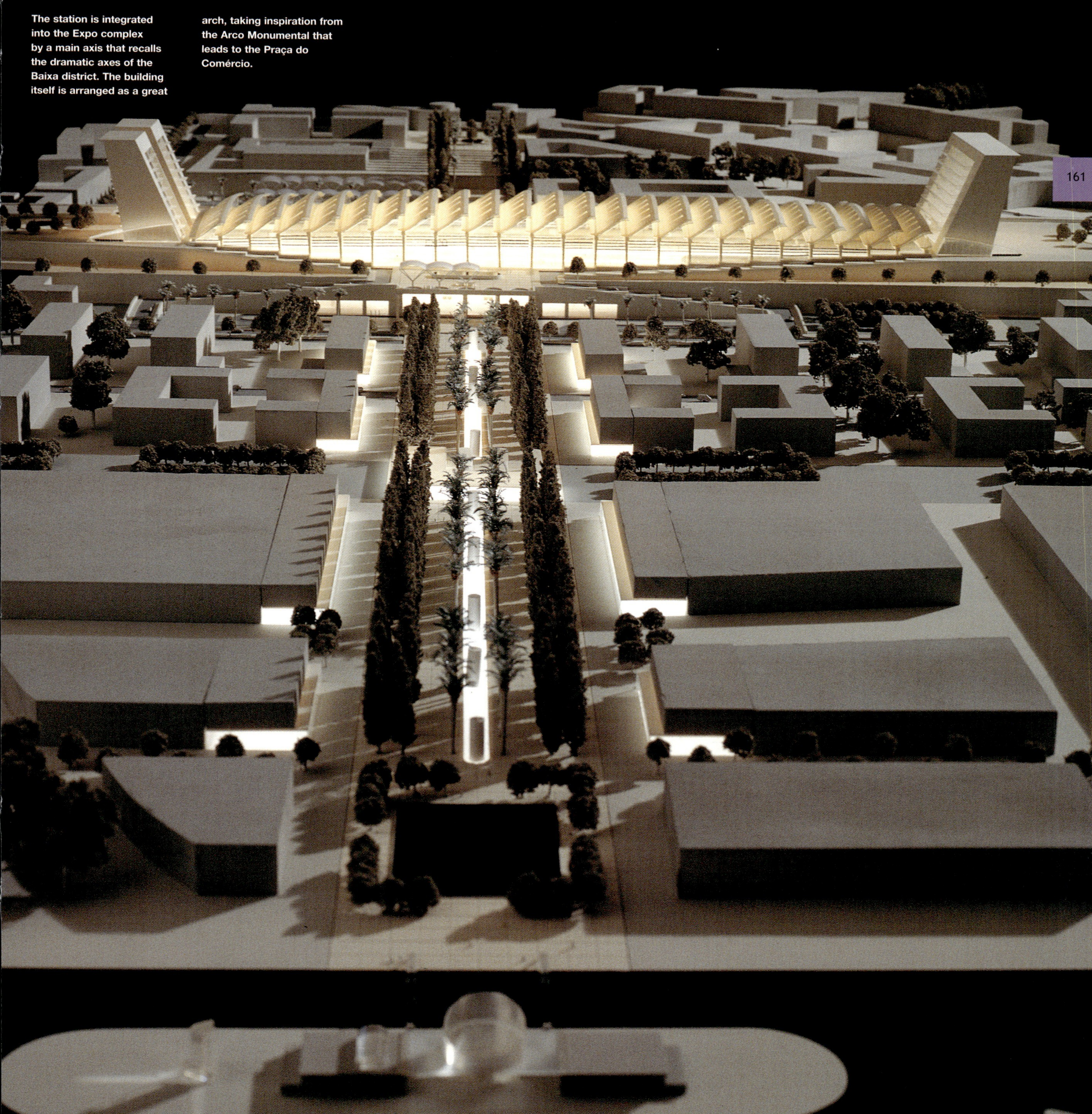

The station is integrated into the Expo complex by a main axis that recalls the dramatic axes of the Baixa district. The building itself is arranged as a great arch, taking inspiration from the Arco Monumental that leads to the Praça do Comércio.

DO ROSSIO STATION + MASTERPLAN

Do Rossio station is situated on the side of one of Lisbon's distinctive hills in the Baixa valley, high above the central square of Rossio. Trains arrive through a tunnel carved out of the mountain face and stop on the carved-out ridge, resembling a table top, on which the station is located. The station reflects the unevenness of the site – its principal street entrance is four storeys below platform level.

As Lisbon expanded around it, Do Rossio station became a major landmark in the city, providing an important link between the Baixa and Bairro Alto districts. Do Rossio's prominent roof reinforces the building's presence, particularly when viewed from the castle and Santo Mote areas.

The Do Rossio station area took shape in 1755, after a disastrous earthquake had destroyed a large part of Lisbon and a grid of new streets was laid out to form the modern city. The railway tunnel, opened in 1889, and the station, with its span shed that draws parallels with London's King's Cross, was designed by José Luis Monteiro in 1890. The station's main façade is a highly individual interpretation of the 16th-century Manueline (or late Gothic) style, with embellished stonework, expressed buttresses and an exotic horseshoe-shaped double entrance portal. Improvements to the station infrastructure in 1959 resulted in the

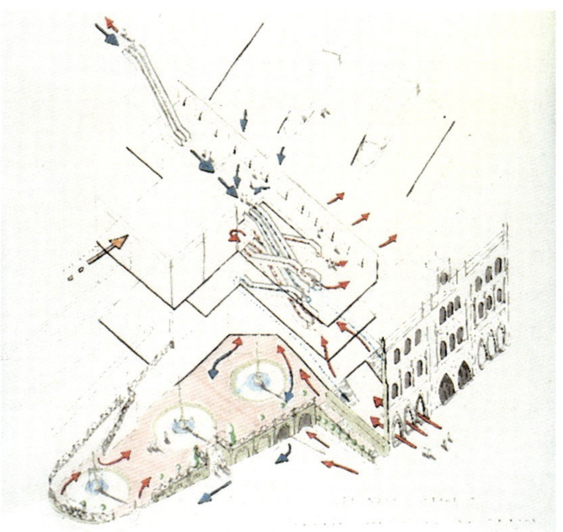

Rossio's wonderful main elevation faces into the town. The concourse sits at the bottom of the multi-storey complex and escalators lead up to the platforms, which reach almost to Lisbon's roof tops.

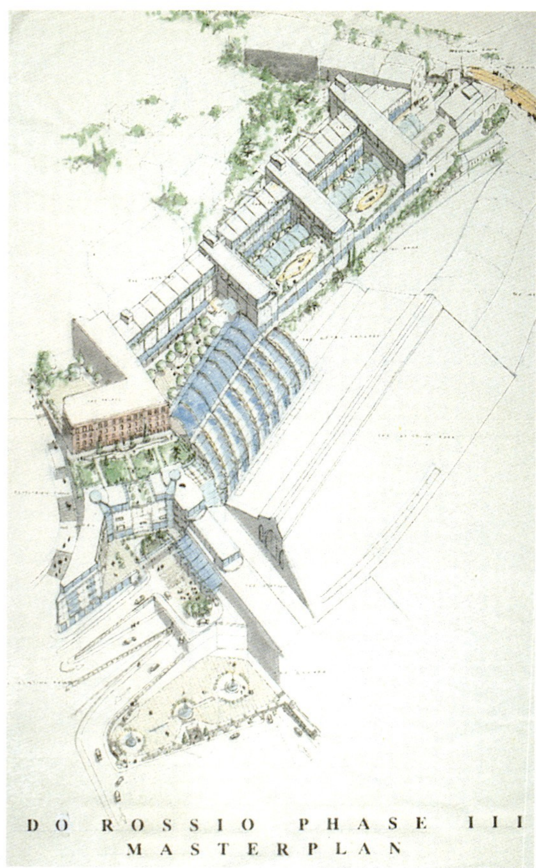

TFP's masterplans for Rossio rejuvenate the station's circulation system, as well as the surrounding area.

building of a transport interchange, used by about 250,000 passengers a day. The Rossio metro station was opened in 1963.

In 1993 Caminhos de Ferro Portugues, the Portuguese national railway authorities, commissioned Terry Farrell & Partners and Ideias do Futuro, Lisbon to produce a masterplan for redeveloping the area around Do Rossio station, a familiar part of Lisbon's townscape for more than a century. The proposal to rationalize the lands adjacent to the station and owned by the national railways organization provided an opportunity to link the Baixa district to Do Rossio and beyond to Bairro Alto. The intention was to restructure the area to the benefit of both pedestrian and motorized traffic.

The commission, in several distinct phases, incorporated climatic, economic and performance issues. The appraisal looked at the refurbishment of land surrounding the station, including the improvements to Do Rossio Station Square (the provision of lower-ground level parking and pedestrian circulation links) and proposals for a mixed-use development relating to the station. A new passenger circulation scheme was implemented in the station building. In collaboration with the Lisbon-based Ideias do Futuro, TFP undertook the design of new concourse and platform finishes, combining new-build elements with existing interiors.

The existing station roof – designed by Alexandre Gustave Eiffel – was reclad and enlarged to cover platform extensions and connect the station directly with the tunnelled-out mountainside. The roof extension had to be sympathetic in scale and character with the existing roof, so TFP designed it with a central curved vault made up of separate segments, the geometry of which reflects the central arch in the existing roof's end screen, its central axis and the tunnels.

Cooling breezes had been a feature of the old station's natural environmental control, and the design had to take account of the fact that the roof extension restricted the free passage of air. TFP's interventions provided controllable ventilators that allow cool night air to pass through the station structure. During the day, ventilation is restricted to allow cool air to radiate from the structural mass.

The Rossio commission allowed TFP to implement a design that seamlessly integrated the historic landmark station in its surroundings.

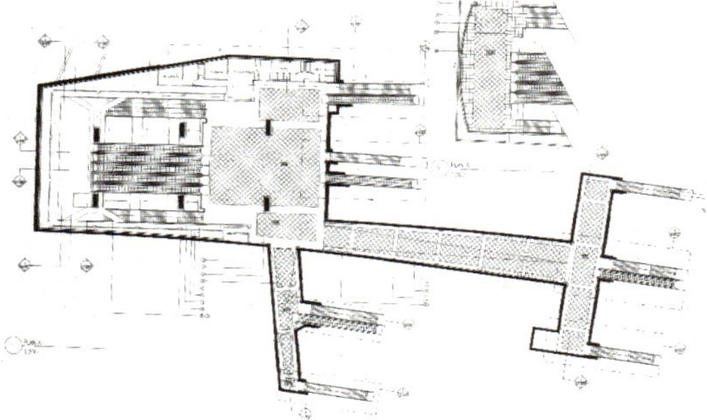

Part of the project was to design the entrance to a new metro station. This parallel sequence to the main station is similarly characterized by a dynamic sequence of escalators.

Top: The station under construction looking towards the Eiffel railway shed.

Centre: View from the shed towards tunnels bored out of the hillside.

Bottom: The interior of the restored railway shed by Gustav Eiffel looking towards the extension of the station and the tunnels.

Interior of the extension area looking towards the tunnels. The curved roof section adjusts to the geometries of the main shed and the tunnel alignment.

BARREIRO FERRY STATION + MASTERPLAN

Barreiro is set on the south bank of the Tagus, across the river from Lisbon. Once a small 19th-century waterfront settlement based on boat building, fishing and cork manufacture, the town is now home to a large number of commuters. It has also become an industrial focus, with a 300-hectare chemical plant to the north-east.

Barreiro's railway terminus was established in 1863 and the original ferry terminal building, built on a peninsula of reclaimed land with adjoining ferry-landing stages, was inaugurated in 1884. In the absence of a road bridge linking Barreiro with Lisbon, ferries have always been a strategic part of the area's transport infrastructure, but by the early 1990s the existing rail and ferry terminus had become unable to cope with the intense growth in commuter traffic.

In 1993, Terry Farrell & Partners and Ideias do Futuro were commissioned by Caminhos de Ferro Portugues, the Portuguese national railway authorities, to design a development concept for the Barreiro waterfront. The masterplan transforms a formerly underused 20-hectare site into a flourishing ferry port, which is strategically linked to southern Portugal's railway network.

Following the construction of railway tracks under the great bridge called the Ponte 25 de Abril, Barreiro's ferry and train stations had to find a new role. The masterplan provides regeneration and new mass-transit ferry links to central Lisbon. Transport links between Barreiro and Lisbon links were further strengthened by the opening of a railway bridge across the Tagus in 1998.

Top and above: Aerial views of Barreiro prior to the landfill that made the new masterplan area possible. The railway station is clearly visible on the peninsula stretching out to sea.

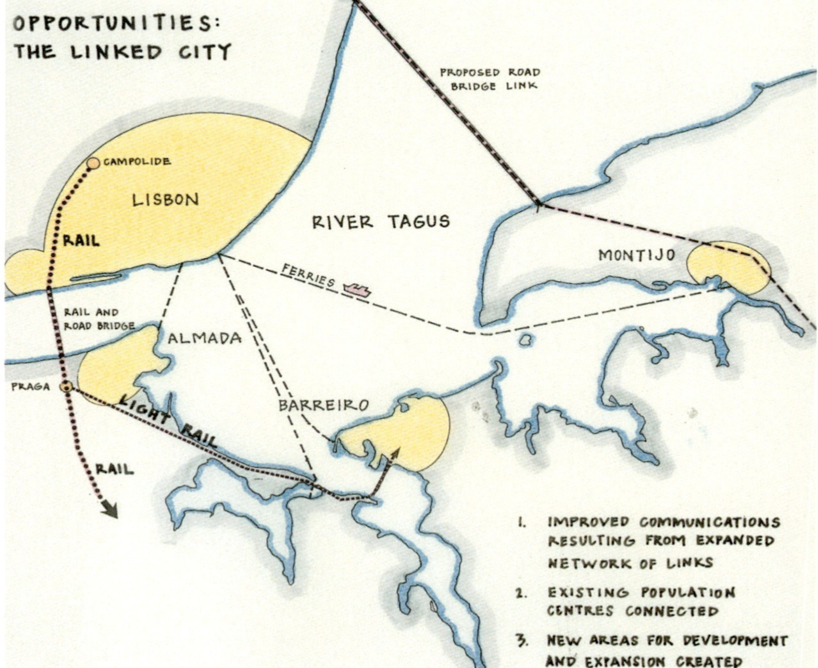

Diagram outlining different ferry connections across the Tagus from Lisbon to Barreiro, with the proposed future rail connecting the north and south sides.

TFP's masterplan responds to a framework plan drawn up by the municipal council of Barreiro, which envisaged the urbanization and expansion of the surrounding region for residential, business, social and amenity uses. Devised in collaboration with local architects Ideias do Futuro, the first phase of the masterplan comprised a transport interchange, with private and public transport zones providing drop-off and pick-up facilities and improved pedestrian access. A potential residential and commercial development along the waterfront, with views over the Tagus to the north, was considered as part of TFP's proposals. The area of the new terminal was therefore zoned for development to the south.

The masterplan divides the site into a main square and a series of secondary spaces partitioned by avenues of trees and landscaping. Forming a main interchange between the ferry and railway stations, the square is equipped with public amenities and retail accommodation. Ticketing and operational areas are housed in a shared concourse, which acts as a visual focus for the masterplan.

Marking the entrance to the site, at the intersection of the pedestrian route and Avenida da Republica, is a large garden square that separates the site from other areas of the town with different identities and functions. The garden also provides a recreational space for passengers and residents, and screens bus and car parking from the development area. During peak hours, the new interchange handles around 15,000 passengers per hour, who arrive or leave by ferry to make connections with other forms of transport or to continue by foot into Barreiro.

After the masterplan was approved, TFP and Ideias do Futuro were commissioned to create a new ferry terminal. The linear building, completed in 1995, was designed with both urban and waterfront faces. It is a simple but elegant structure that strongly advertises its function. The double-span roof, designed in association with engineers Battle McCarthy, optimizes structural efficiency, and its lightweight steelwork allowed foundations to be constructed economically in difficult ground conditions. To offset the potentially oppressive nature of a 32-metre span enclosure, an open slot was created at the middle span to introduce light and ventilation into the centre of the building.

Masterplan diagram showing the new light-rail bridge in the foreground and the first concept for the ferry port terminal on the water's edge.

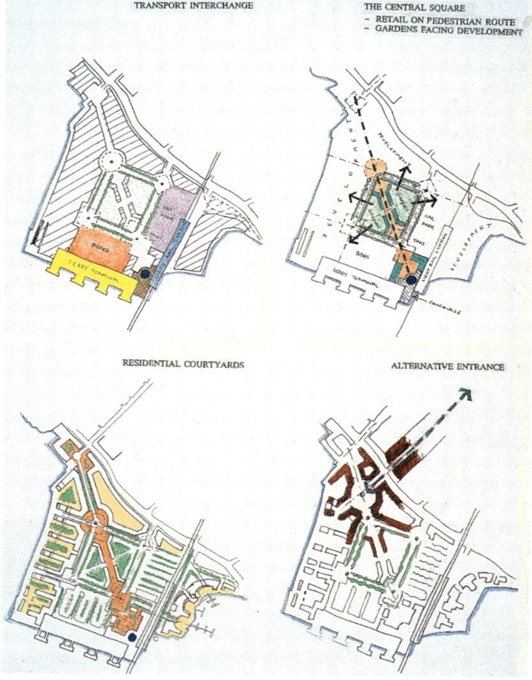

Scheme development drawings.

Bottom: Sectionalized elevation of the ferry terminal.

View of the ferry terminal from the new square.

Bottom left: Site plan.

Bottom right: Aerial view looking across the ferry terminal with the historic station in the distance.

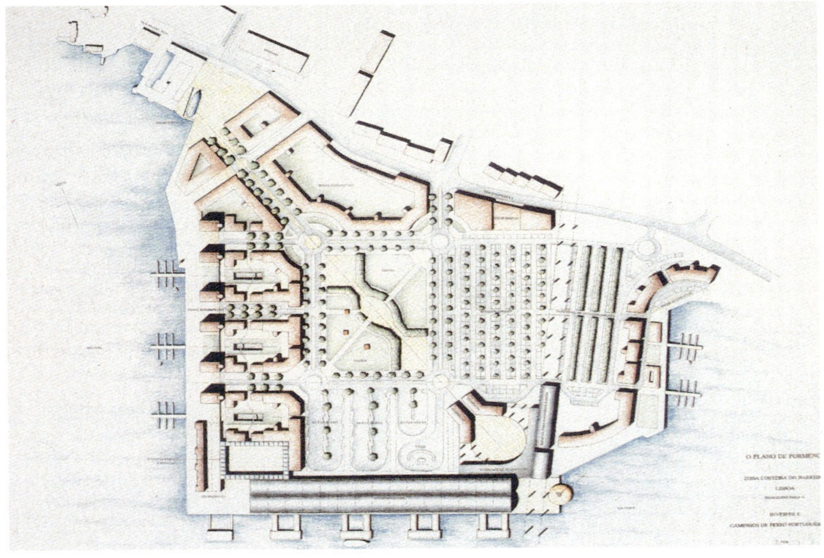

View from passenger entry side towards the main square.

Finger bridges lead to floating passenger decks on the water's edge.

Inside the main pre-paid ticket entrance area.

Post-paid ticket area
showing entry to new
access finger bridges.

EDINBURGH

EDINBURGH

Top left: The stages of Edinburgh's development: Old Town, New Town, arrival of the railway and, most recently, TFP's International Conference Centre masterplan on Lothian Road, linking Old and New Towns.

Top right: Satellite photograph. Edinburgh is to the right, bordering on the Firth of Forth estuary. While suburbs spill out from the centre, most of the land around the city is countryside.

Bottom: Skyline studies by Terry Farrell for the new masterplan.

Seen from the vantage point of Edinburgh Castle, central Edinburgh is one of the simplest 'city faces' to understand. Originally a fortified settlement built on a rocky outcrop and surrounded by low-lying land, over time it has come to comprise four elements: the Old Town, spreading from the castle down the Royal Mile to the Palace of Holyrood; the loch – or gardens in a valley, as they are now – with the railway lines that run through it; the linear New Town; and the Firth of Forth, visible in the distance.

The fortified nature of the Old Town meant that opportunity for expansion was limited – so, from the late 18th century, the neoclassical New Town was built on flat land almost half a mile from the Old Town, linked by striking elevated bridges spanning the loch, which was then drained and landscaped. At the fringe of the New Town runs the irregular Water of Leith, which winds around a gorge before reaching the Forth. Each element – the Old Town, the loch (or gardens), the New Town and the Firth of Forth – runs east–west in a four-layered sequence. It is a sublime composition, making Edinburgh truly one of the great cities of the world.

Edinburgh's ordered core belies a disordered perimeter. The city centre embraces a philosophical enlightenment vision of the urban ideal, whose wealth was dependent on its hidden opposite: the vast, chaotic, dynamic and fragmented industrial suburbs that are etched far into the landscape, and that eventually reach out to unite Edinburgh with its age-old rival, Glasgow.

The city's diversity is reflected in Terry Farrell & Partners' Edinburgh projects, where the picturesque setting of the Dean Art Gallery, adjacent to the Water of Leith, is seen to evoke a very distinct architectural response from the urban location of the Conference Centre and the Health Club and Spa.

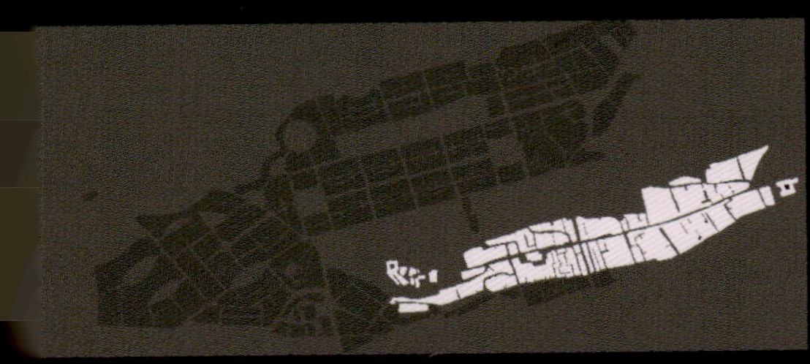

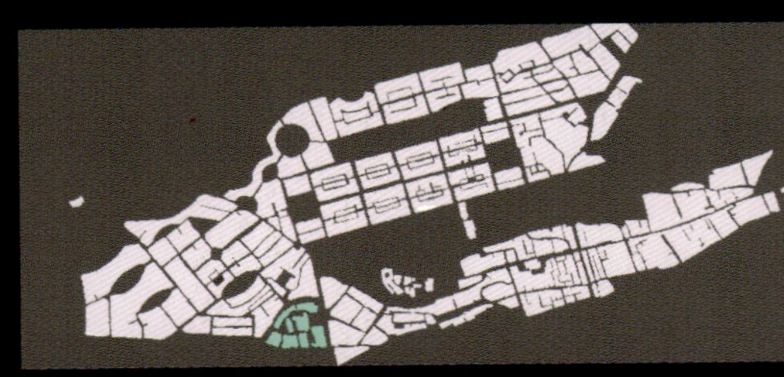

Top left: Aerial view showing the castle looking towards the gridded New Town.

Top right: View looking down Princes Street with the castle in the distance.

Bottom: Location of TFP's three schemes. From left to right: the Dean, Exchange Financial District masterplan and the Mound.

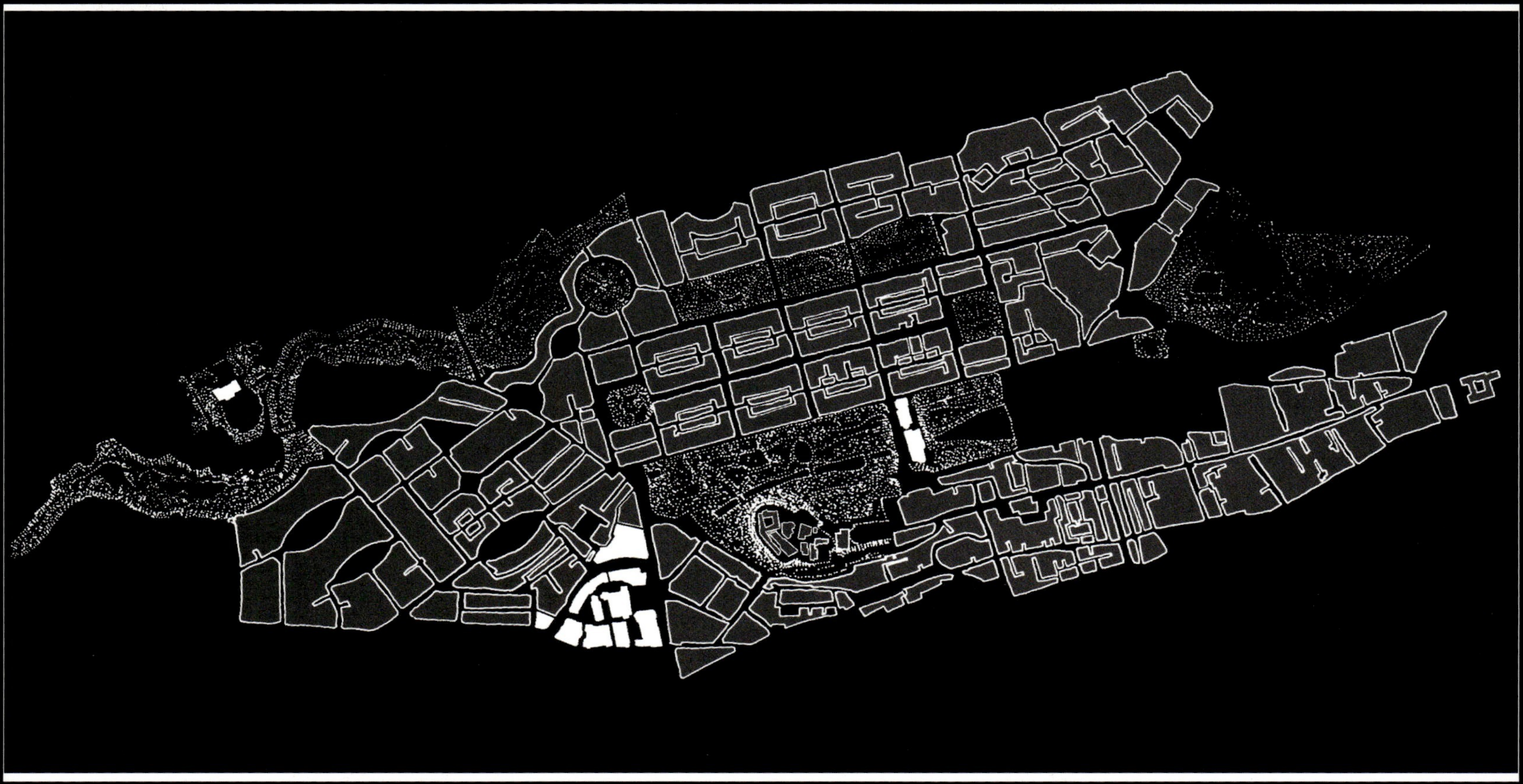

INTERNATIONAL CONFERENCE CENTRE + MASTERPLAN

The 4.2-hectare site, located in west central Edinburgh on former railway lands that included the Caledonian railway station, offered the potential for a significant inner-city development.

Edinburgh has an inspired tradition of careful and skilful town planning that has resulted in a harmonious juxtaposition of organic medieval street patterns and ordered Georgian planning. However, this harmony had been marred by the building of the Caledonian railway station in 1870 at a point where the Old Town meets the New, and which acted as a significant barrier between the New Town and the triangle of land between Lothian Road and Morrison Street.

TFP's masterplan heals this divide by re-establishing links across the former railway land towards the New Town, at the same time as restoring an appropriate urban grain and density for the area. The new quarter is designed to extend the city of Edinburgh to the west: TFP's masterplan opens up land that, for the most part, has been inaccessible to the public for a century.

Aerial view of Edinburgh showing the site's former use as a goods yard. The railway ran between the New and Old Town up to Waverley Station in the distance, creating a depressed industrial area within beautiful urban surroundings.

Aerial view of the masterplan showing the Conference Centre, Health Club and Spa.

Top: View of the Conference Centre, Sheraton Hotel and Usher Hall.

The Exchange Financial District masterplan was the first major British commission undertaken by TFP outside London. Won in competition in 1989, the commission drew on Terry Farrell's enthusiasm for 'gentle architecture', a theme evident in his earliest work, as evidenced by the knitting in of the masterplan to its surrounding context. In 1984, Farrell wrote in a practice monograph: '"Gentle architecture" implies that which is accessible to a wide range of people; is non-alienating in contextual handling and external expression of internal use and entrance ways; is unassertive and familiar in colour, form, imagery and formality of arrangement, sane and humane in terms of non-extreme theoretical or technological interpretations; and is above all an anxiety-free architecture which doesn't feed off any crisis cultivation.'

Drawing on lessons learned from masterplans for other London developments such as King's Cross railway lands, Tobacco Dock and Charing Cross, and the masterplan for Comyn Ching Triangle, Covent Garden, the scheme reflects Edinburgh's great tradition of city planning.

The masterplan provides plots for seven office developments and a leisure pavilion arranged around three public spaces – Conference Square, Festival Square and the Morrison Street entrance to the conference centre – incorporating pedestrian routes and car-parking facilities.

The distinctive drum-like form of the Edinburgh International Conference Centre, completed in 1995, landmarks the site and forms a set piece within the urban mass. Reflecting the differing needs of those who work, visit and stay on the site, the TFP scheme accommodates a mixture of uses, including office and conference facilities, retail space, leisure facilities and car parking, as well as carefully integrating the existing Sheraton Hotel.

Drawing on the city's vernacular tradition of terraces and crescents enclosing urban spaces and gardens, the building blocks are set up in a gently sweeping curve that define the site envelope. At the

Aerial view looking south with Atholl Crescent in foreground. The curves and crescents of the new masterplan harmonize with the city's existing layout.

Drawing of the masterplan showing the elements designed by TFP.

KEY:
1. Conference House
2. Conference Centre
3. Sheraton Spa
A. Conference Square
B. Festival Square
C. West Approach Road bridge

heart of the project is the triangular Conference Square, which forms the main public space for the conference centre. Nearby is a diversity of public spaces and walkways that resemble public rooms and corridors within a building. Rather than providing an impersonal expanse with buildings around the edge, TFP's masterplan incorporates elements of contrast and surprise. For example, the angular Sheraton Spa, squeezed into an uncompromisingly small plot of land, provides a startling visual juxtaposition with the circular conference centre. Likewise, the intimate footpath that comprises the crescent opens up into the grand space of Conference Square.

Creating a tangible public domain for pedestrians is central to the masterplan – its success depends on good ground-level connectivity. Urban development that strives to accommodate motorized traffic, together with the fracture between past and present, has made Edinburgh a less enjoyable place for pedestrians. The quality of the pedestrian domain relies on the design and form of individual buildings.

Within the Exchange, extensive pedestrian and cycle routes form connections with existing streets beyond the site. Conference Square and Festival Square are linked by the crescent, and in this way the conference centre is directly linked to the Sheraton Hotel and Usher Hall, as well as to the West End and the New Town via a new pedestrian bridge and Rutland Square. Internal spaces and the areas around buildings are regarded as equally important.

The driving forces behind the Edinburgh masterplan are historical continuity, the integration of old and new, pedestrian connectivity, and the quest for richness and diversity. TFP's singular concept of urban design allows an incremental approach that encourages the area to take shape in its own way. Confronting the reality of the urban situation – rather than prescribing utopian visions – is an integral part of TFP's outlook.

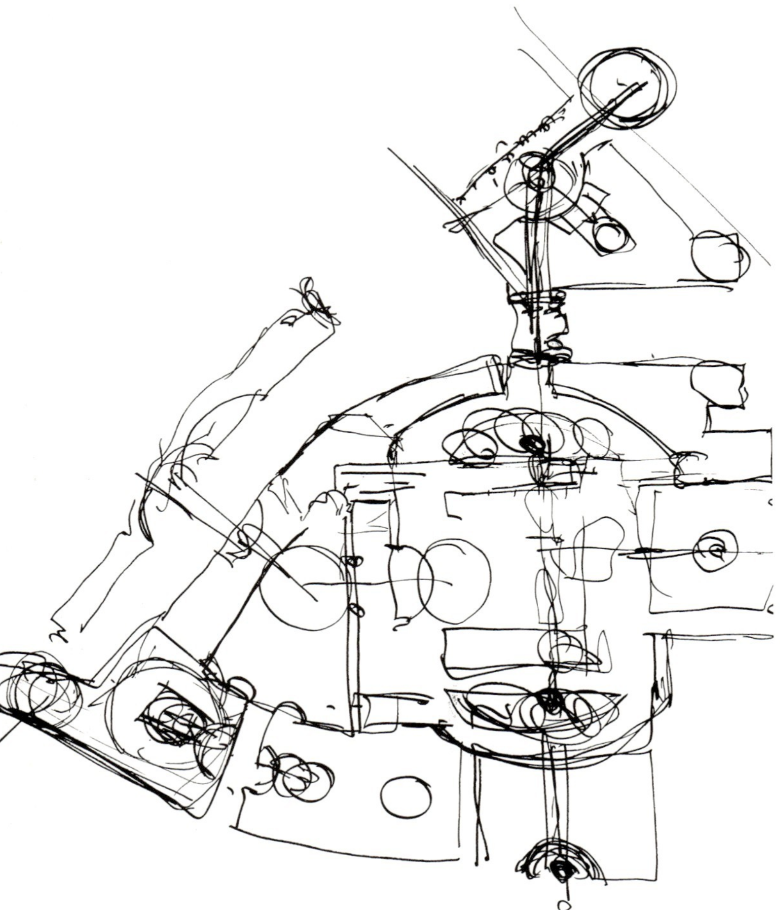

Early concept drawing of the masterplan by Terry Farrell showing key linkages.

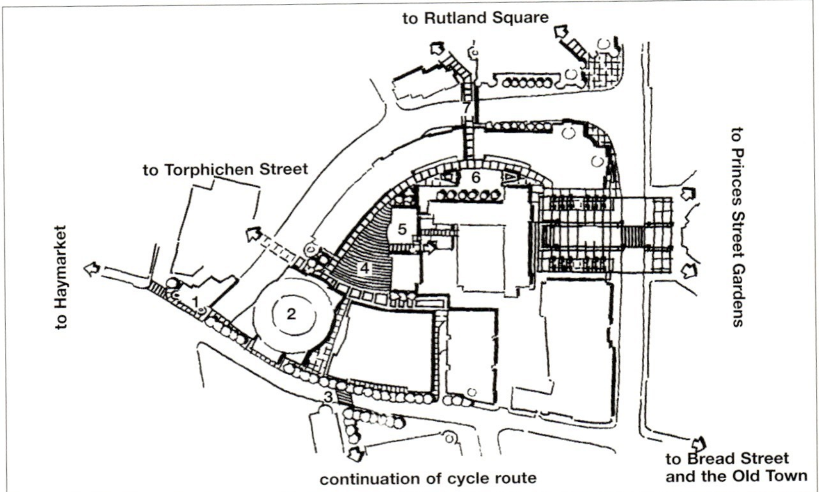

The masterplan's public realm:
1. Conference House
2. Conference Centre
3. Morrison Street
4. Conference Square
5. Sheraton Spa

Bottom: The redesigned Festival Square from the steps of the existing Sheraton Hotel.

Festival Square after TFP's masterplan.

The completed Conference Centre.

Bottom left: Ground plan.

Bottom right: Cross section with Conference Square on the right and West Approach Road on the left.

Opposite: Entrance elevation.

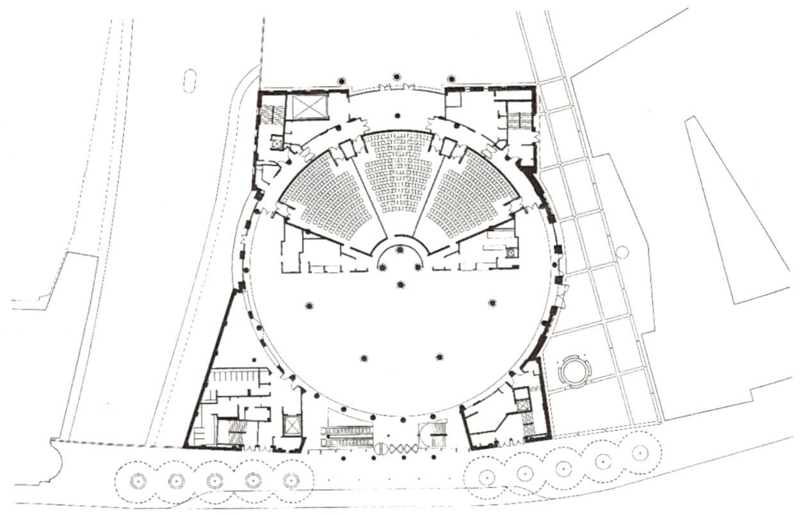

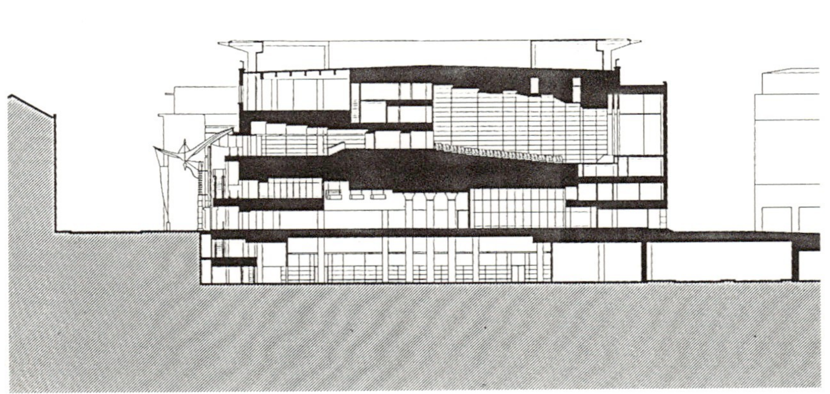

E I
EDINBURGH INTERNATIONAL
C C

Design development sketches by Terry Farrell.

Bottom: Study model photographs.

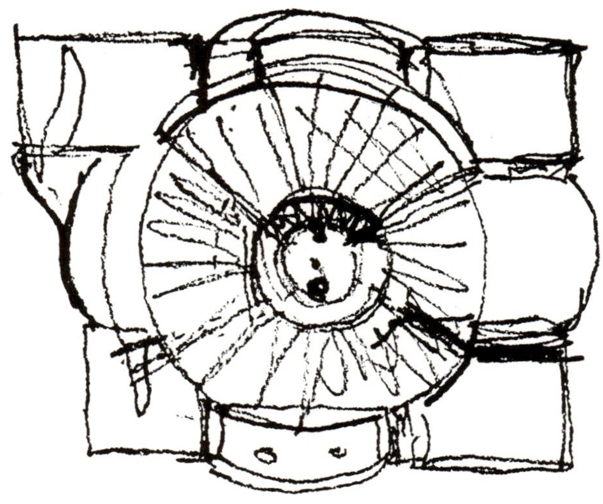

The Conference Centre's main auditorium can be subdivided from a 1200-seat space to two 300-seat spaces and one 600-seat space, or one 900 and one 300-seat space.

Top left: Open auditorium with 1200 seats.
Top right and centre left: Two variations of 900 seats.
Centre right: Two separate 300-seat auditoria and one 600-seat auditorium.

Note that the moving walls of the small auditoria echo the exterior architecture of the outside drum of the Conference Centre.

Bottom: Design development sketches and Level 3 plan.

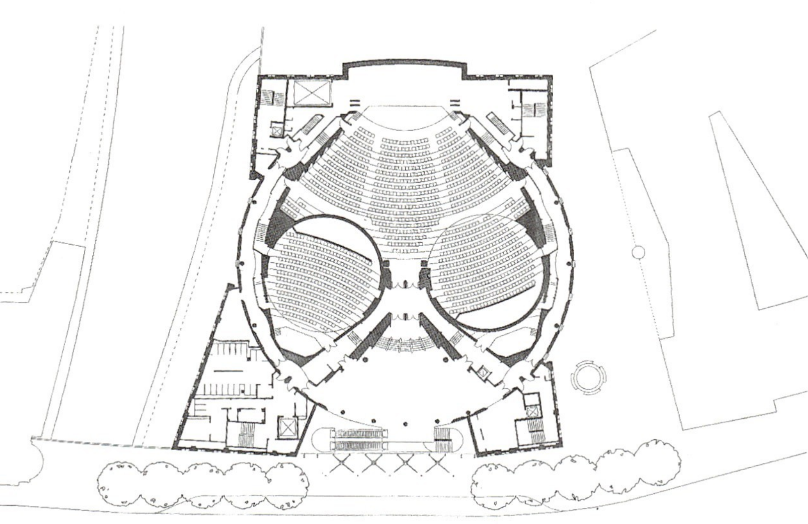

View into the café from the main ground-floor corridor looking through one of the vitrines to the sculpture placed on the café table.

THE MOUND

The Mound is at the heart of Edinburgh's history and its urban story. James Craig, architect of the New Town, saw this 'land bridge' – constructed from the rubble used to make the New Town between 1781 and 1830 – as a temporary structure, while William Playfair built three buildings on it: the Royal Institution, later reincarnated as the National Gallery of Scotland, and the Royal Scottish Academy. He also designed the Edinburgh railway, which runs below the Mound. The tension and balance of the landscaped valley (the former Nor Loch), interrupted by a land bridge between the Old and New Towns, is the key to the Mound's urban drama. Playfair's placing of two buildings as points in space – the National Gallery of Scotland and the Royal Scottish Academy – celebrates the valley as a continuous expanse and acknowledges the power of landscape, rather than urban or architectural

Top right: TFP's 1993 design for the National Galleries of Scottish Art and History in Glasgow's Kelvingrove, which formed part of a study for the future of the NGS's collection. The site was abandoned in favour of expanding existing galleries in Edinburgh and TFP's Mound scheme continues on from its involvement in this project.

1

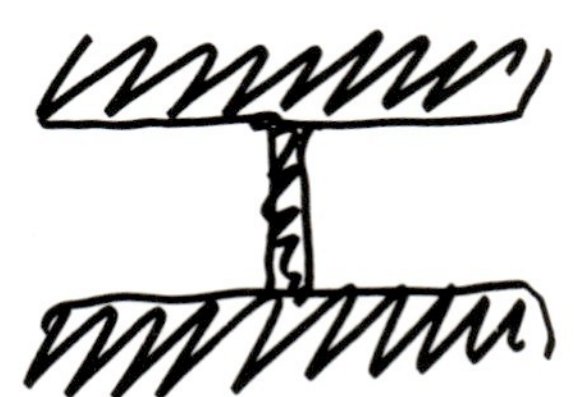

2

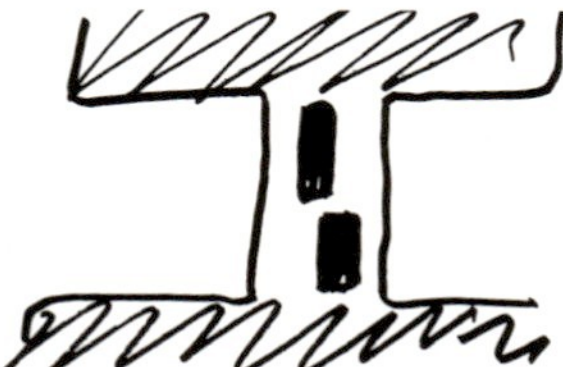

3

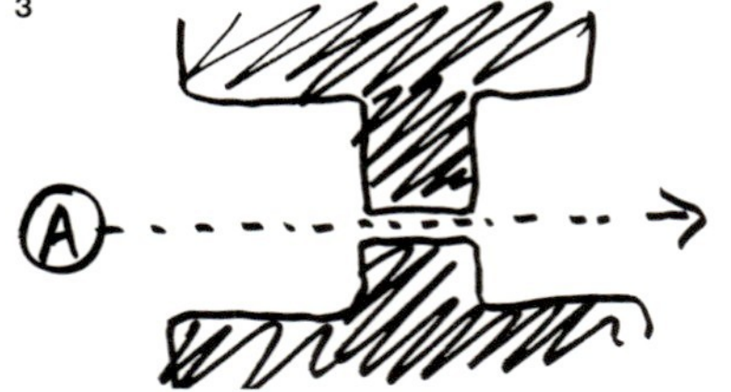

4

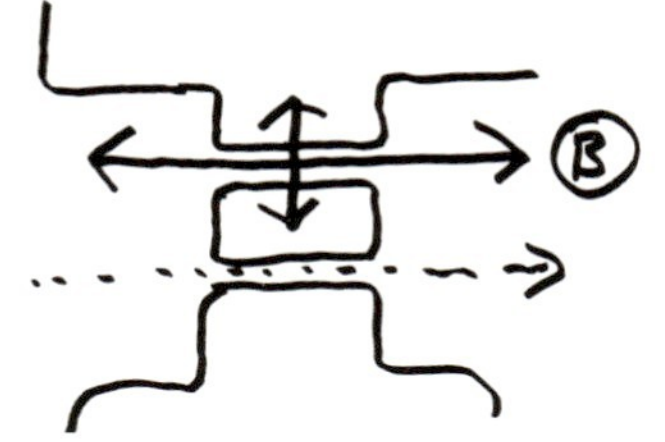

Aerial view showing the Mound as it exists. William Playfair's two great galleries – Scottish Academy and NGS – form a bridge between the Old and New Town. The railway arch penetrates beneath.

Centre right: Historical drawing showing the landfill from the New Town, which formed the bridge on which Playfair's two galleries would be built.

Sketches showing stages of the Mound's development as part of TFP's proposals:

1. Land bridge built to connect New Town and Old Town across the valley.

2. Bridge with the Royal Scottish Academy and the National Gallery of Scotland – two major public buildings by Playfair built on the Mound to create an arts acropolis.

3. The railway travels along the bottom of the valley gardens to Waverley Station, perforating the land bridge.

4. Proposed connections link both sides of the valley gardens and the RSA and NGS below ground.

Top: Cross section proposal for the two gardens.

Below: Plan of the Mound's lower level. Connections are made between the gardens to the east and west and the galleries to the north and south. A shop sits in the centre.

Centre: Upward view.

Bottom: Plans.

links, to connect the Old and New Towns.

TFP's competition entry focused on a celebration of connectedness, in the style of the Mound itself. The National Galleries of Scotland's brief was for a building that would act as a catalyst to revitalize the Royal Scottish Academy and the National Gallery of Scotland. TFP were asked to provide a façade-less solution that would not compete with Playfair's neoclassical set-piece at high level. The solution was an underground grotto, or undercroft, linking the Mound's east and west gardens through a sequence of inspirational spaces, which also forms a strong directional axis on either side of the Mound. The grotto has the same crowd-pulling effect that the new railway, running through the Mound, had for 19th-century visitors.

Illuminated by natural light from a glazed roof, the grotto provides a shared entrance to the National Gallery of Scotland and the Royal Scottish Academy, along with a ticket office and cloakrooms. Gallery shops occupy underground spaces. A backlit wall 60 metres by 4.5 metres is used as a display area for prints and photographs, and for video and film projection. This central section is linked with the entrance space above by transparent sculpture plinths that act as light wells. Sloping public walkways lead down to the gardens at either end, providing bright, daylit spaces for the building's interior. The east end's café and the west end's restaurant engage with existing and re-routed footpaths on the Mound. The largest spaces are the lecture theatre and education suite, located in the south-eastern corner of the Royal Scottish Academy.

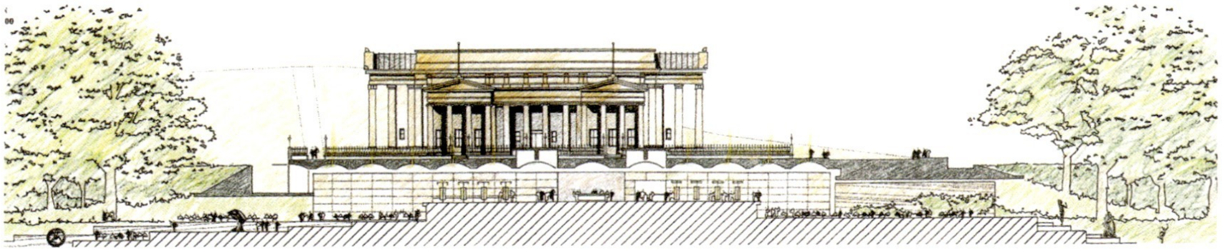

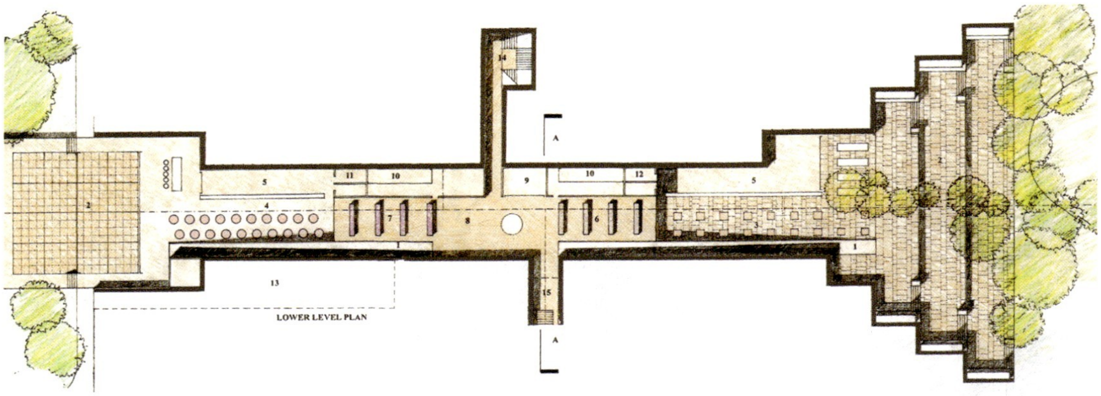

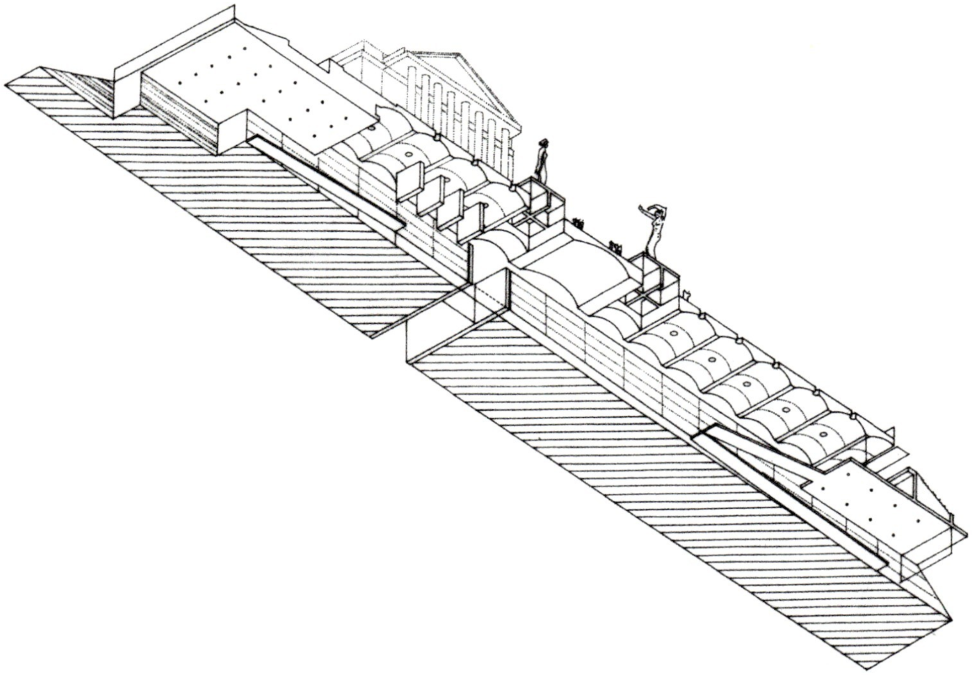

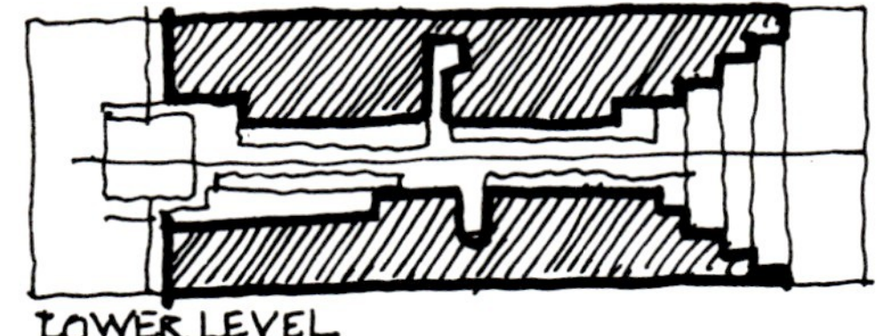

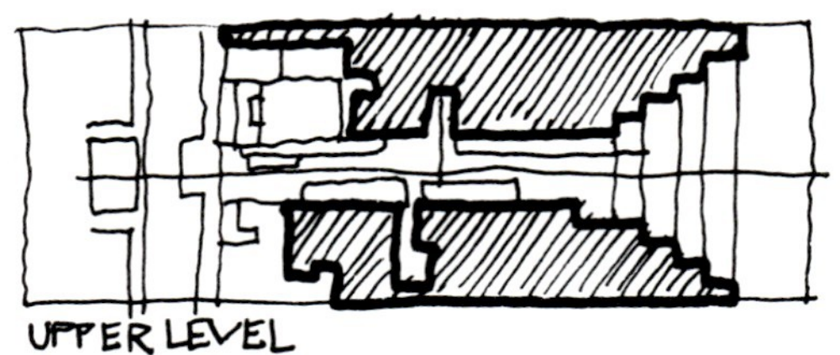

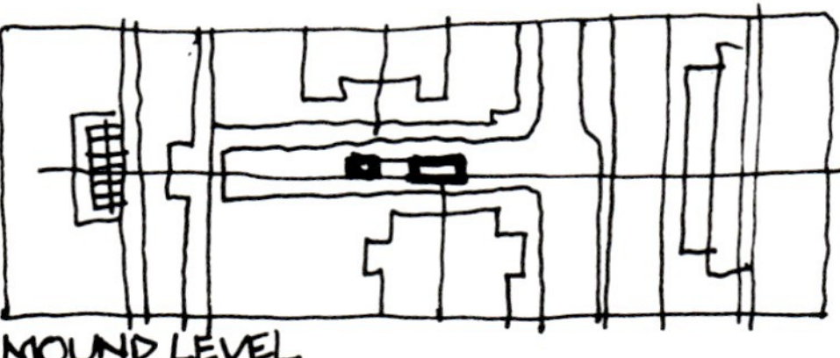

Top left and right: Construction drawings showing the engineering of the slot between the NGS and the RSA.

Bottom left and right: Concept drawings by Terry Farrell.

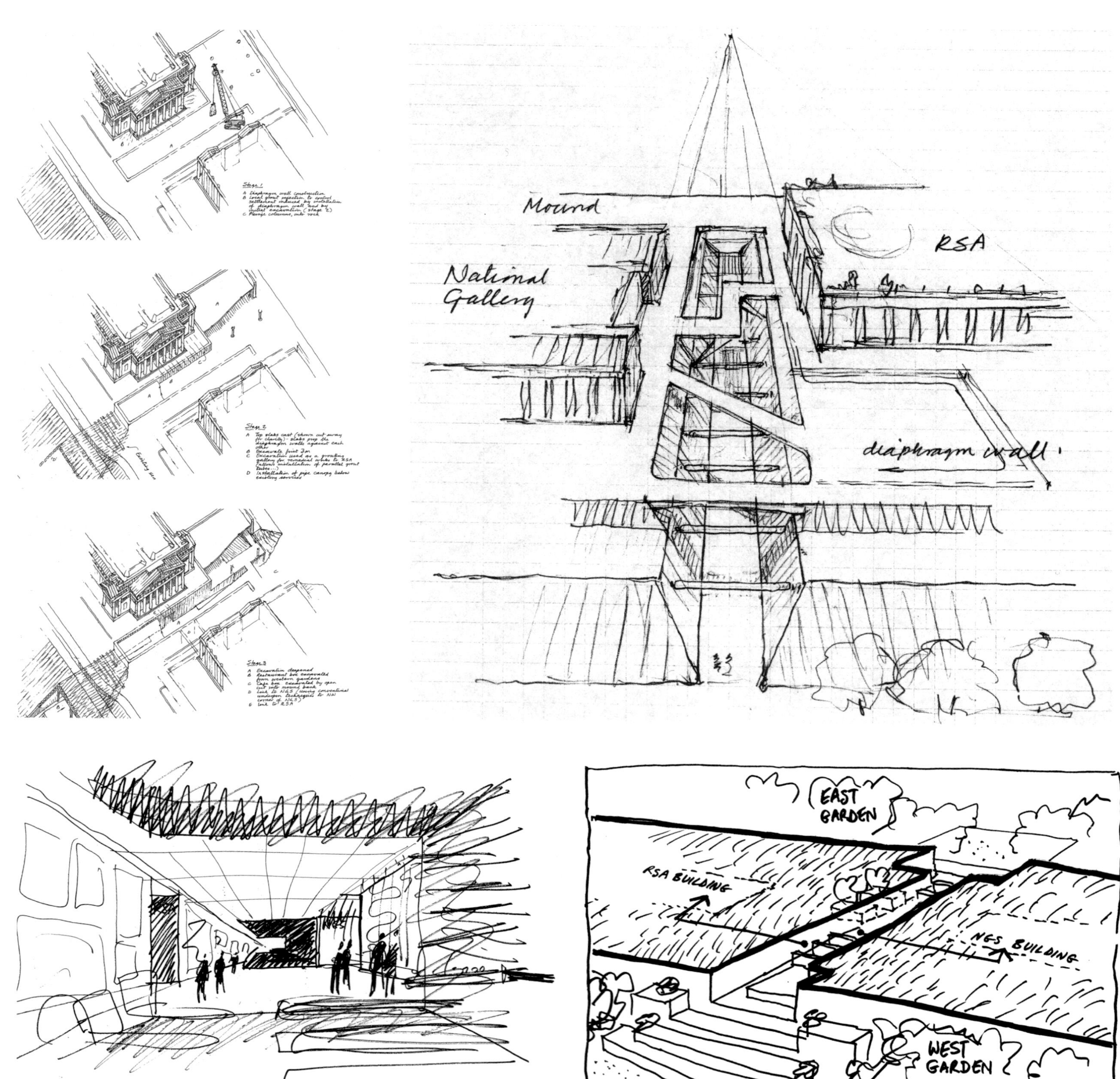

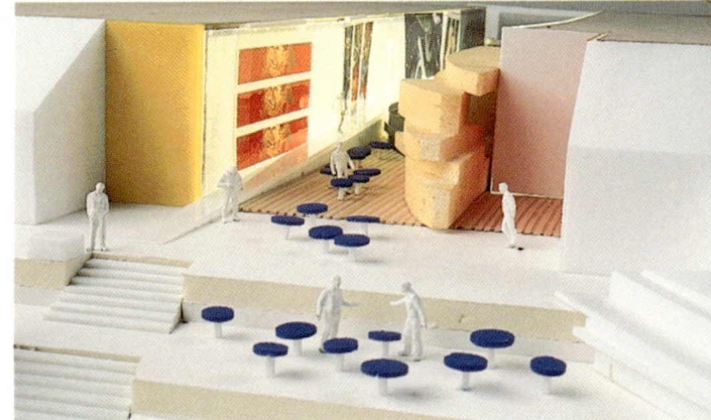

Views of study model interior constructed from the connecting route between the two gardens.

Aerial view of model.

Top: 1:500 model showing connection to gardens with galleries above.

NEWCASTLE

NEWCASTLE

Until the arrival of the steam train, Newcastle was a linear city that had developed along the banks of the River Tyne (the Quayside) at the bottom of a deep gorge. The vast industrial expansion of the new town resulted in a dramatic change of scale for the city in a triumph of engineering over nature. Robert Stephenson's High Level Bridge of 1846–49, with its twin decks, one each for road and rail, resulted in the old town being bypassed. A fine new city was created on the flatlands above the gorge, while the Quayside was neglected and gradually abandoned. Emblematic of the city's post-war industrial collapse, motorways created further barriers between the Quayside and the rest of the city.

The late 20th century saw the rediscovery of the Quayside as a district of great interest and quality. Reuniting old and new parts of towns has been, and continues to be, an exhilarating challenge of urban planning. In the past ten years, however, progress has been dramatic and, with the rejuvenation of Gateshead's banks opposite the Quayside, on the south bank of the Tyne, Newcastle is experiencing a true urban renaissance. This rediscovery has grown up around the new leisure-based economy, which forms the context for Terry Farrell & Partners' Quayside and International Centre for Life projects.

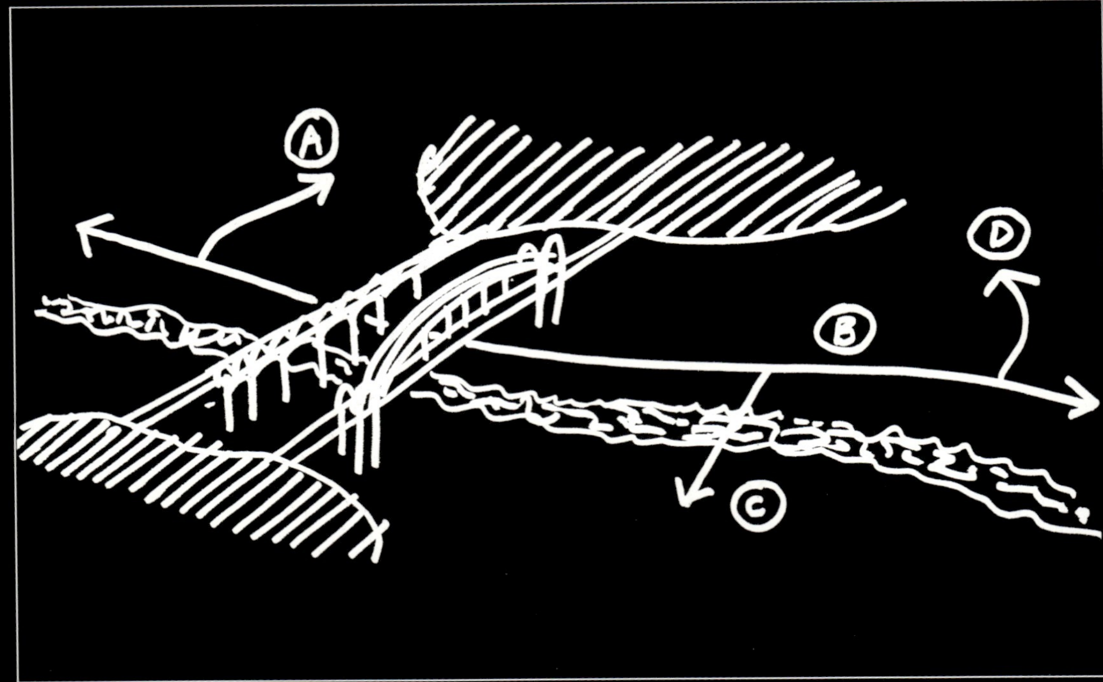

Top: Satellite image. The River Tyne flows through Newcastle into the North Sea. Newcastle and Gateshead are located either side of the river.

Above: Sketch by Terry Farrell. The 19th- and 20th-century bridges effectively bypassed the historic city on the Tyne riverbanks. With four new projects, the lower city has not only been revitalized but has become more central, better planned and connected than ever – a true urban renaissance.
A. ICL (infill)
B. East Quayside masterplan
C. New bridge to arts centre and music centre on the south bank of the Tyne
D. Ouseburn masterplan

Top: Newcastle grew up along the north bank and Gateshead along the south bank of the Tyne. Spanning the two are the city's distinctive bridges: Redheugh, King Edward, Queen Elizabeth II, High Level, Swing, Tyne and Millennium.

Bottom: In the mid-18th century, the Quayside was the city's commercial hub.

Top: Grey Street is one of Newcastle's finest streets. TFP's mixed-use renovation of numbers 52–60 focuses on incorporating new buildings into the historic fabric and recalls its scheme at Comyn Ching Triangle, London.

Bottom: View of Tyne Bridge, a Newcastle landmark since its opening in 1928. In the distance is Stephenson's High Level Bridge of 1846–49, and below that, the Swing Bridge.

EAST QUAYSIDE MASTERPLAN

Located east of the city's historic walled boundary on the north bank of the Tyne, the Quayside was a populous suburb until the 1840s, when it was transformed by industrialization. As New Quay was constructed, extending from the Swirl (the old town boundary) towards Ouseburn, homes were moved and the land was redeveloped to accommodate grain warehouses and industrial sites. Construction of the High Level Bridge in the 1840s severed the Quayside quarter from the city centre.

In 1991, on winning the commission to redevelop the Quayside, Terry Farrell & Partners set out to establish a new 'place' in Newcastle, based on a series of urban spaces and pedestrian routes that would act as a framework for a phased mixed-use development, which would then become the focal point of what was then a rapidly changing quarter of Newcastle.

Public spaces, pedestrian routes, roads, car parks and other civil engineering infrastructure, as well as individual buildings, were designed and built, and artistic and sculptural projects were commissioned for the site. A set of development guidelines for each plot included details of density, height, massing and general architectural arrangement.

The TFP scheme reflected the site's historic use as a dock: the buildings are arranged to resemble the urban blocks of warehouse architecture, and the spaces between them reflect the narrow routes between old warehouses. The materials for the hard landscaping, furniture and special features support the character of warehouse and dockside. In this way, rather than competing with adjacent buildings, the Quayside development restores the area's traditional urban grain, scale and mass.

The masterplan evolved into a linear arrangement of buildings and public spaces set back from the Quayside edge. In Terry Farrell's words, the layout is 'like the beads of a necklace'. Running parallel to the river's natural contours, the kilometre-long plan (covering 10 hectares in all) reflects and enhances its location, as well as emphasizing the great curve of the Quayside wall and maximizing views of the water. The linear organization reinforces an unobstructed pedestrian route along the riverside. Breaks between buildings offer easy pedestrian access through the site from City Road to the river. Visual and physical links with historical landmark routes (the Chair and Swirl) have promoted close integration between the scheme and the surrounding urban fabric.

The masterplan narrows towards its mid-point, opening up views of the River Tyne and of Newcastle's landmark bridges, the Tyne, the Swing and the High Level. Two curved pockets of public space along the riverfront are focal points of the scheme and draw attention to the front doors of individual buildings – all buildings are planned with front doors opening onto the Quayside.

TFP has designed a residential phase of 111 flats at the eastern end of the masterplan, adjacent to the Ouseburn inlet. Following the masterplan guidelines, the 9800 square metre building is in the form of a crescent to make the most of the river views. Starting at the same height as the adjacent four-storey flats, the building gently slopes up as it approaches the waterfront to a maximum height of 11 storeys. The development wraps around a landscaped semi-private open space that banks up to a turf roof over external garages.

The completed masterplan – which received a number of awards – creates a vibrant new quarter that complements Newcastle's city centre. The development's identity derives from its sequence of landscaped squares and urban spaces along the river, and is linked to surrounding neighbourhoods, thereby making itself an integral part of the city. East Quayside has had considerable impact as a regenerative force. The city now offers a wonderful walk from the landmark Swing Bridge through the revitalized Quayside, and across, via the new Millennium Bridge, to Gateshead, which features Norman Foster's music centre and Dominic Williams's Baltic Mills. Together, these projects are transforming Tyneside.

Bottom left: The Tall Ships race, which took place along the Quayside in 1993.

Bottom right: The Millennium Bridge, by Wilkinson Eyre, creates a vital connection between the completed East Quayside masterplan and Gateshead.

Top: View of the Quayside from Gateshead, with the Millennium Bridge in the foreground.

Centre: The completed Quayside. The retaining wall has been carved in relief, part of a programme of art works that are used to define site boundaries and act as landmarks.

Bottom left: View of the Quayside. Panter Hudspith's Pitcher & Piano bar is to the right.

Early concept drawings.

Bottom: Quayside masterplan drawing.

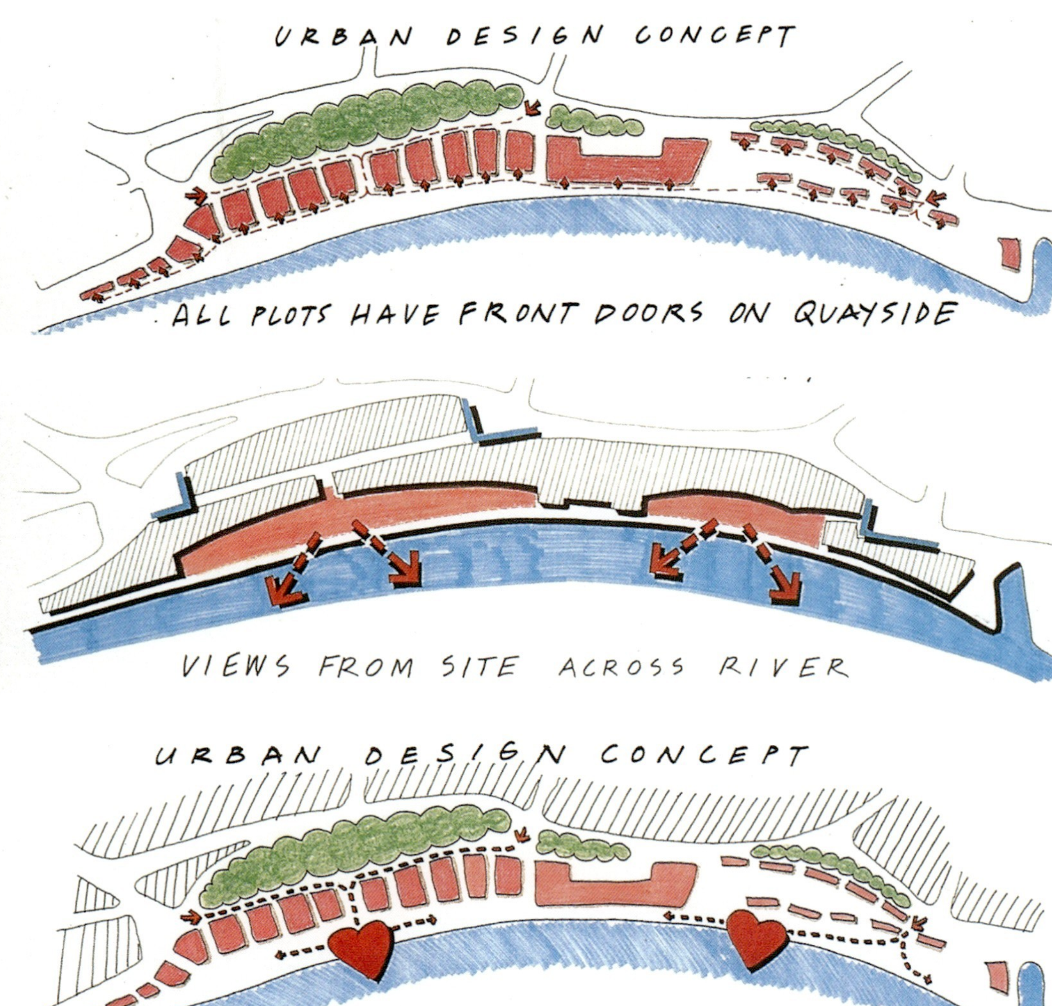

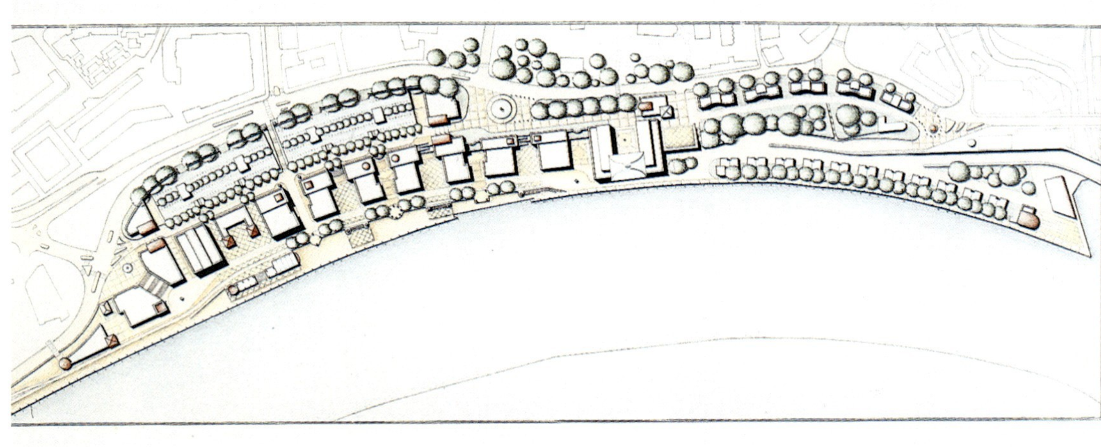

The 'red line' boundary defining the Quayside site before construction. The Quayside has had a great impact on the regeneration of the Newcastle/ Gateshead area.

Bottom left: Dilapidated wharves and disused docks characterized the area before its transformation.

Model of the masterplan.

Bottom right: The completed masterplan aims at a seamless integration between the existing context and new interventions.

Adjacent to the Ouseburn inlet at the eastern end of the site, the Crescent Housing is part of the masterplan's residential phase.

The Quayside masterplan anticipated the transformation of Tyneside, which includes such buildings as (from left to right) Dominic Williams's Baltic Mills, CZWG's St Anne's Wharf, Wilkinson Eyre's Millennium Bridge, Panter Hudspith's Pitcher & Piano, and Norman Foster's Gateshead Music Centre.

PITCHER & PIANO

INTERNATIONAL CENTRE FOR LIFE

The International Centre for Life (ICL) is located at Forth Banks, an area of Newcastle with a rich and intriguing history. For hundreds of years it was noted for its health-giving parklands and for the Newcastle Infirmary, built there in 1752.

Forth Banks was rural until the early 1800s, when it became the scene of many important early industrial ventures. John Dobson's Central Station was built in 1830. Neville Street and Scotswood Road, thoroughfares that now impact on the site, were opened in 1835. The area also became home to the locomotive industry, notably Hawthorne's Engine Works, Stephenson's locomotive works and Joicey's Engineering Works. To the west was the 1830 cattle market; the historic Market Keeper's House, also by Dobson, was incorporated in the ICL complex. As industry expanded, railways and high-level bridges cut through Newcastle, isolating the east and west quaysides. The building of major roads in the 1960s created a further barrier between the west and the rest of the city.

Over the course of its history, Forth Banks has also been the site of cattle and pig pens, a petrol station, a bus station, an abattoir and a burial ground. By the time the ICL project began in 1995, much of the railway activity and engineering had been replaced with the dereliction that has come to characterize many inner-city brownfield sites.

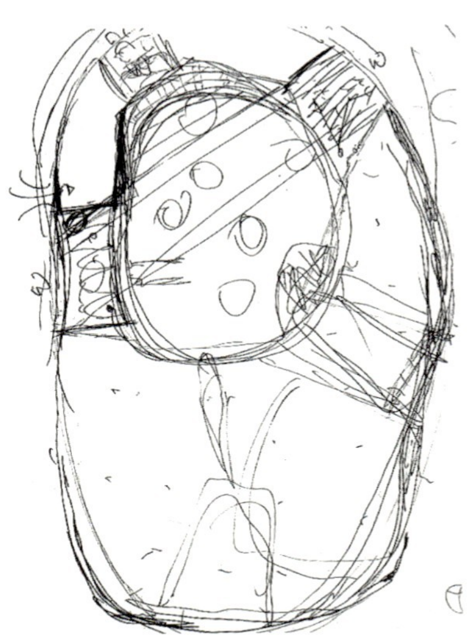

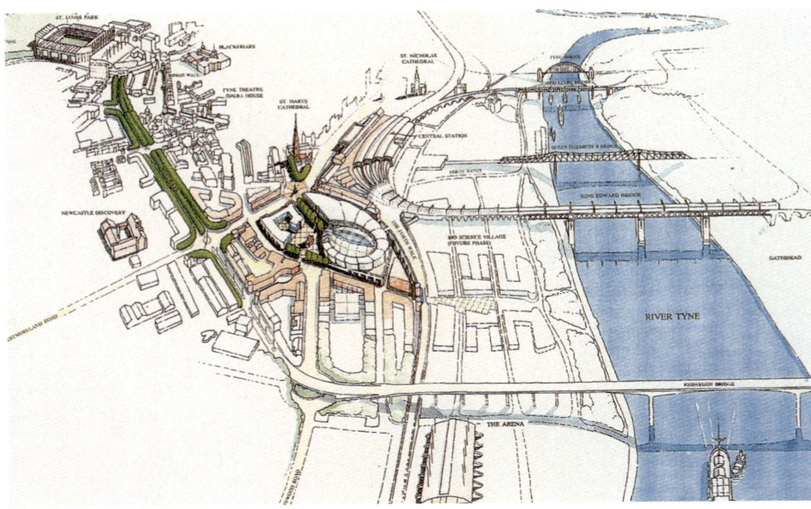

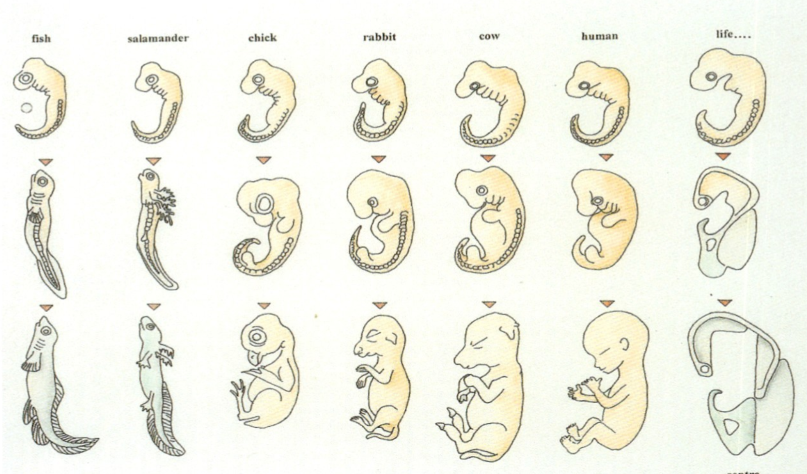

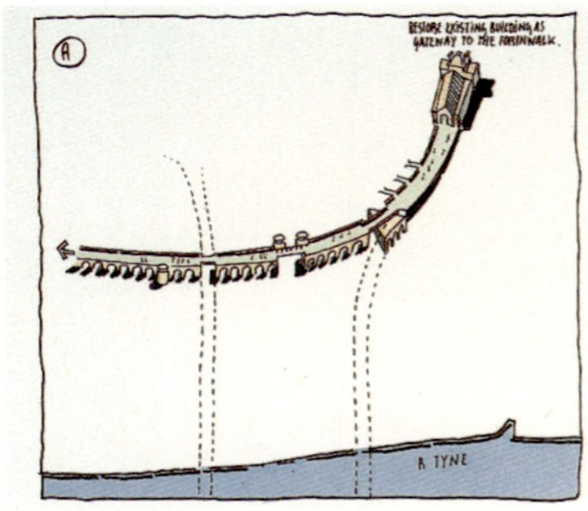

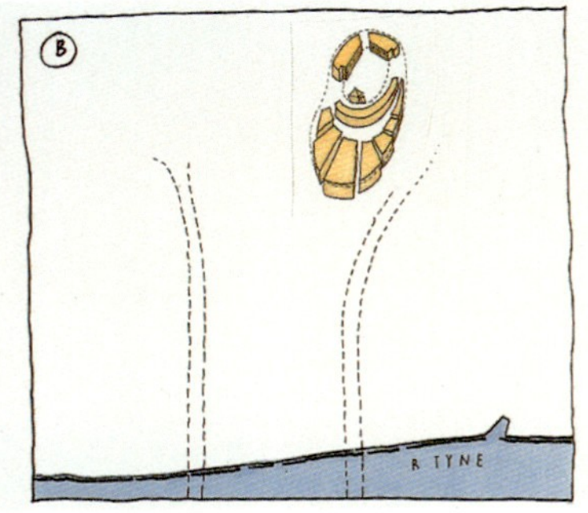

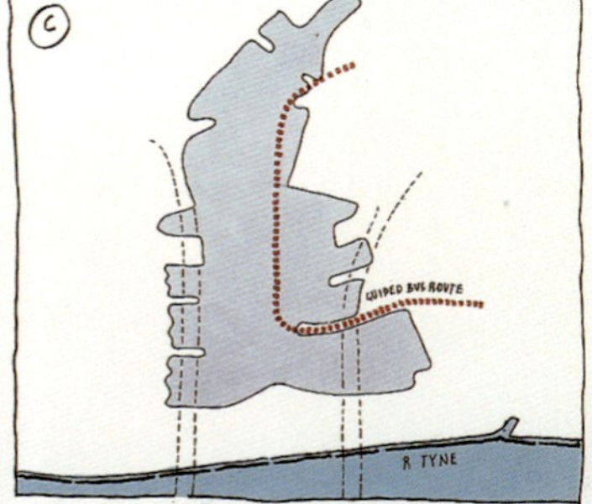

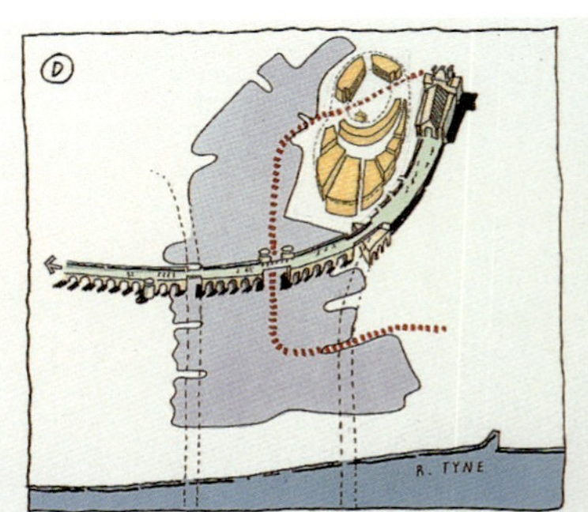

Top: Early concept masterplan drawing.

Above: Right from the start, the masterplan was designed to impact on the regeneration of a large section of the city.

Top: First concept sketch by Terry Farrell, summer 1996.

Centre: The design concept takes as its form an embryo motif. The illustration is based on an idea originating from Mahlon Hoagland's *The Way Life Works* of 1995.

The ICL site merges with the curving cityscape of crescents and railway lines. Newcastle Central Station is to the east, Pugin's celebrated St Mary's Roman Catholic Cathedral from 1842 is to the north east and Newcastle City football ground (St James' Park) is to the north.

The International Centre for Life is testimony to Terry Farrell's support of Robert Venturi's much quoted manifesto in his book *Complexity and Contradiction in Architecture*: 'I like elements which are hybrid rather than "pure", compromising rather than "clean", distorted rather than "straightforward".... I am for richness of meaning rather than clarity of meaning; for the implicit function as well as the explicit function. I prefer "both–and" to "either–or", black and white, and sometimes grey, to black and white.'

The writer Kenneth Powell has described Terry Farrell as Britain's leading 'architectural outsider', and ICL, which defies the usual architectural typecasting, recalls this statement. An example of Farrell's fascination with contextual architecture at its most literal, ICL is the product of a collection of diverse narratives. The project gives form to theories of urbanism and regeneration, reflecting Newcastle and its local history as well as elements of bioscience.

An example of the ambiguity embraced by Venturi, ICL is a building designed to avoid categorization. In fact, it is not one building but a complex of three. Its style combines organic exuberance with the pared-down and functional. ICL is a wholehearted response to its setting on the western edge of Newcastle, beside the River Tyne. For the practice, ICL is above all about using architecture as a catalyst for regeneration and repair.

ICL was intended to knit the dislocated western central area of Newcastle into the fabric of the city while providing a centre for genetics research. The scheme cost £60 million in total, 50 per cent of which was funded by revenue from the National Lottery. Its phased masterplan consisted of three elements: an exhibition space with an educational facility for schools and universities (LIFE Interactive World); Newcastle University's Institute of Human Genetics; and commercial laboratories/office space (Bioscience Centre).

The copper-clad roof of LIFE Interactive World is based on the curving geometry of a leaf.

Design development studies by Aidan Potter.

Already involved in masterplanning the city's east quayside, TFP won the commission in competition in 1996, and on-site work began within three months.

The scheme comprises a collage of buildings arranged in a great curve around a public open space – a robust and flexible design that could be completed in separate phases. There is no iconic building at the centre of the complex. The focus of attention is the pedestrianized Times Square, the first major square to be built in Newcastle for more than a century.

From the beginning, the curved layout of Times Square appeared to resemble an embryo. An image that recalled the early stages of biological growth seemed to be a fitting motif for a 'centre for life' and for the regeneration of a derelict urban quarter. The curved form is used as a metaphor for continuity, and the ICL masterplan seeks to embody a cohesion between the city's past and its future. The embryonic form is not only symbolic, however; it responds to the great sweeping railway lines, elevated viaducts and crescents that characterize the west end of Newcastle.

Beside the site runs the route of the historic Scotswood Road, which Terry Farrell, who grew up in Newcastle, was keen to incorporate in the masterplan. Scotswood Road is a symbol of Geordie culture immortalized in the 'Blaydon Races' anthem ('Gan alang the Scotswood Road to see the Blaydon Races'). Its route, which bisects the ICL site at the centre's entrance, is marked by memorial paving stones. The Scotswood Road entrance to the site is also adorned with an open-metalwork screen – a modern reflection of Dobson's similar screen at the entrance to the neighbouring Central Station.

Bordering two sides of Times Square is the four-storey Bioscience Centre, the first building on the site. Used as commercial laboratories and office space, the centre is a functional building faced in sandstone and, on the street elevation, render and glass blocks. It was completed in 1998, around the time when TFP received the final brief for the research and visitor-attraction elements of the project.

The brief said that the visitor attraction was to be 1.5 storeys high – lower than originally envisaged, thereby disrupting the continuity of the curved envelope. This resulted in what was called the 'ski slope' that links the Institute of Human Genetics to the single-storey visitor attraction in the style of a 'black box'. The 'ski slope' device is one of the most interesting sculptural junctions of the scheme – the start of a visual spiral that cascades down to the lowest curve of the visitor attraction. At this point, the floor-sweeping geometry fits the domestic scale of the original Market Keeper's

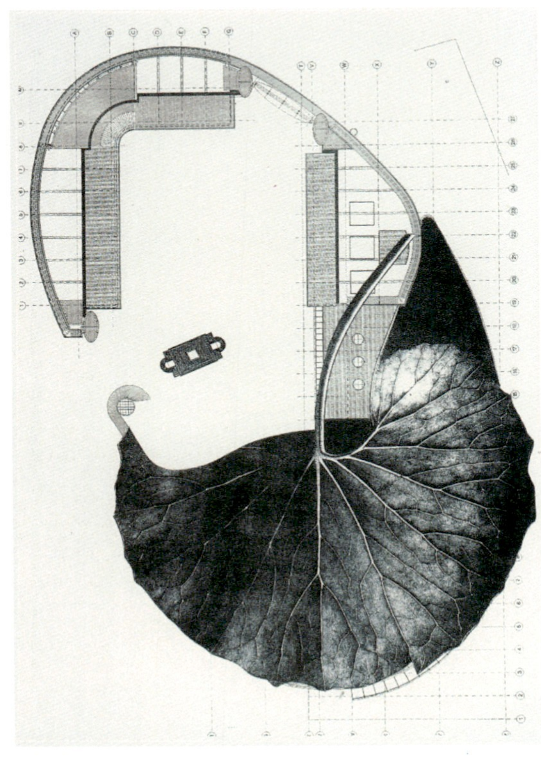

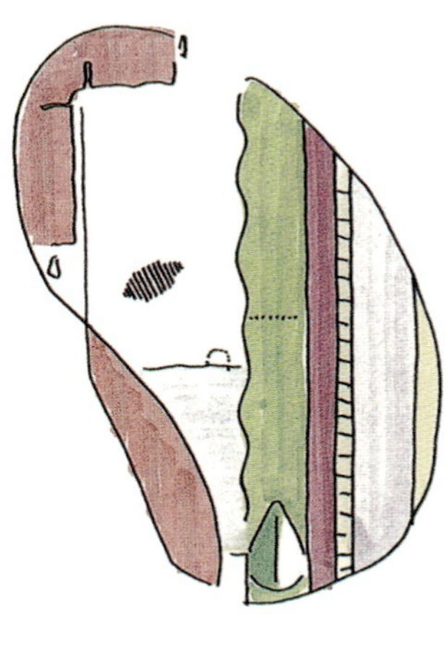

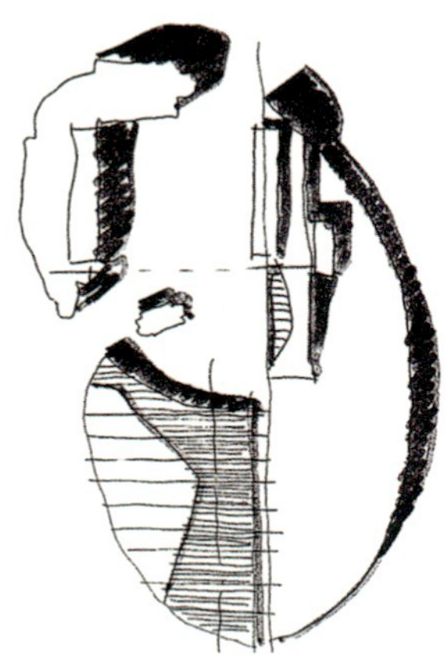

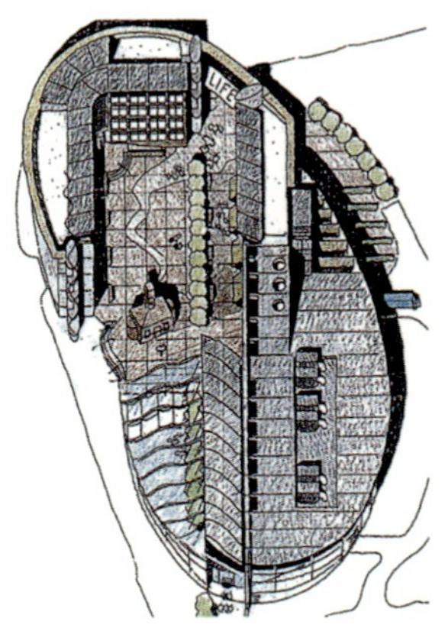

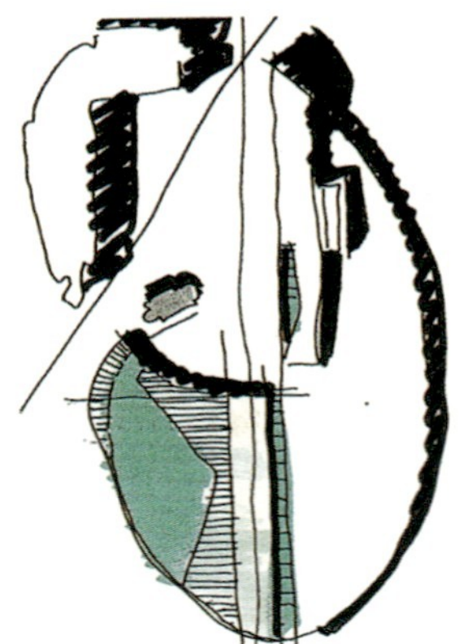

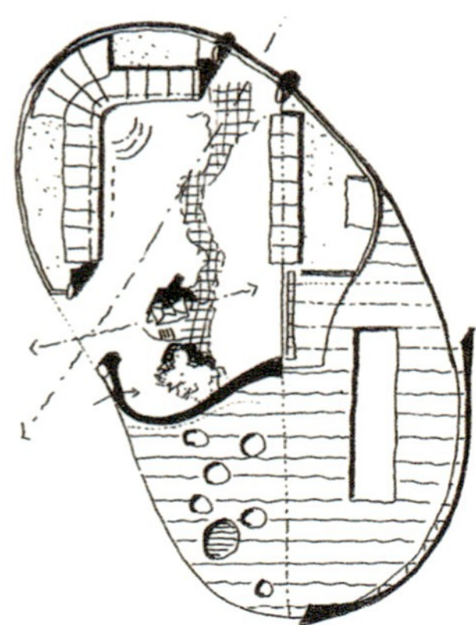

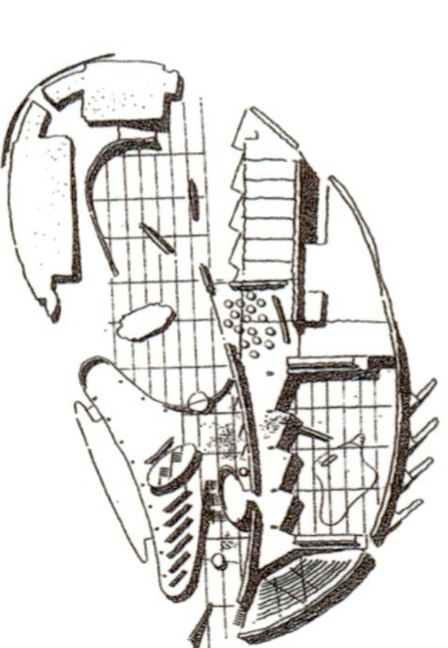

The ICL complex acts as a landmark set within surrounding road and rail links.

House, and this serves to anchor the historic building in the scheme. This helical shape is adjacent to the elevation of the Genetics Institute, which runs on, straight as a rifle shot, into the visitor-attraction component of the scheme.

The 'black box' contains multimedia displays that do not require architecture or context. This part of the complex is unashamedly functional and recalls some of the Farrell/Grimshaw buildings designed in the 1960s and 1970s. Designed out of profile metal, with servicing on its flat roof, the building has a box-like industrial aesthetic that is a fitting reference to Newcastle's railway legacy.

The entrance hall to the visitor attraction is an entirely different space from the enclosed architecture of the black box, resembling an inside–outside expanse flooded with natural light. Its flat, free-form roof is seemingly warped over many columns, resulting in a soft canopy effect that extends almost to the ground. The inspiration for this unusual organic form derives from the structural complexities of a leaf. (Nature produces highly efficient structural forms that have refined themselves over years of development, and the roof concept was meant to be sympathetic to those life-affirming principles.)

The green pre-patinated-copper roof is engineered to cover its timber skeleton like a giant water lily, making it one of the most complex geometrical roofs yet created in timber and steel. The sectional form constantly changes along its length and has no mathematical or analytical shape. The design was developed using advanced computer techniques to translate study models into a series of sectional profiles and grid nodes, which were then transformed into structural models on which loads could be imposed. The exhibits housed in the pre-patinated-copper structure celebrate the amazing diversity of life, and the building's organic design is intended to echo this.

TFP has used a bold colour scheme to separate different elements of the complex and reinforce its collage-like character. Representing the DNA coding colours of green (roof of the visitor attraction), yellow (Bioscience Centre and Genetics Institute), blue (Genetics Institute) and red (internal wall of the visitor attraction), the vibrant elevations introduce a further element of richness that reflects the fundamental variety of the brief.

The architectural design of the complex responds to its context, while creating sufficient coherence and identity to establish a new quarter. ICL is a landmark urban regeneration project that celebrates and revives elements of Newcastle's past. The architecture and urban planning actively promotes renewal, evolution and development, thereby mirroring the life-giving function of the site.

ICL's four buildings are arranged around Times Square, Newcastle's first public square for over a century.

Bottom: Context elevation.

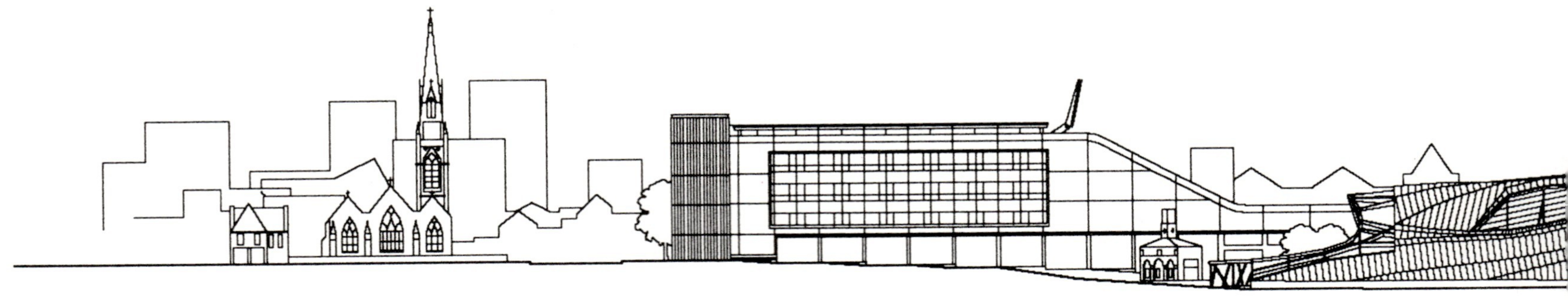

Top left: The square preserves John Dobson's historic Market Keeper's House and incorporates Charles Jencks's sculpture of a DNA helix.

Centre left: ICL comprises four buildings:
1. Bioscience Centre
2. Institute of Human Genetics
3. LIFE Interactive World 'black box' gallery
4. LIFE Interactive World entrance

Centre: The four generating geometries.
1. Scotswood Road
2. Embryo form
3. Spine
4. Axis of Market Keeper's House

Top right: View of the complex from Newcastle Central Station.

Centre right: Pedestrian permeability.

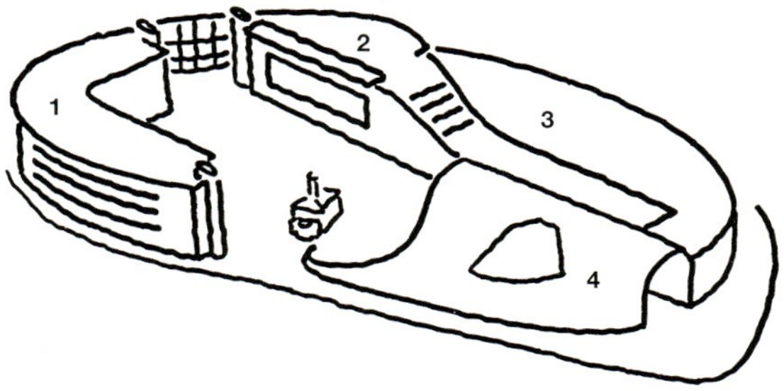

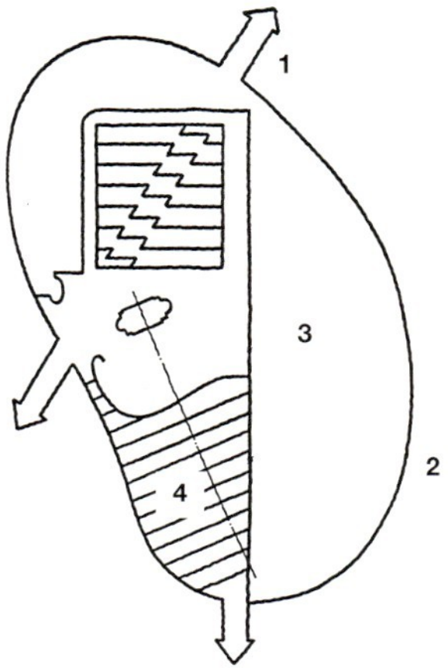

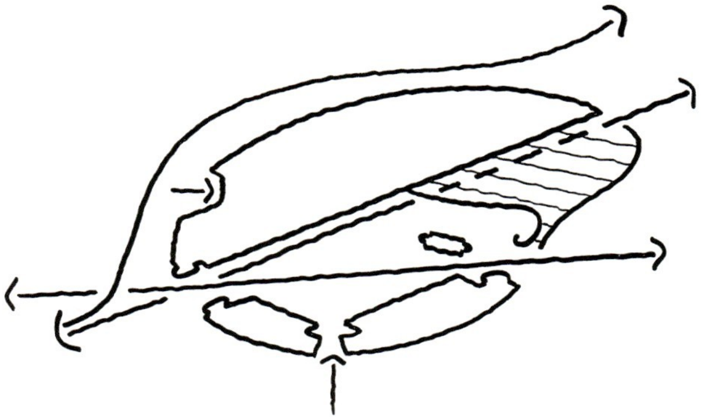

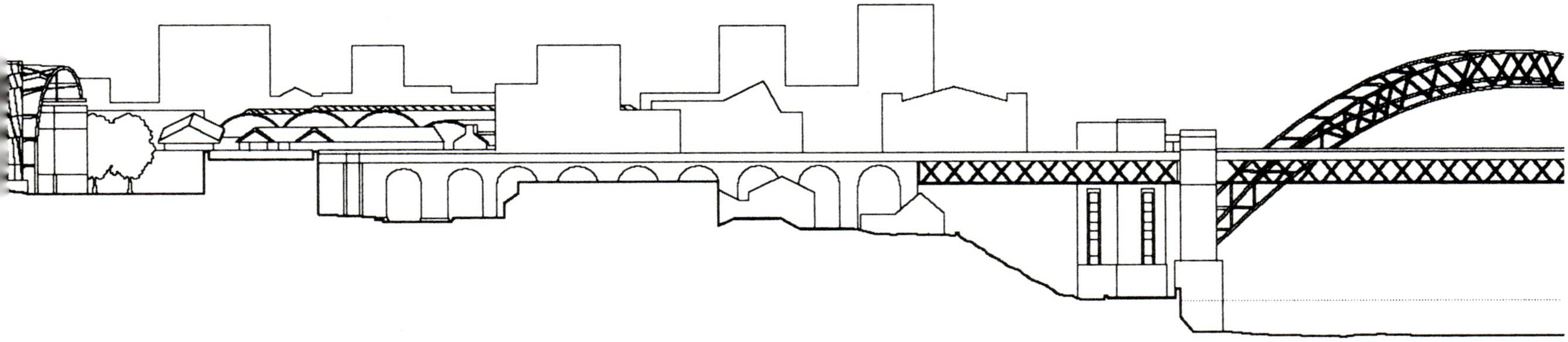

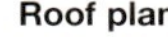

Ground-floor plan
1. Bioscience Centre
2. Times Square
3. Market Keeper's House
4. Retail Units
5. Genetics Institute Entrance
6. Conference Suite
7. Visitor attraction 'black box'
8. Visitor attraction

Bottom left: Landscape montage.

First-floor plan
1. Bioscience Centre
2. Genetics Institute
3. Consulting Clinic
4. Education Suite
5. Helix Gallery
6. Visitor attraction 'black box'
7. Visitor attraction

Roof plan.

Bottom right: Structural diagrams.

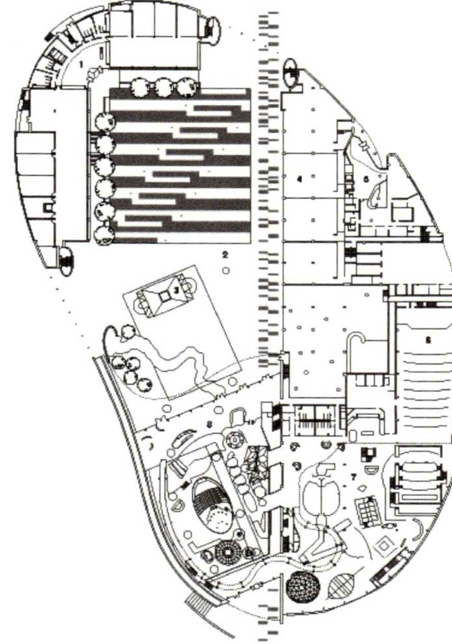

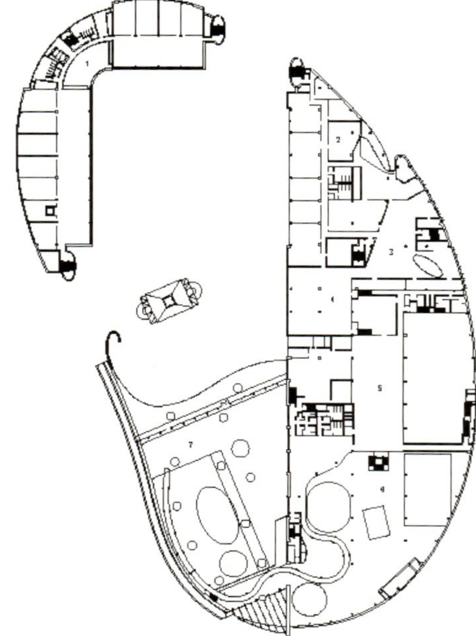

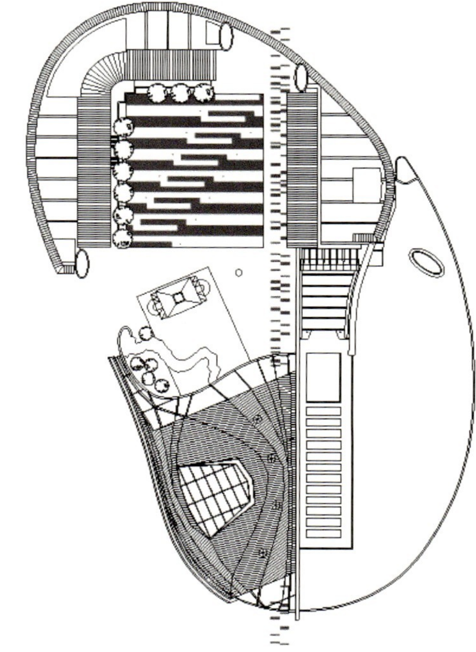

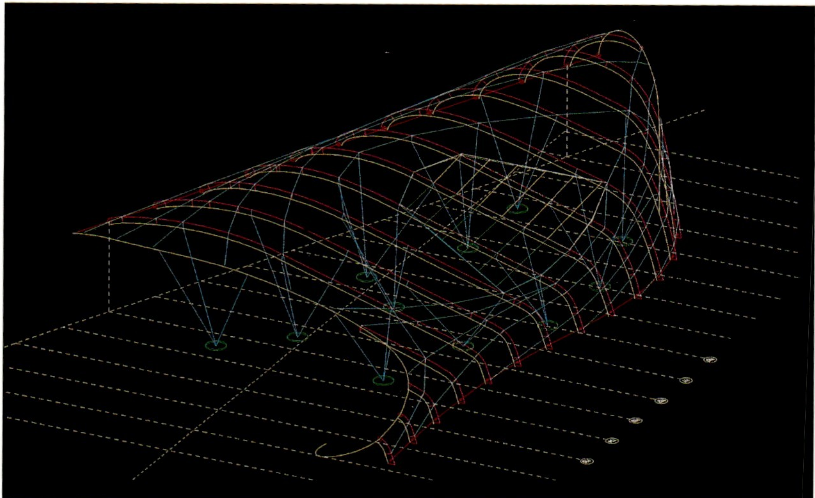

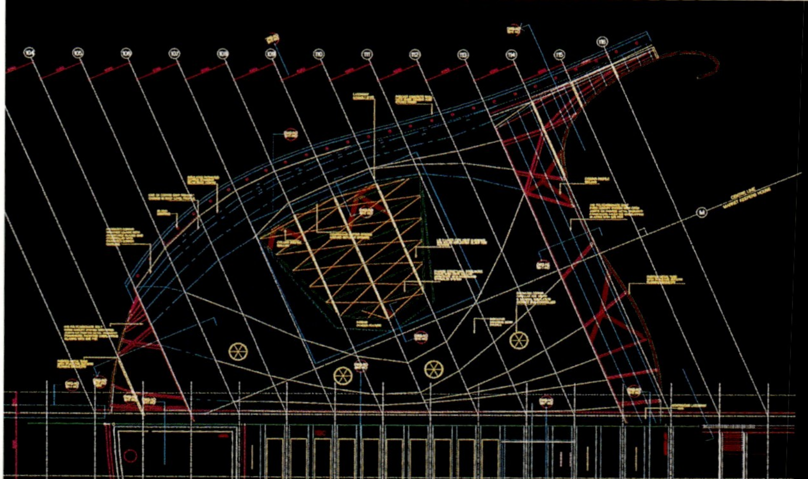

Top left: Cross section perspective through visitor attraction.

Bottom: Long section perspective.

Top right: Worm's eye view of visitor attraction.

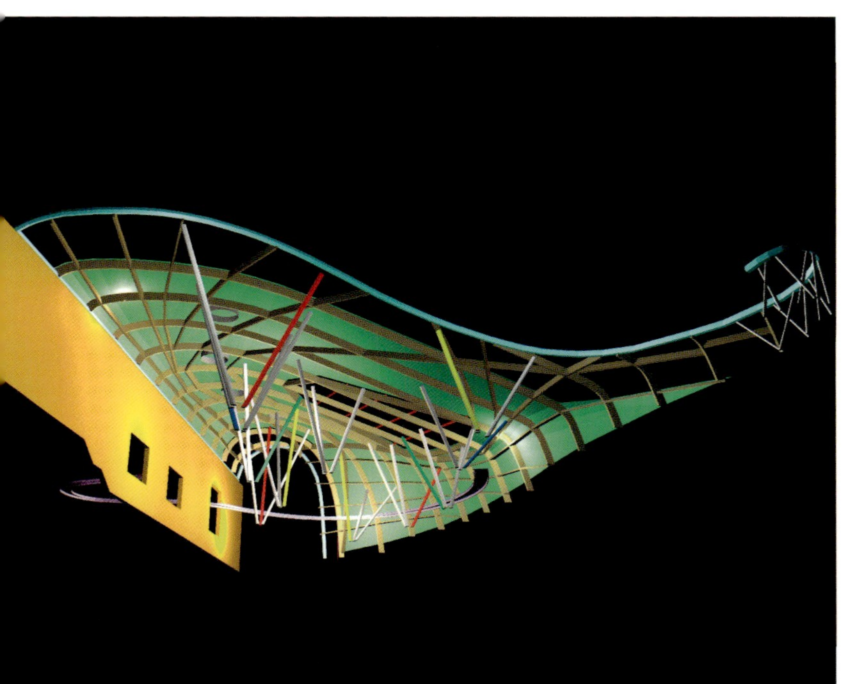

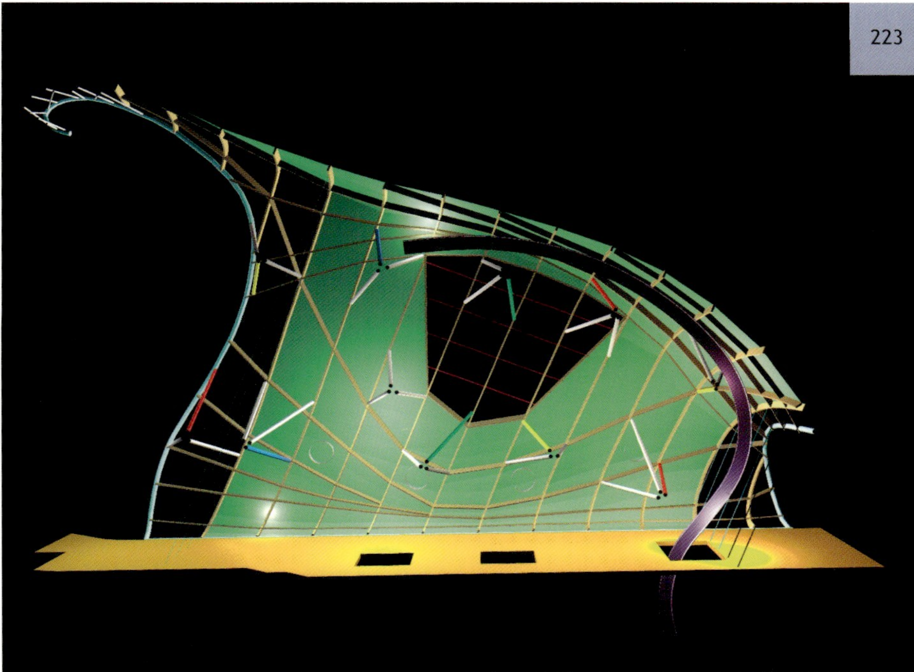

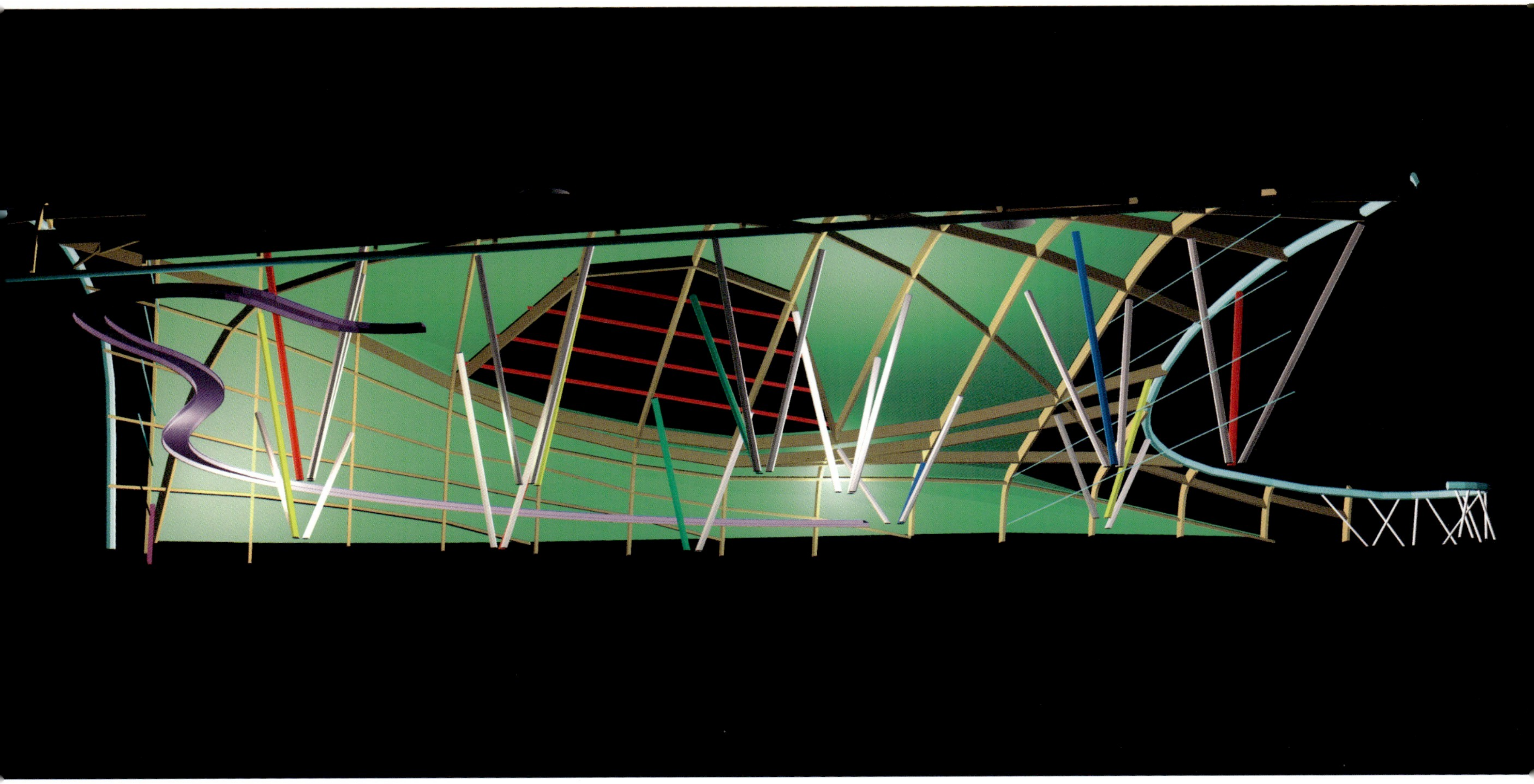

The entrance to LIFE Interactive World.

The east wall of LIFE Interactive World.

Bottom: The main entrance to the complex is marked by a steel screen that spans 23 metres between the staircase towers of the Institute of Human Genetics (left) and Bioscience Centre (right).

Street front detail of the Institute of Human Genetics and the 'black box' visitor attraction.

Bottom: Institute of Human Genetics.

Detail of the Bioscience Centre looking towards LIFE Interactive World.

The Bioscience Centre. Pugin's celebrated St Mary's Roman Catholic Cathedral is to the left.

Main image: View of the main entrance. The Bioscience Centre is to the right and the Institute of Human Genetics is to the left of the screen.

Inset left: Street entrance to the Bioscience Centre.

Inset centre: Detail of the termination of the visitor attraction roof structure in Times Square.

Inset right: Detail of the Scotswood Road screen.

Inset left: Glazed screen walls at either end of LIFE Interactive World provide a naturally lit experience for the visitor.

Inset right: The glue-laminated timber roof structure forms highly sculptural geometries.

Interior volume of the naturally lit visitor attraction with its glue-laminated timber roof structure.

Bottom: Model showing the roof structure and exhibition contents of the visitor attraction (left) and the 'black box' exhibition display (right) of LIFE Interactive World.

Simple glass blocks provide the defining character of the Bioscience Centre.

Bottom: Details of LIFE Interactive World's glue-laminated timber roof structure and coloured steel columns.

Details of the visitor attraction and Scotswood Road screen.

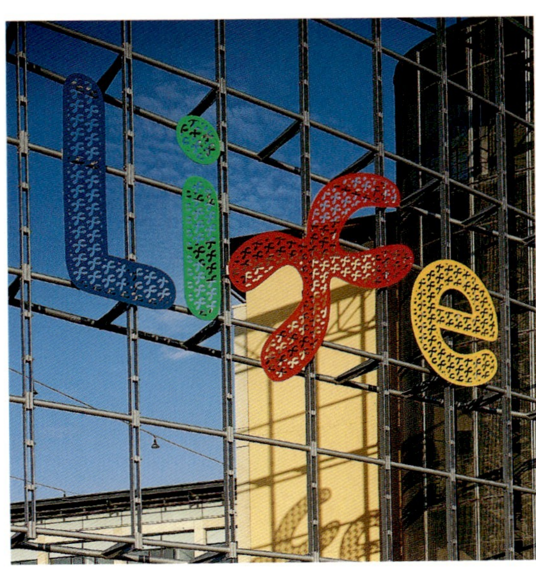

Detail of visitor attraction roof.

The new ICL sits at the western edge of the city with vacant sites beyond, awaiting urban regeneration. The project's aims are as much about urban renewal as about buildings and architecture.

Welcome to Life
Life

HULL

HULL

Hull is an isolated outpost city set on the north shore of the Humber estuary where it meets the River Hull. Founded in the 13th century, the city grew out of what came to be a series of connected harbours extending along the Humber. Vulnerable to attack from the sea, a walled city was built to protect both its urban settlement and the Humber Estuary and Eastern Seaboard from European invasion. Closely oriented to the water, Hull once boasted the world's biggest fishing fleet and, during the 18th century, was Britain's third largest shipbuilding city.

The city is now one of lost identity. Industrial growth followed by 20th century decline has led to its abandonment, dereliction and collapse. These are the legacies passed on to a new generation of urbanists, whose task is to serve a process by rediscovering the city's origins and remake its historic core.

Civic wealth generated from Hull's telecommunications industry has enabled urbanists to reassess and repair past mistakes. Terry Farrell & Partners' design approach for the Deep sits within this context. Applying a long-term commitment towards the masterplan process, the building is part of Hull's bid to become one of Europe's foremost cities.

Above: Sammy's Point, named after the historic Samuelson's ship yard, marks the point where the River Hull meets the Humber estuary. The former ship yard is now the site for TFP's new millennium project.

Top: Satellite image showing the Humber estuary flowing into the North Sea. Hull is on the north bank of the River Humber and the Humber Bridge is to the left.

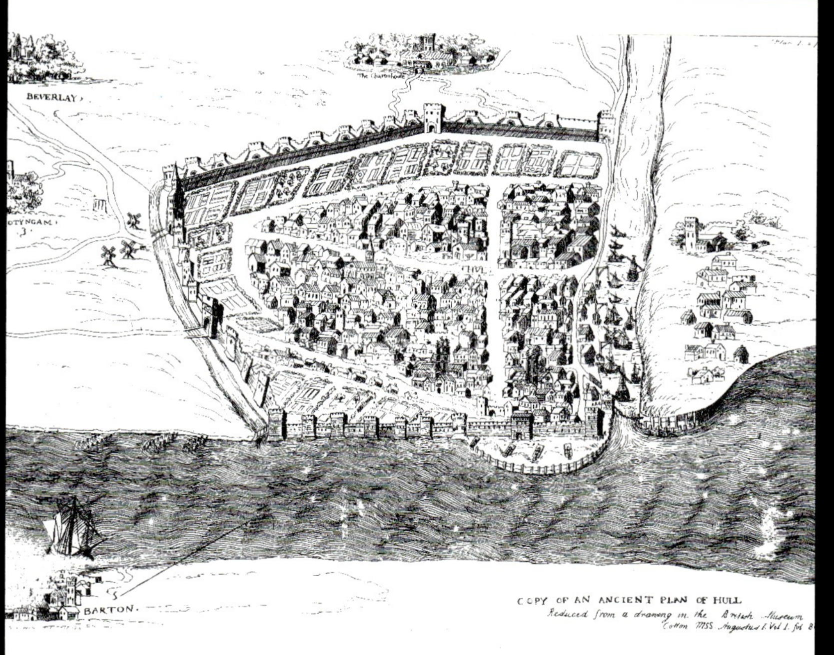

Historical view of the walled city.

Below and bottom: Masterplan completed by TFP sfor Hull City Vision. The study developed an approach for the whole of Hull, focusing on the removal of pocket car parks that had created empty plots in the town centre.

THE DEEP
WORLD OCEAN DISCOVERY CENTRE

Situated on a 2.45-hectare brownfield site at Sammy's Point, at the confluence of the River Hull and the Humber estuary, the Deep began its life as an urban renaissance scheme. In this respect, it reaches beyond architecture to become enmeshed with the infrastructure of the River Hull corridor, as well as the economic, social and cultural renewal of the city in general. Now recovering from its status as recession-hit, Hull was once an economic powerhouse. Its decline over the last 50 years has been extreme; the development of the Deep had to be viewed as part of a large-scale urban strategy.

The Deep is one of three aquarium commissions so far undertaken by Terry Farrell & Partners; the other two projects are in London and Seattle. This type of leisure building is public architecture at its most populist. As Terry Farrell has repeatedly stated, his aim is to create buildings that win popular support by bridging the gap between elite and populist causes. As a comprehensible, iconic building, the Deep looks for inspiration to a range of precedents and the design conjures up metaphorical associations with wave or glacier-like forms.

The £40 million scheme is the second of TFP's landmark millennium projects (the other being the International Centre for Life), based in two buildings. The main building, located at the south-west point of the site, houses the visitor attraction, the Learning Centre, the Total Environment Simulator and the University of Hull's research facility. The other building, a simple linear structure close to the site's western edge, is a business centre that will help fund and contribute research to the educational part of the scheme. Designed to nurture fledgling companies in the commercial application of marine science research, the business centre houses both laboratory and office space within a campus-style environment. TFP has also designed a pedestrian footbridge across the River Hull that links the city to the underdeveloped east bank.

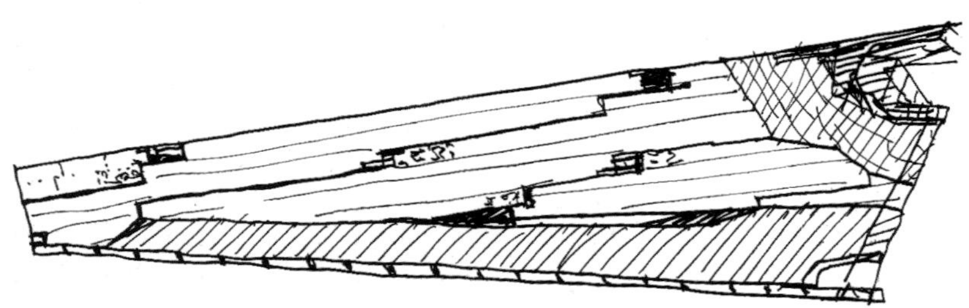

Concept sketches by Aidan Potter (top) and Terry Farrell.

Top left and centre: Concept sketches by Terry Farrell.

Top right: The barrenness of the site and its dramatic seacapes led TFP towards a free and imaginative form: the design bears a resemblance to *The Ice Sea* (*Dashed Hopes*) by Caspar David Friedrich.

Bottom: Early concept model.

A central objective was to create a building with a bold, pioneering image for the city of Hull. The four-storey visitor attraction housing a world-class aquarium exhibition is therefore designed to be a dramatic icon. The barrenness of the site and its dramatic seacapes led Terry Farrell towards a free and imaginative form and the resulting design has been likened to *The Ice Sea* (*Dashed Hopes*) by the 19th-century German Romantic painter Caspar David Friedrich (illustrated far right).

The design of the Deep captures the image of an eroded monolith. Over time, fractures, fissures and fault lines will create a complex pattern on the monolith's surface. Man's intervention halts the process of decay and transforms the vision of abandonment into one of optimism and regeneration. The design exploits the natural metaphor of land form versus sea form. Like the Peak Tower in Hong Kong and Newcastle's International Centre for Life, The Deep is a building that revels in its metaphorical associations. At an extreme point in the landscape, the visitor attraction rises in a wave-like form, amplifying the geography of the site and the oceanographic function of the building. The exterior is treated as an eroded rock face using organic forms and lines, while irregular recessed strata on the façades provide points of access and openings for windows. The roof plane is treated similarly to the wall surfaces so that the building is read as a three-dimensional object rather than as a series of two-dimensional planes.

Similar qualities of natural erosion inform the interior spaces, where a rich and varied spatial sequence makes the most of the views. The interior spaces were strongly influenced by the physical nature of the ocean: rather than imitating the usual aquarium form of a linear procession of tanks, TFP made full use of the three-dimensional space. The building's section offsets the solid (water) and void (circulation space), giving visitors a sense of immersion within an ocean environment.

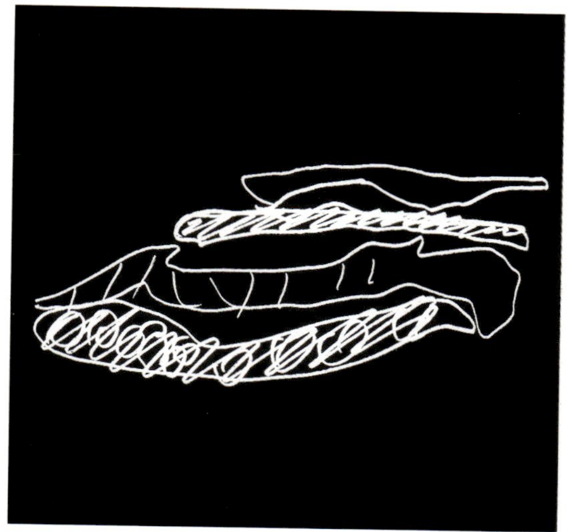

Sequence showing the erosion of the monolith.

While the main mass of the building is treated as natural metaphor, two architectural elements are placed within the composition. These are an observation point at the form's pinnacle, with unrivalled views across the River Humber to the great Humber Bridge, and an entrance lift, stair core and walkway that bridge out of the main structure. The urban boundary of the site is marked by the business centre, which offers highly flexible office space for young businesses and larger spaces for established anchor tenants.

As Terry Farrell sees it, one of the great products of urban regeneration is the knock-on effect that one development can have on a whole city – as typified by the transformation of Bilbao since the building of the Guggenheim museum in 1999. It is hoped that, following its completion in 2001, the Deep will be a symbol of regeneration that will contribute to the revival of Hull as one of Europe's foremost cities.

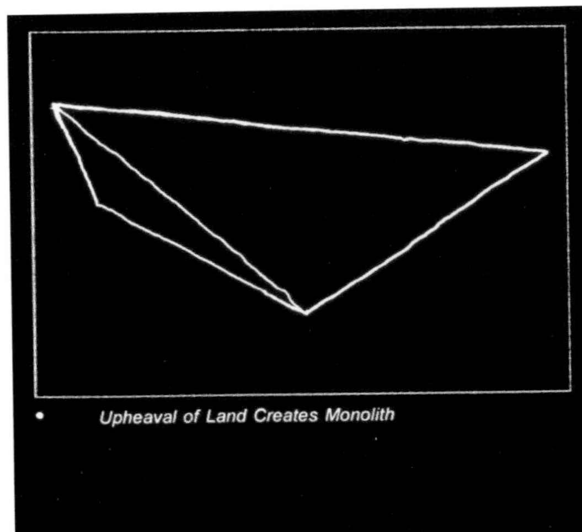

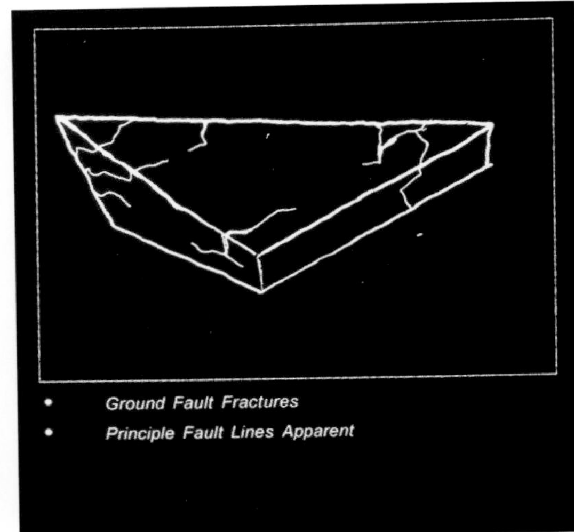

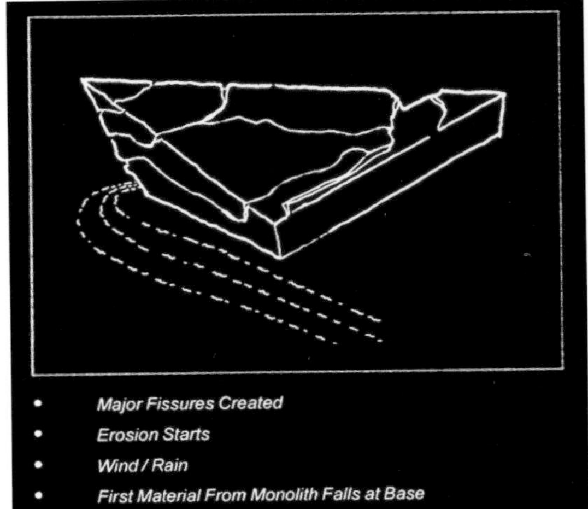

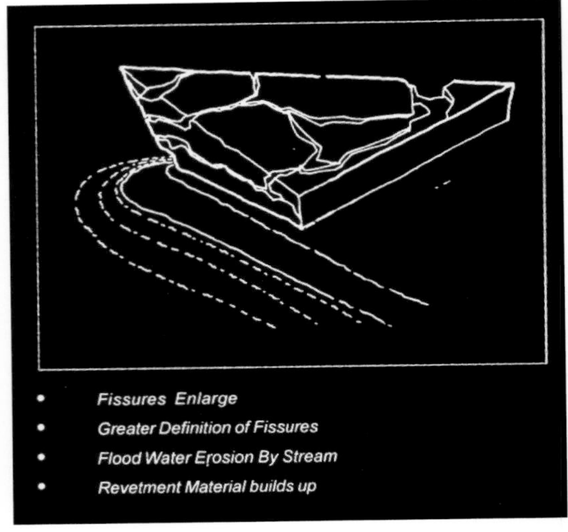

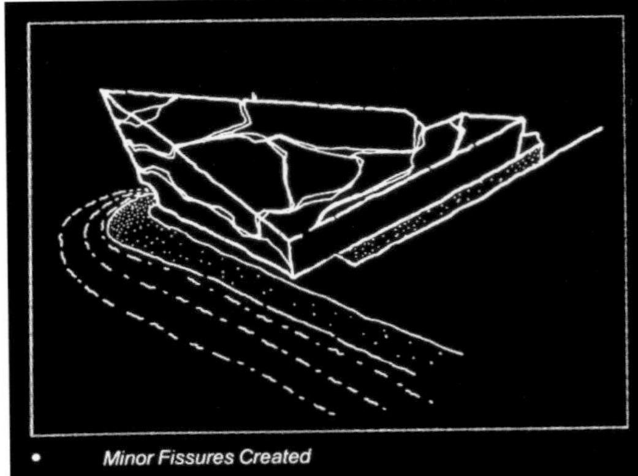

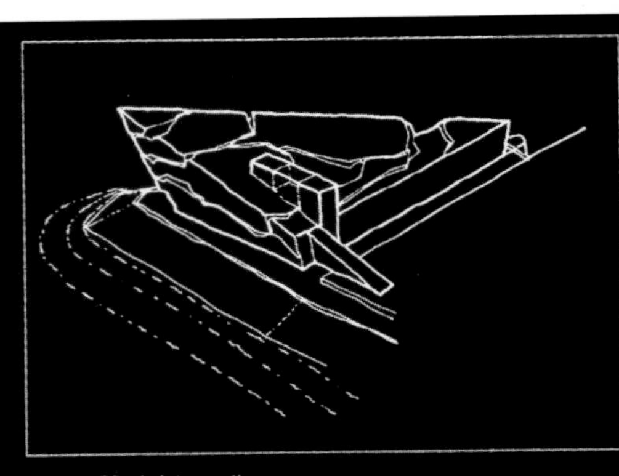

Interior perspective views.

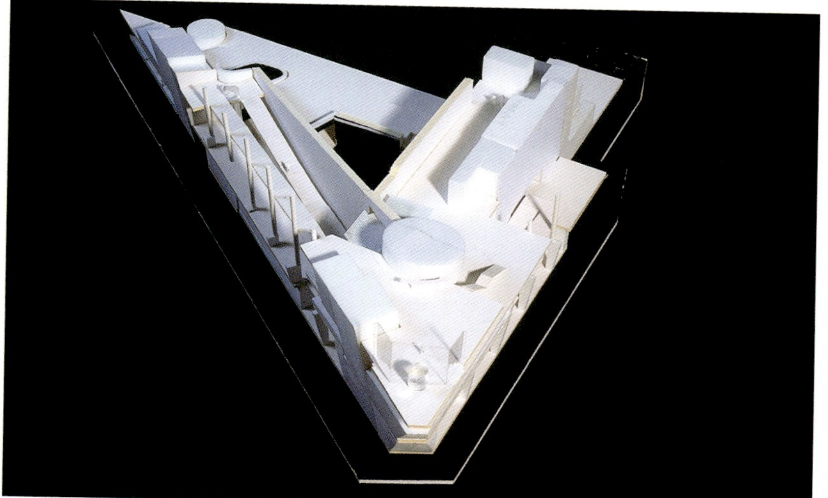

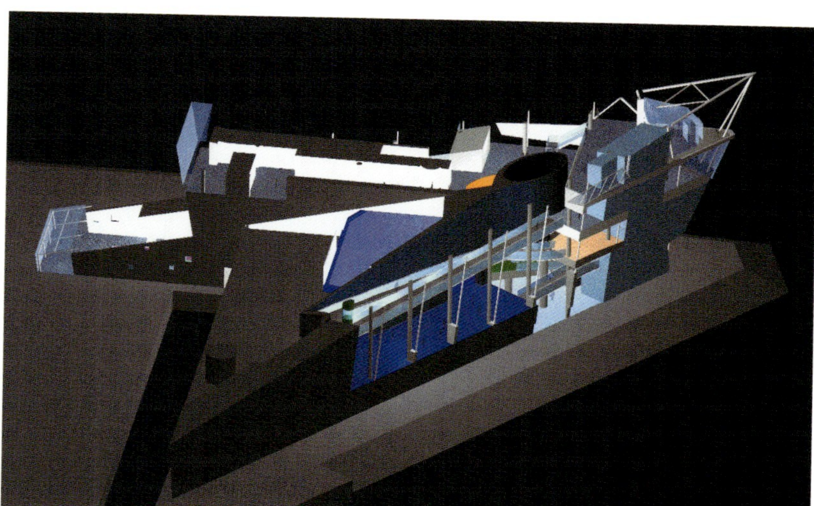

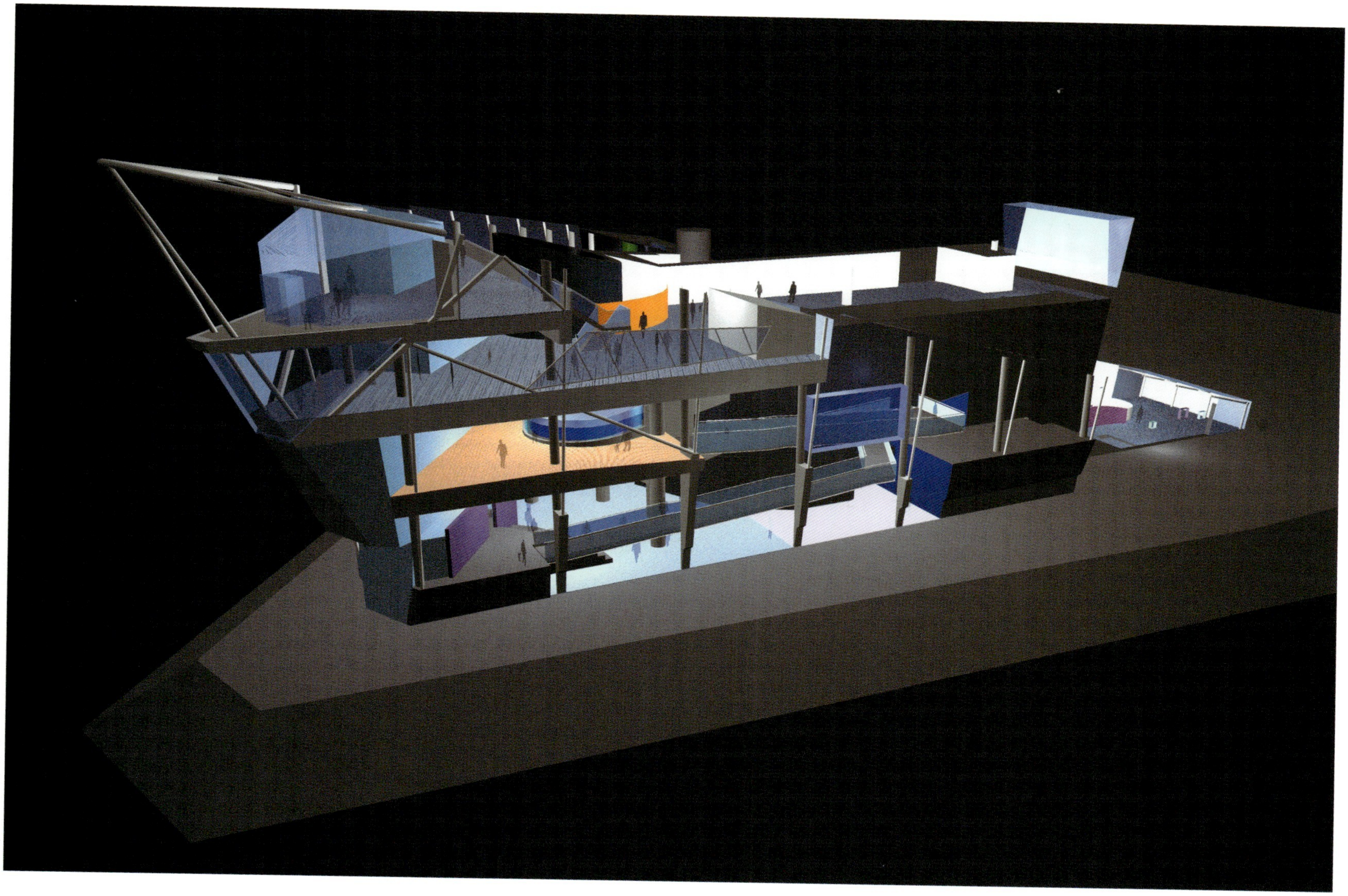

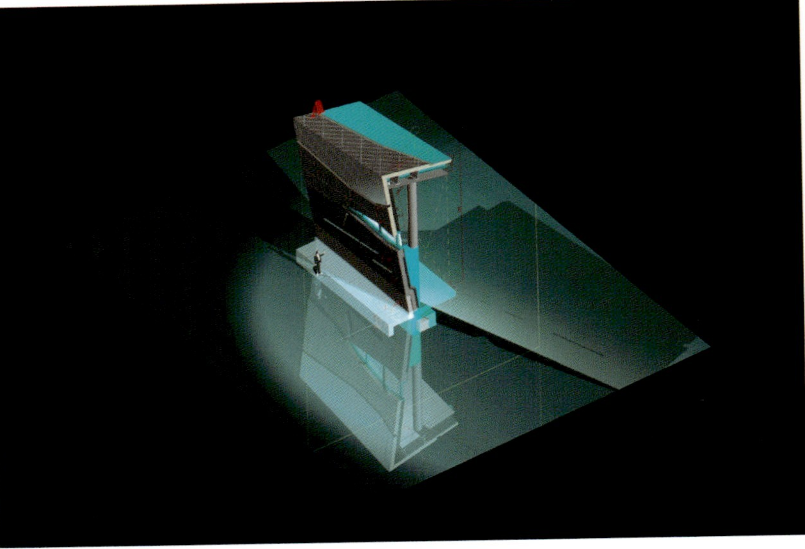

Study models assessing cladding and internal features.

Above: Construction photographs, January 2001.

Top: South elevation.

Bottom and opposite bottom: Construction photographs from May 2001.

Top: Perspective from the River Humber.

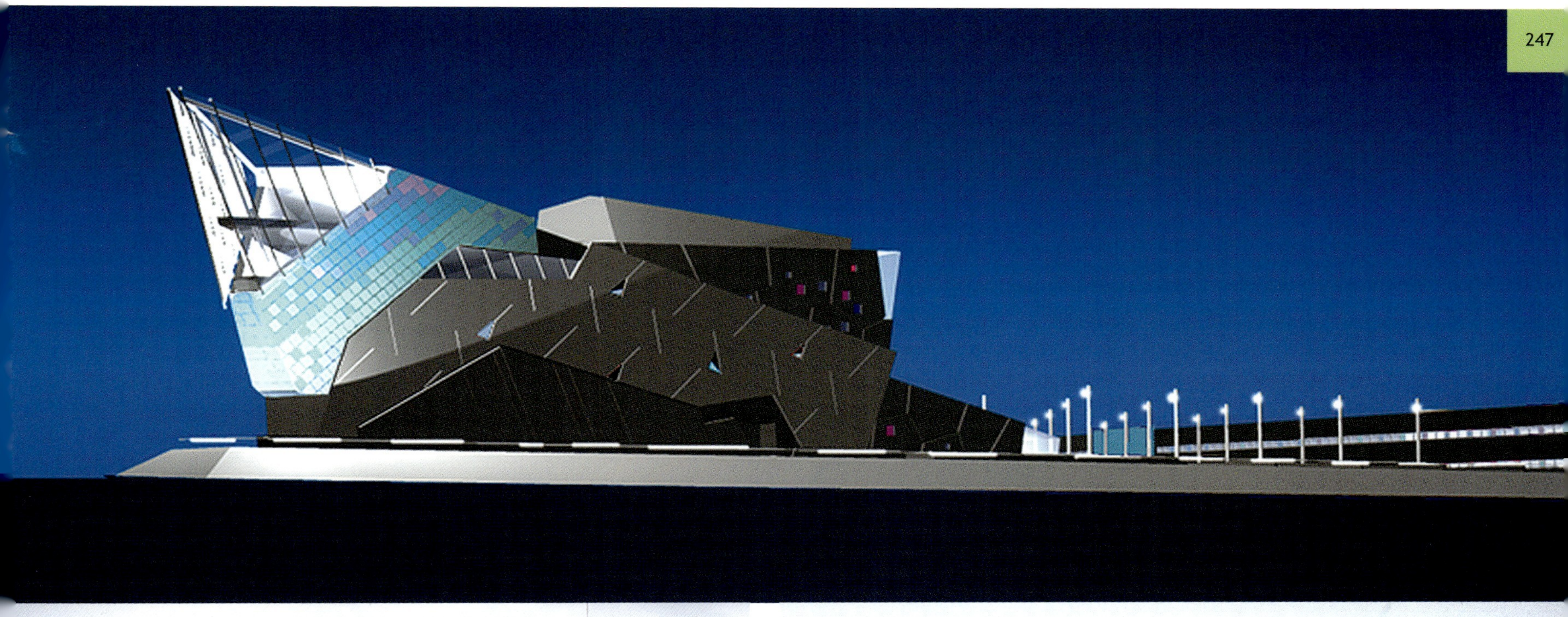

Below and opposite: The completed business centre for marine research and application.

Bottom: Ground-floor plan (above) and east elevation (below).

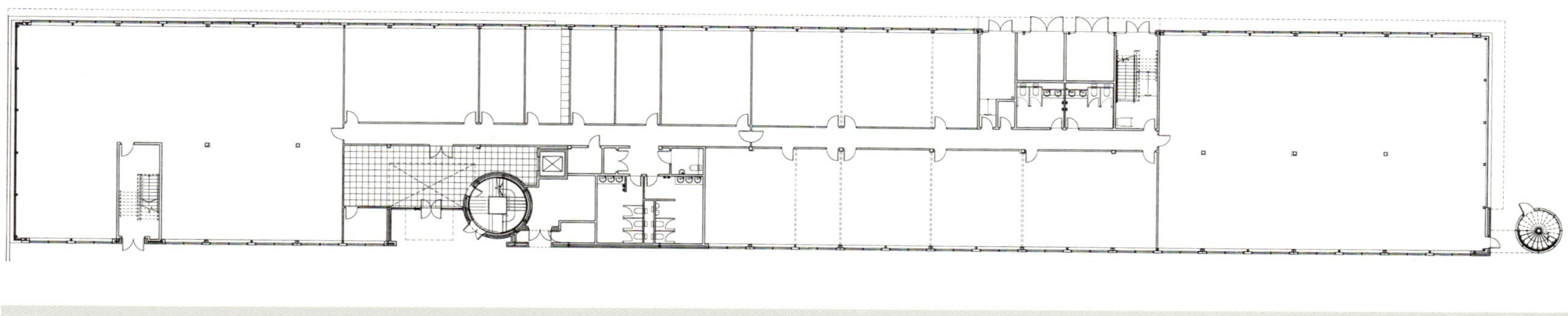

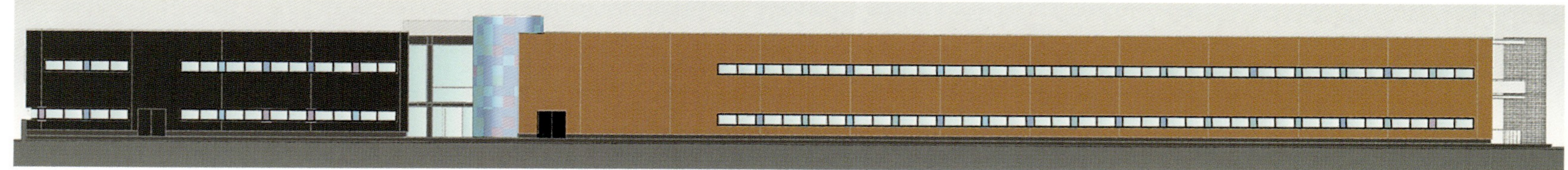

LONDON

LONDON

London's urban makeup arises from an existing template of rules and narratives comprised of rivers, marshes, field patterns, rights and customs, market fairs, villages and changes in land ownership. These shifting themes and uses, recurring over generations, form historical traces upon which new and evolving urban design responses are superimposed. The city's eccentrically planned streets and places reflect an intricate layering of history and change. It is a story of continual making and unmaking; an uneasy truce between chaos and order.

Unlike many great cities, London's plan originates from a process of incremental growth rather than from the implicit imposition of a formal layout. Where Paris, Beijing or Seattle are composed around a visible plan, London is process driven. In this way, the industrial revolution, growing transit systems and the twentieth-century car-based suburban sprawl have surrounded and enveloped – rather than carved out and defined – the city into a web of complex villages.

Significant structures and features are only revealed to those who make the effort to discern them. The Thames and its connecting bridges provide the anchor from which the city's disparate villages stem – Westminster and 'the City' followed by subcentres – villages such as Hampstead, Notting Hill, Hammersmith and Brixton, which in turn grew up along the path of the Thames's ancient tributaries. As a city of edges, London is contained by its City wall, the Circle line, North and South Circular and the M25. Divisions, in the form of the Thames and Lee rivers, rail viaducts and arteries, create further patterns. Great highways – the Roman roads, Westway, radial interchanges – and high streets – Kingsland, Edgware and Walworth Roads, among many others – drive through the metropolis, tracing topography and linking distances. Parks and undulating land masses offset the urban grain. As a counterpoint to the apparent chaos, planned estates in the form of Belgravia, Mayfair and St James's provide pockets of order and tranquillity. The great Victorian stations, together with an ever-expanding Underground system, contribute to a further shift in the city's urban layout and overlay another distinctive pattern. In more recent times, an emerging motif of tall buildings has created a new narrative on the London skyline. Post-war redevelopment – on-going plans for the South Bank, gentrification of the East End and colonization of the Thames Gateway, along with the regeneration of many brown-field sites – evidence another turn in London's restless evolution, ensuring a further display of intervention within its urban form.

Left: Satellite image of Greater London locating TFP's projects within the context of the Thames Gateway to the east and central London.
Left to right: Samsung Headquarters, Boston Manor; Swiss Cottage redevelopment; Paddington Basin; power station, Lots Road; Home Office headquarters, Marsham Street; Three Quays Hotel, Tower of London; headquarters building, Canary Wharf; Greenwich Promenade; Greenwich Peninsula; National Aquarium, Victoria Docks; Royal Docks; Bluewater; Bluewater Valley; Ebbsfleet; and Springhead.

Centre: Satellite image showing TFP's projects within the context of 'village' London: Swiss Cottage, Paddington Basin, Lots Road, Marsham Street and Three Quays hotel.

Right: City of London plan from 1943 showing community and urban space analysis.

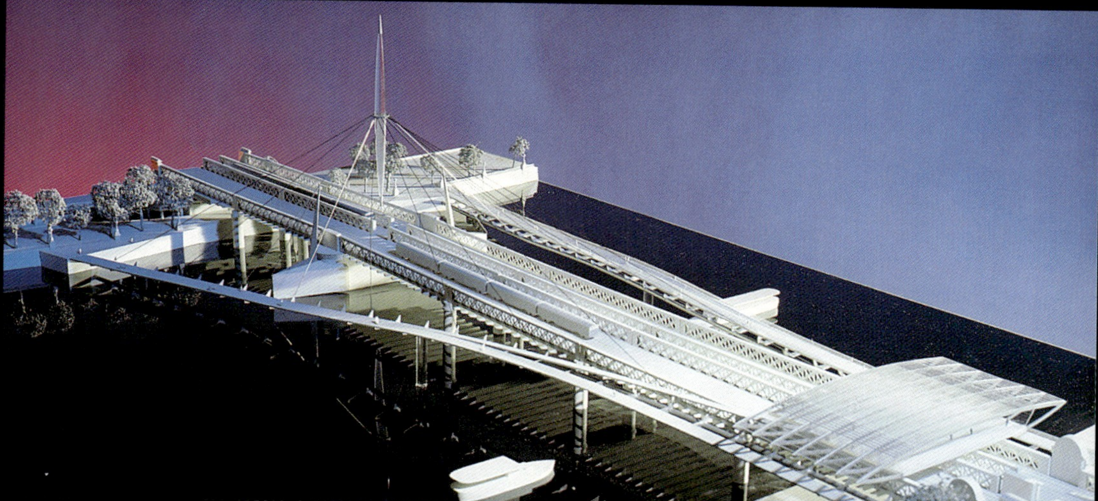

City of London plan from 1943 showing social and functional analysis.

Centre: Historical view.

Above: TFP's Blackfriars Bridge proposal of 1993.

Top: TFP's Hungerford Bridge proposal of 1993.

DOCKLANDS/THAMES GATEWAY

While the wealth generated from trade has always flowed into the city from the east via the Thames, London's east side is historically its poorer side. Down wind of smoke and pollution, and down river of waste dumped into the Thames, the east has always been the less desirable location. The decline of 'smoke stack' industry and the ending of almost 200 years of cement-making in north Kent has released vast areas of land for redevelopment. The greater focus on connections with Europe, the construction of the high-speed Channel tunnel rail link and pressures for the economic growth of the south-east have combined to create the conditions for a new phase in London's evolution, resulting in its expansion and growth eastwards. Terry Farrell & Partners' projects in eastern London are engaged in the definition, articulation and design of this new direction for the city.

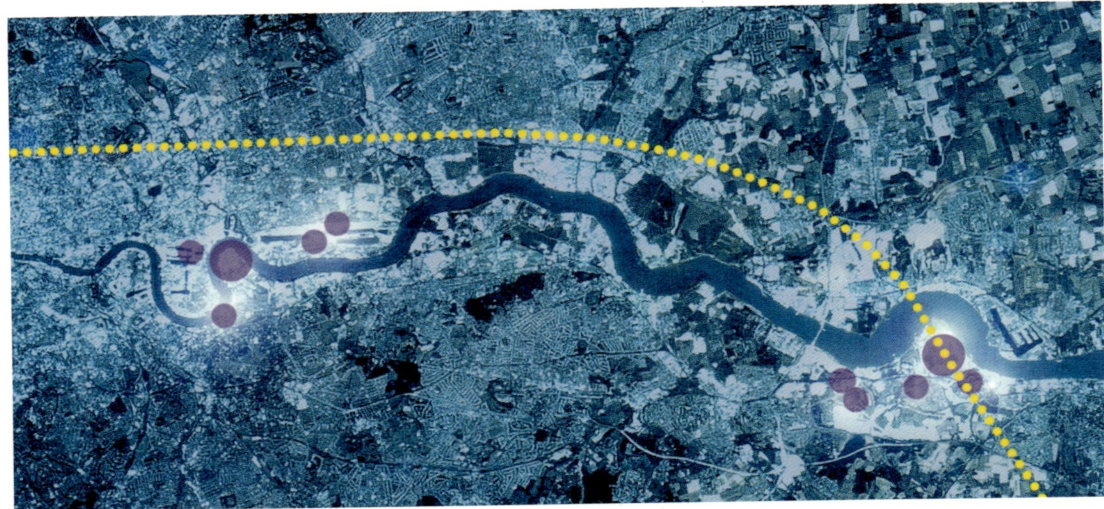

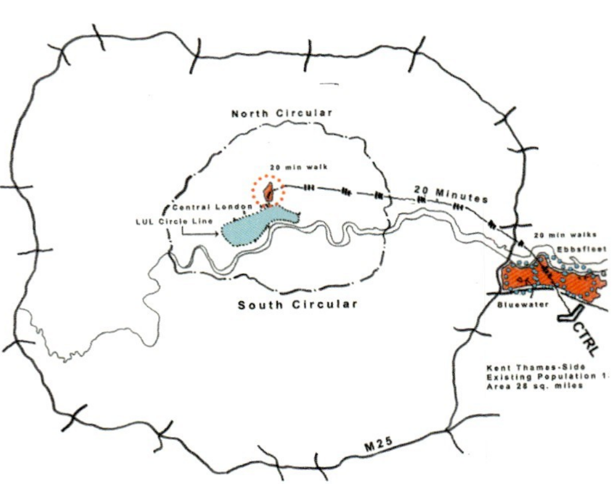

Top left: The Thames Gateway corridor, connected to central London by the proposed Cross Tunnel Rail Link (CTRL), has been identified as the focus of London's future economic growth. An arc, reaching from Stratford to Beckton via the Lower Lea and the Royal Docks, provides the opportunity for the City to expand east. TFP's projects are grouped around Thames Gateway and Canary Wharf.

Bottom left and right: Masterplan for Bluewater Valley.

Top right: The CTRL is the regenerating catalyst behind the new Thames Gateway area.

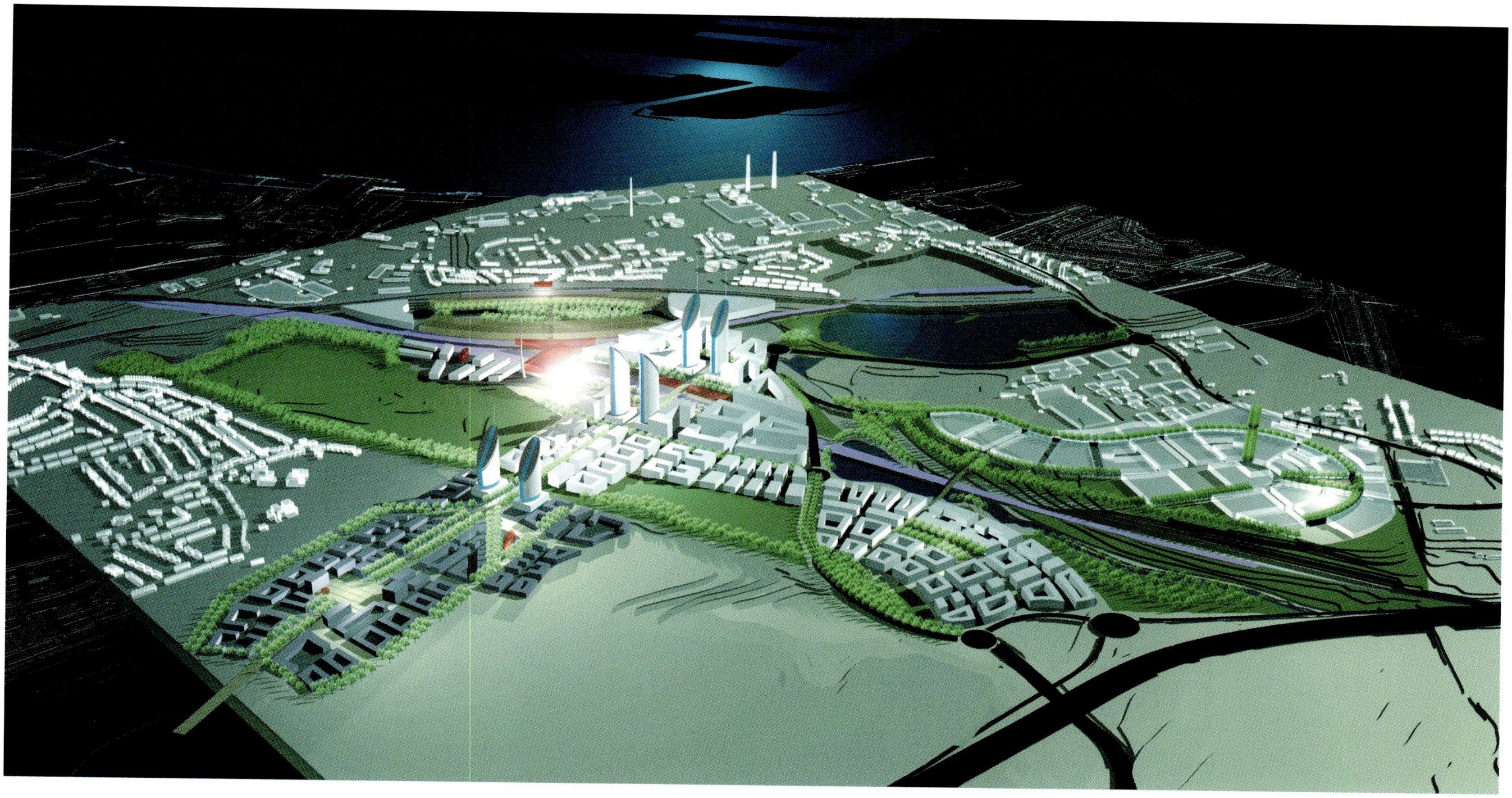

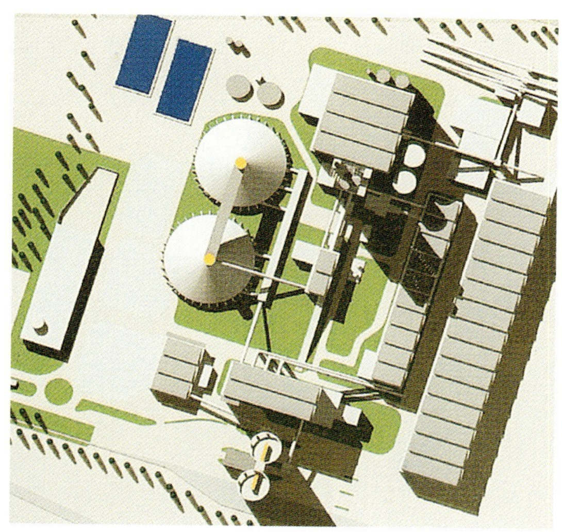

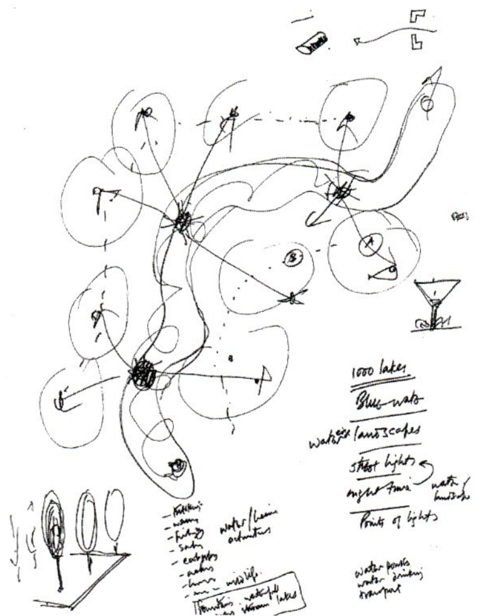

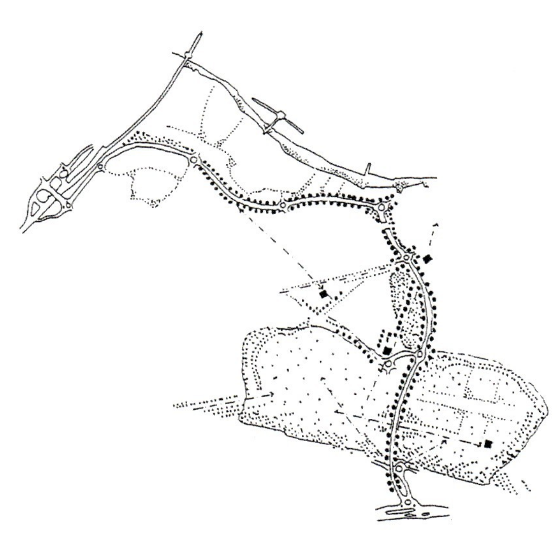

Bottom left: TFP's proposal for the Blue Circle Cement Works in Medway, Kent.

Top: TFP's Ebbsfleet masterplan provides the structure for a new urban district linked to and from central London and mainland Europe by the proposed Channel Tunnel Rail Link.

Bottom right: Concept sketch (left) by Terry Farrell and sketch (right) showing landscape proposals for Bluewater Valley.

Top left: Recent infrastructure projects, including (from top) Stratford town centre with its CTRL, Canary Wharf and the Jubilee Line extension.

Bottom: The Royal Docks before regeneration. Built in the 19th century to heroic scale, these estuary docks – once bleak and abandoned – are now being re-urbanized.

Top right: TFP's masterplan for Greenwich Peninsula.

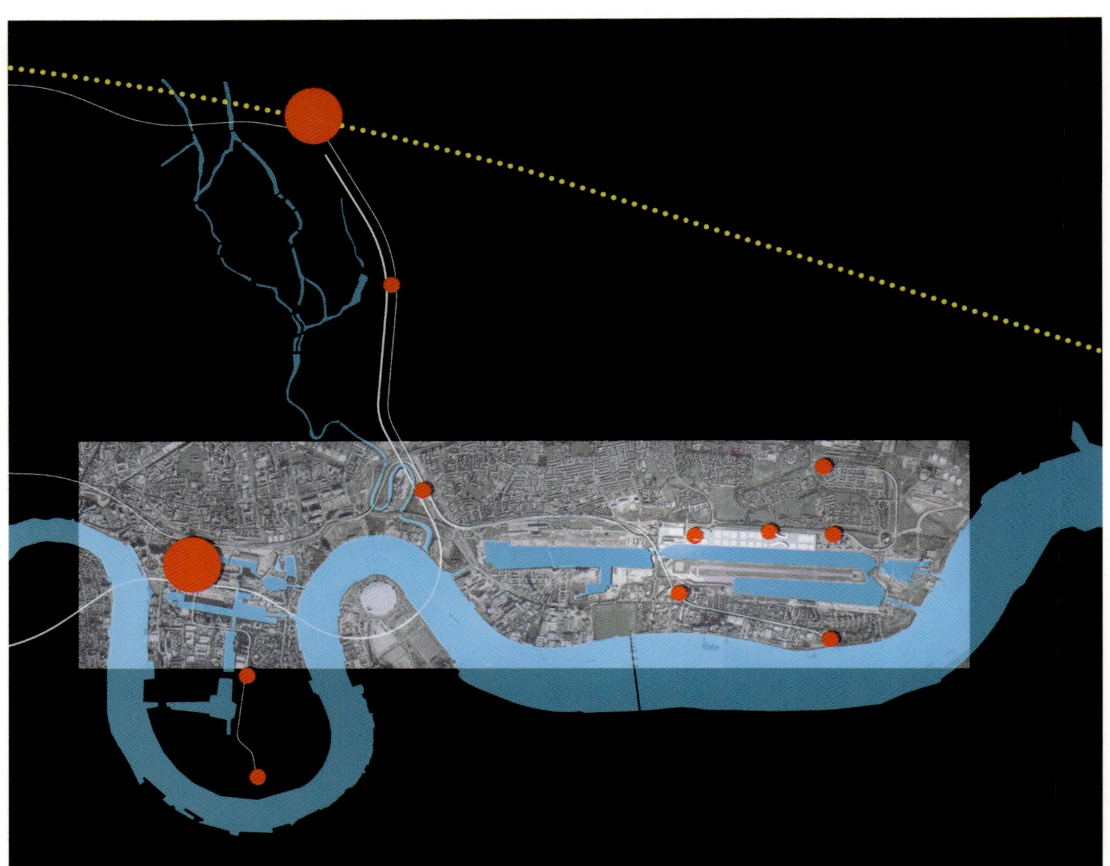

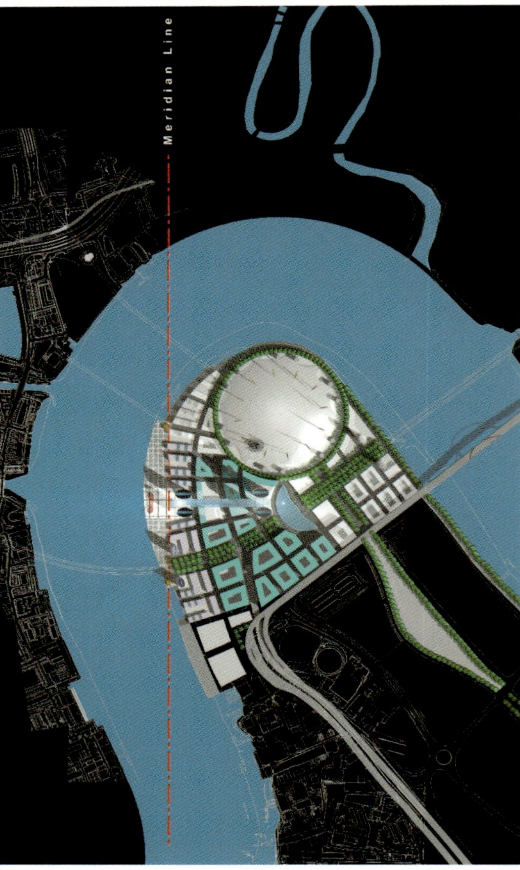

Top: TFP's masterplan for Greenwich Peninsula.

Bottom: Sketch by Aidan Potter. TFP's Royal Docks scheme takes the linearity of the great docks as its main theme.

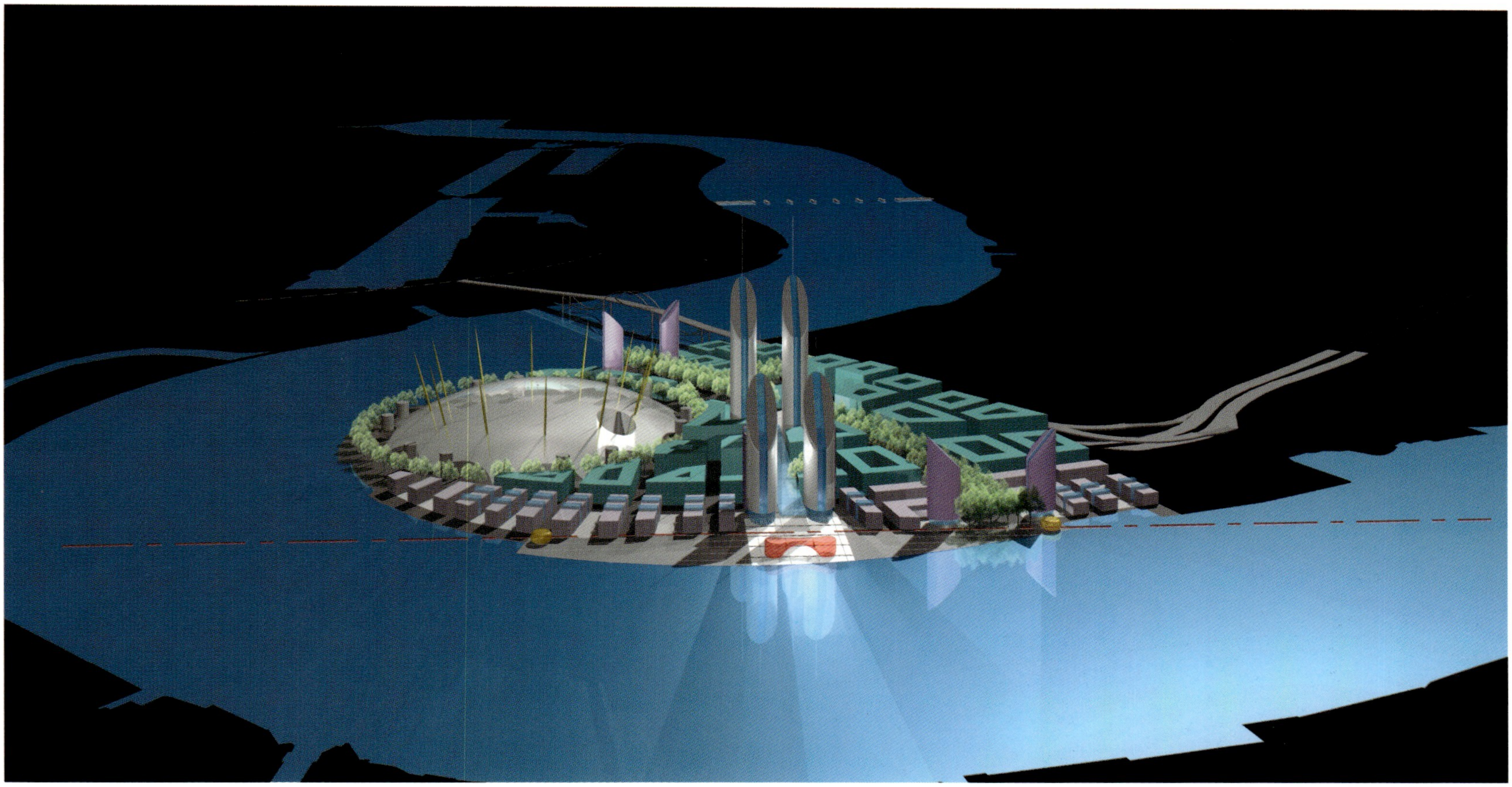

NATIONAL AQUARIUM

Not far from the Thames flood barrier on the north bank of the river, the National Aquarium is sited on a peninsula bordered by water on its north, south and west sides. Responding to the edge of Victoria Dock, the aquarium is intended to play a key part in the regeneration of the Royal Docks as a whole. The building's location at the extreme end of the peninsula dictates its long, narrow footprint. On its main, eastern approach elevation, the building appears to be set on an island, and its entrance is reached by a combination of paths and bridges.

Site plan.

Top: Concept sketch by Terry Farrell.

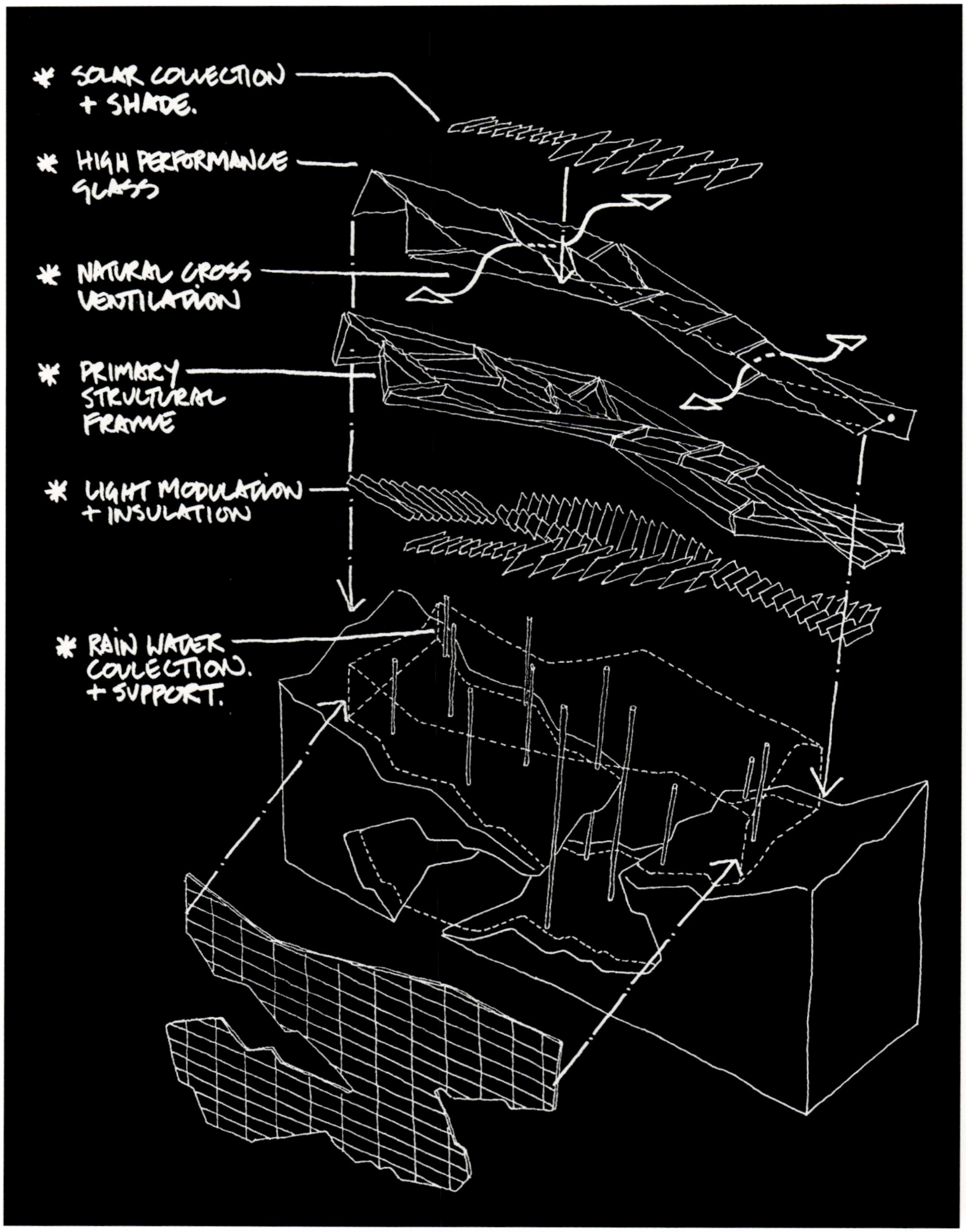

The elements of the building are a metaphor for the earth's habitat. The building reflects a slice of the earth's crust.

The metaphor for the design concept is the earth's environment in microcosm – land, water, vegetation, air and clouds – and the building's base is reminiscent of fissured rock strata. Reflecting the movement of the earth's plates, the core of the building appears to contort, creating a dynamic land and water form within its centre. The roof form resembles a cloud that moderates the climate below. In summer, the 'cloud' collects solar energy and adjusts artificial illumination and temperature controls according to the intensity of light and solar gain, as well as naturally ventilating the spaces below. In winter, transparent blankets of insulation reduce heat loss, in keeping with the project's aim to create a sustainable environment.

The exhibition areas of the 15,500-square-metre building are in four parts – UK, India, Red Sea and South Pacific – reflecting four representative world habitats. The UK exhibits spill out from the centre of the building to the entrance, with the India exhibits located above it. The north and south elevations are dedicated to the tropical and subtropical areas of the Red Sea and the South Pacific. Internally, the east–west orientation of the glazed areas allows cross-ventilation in summer, and air also rises up from the cooler UK exhibits to ventilate the warmer Ganges exhibits. The two internal exhibition areas of the South Pacific and the Red Sea act as thermal buffers across the two extremes of heat gain from the south in the summer and heat loss from the north in winter. Solid masonry walls balance the temperature by becoming natural heat sinks. As Sir David Attenborough wrote of the National Aquarium project: 'Nothing reveals the dazzling beauty of the natural world more sensationally than the modern high-tech aquarium. Londoners will be astonished and delighted – and not before time.'

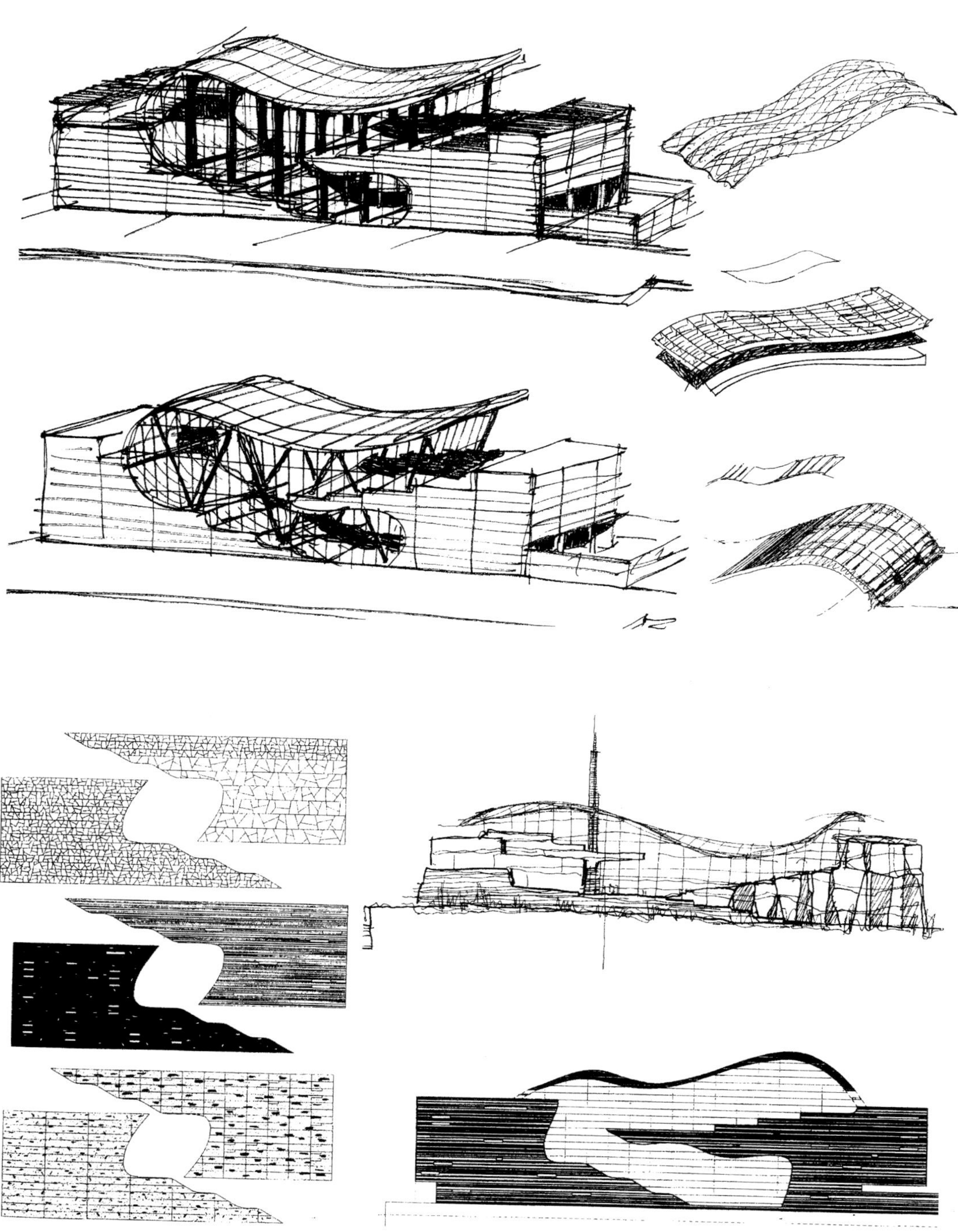

Early concept drawings by Doug Streeter.

Top: Analysis of the building's skin and interior.

Concept sketches by Doug Streeter demonstrating the evolution of the scheme.

View of the model.

Top left and right: Cross sections through the building.

Bottom: View of the aquarium with the car park in the foreground.

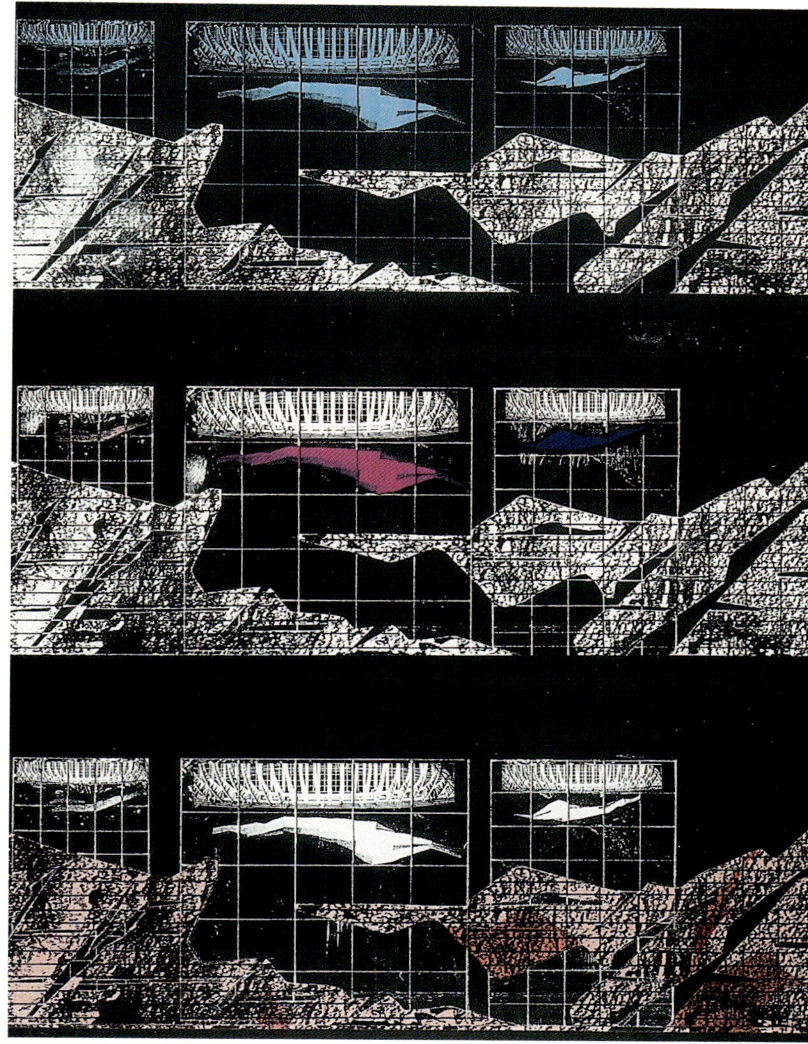

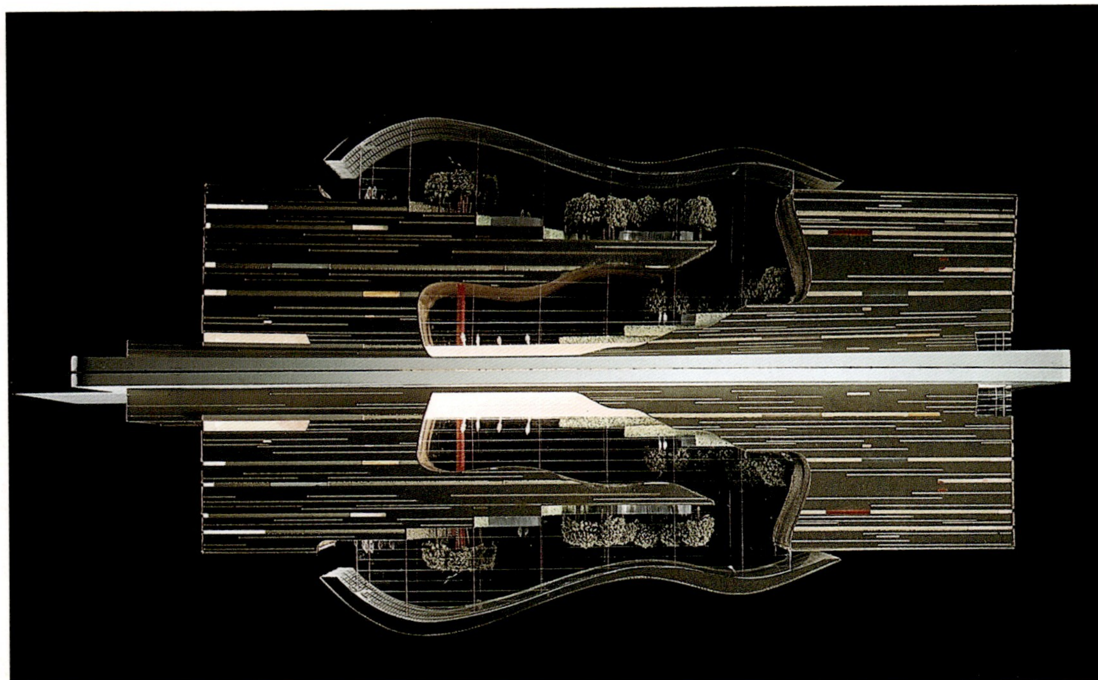

View showing the added Antarctic pavilion, which would be floated into place and added without disruption to the construction process.

Top: Model shot before the inclusion of the Antarctic pavilion, the scheme's final phase.

Right: Western views of the model.

GREENWICH PROMENADE

PIER + RESTAURANTS

Greenwich Promenade has its roots in a body of recommendations made by Terry Farrell & Partners in 1994 arising from the practice's Royal Parks study. In the report, TFP proposed an axial progression linking the grand architectural composition of the Queen's House and park with the River Thames. A restored river landing stage was the starting point, or 'front door', which led to the unfolding of a series of great public spaces.

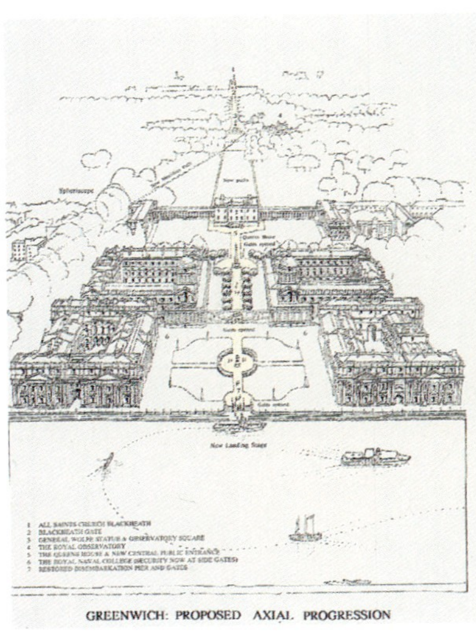

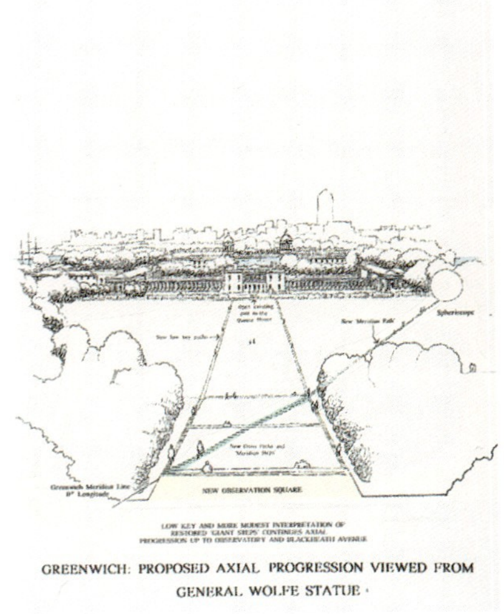

Bottom left to right: Illustrations to the Royal Parks review (see pp 270–71). TFP's proposals show how the approach to Greenwich's great complex – Britain's Versailles – has been obscured. With TFP's pier and Rick Mather's new visitor's centre, Greenwich's approach and formal arrangements become clear, creating a 'front door' for the millions of tourists who visit the site each year.

Top left: As a gateway building, Greenwich Promenade's ground-scraping form recalls that of Kowloon Station.

Top right: The scheme within the planning of Greenwich. The World Heritage Site contains the works of Jones, Vanbrugh, Hawksmoor and Wren, and commemorates great astronomical and maritime events.

Greenwich Promenade fits into a tradition of much loved small-scale buildings that the practice has completed during its history. The Bayswater and Covent Garden Clifton nurseries, the interior of the Crafts Council gallery, Henley Royal Regatta headquarters and a handful of private houses have become landmarks as rewarding as – though in a different way from – the grander projects of Charing Cross and Vauxhall Cross.

Greenwich Promenade is also the latest in a line of Thames-side buildings designed by TFP – starting with Terry Farrell's first built work, the Blackwall Tunnel Ventilation Towers, and continuing with Charing Cross, Vauxhall Cross, the Three Quays Hotel near the Tower of London and Lots Road Power Station.

The aim of the scheme was to create a gateway to Greenwich from the river within the West Greenwich Conservation Area, which faces Island Gardens across the river on the Isle of Dogs. A World Heritage Site, the conservation area encompasses such historic landmarks as the Royal Naval College, Cutty Sark Gardens, the Royal Park, Greenwich Observatory and The Queen's House.

The new building is sited just north of the *Cutty Sark* tea clipper and Sir Francis Chichester's *Gipsy Moth* yacht. Monument Gardens provides a leafy backdrop to the south, with Pepys's House beyond; Brunel's Portal Rotunda, the entrance to a foot tunnel under the river linking Cutty Sark Gardens with Island Gardens, is to the west.

Although accommodating some of London's most prestigious attractions, the site takes little advantage of the riverfront as a whole and currently provides only modest facilities for fare-paying ferry passengers. The TFP-designed scheme will optimize the potential of the site, as well as being a primary orientation and destination point for locals and visitors.

In practical terms, this involves the construction of new pierhead amenities, including a restaurant and four ferry-ticket offices, as well as the coordinated design of railings, steps, ramps, signage, street furniture and lighting. Greenwich Promenade will revitalize the site, signalling an end to its role as an isolated enclave for ferry users.

The main focus of Greenwich Promenade is two lightweight glazed pavilions connected by a continuous roof. The opening between the pavilions creates a partially covered piazza that frames and encloses panoramic views of the River Thames and the gardens of Pepys's House. The softly rounded form of the pavilions is designed to encourage free circulation of people around all sides, enhancing existing connections and routes through the site. This layout provides 1741 square metres of public open space – 1196 square metres more than that provided by the existing building. The height of the pavilions was dictated by the need for them to be easily perceived from the river without obscuring historic views. After careful study, the height was set at two storeys, which offered the advantage of wider views from the upper level. Planned external balconies and seating areas will enhance the liveliness and vibrancy of the architecture.

The forms and palette of materials are nautical in spirit, referencing Greenwich's maritime heritage. A continuous aluminium horizontal 'skirt' around the glass perimeter will be supported on a lightweight steel frame. The external cladding will be anodized aluminium curtain walling with clear glazing, while the solid elements to each pavilion

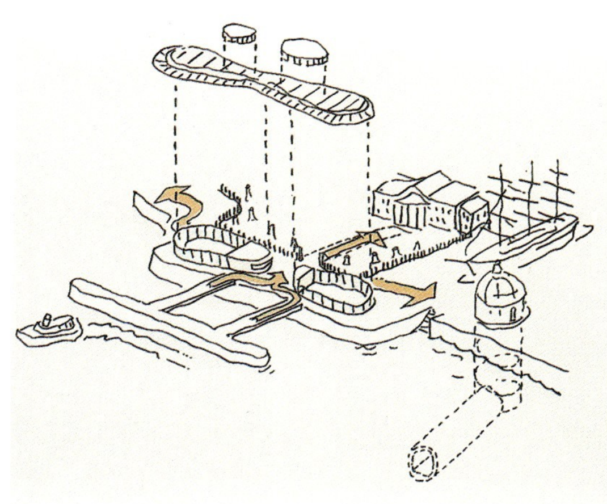

The pier is a gateway.

The portal roof connects two pavilions containing ticket offices, restaurants and a café that will accommodate passersby and ferry users.

The pavilion in relation to adjacent landmarks: the *Cutty Sark*, the cupola to Brunel's foot tunnel and the *Gipsy Moth*.

Upward view explaining the structure and interior.

Bottom: Perspective view.

will be clad in white American oak. Terraces will be constructed from timber boarding on cantilevered steel supports with handrails of clear glass and steel.

The designs for Greenwich Promenade also include a wider masterplan proposal to provide a pedestrian route linking the pier site with Pepys's House through Monument Gardens. The route will start from a gate in the listed Monument Garden railings adjacent to Greenwich Promenade.

The design of Greenwich Promenade looks to an architectural language that shows respect for its stately surroundings. Terry Farrell has said that 'An architect's task is to develop form which follows function but also form following context. It is not a question of choosing between the two, but of doing both.' An open mind, signified by a diversity of architectural approaches, is a prerequisite to successful interpretation of a client's brief and to producing work that is in sympathy with its location as well as its historical and social context. Architects are confronted with many different architectural challenges. In Terry Farrell's words, 'To try to produce an architecture which follows only one rule, whether constructional or functional, is simply escapist.'

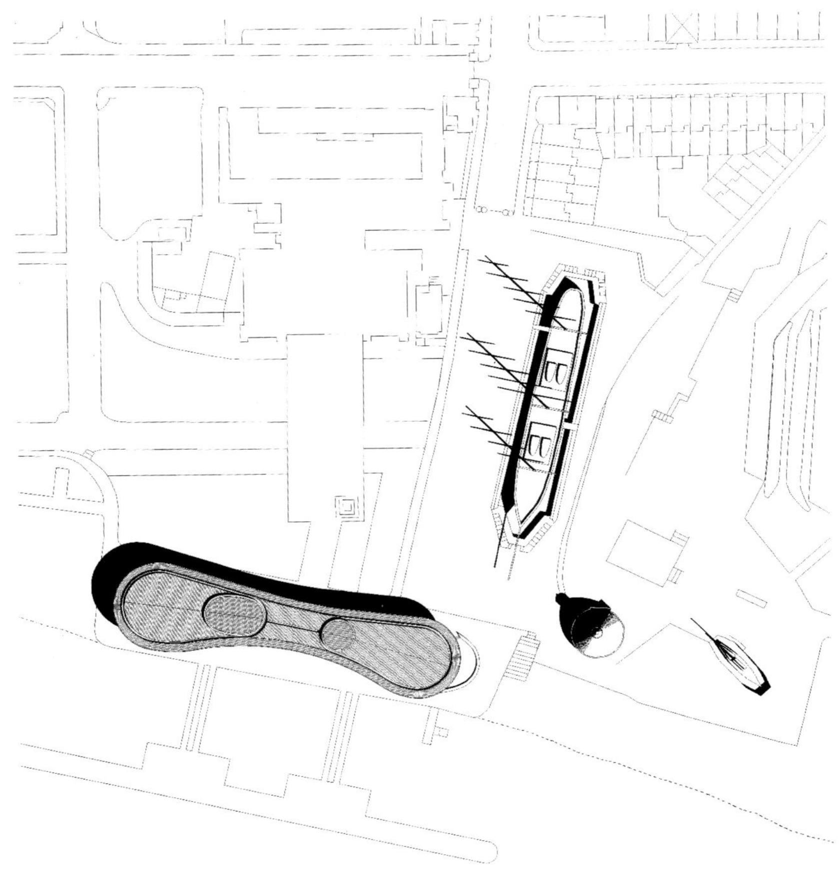

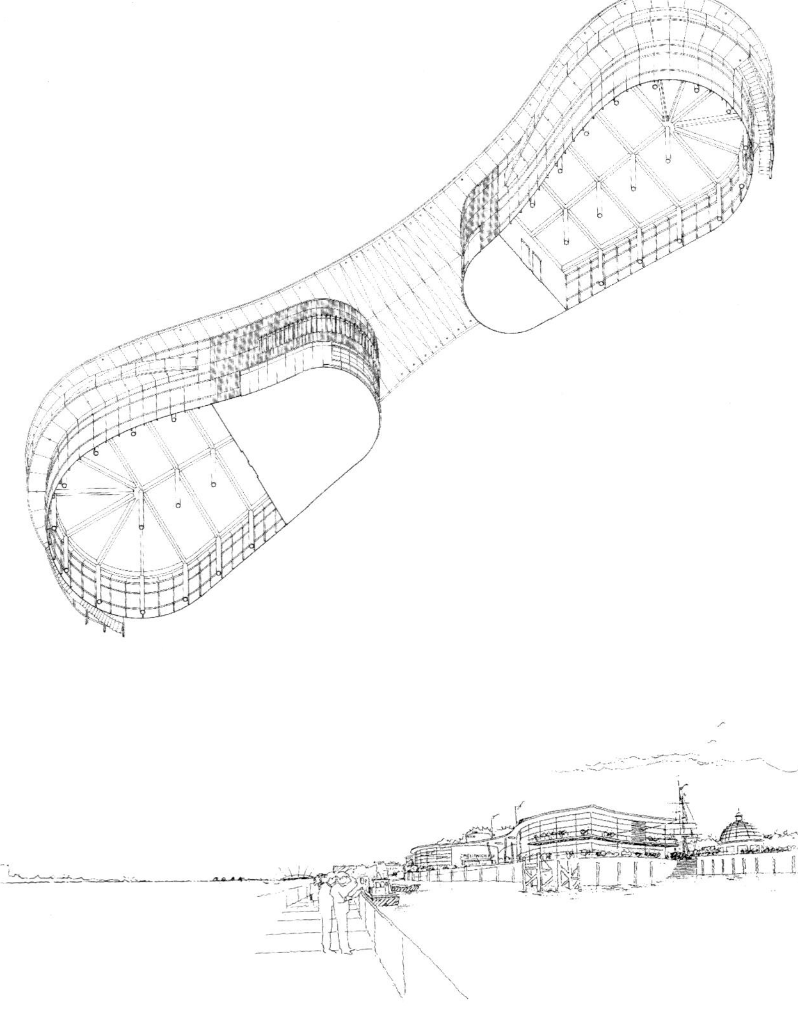

Greenwich pier acts as a portal to Monument Garden, leading to Pepys's House, the *Cutty Sark* and Greenwich beyond.

Top: Ground-floor plan. **Bottom: Context elevation.** **Opposite: Model view.**

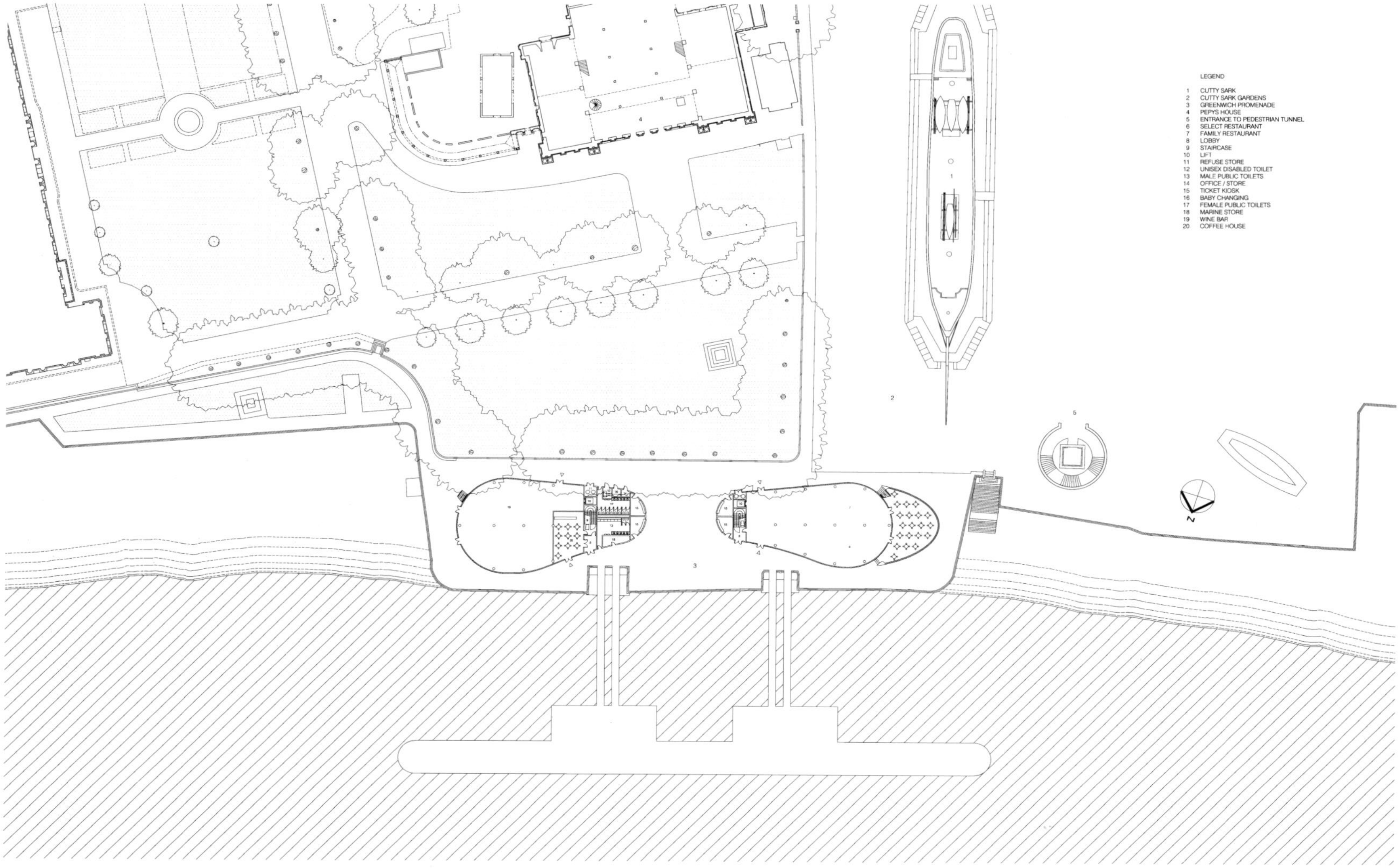

LEGEND

1 CUTTY SARK
2 CUTTY SARK GARDENS
3 GREENWICH PROMENADE
4 PEPYS HOUSE
5 ENTRANCE TO PEDESTRIAN TUNNEL
6 SELECT RESTAURANT
7 FAMILY RESTAURANT
8 LOBBY
9 STAIRCASE
10 LIFT
11 REFUSE STORE
12 UNISEX DISABLED TOILET
13 MALE PUBLIC TOILETS
14 OFFICE / STORE
15 TICKET KIOSK
16 BABY CHANGING
17 FEMALE PUBLIC TOILETS
18 MARINE STORE
19 WINE BAR
20 COFFEE HOUSE

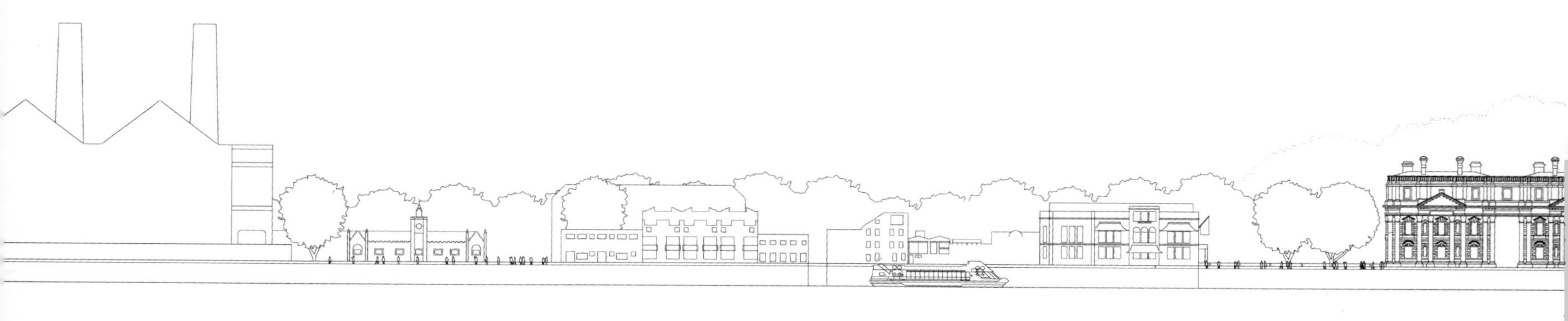

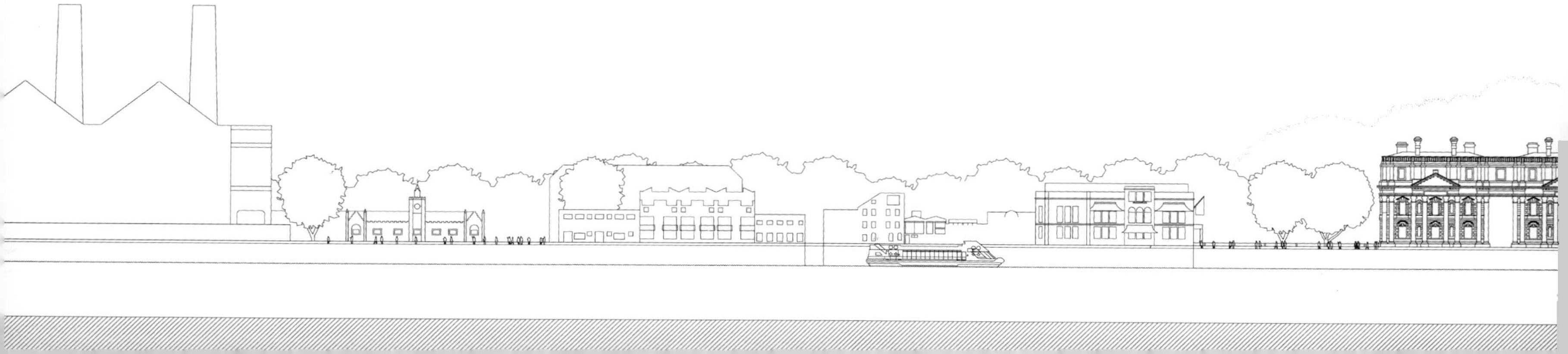

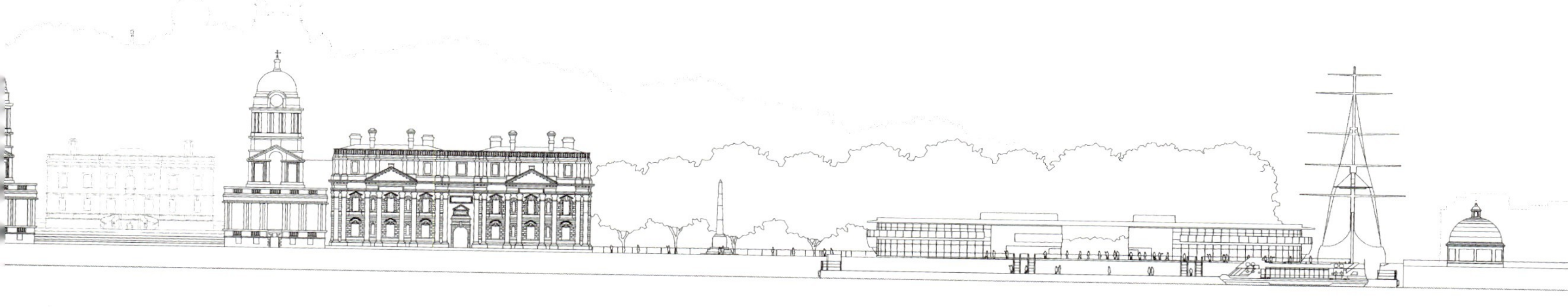

ROYAL PARKS STUDY

+ WORLD SQUARES STUDY

Top left: 18th-century view of St James's.

Bottom left: Study for the 1999 World Squares competition to bring together London's squares and ceremonial routes.

Right: World Squares study of St Martin's Place with view to Trafalgar Square.

The Royal Parks are one of London's greatest assets. These areas of trapped countryside cover 2000 hectares and provide the setting for many great buildings and institutions, including Kensington and Buckingham Palaces, London Zoo and the Albert Memorial.

Properly implemented, the parks contribute to the art of the public realm yet they are no longer linked to each other and their original grand circulation routes are given over to multiple access points. As a member of the Royal Parks Review Group, Terry Farrell campaigned during the 1990s for the large-scale design of landscape and buildings within the parks. In particular, he looked at how to make the best use of what is considered to be royal (and private) land but is now in the public realm. Just as Greenwich should be able to rival the awesome qualities of the Palace of Versailles, the other parks need to recapture their particular splendour for the benefit of all.

The future of the Royal Parks should be viewed as part of a grand strategy for London rather than made dependent on piecemeal development. The view from Primrose Hill and the Broad Walk should be linked directly with a pedestrian avenue through London Zoo. Further south, the Broad Walk should continue through Park Square and Park Crescent gardens. This would link Primrose Hill, Regent's Park and Portland Place with Piccadilly Circus, Waterloo Place and St James's Park in a tremendous route that would extend and build on John Nash's original great design.

TFP also considered a new role for the royal residences. Today, the social and political conditions that made possible the urban masterpieces of linked parks and palaces no longer prevail, but the parks and palaces continue to distinguish London from other cities. The gardens of the residences are hidden behind high walls, with the result that few people can enjoy their glory. This is the opposite of what was originally intended. Terry Farrell's simple proposal opens up the palaces and parks to public gaze. Buckingham Palace and its grounds would be integrated with the rest of central London and open for all to walk through. The suggestion is for a great promenade from The Mall, up Constitution Hill, across Hyde Park Corner, through the Wellington Arch and Decimus Burton's screen, and along Rotten Row to Kensington Palace. With the walls encircling the palace gardens removed, Buckingham Palace, St James's Palace and Kensington Palace could be largely open to the public, and galleries, museums, concert rooms, education and conference facilities could be installed in the palaces themselves. Care would be taken to preserve the privacy and security of the Royal Family.

These plans would reintegrate large areas of London, extending and building on original designs. The parks are an essential part of London's urban design: it is only through such brave physical changes that the city will develop to embrace the needs of the new century.

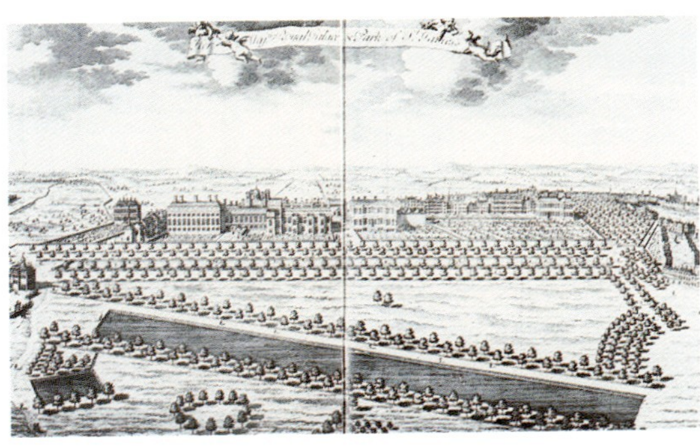

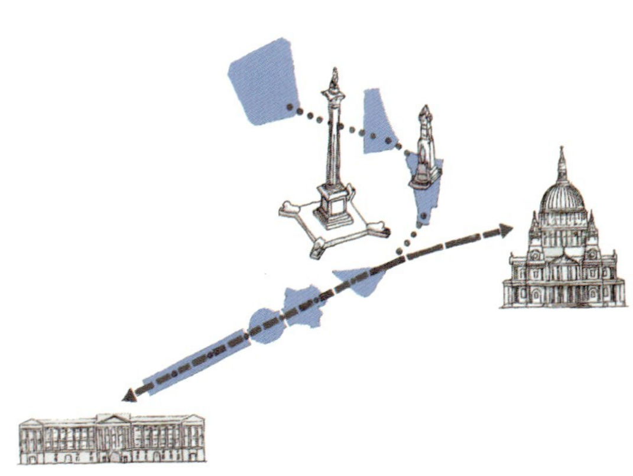

Top left: Location of London's Royal Parks in relation to the Thames.

Centre left: St James's, Hyde, Kensington and Regent's Parks connected up again by walkways to become part of a World Heritage sequence.

Centre right: Accessibility across Park Lane.

Bottom left: Two detailed proposals for part of Kensington Gardens.

Proposals for linking Green Park to Buckingham Palace with new gateways, open railings and access to Buckingham Palace Gardens at certain times of the year. St James's and the Mall are made more accessible.

Top and centre right: Completion of the Nash route through Royal Crescent to Park Crescent and Park Square. This would make Primrose Hill accessible from Regent's Park.

Bottom right: Proposals for Bushy Park.

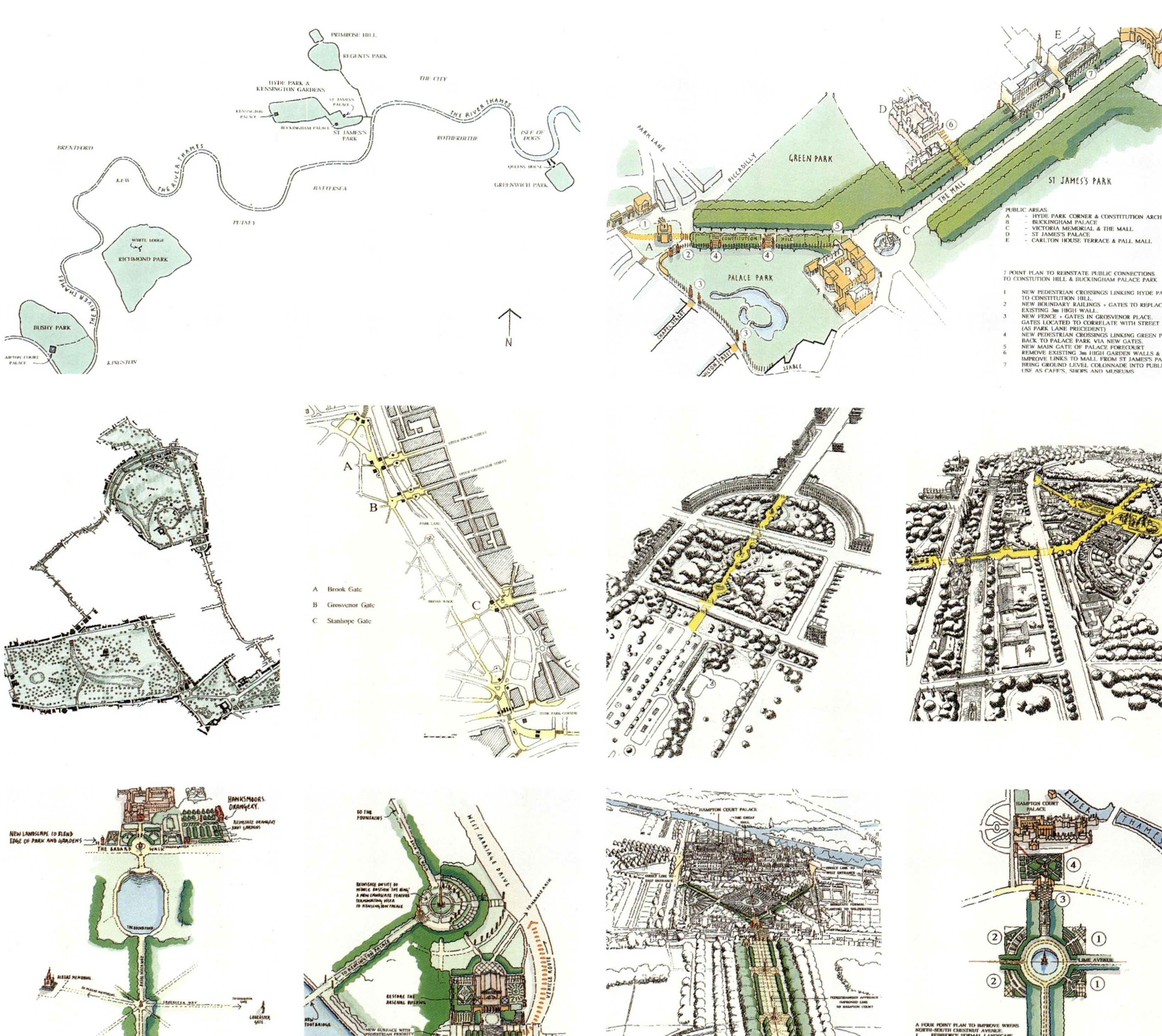

LOTS ROAD

POWER STATION + NEW HOUSING

Situated on a wide concave bend of the Thames, the Lots Road Power Station occupies a highly visible location which, after a century of industrial use, has remained largely undeveloped. Together with Battersea and Bankside, the majestic building is one of three great power stations on the Thames. The other buildings on the site – facilities for oil and gas storage, a waste transfer depot, and a Thames Water pumping station – make no aesthetic contribution to their location and, because of their use, create a physical and visual barrier between the surrounding area and the river.

The redevelopment of the power station and site will unify an important but fractured district of London with physical, social and visual permeability. It will create one of the largest covered public open streets in London and open around 600 metres of river and creek to public use for the first time in over a hundred years. The creek

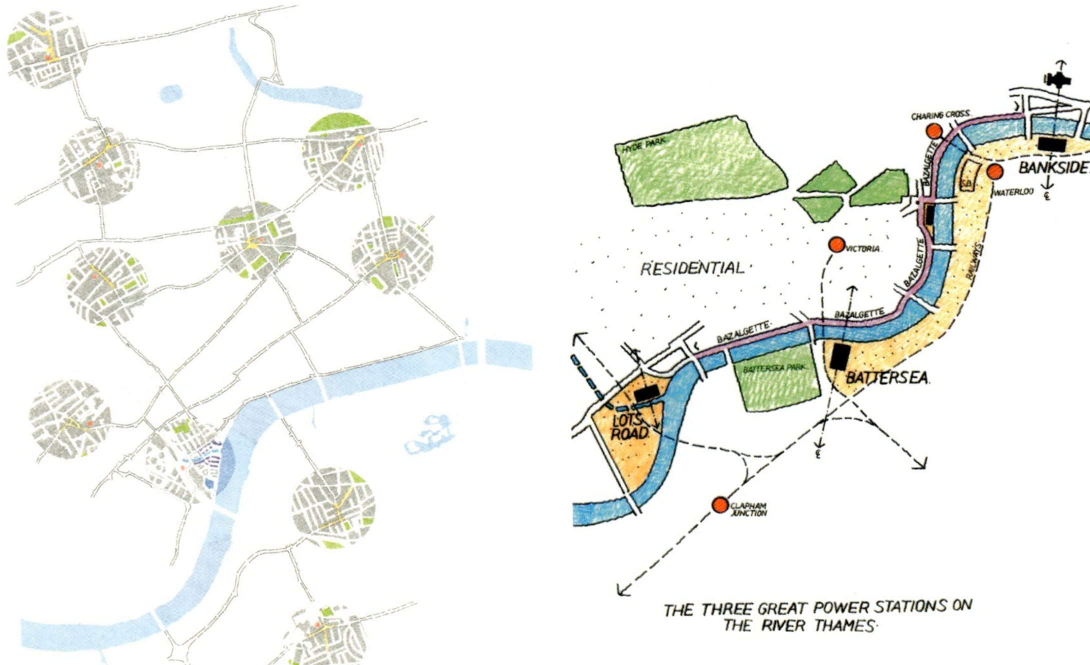

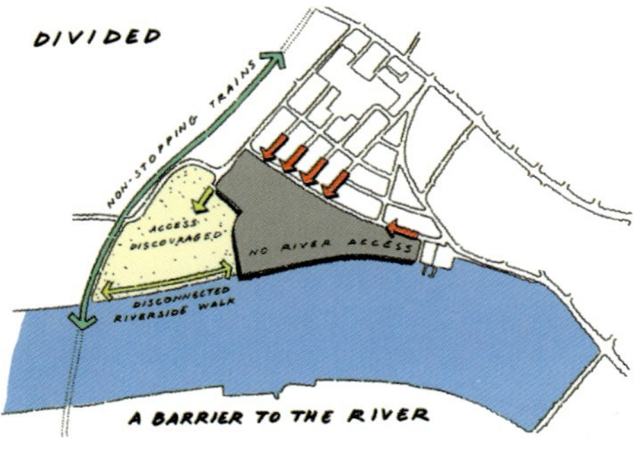

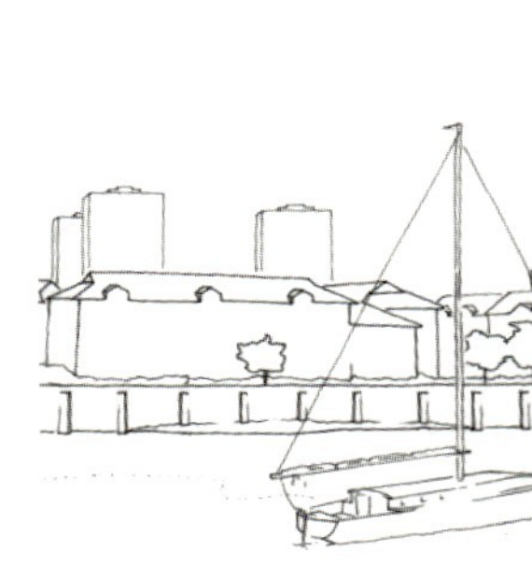

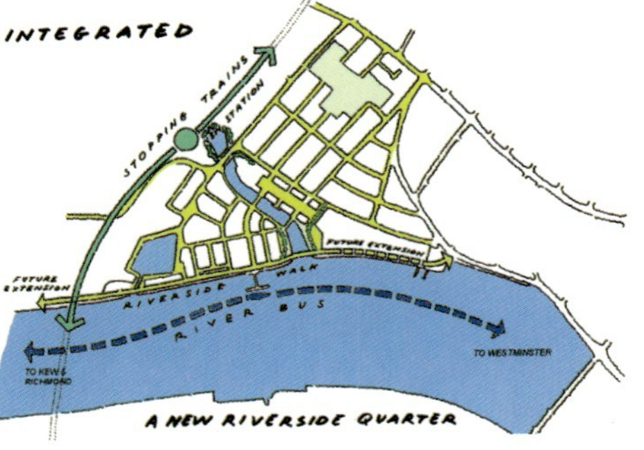

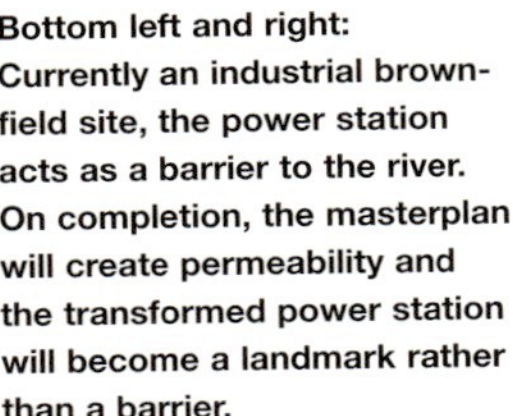

Bottom left and right: Currently an industrial brownfield site, the power station acts as a barrier to the river. On completion, the masterplan will create permeability and the transformed power station will become a landmark rather than a barrier.

Top left: Together with the adjacent developments at Imperial Wharf and Chelsea Harbour, Lots Road creates a complete new urban village, surrounded by the existing villages of South Kensington, Earl's Court, Fulham, Battersea and Clapham.

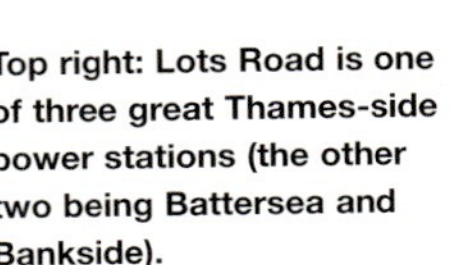

Top right: Lots Road is one of three great Thames-side power stations (the other two being Battersea and Bankside).

Panoramic view looking towards Lots Road power station from the north end of Battersea Bridge.

will become a new linear park and water garden, which will also promote new wildlife habitats.

When the power station was completed in 1904, it was the biggest generating station in the world – biggest not only in terms of size and output, but also in terms of cost, which amounted to £2.5 million. Around 135 metres long, 54 metres wide and 42 metres tall at the roof's apex, the building is colossal, and its four chimneys were, at 83 metres, the highest in Europe. Of extra significance to building historians is the fact that Lots Road was one of Britain's first steel-framed buildings. It is still used to power the Underground system.

Terry Farrell & Partners' proposals focus on the retention and conversion of the historic power station building, which will be decommissioned, decontaminated and cleared of internal plant. The shell will then be transformed into a mixed-use development comprising community uses, a doctor's surgery and dental practice, local shops, loft offices, an internal street, live-work units and private apartments. The ground level will be opened up to create permeability across the site from Lots Road to the river and creek, while the tops of the two remaining chimneys will be converted to house public viewing galleries offering spectacular views of the Thames and across London.

Two new residential towers located on either side of the creek entrance have been carefully conceived to form a powerful visual grouping with the power station. The ridge height and chimney tops of the power station determine the springing point and culmination of the 39-storey north tower which in turn generates the height of the 25-storey south tower. The slim towers are around four times smaller in plan and around 25 per cent lower in height than a typical office tower. Containing a mix of apartments with penthouses under sloping glass roofs, the towers' east-west orientation ensures optimum views.

The southern end of the development is long and thin, following the line of the creek. Residential buildings, arranged in sequential blocks to continue the permeability from Lots Road, follow the creek's curve, creating a broad public frontage to the new water garden.

Social housing is principally arranged in a new low-rise building adjacent to the power station, carefully designed to mitigate the scale of the existing building, act as a counterpoint to the northern tower and create a courtyard at the eastern end of the power station. This building also contains a crèche and a local museum. The riverside scheme will add an expanded village centre to a mixed-use urban quarter within walking distance of local transport, rail network and bus routes.

Top left: TFP's transformed power station creates one of the largest covered public open streets in London.

Centre left: View of the existing building.

Top centre: The generator room that powered the London Underground.

Centre right: CAD image of the converted power station.

Top right: The power station is an integral part of London's transport heritage. Poster from 1930 by E. McKnight Kauffer.

Bottom: Context section.

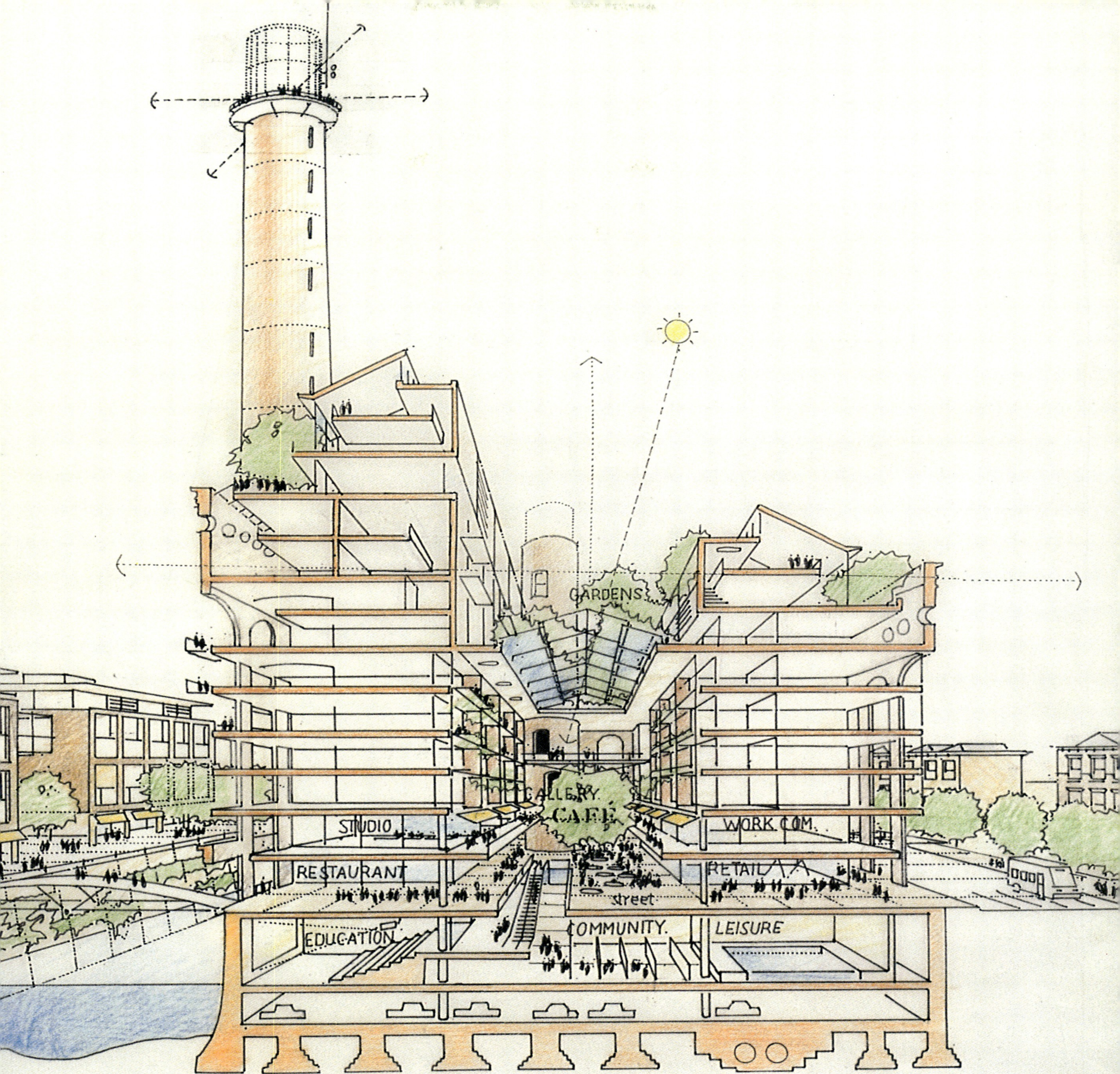

Drawing by Aidan Potter showing cross section.

Top: Aerial perspective from the south.

Centre left: A cluster of tall buildings exists alongside the proposed Lots Road towers, forming a gateway at the elbow of the Thames.

Centre right: Concept sketch by Terry Farrell.

Bottom: Rotated views. Like a dancing couple, the pair of towers creates a dynamic form when seen from different viewpoints.

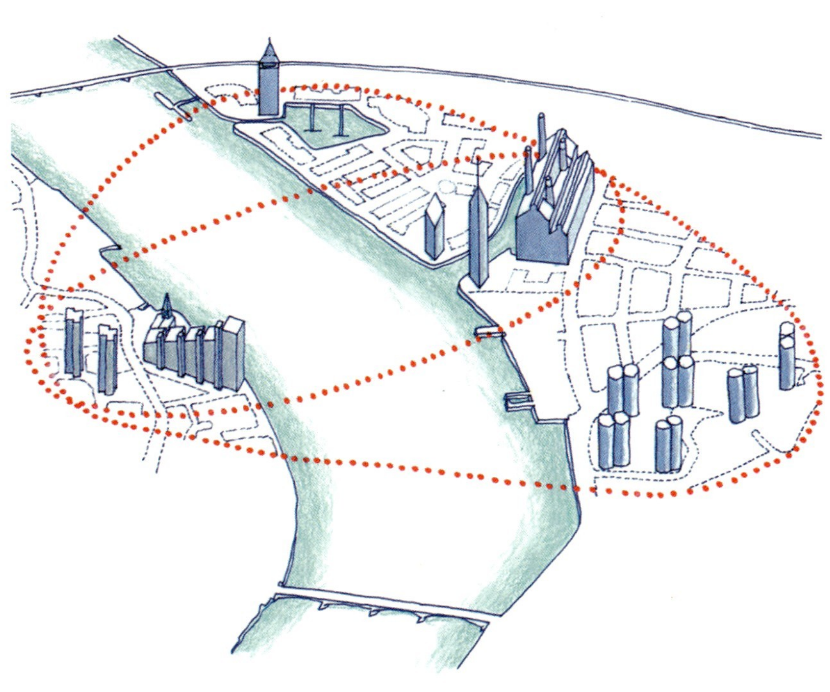

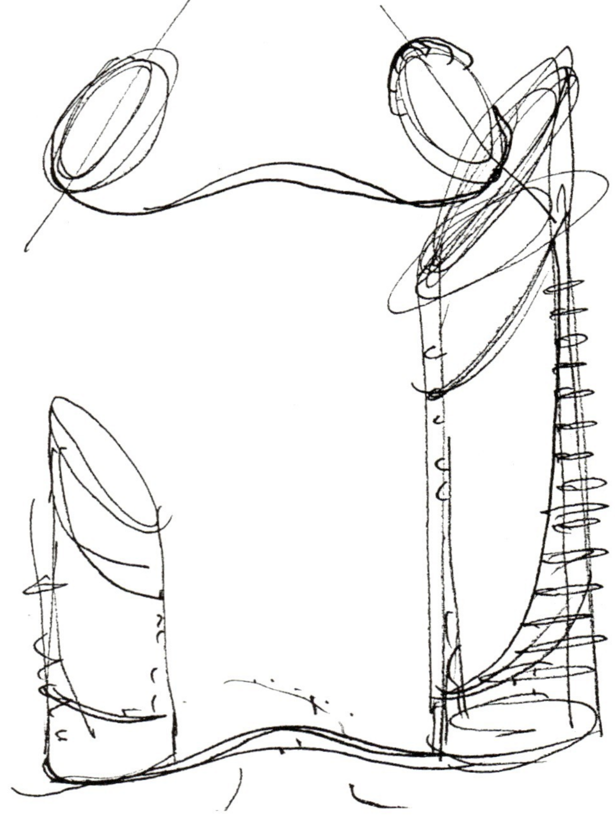

Tower-top studies.

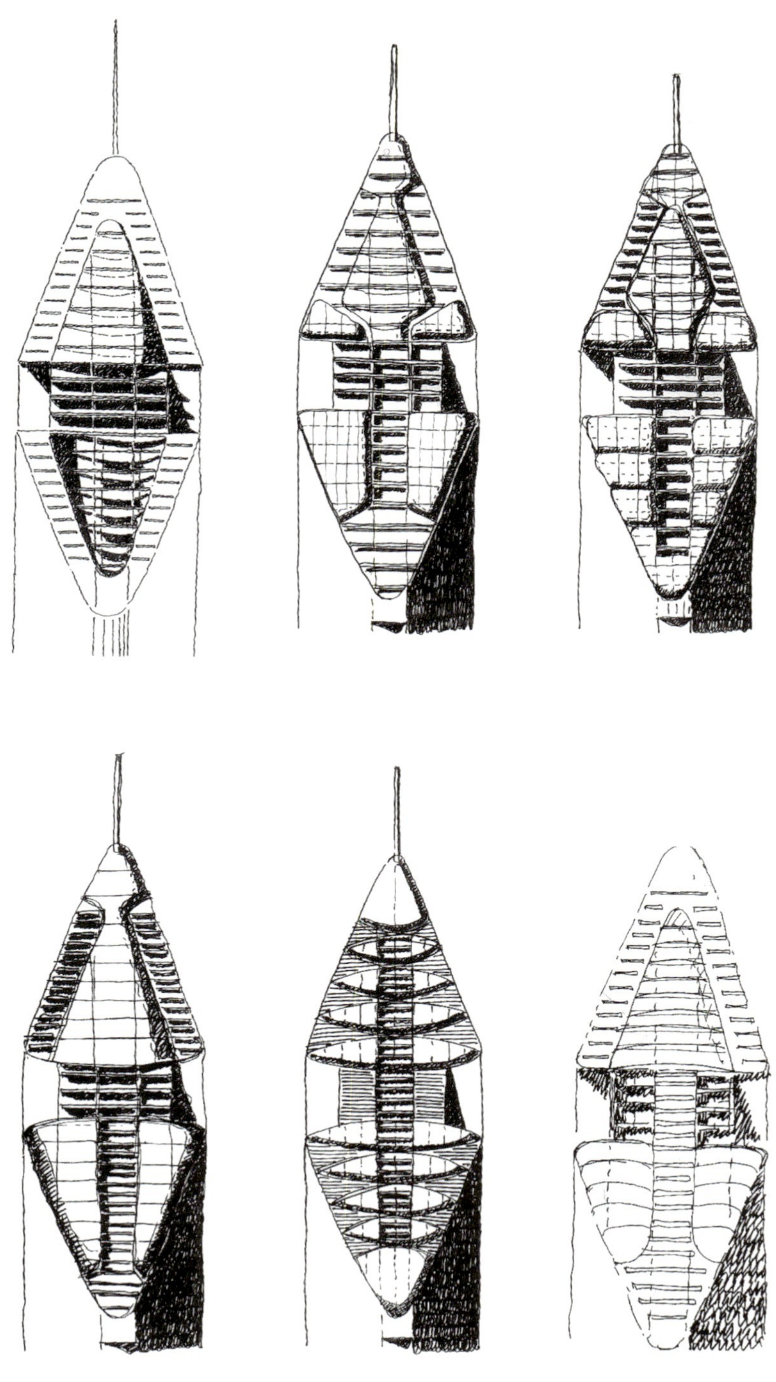

Tower study.

Top: Sketch by Aidan Potter showing sectional study of typical bay.

Bottom left: Terrace study.

Bottom right: Creek study.

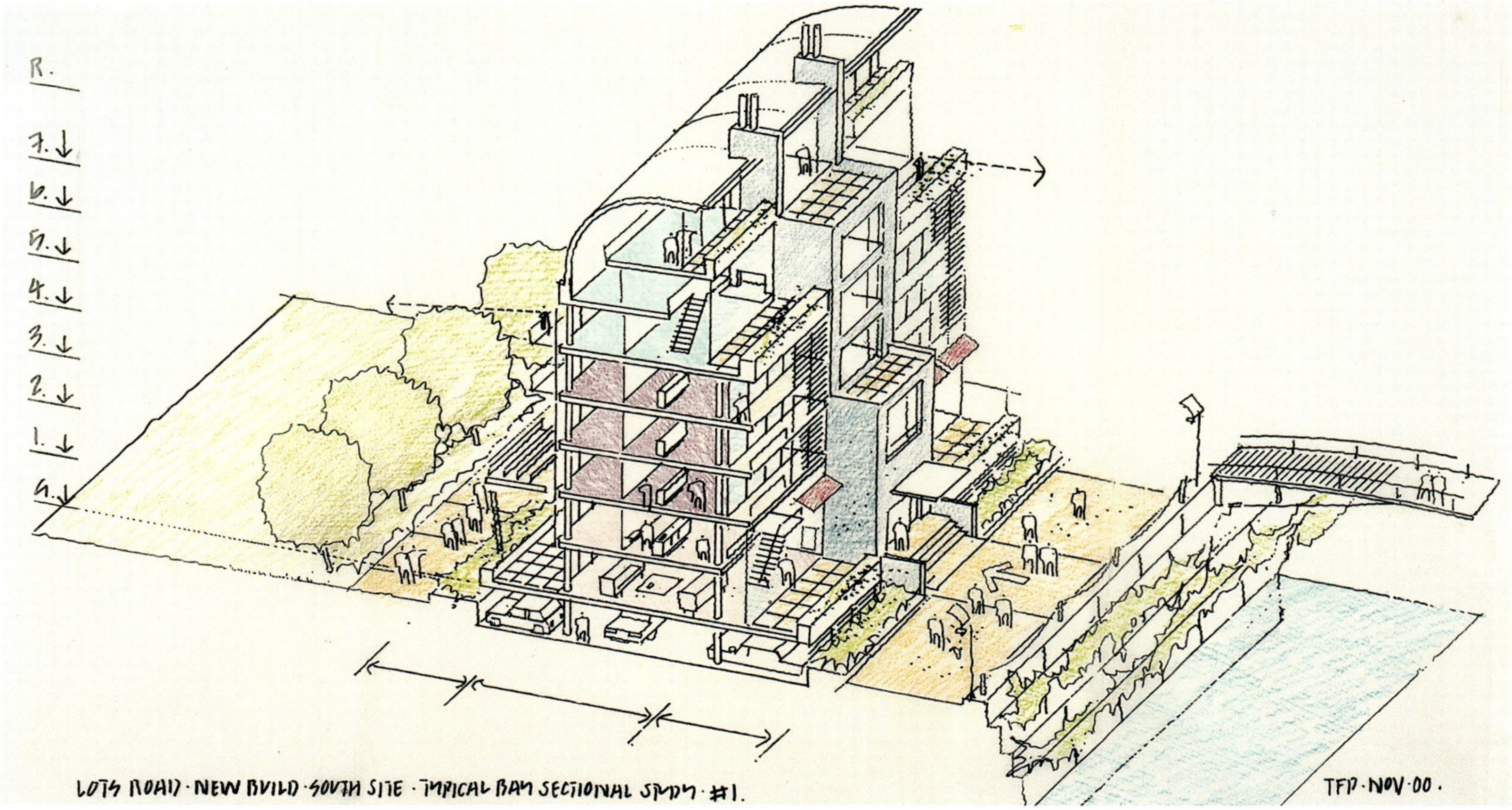

R.
7.
6.
5.
4.
3.
2.
1.
G.

LOTS ROAD · NEW BUILD · SOUTH SITE · TYPICAL BAY SECTIONAL STUDY · #1.

TFP · NOV · 00.

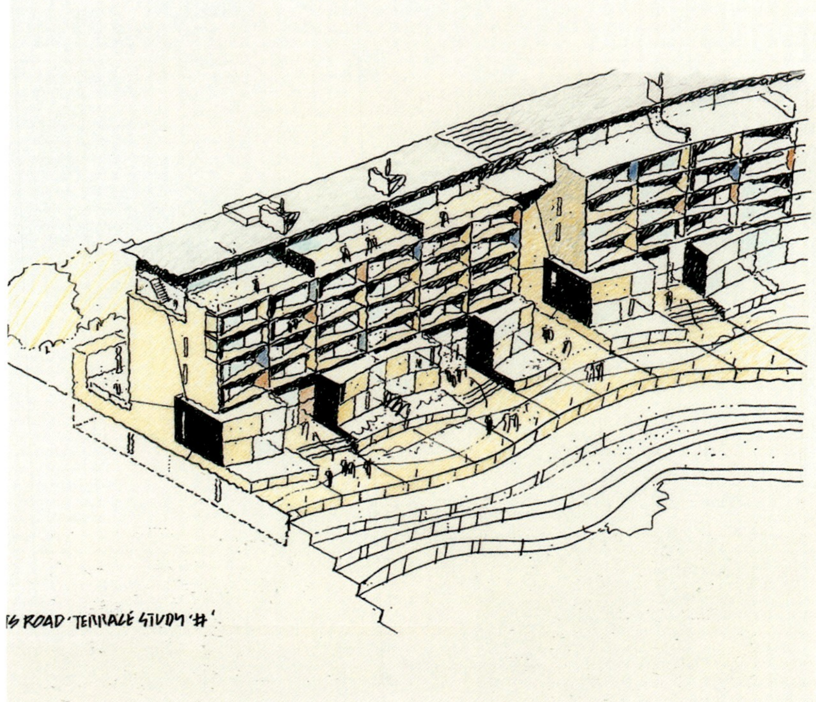

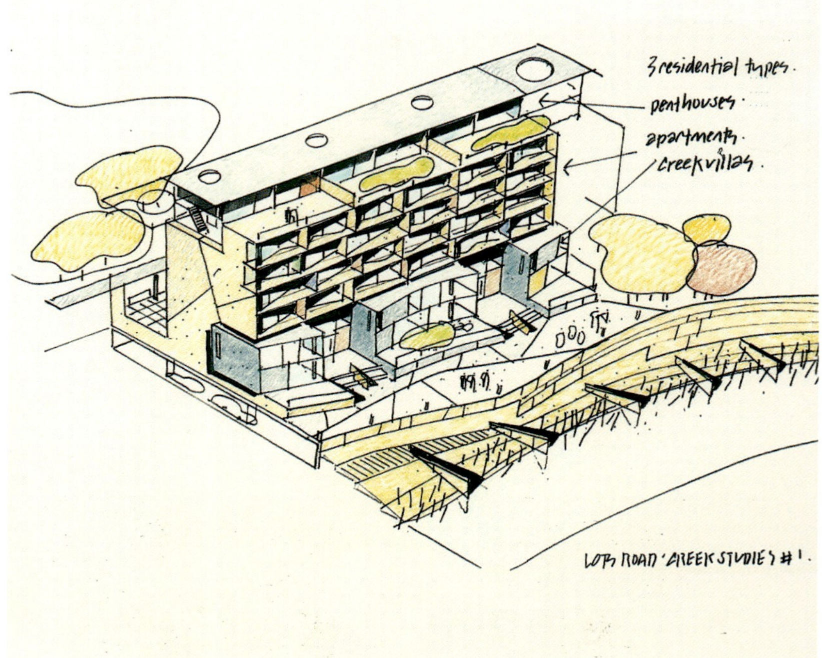

Top left: Concept sketch by Terry Farrell showing a sequence of water gardens.

Bottom: Sketch by Charles Jencks showing water garden proposal for the creek at Lots Road.

Centre: Sketch proposals for landforms and water gardens.

Top right: Landscape study for the areas surrounding the power station.

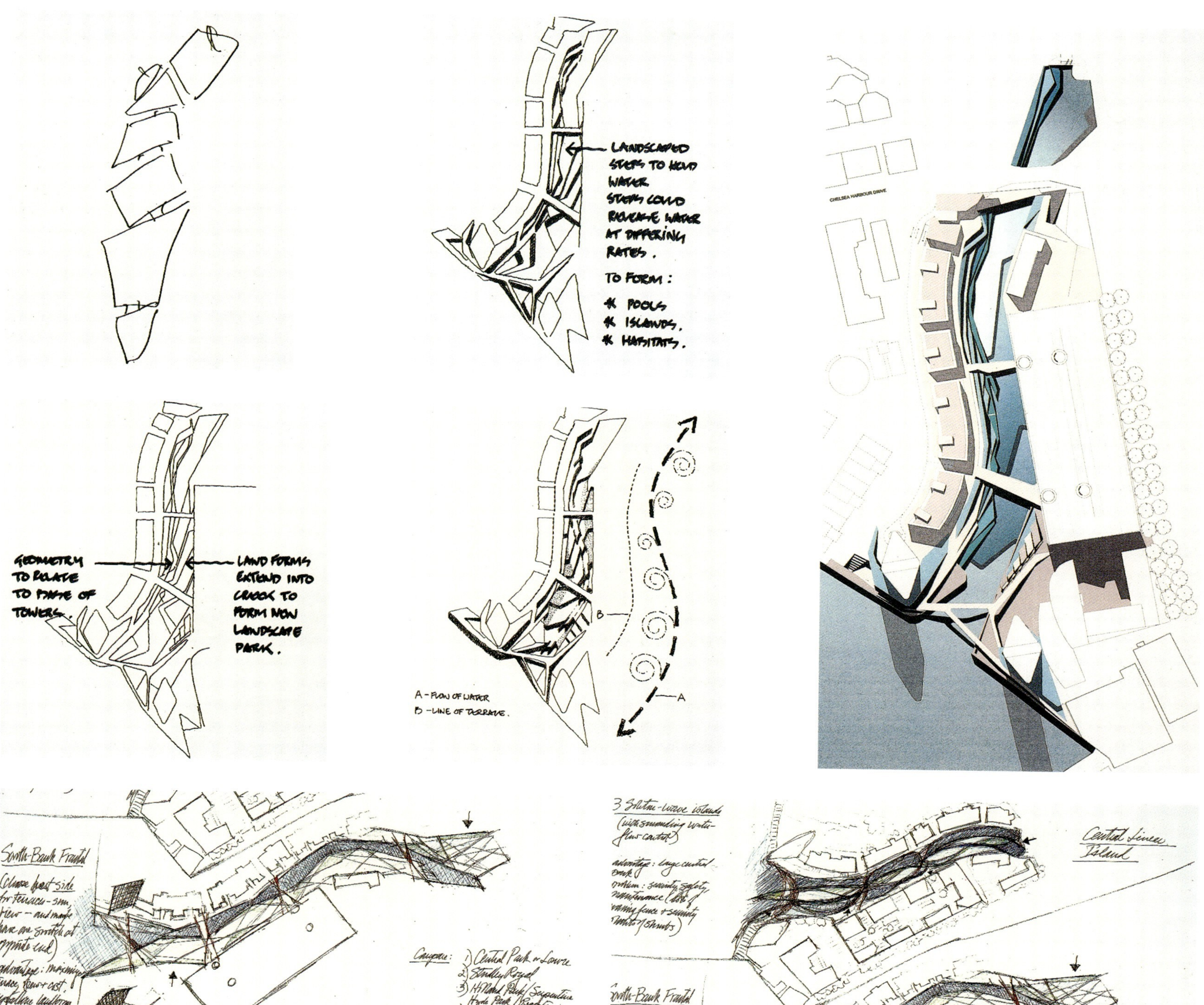

Photograph of study model.

HOME OFFICE HEADQUARTERS

The Marsham Street towers, situated parallel to the River Thames in Victoria – and infamously nicknamed 'the three ugly sisters' – have been creating a negative impact on the area for the past three decades. Built for the Department of the Environment between 1963 and 1971 to the designs of Eric Bedford and Robert Atkinson & Partners, Marsham Street was described by the former Conservative environment secretary Chris Patten as 'a building which deeply depresses the spirit'.

Balanced on top of a gigantic podium, occupying a two-hectare site, the three linear slab blocks rise 68 metres above street level. Although adjacent to conservation areas, listed buildings and historic landmarks such as Westminster Abbey, St John's Smith Square, the Houses of Parliament and Lambeth Palace, the towers have an impermeable aspect that suffocated signs of the area's historical importance. They have languished since 1997, when they were condemned to demolition. The Department of the Environment moved to new headquarters in Victoria, freeing up the site for a new Home Office building.

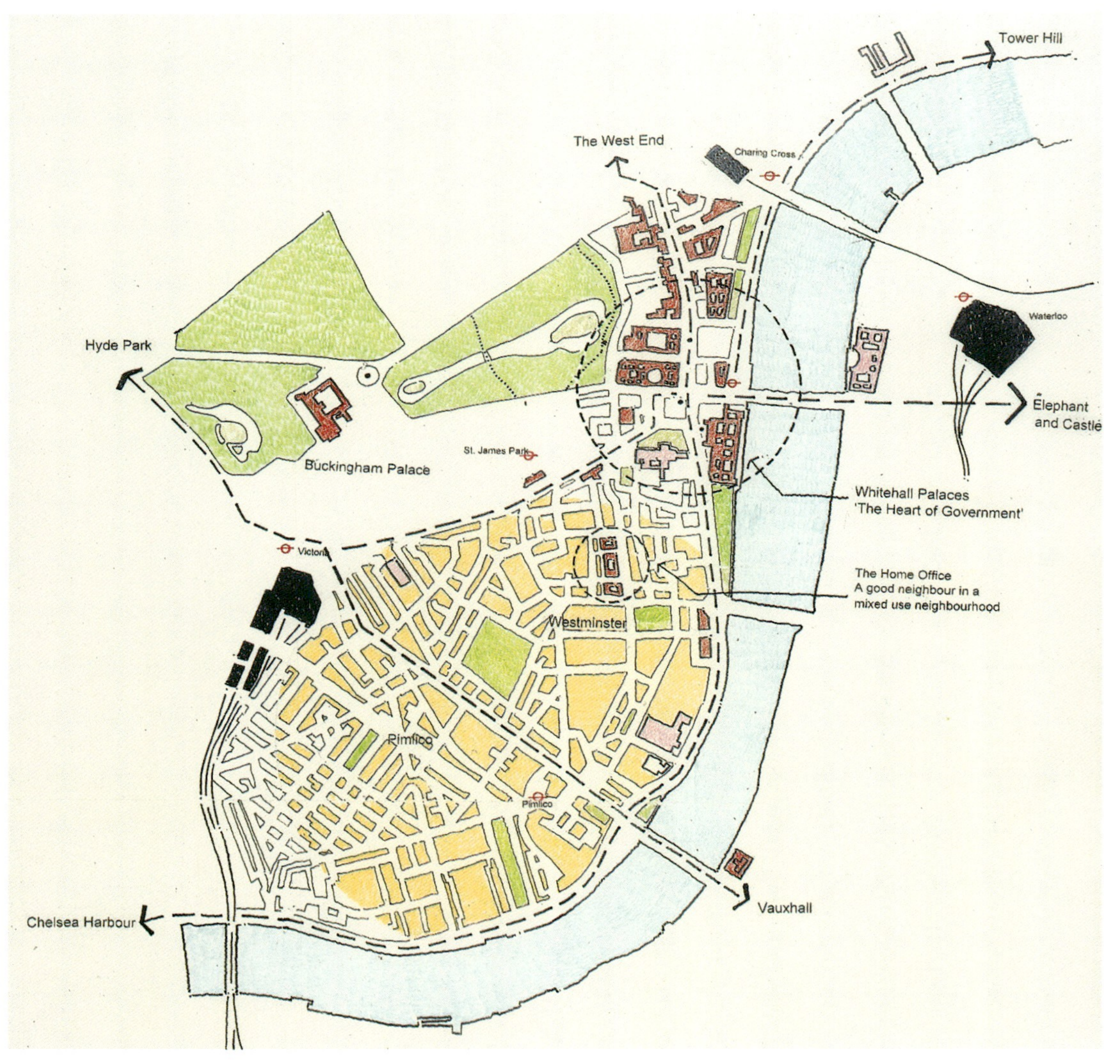

The new Home Office is located within an urban district of Westminster, a neighbour to schools, hospitals, housing and listed buildings. Its setting is quite distinct from Whitehall's monocultural environment, a highly specialized arena of state buildings that includes the Royal Horseguards, Banqueting Hall and Palace of Westminster. The Department of Environment was built in the 1960s at the scale of the Whitehall buildings. Its legacy is an urban planning exercise that inserts a non-pompous 'gentle giant' headquarters building into the neighbourhood.

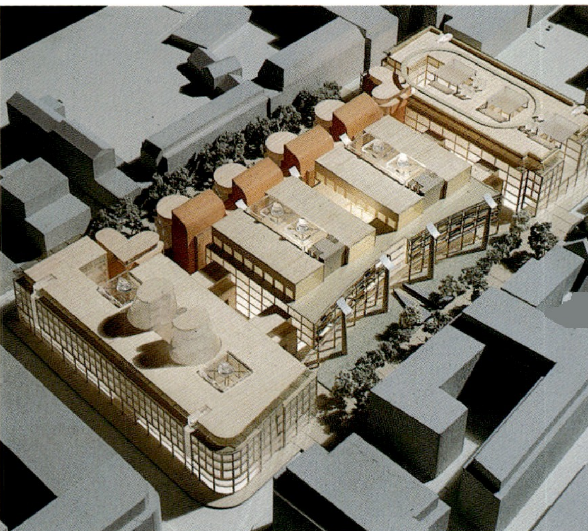

Bottom: TFP's proposals for the site predated the Home Office decision to occupy the building, demonstrating that studies of the urban form can lead to a final design even with the occupier unknown – a good example of urban design leading architectural form.

Top: The 'gentle giant' concept informed TFP's study for the Hong Kong and Shanghai Bank's City headquarters, a permeable building in Gresham Street that was designed to be a good neighbour.

Various architects submitted proposals for Marsham Street, but Terry Farrell & Partners was involved in the redevelopment of the site from its inception in 1991, when the practice prepared outline masterplan principles for British Land. There is much continuity between the urban intentions outlined in this early scheme and TFP's current proposal.

The 1991 masterplan focuses on reinstating the area's historical pattern, which was swept away by the giant linear block of the current buildings. The idea was to tie the site back into its surroundings by creating a number of separate buildings that would remake lost street frontages and public spaces. The early scheme also acknowledged the restricted public circulation offered by the existing buildings and planned a network of pedestrian routes through the site. It proposed that the site should support a diversity of uses, with retail and commercial functions being linked by public spaces. The low-rise massing of the proposed buildings reflected a 1991 study by Arup Associates, which concluded that the existing nineteen-storey towers were so wasteful of space that a proposed replacement building only eight storeys high could accommodate 50 per cent more people.

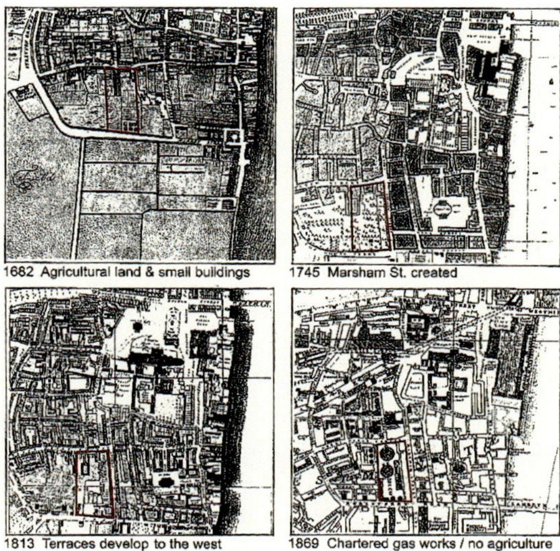

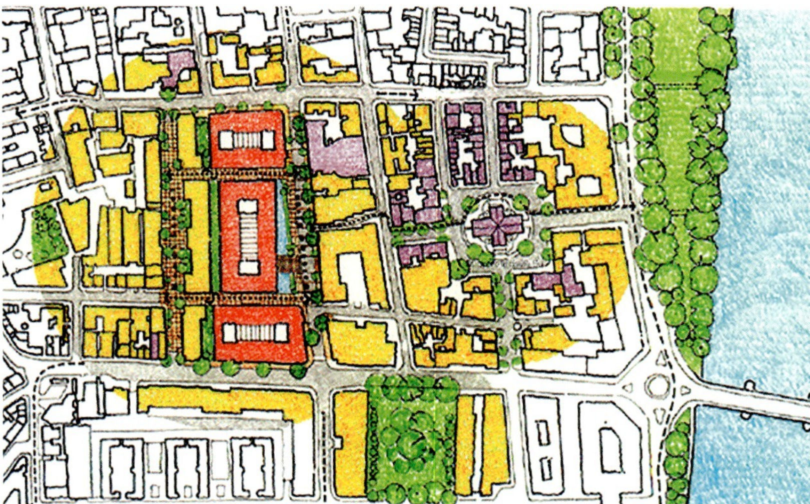

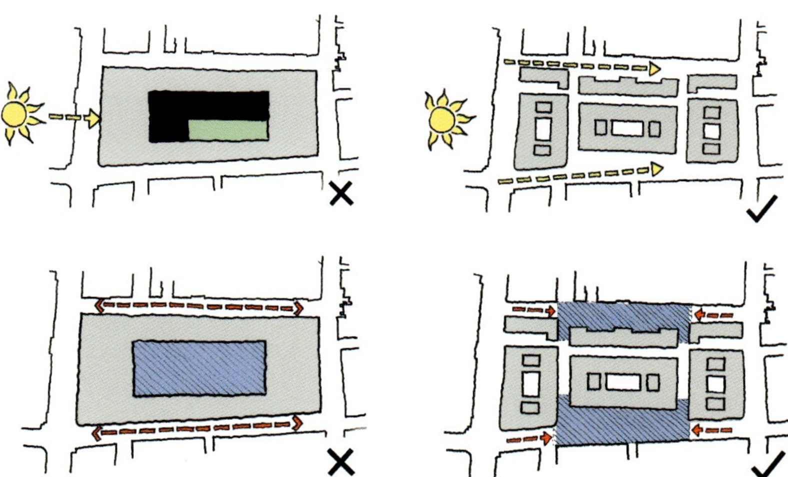

Bottom left: Concept plan.

Top: The 'three ugly sisters' are to be seen at the top right of the image.

Bottom right: The site envelope is planned to be permeable and open to sunlight.

Top: Evolution of the site.

In September 1994, TFP was commissioned by the Department of the Environment to prepare an illustrative scheme to accompany the outline planning application. This followed a massing study completed by Fitzroy Robinson Partnership of 1992. TFP's brief was to assess the parameters set by the level of floor space and mix of uses, the building envelope and the development principles. The practice tested these parameters to see whether they provided a robust and flexible programme for working up a detailed scheme. It confirmed that the development proposed in the application could be achieved and that it offered scope for innovative design solutions. TFP saw the commission as an opportunity to test theories of sustainability at one of the few inner-city sites large enough to permit it.

In January 1995, a model by TFP went on show at the Houses of Parliament, alongside the bulk and massing studies by Fitzroy Robinson. The new design differed from Fitzroy Robinson's in moving the open space that had previously been placed at the centre of the scheme to the western and eastern edges, bringing increased benefit to the public. TFP's proposal was noted by Westminster City Council for its low-energy-consuming, mixed-use content.

October 1996 saw the launch of an international competition for the design of the site, which was won by the Italian Gabriele Tagliaventi. Earlier bids also involved IM Pei, BDP and, latterly, MacCormac Jamieson Prichard. In April 1997, outline planning permission was granted for the demolition of the existing buildings and for the mixed-use redevelopment incorporating office, residential and retail elements.

In 1998, TFP – working within the framework of the existing outline planning permission and statement of development principles – produced a revised scheme to accommodate the Home Office. The scheme allowed for the accommodation of 3000 staff on one site, whereas the department is

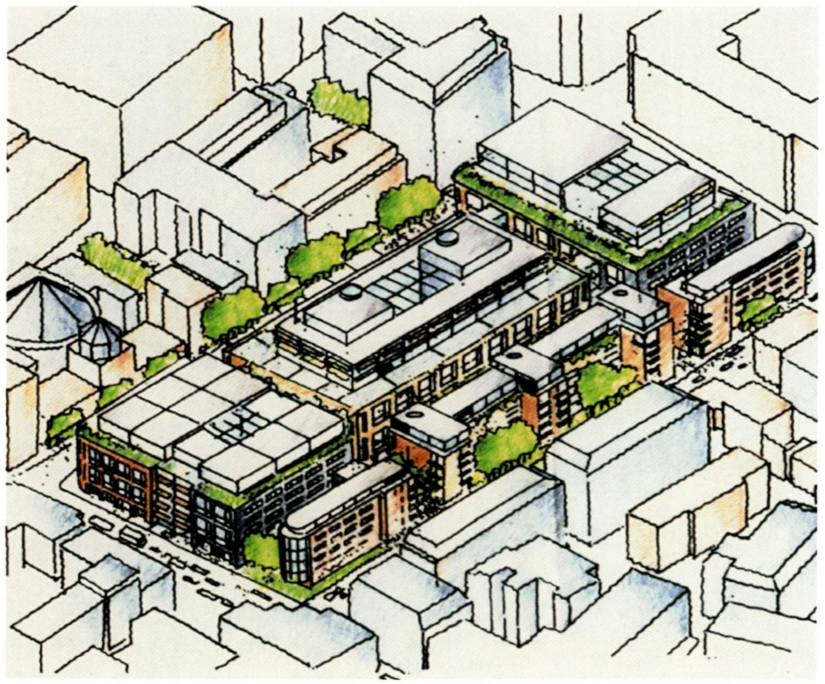

Axonometric from the north west by Aidan Potter.

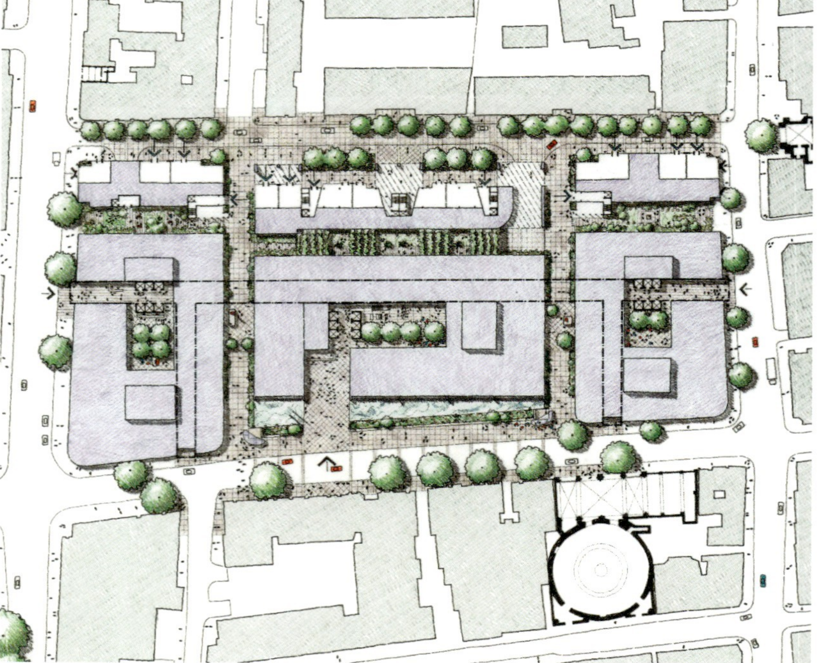

Urban design site plan. Permeable streets, new squares and mixed-use accommodation harmoniously sit within the adjacent listed buildings and street patterns.

currently housed on six sites. Westminster City Council was encouraged by this approach and acknowledged that the scheme complied with outline planning consent.

After receiving a positive response from Westminster Council planning department and English Heritage, TFP developed its 1998 proposal for its final submission in March 2000. While retaining the main features of its original scheme, the new submission made substantial improvements to the elevations and landscaping. In August 2000, Home Secretary Jack Straw named Anne's Gate Property as the preferred bidder, with TFP as lead architect.

TFP's new masterplan for Marsham Street addresses the transition between the existing built forms surrounding the site and the new buildings. The essence of the scheme is to provide a long-term solution for a government headquarters building that uses the latest thinking about urban design to restore an area to its original diversity. The proposals aspire to create a vibrant civic community with a strong sense of place. The components are there: pedestrian connectivity; a tangible public realm with open spaces that encourage people to commune and communicate; mixed-use planning that promotes inclusiveness; and high-quality architectural design.

At the centre of the masterplan are three linked low-rise buildings comprising a central block and two 'bookend' pavilions linked by glazed bridges. The pavilions, which provide access to Horseferry Road to the south and Great Peter Street to the north, step down at the ends, allowing the central Marsham Street elevation to relate in scale to the neighbouring Georgian terraces. The central block includes a conspicuous public entrance, framed by a simple stone portico supported on stone piers and dignified by a five-storey-high glass screen and grand public space. Juxtaposed with the grandeur of Marsham Street's civic-style forecourt, the more informal Monck Street elevation – which will be

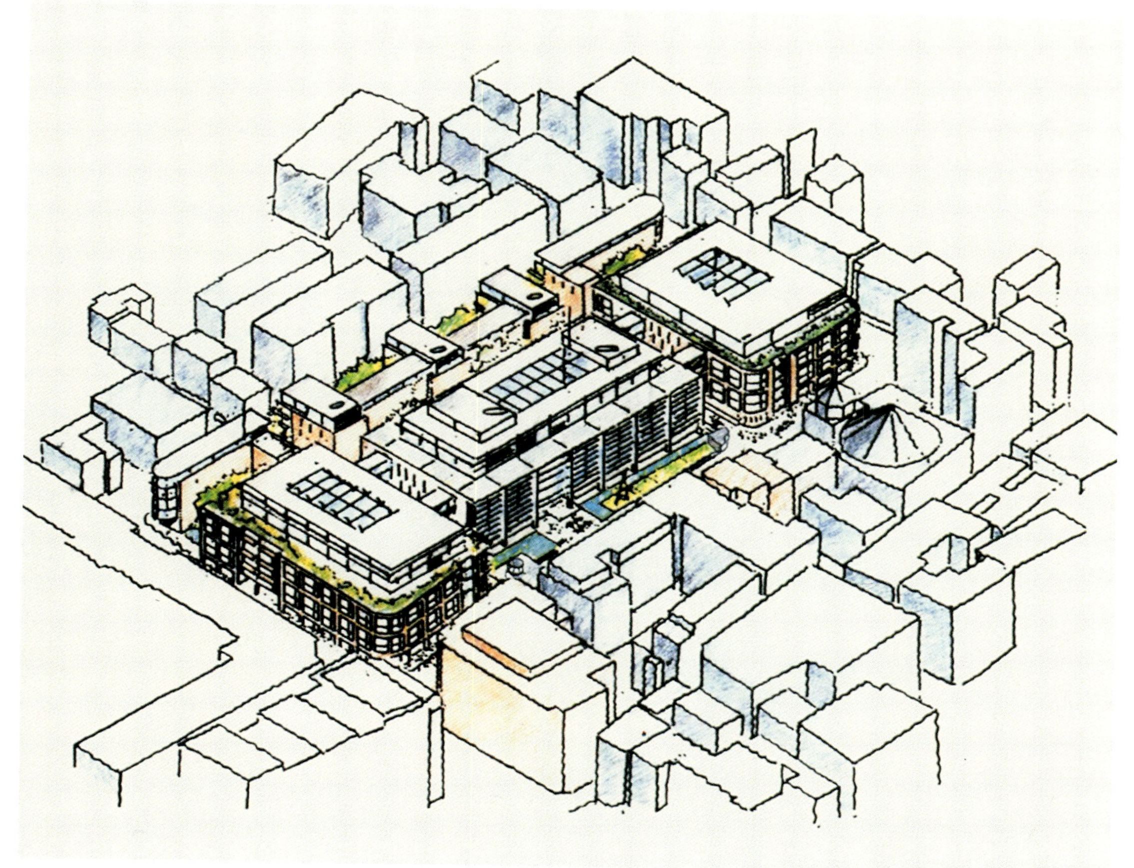

Axonometric from the south-east by Aidan Potter.

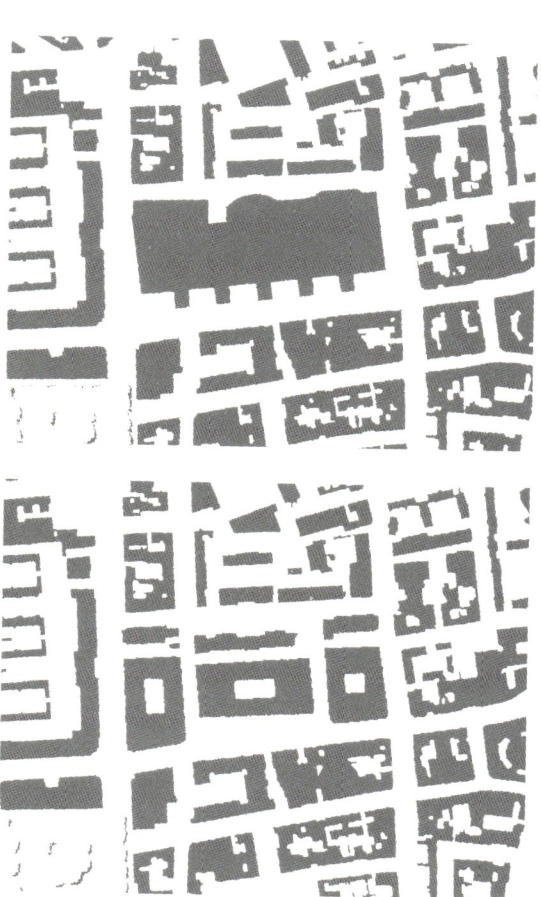

Top: Figure ground before conversion.
Bottom: Figure ground after conversion.

given over to residential use – is complemented by a 1430-square-metre public garden.

Rather than being designed as inward-looking courts, these public spaces are oriented towards the street to maximize accessibility. Three 'pocket parks' within the site envelope create additional external space and pleasing views for office workers. In contrast with the existing building, which discourages public access, routes that give priority to pedestrians have been carved through the new site to link Marsham Street with Monck Street – reflecting Terry Farrell's belief that great towns are places where wheels take second place to feet as a mode of transport.

Inside the building, excellent levels of natural light are provided by glazed atria, which ensure that 95 per cent of occupants are within 6 metres of daylight. A naturally lit internal 'street' runs the length of the three buildings. Equipped with amenities such as a library, a café and a print shop, and giving access to the pocket parks – this central axis is a place for office workers to meet.

Marsham Street demonstrates a relatively pared-down design approach by TFP but retains many of the practice's signature touches. The building's form – three simple glazed boxes – recalls the lightness and transparency of the

Long section through the site.

recently completed Sheraton Spa building in Edinburgh, but is devised on the grander scale appropriate to a government headquarters building. Marsham Street also reinforces the practice's reputation for 'groundscrapers' – low-lying buildings designed for city life that were first seen at Vauxhall Cross and which now characterize TFP's architectural style in cities from Seattle to Seoul.

As in all of TFP's current work, Marsham Street combines architectural innovation with a resolution of urban design issues. The scheme will not only provide a flexible and cost-effective state-of-the-art headquarters building, but will also foster a new community-oriented district far from the shadows of the three 'ugly sisters'.

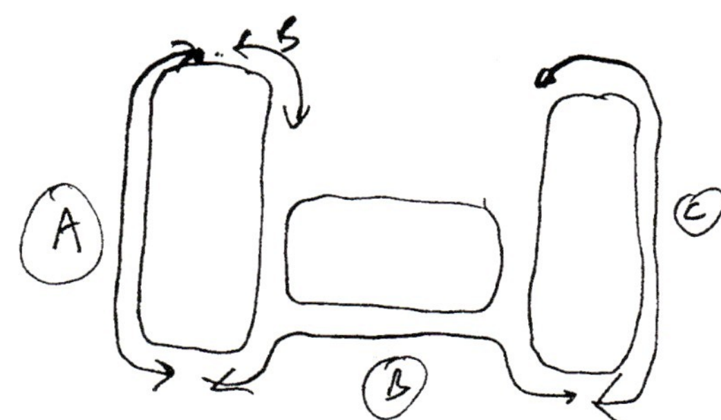

Top right: Concept sketch by Terry Farrell showing elevational variety.

Top left: Model view.

Bottom left: The urban design of the exterior is followed into the building's interior planning. An internal street with subsidiary side streets and main squares form community spaces – accommodating up to 5000 people, the headquarters is like a village in its own right. The internal urban design disciplines the three buildings and connects the internal with the external urban design story as one of the scheme's most powerful elements.

Top right, bottom right and opposite: On one level, the large-scale building, or 'gentle giant', sits within the neighbourhood with its own urban design story broken down in scale to form neighbourhoods, squares and streets at an appropriate scale. At another level, it functions as a large-scale linked-up headquarters building. The result is a reduction in scale that makes for a habitable headquarters building.

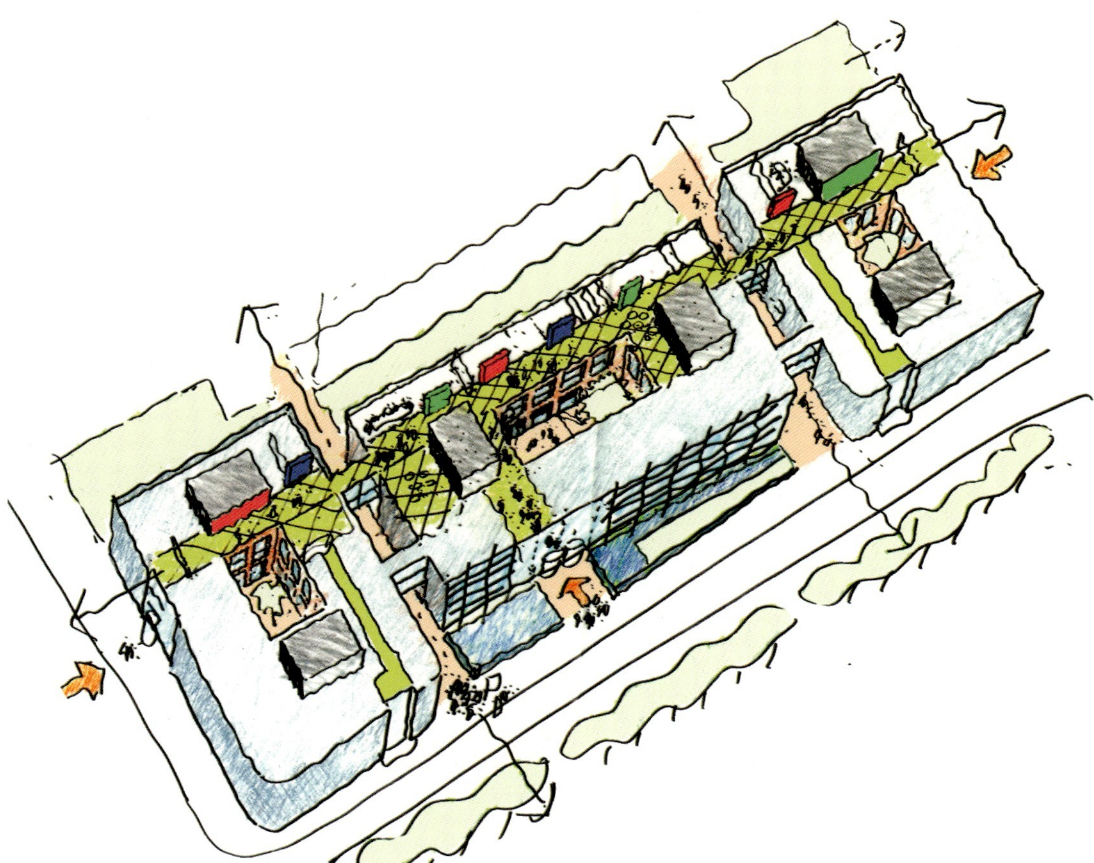

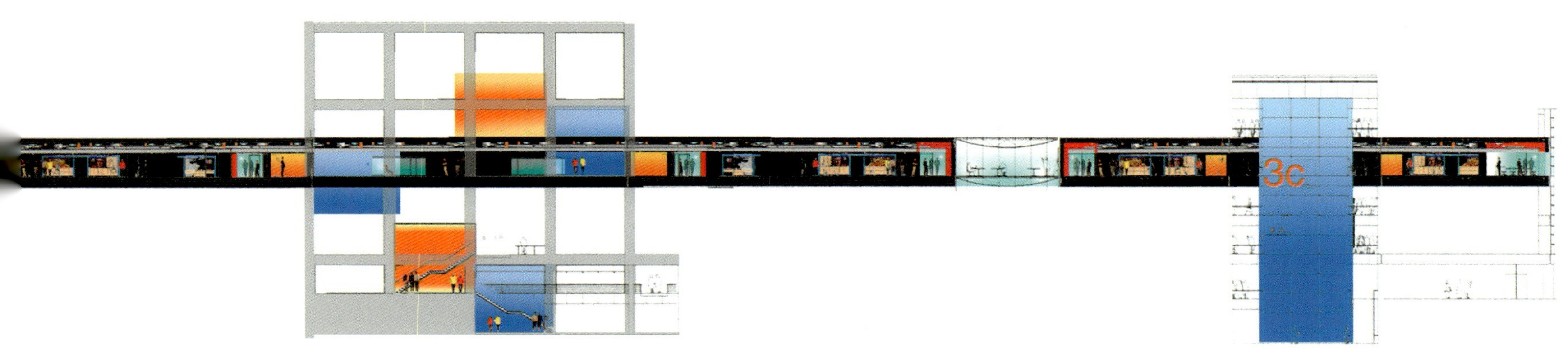
3c

THREE QUAYS HOTEL

Designated a World Heritage Site, the Tower Environs quarter is bounded by the edge of the Tower precinct, the walls of the Tower of London and the River Thames. The whole complex is encircled by two major traffic arteries. In a feasibility study of 1996, Terry Farrell & Partners suggested ways of breaking through these barriers by introducing pedestrian routes and a new link to St Katherine's Dock. Other proposals included improvements to Tower Wharf, East Gate and Tower Bridge Approach, Tower Hill and West Gate, and Trinity Square.

The 3879-square-metre Three Quays site – visible from Greenwich Park in the south and from Primrose Hill in the north – occupies a rectangular patch of land, largely reclaimed from the river, on the north bank of the Thames. The existing office building, Three Quays House, will be redeveloped to provide hotel and retail use. The scheme is separate from, but compatible with, proposals for enhancing facilities at the Tower of London as an engine for economic regeneration within the Pool of London (the area between London Bridge and Tower Bridge).

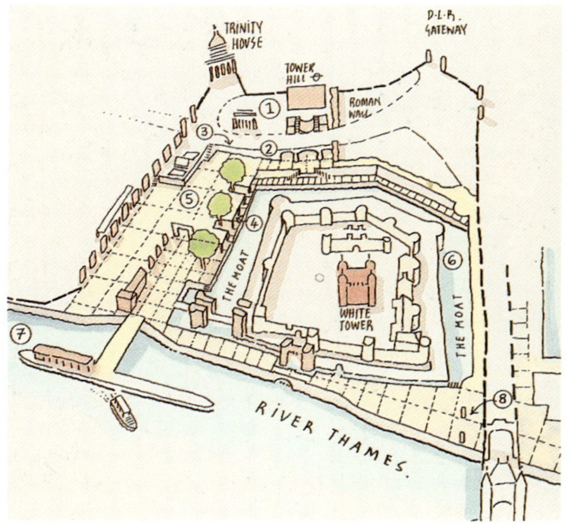

Above and top right: Three Quays is located next to the Tower of London and Tower Bridge, with HMS Belfast opposite.

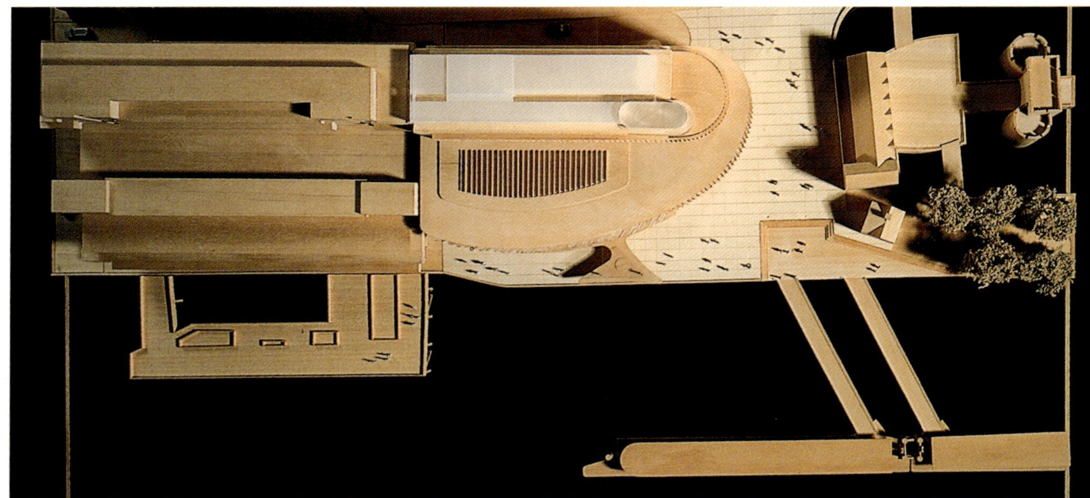

The scheme creates the opportunity to provide a better entrance, new pier and access to the Tower complex.

The design of Three Quays Hotel represents a calm and ordered statement that respects the river frontage in its massing and intention and makes an appropriate terminal point for the riverside 'terrace' that runs between London Bridge and the Tower. A new public square, to be built alongside the pump house at the Tower's western entrance, will add animation to the riverside walk and provide a focus for a new Tower Pier and improvements to the Tower's entrance. Horizontal massing ensures that the building will blend into its surroundings, and its overall scale is designed to harmonize with, rather than shrink from, the Tower itself.

Articulated into two distinct and contrasting elements separated by an expressed stone cornice, the building's primary mass comprises a lower five-storey block on its south side, lining the river, which is surmounted by three storeys of guest accommodation on the north side, facing Lower Thames Street. These two volumes allow the scale of the hotel to reflect the varying scales of its immediate neighbours.

The scale and form of the street front are quite distinct from those of the river front. The street front provides an anchor for the building and a strong corner entrance, while the river front shows how the building breaks downs into separate components. In this way, the form of the building has been manipulated to maximize views of the Tower of London: gently curving along a sight line dictated by the view from London Bridge towards the Tower, the south elevation is designed to reveal the whole of the White Tower. Additionally, the eastern end of the upper volume terminates in a radial form and steps down to reveal views of the pump house, while the upper, three-storey volume is set back from the river front to maintain its sight line to the Monument and allow a full view of the Pool of London in front of Tower Bridge. The east elevation, adjacent to the Tower, is characterized by vertical stone fins that provide a private and solid front. Behind these fins are patterns expressing the building's underlying horizontality, with the alternating patterns of windows and balconies maintaining the same rhythm as expressed on the north and south elevations.

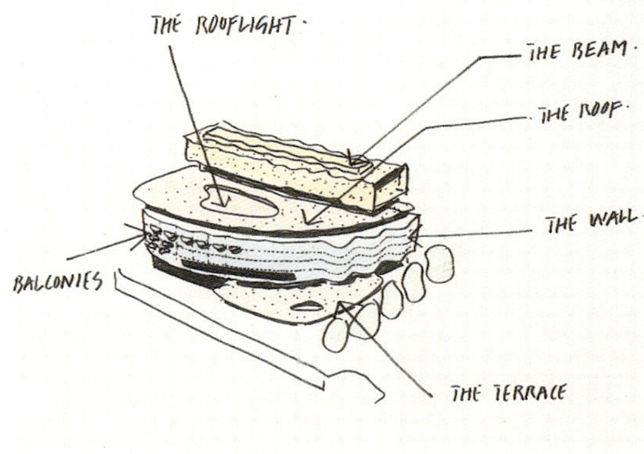

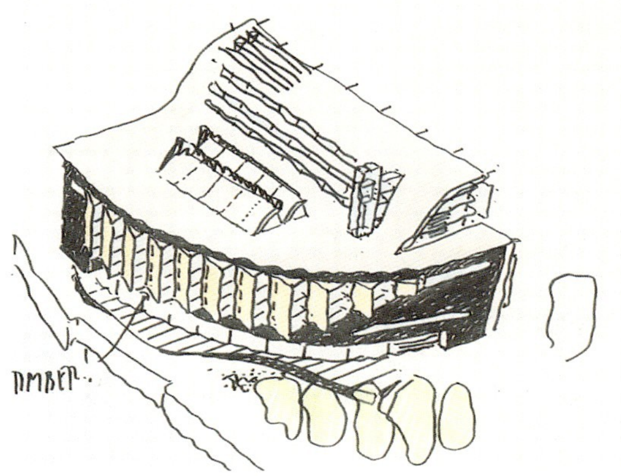

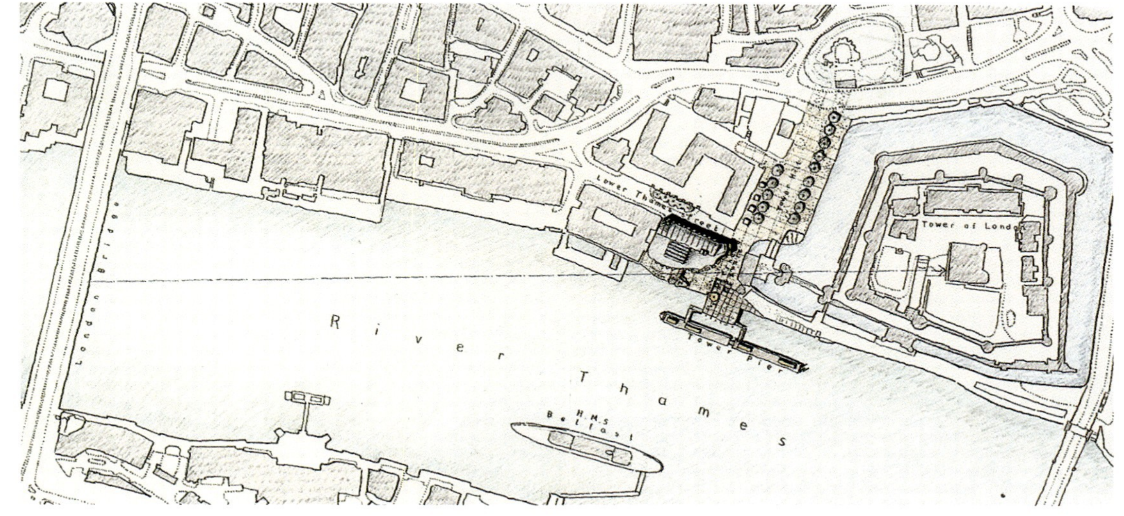

Site plan.

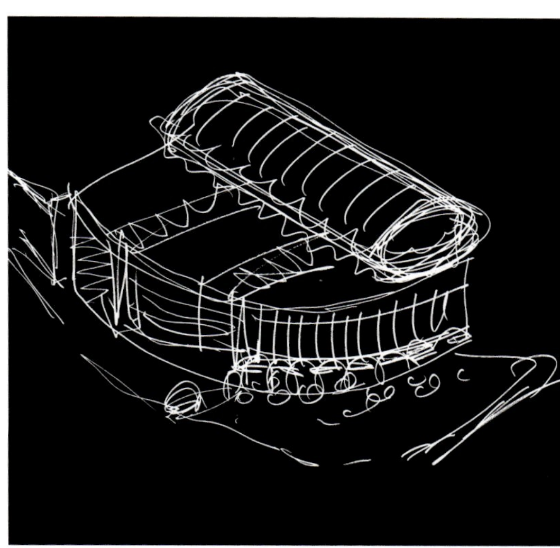

From top to bottom: Initial sketch by Terry Farrell and concept sketches by Aidan Potter.

Various views of the building. The stone and glass façade provides different expressions for each elevation.

PADDINGTON BASIN
+ ORANGE HEADQUARTERS

Top left: Paddington Basin in the context of London's urban villages and parks.

Bottom right: Perspective.

Top right: Context plan by landscape architects Gillespies. TFP's scheme is part of an assemblage of five masterplans designed by individual architects in collaboration.

Paddington Basin, a five-hectare site on the Grand Union Canal in West London, has had a rich and varied past. This one quarter symbolizes the historic village of Paddington as well as a 2000-year old point of exit and arrival for London, marked by Watling Street, one of the city's few Roman roads. The 18th-century canals, Brunel's railway station and the 1960s Westway represent three further layers of history. With the advent of the railways in the 1850s, the basin faced an early decline. By the 1940s the land bordering the canal banks and the industrial facilities at Paddington Basin lay neglected. Over the next 30 years, almost all the old buildings were demolished. The final blow came in 1970, when the opening of Westway, a major traffic artery, sliced off a key quarter of north Paddington. In the 19th century, the basin was a busy thoroughfare; today, with Westway soaring above and traffic on Harrow Road speeding past, it is a cut-off quarter badly in need of regeneration. Paddington Basin is now being stitched together again. The Heathrow Express, based at Paddington Station, brings the airport into the town, and Orange Communications has chosen to set up its corporate headquarters at this place where so many historic layers converge.

As a direct result of Terry Farrell & Partners' experience at Kowloon Station and its linked air-rights development – the 'in-town' airport – Paddington Station was regarded as a crucial element in the redevelopment proposals. TFP saw that the Heathrow Express would make Paddington a key location, and that the basin's three core sites – the Heathrow Express terminal, Paddington Goods Yard and an air-rights development on top of Paddington station itself – would make the location an even more important gateway to London than King's Cross to the east.

By the early 1980s, Westminster City Council had decided to redevelop the Paddington Basin site. A decade later, after various failed efforts, the new site owner, European Land, brought in TFP as

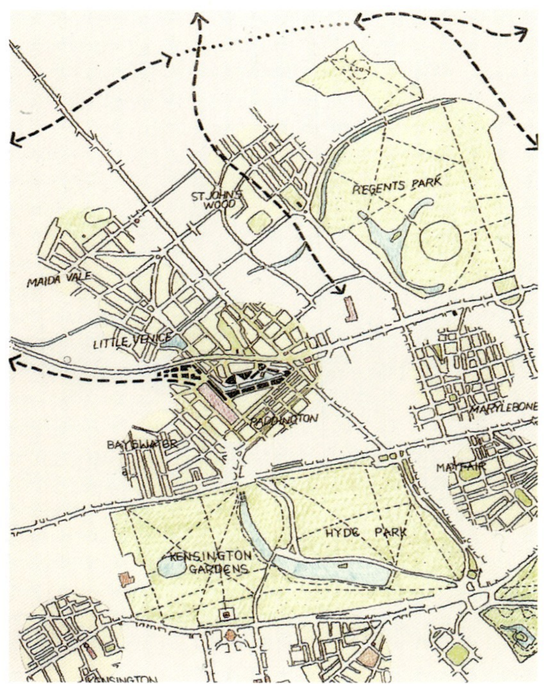

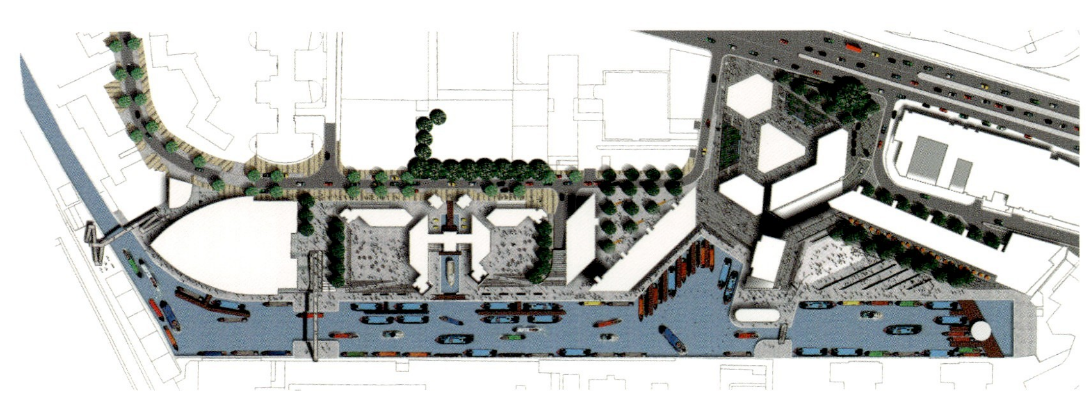

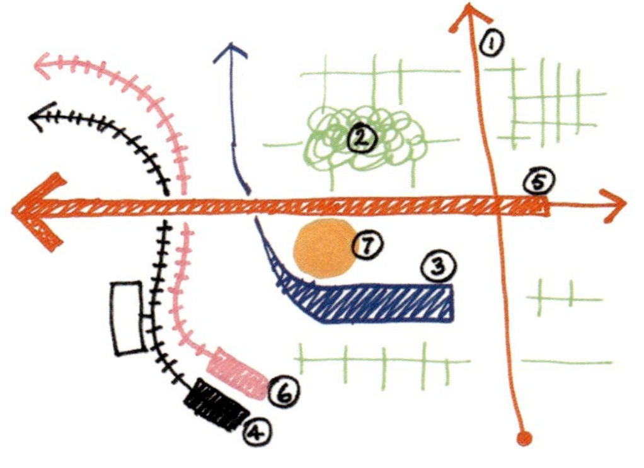

Opposite, bottom left: Concept sketch by Terry Farrell. Paddington Basin has always been a major western gateway to London:
1. The Roman Empire arrival point (Watling Street begins at Marble Arch: 1st century AD)
2. The village of Paddington emerges (centred around Paddington Green: 13th century to present)
3. The Grand Union Canal arrival point (Paddington Basin: 18th century)
4. The Great Western Railway arrival point (Brunel's Paddington Station: 19th century).
5. The motorway network arrival point (A40 motorway and the Edgware Road flyover: mid-20th century)
6. Air travel arrival point (Heathrow Express: late 20th century)
7. Electronic satellite communication arrival point (Orange headquarters: 21st century).

This page: Following the demise of the 19th- and 20th-century transportation industries, the big issue for the masterplan is permeability across all systems, rebuilding the village of Paddington and reconnecting it to London and, via the Heathrow Express, the world beyond.

masterplanners. The initial focus was on lands west of the station. TFP then proposed the inclusion of the area east of the station, the Goods Yard to the north and the St Mary's Hospital lands. In what was to be the defining element of the masterplan, the Heathrow Express terminal was located to the east in order to open up direct access by thousands of users to the basin area. The £400 million mixed-use scheme proposed extensive housing, shopping and waterside leisure facilities and office accommodation. TFP saw the basin as a potential extension of London's West End.

The former industrial nature of the basin meant that the original buildings were constructed hard up to the waterside. Consequently, there are almost no points at which the public can reach the water, which is hidden from view and remains inaccessible to much of the surrounding community. TFP's 1996 masterplan combined a canalside walk with extensive circulation areas at the western and eastern ends of the basin, as well as links with the surrounding area. Local amenities such as shops and restaurants were located within these hubs, functioning as magnets to bring people through the network of pedestrian routes. Planning permission was granted in November 1998.

The architectural character of the scheme is based on four blocks with seven-storey bases, with set-backs to create rooftop expressions. Landscaped roof terraces, pedestrianized open spaces and inlets for mooring boats combine to create a vision of diversity and richness. TFP's masterplan aims for permeability, with links through the buildings to new moorings and across to St Mary's Hospital.

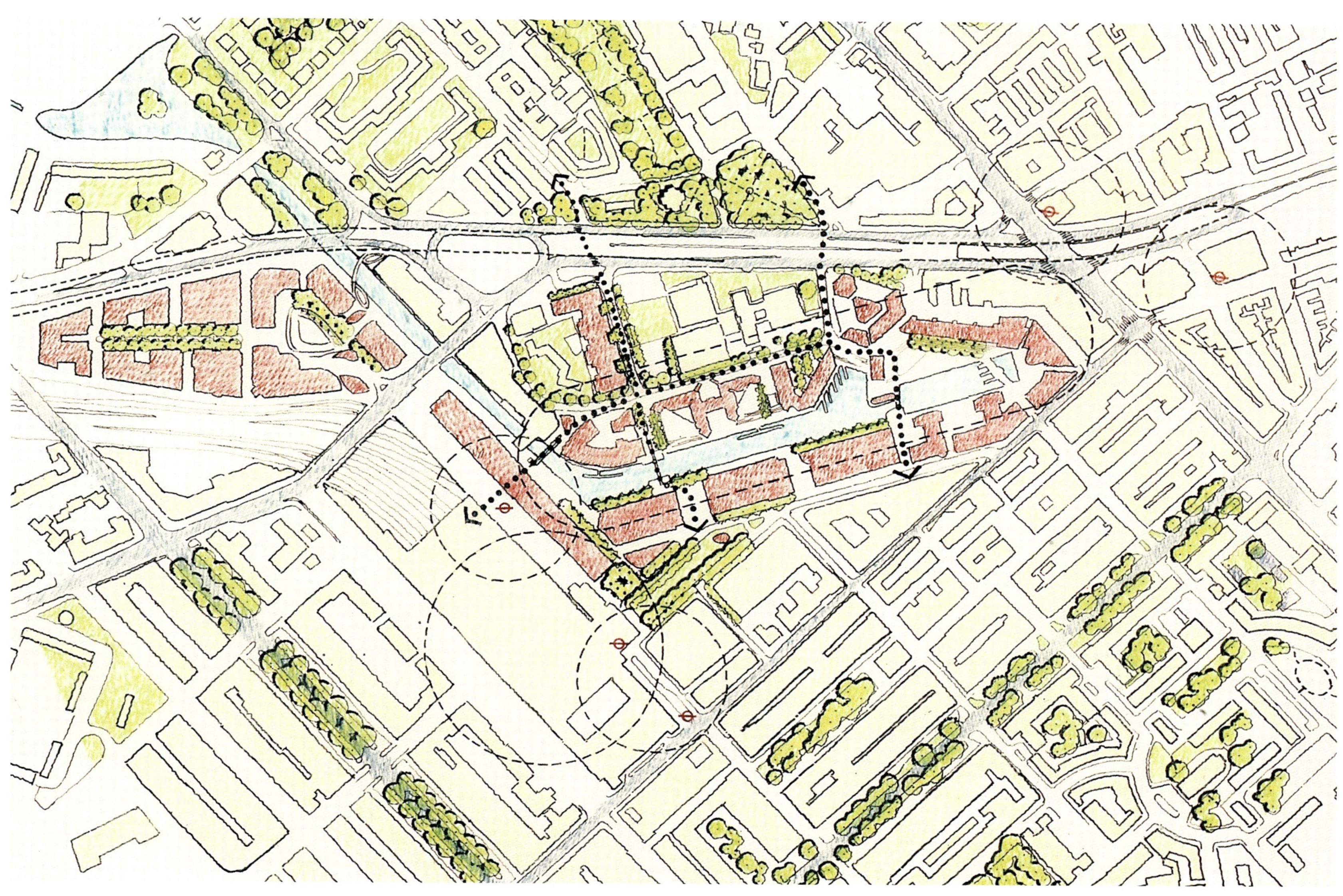

The Point comprises 20,000 square metres of office space over ten storeys in a wedge shape that forms the gateway to Paddington Basin. Located on the western edge of the waterfront next to Paddington station, the flagship office building sets the high standards to which the whole basin development aspires. The building is planned with two main entrances to accommodate different tenancy options, with a central bank of eight lifts, two of which are glazed and situated within a glass atrium.

The triangular massing of the building is a response to the site, with curved sides to the north and south, and two towers, with a recessed entry between them, to the east. The ground and lower-ground levels have full-height glazing recessed behind a colonnade of polished concrete columns. The two curved façades above this, forming levels one to six, comprise full-height glazing behind a frame of expressed vertical metal fins, creating a strong vertical rhythm. When seen from an oblique angle, the fins give an impression of solidity, while giving the building's occupants good views of the basin. Between the fins on the south side is a timber brise-soleil that provides effective solar-energy control to the office space and gives a strong identity to the exterior. On the north side the fins hold a 'light shelf' that reflects light into the office space while maintaining the external expression of the south side.

In contrast with the more modelled lower floors, the upper three floors have a 'smooth skin' climate façade. The east elevation is a simple composition of two glazed towers addressing the adjacent plaza.

It is proposed that the building will become the Orange telecommunications company headquarters. TFP's fit-out proposal for Orange incorporates interactive areas on the ground and lower-ground levels, as well as the terraced seventh level. The atrium is developed conceptually as a vertical street with layout to all levels embracing the transparency of the building. This is achieved by maximizing good views and sight lines, natural ventilation and light. As people move around the building, they will experience the activity generated by its inhabitants and their interactive process.

The forward-looking aesthetic of the fit out reflects the values of Orange in choice of materials and fittings. The relationship of spaces and uses is based on an inherent flexibility that enhances the working structure of the company, thereby promoting innovation and success.

Left: Concept drawing of the Orange headquarters.

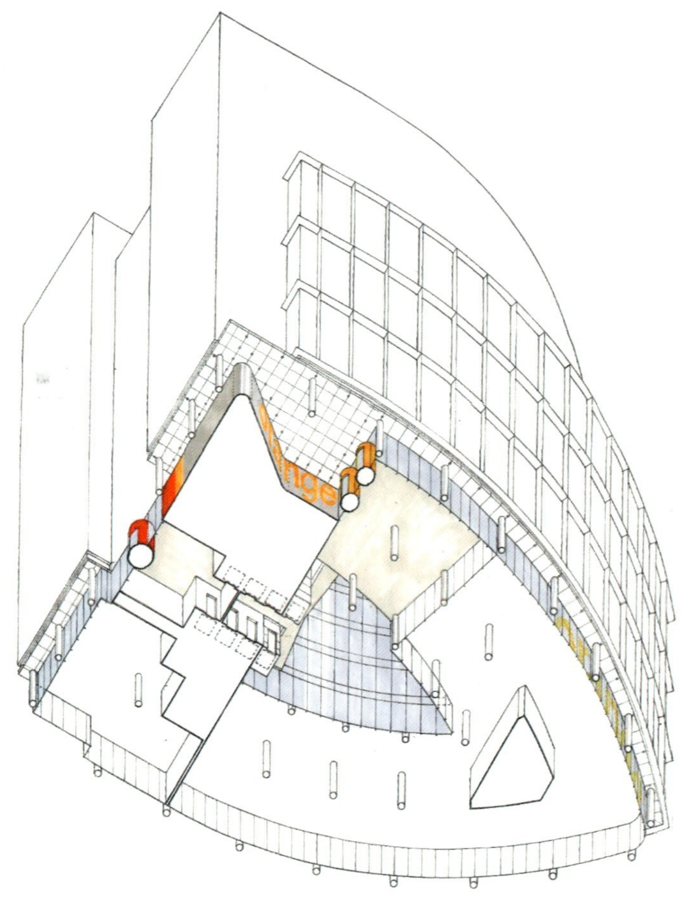

Right: Upward-looking view showing the ground floor.

Model and CAD drawing.

SWISS COTTAGE MIXED-USE DEVELOPMENT

Terry Farrell & Partners are part of an initiative to create a new cultural heart in Swiss Cottage, an existing urban village which, together with Highgate, Hampstead, Chalk Farm, Camden and Kilburn, forms inner north-west London. Through the agency of Public Private Finance, new social and welfare amenities will re-create the original concept for a civic-cultural centre for this central location. The site is currently occupied by the Swiss Cottage library and sports centre, designed by Sir Basil Spence between 1963 and 1964. The library, a Grade II listed building and a modernist icon, will be retained.

The masterplan comprises a new landscaped civic space – the subject of an international competition won by Gustafson Porter – a new community centre, doctor's surgery, café/bar, innovative social housing, private apartments and state-of-the-art leisure centre, designed by TFP and a new regional theatre designed by Rab Bennetts. Combined with existing facilities (sheltered housing for the elderly, a youth centre, restaurants and shops, an outdoor market and local offices) and close to public transport, the scheme will establish a vibrant cultural heart in the new urban quarter.

New routes through the scheme from Adelaide Road, a street between the library and leisure

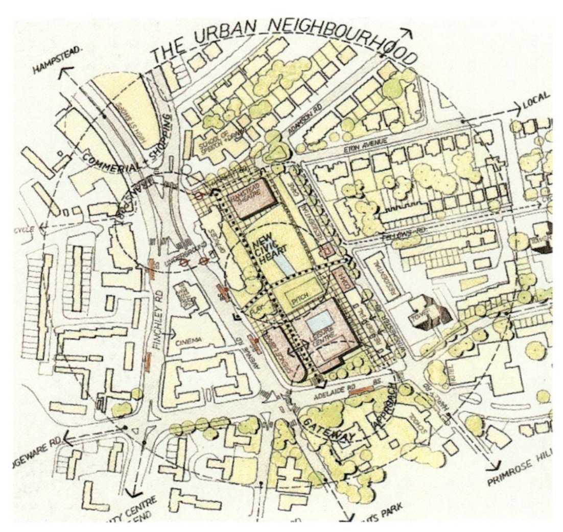

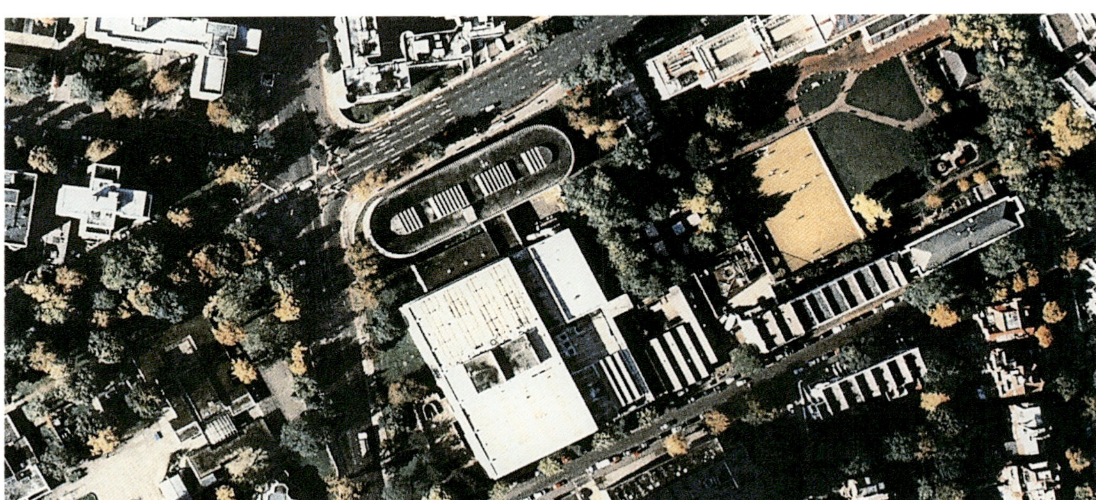

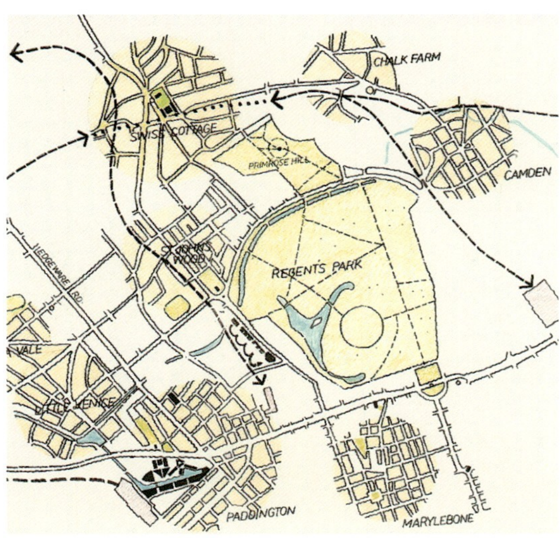

Bottom left: The urban neighbourhood around the Regent's Park area.

Top left: Swiss Cottage is a genuine town centre. The redevelopment project is a good example of architecture growing from urban design and creating – together with Rab Bennetts, John McAslan, Gustafson Porter and the late Basil Spence – one of London's most positive mini urban villages.

Bottom right: Masterplan.

Top right: Aerial view of Basil Spence's existing library and sports centre of 1963–64.

Concept sketches by Terry Farrell.

The existing situation has no permeability. There is a failure at an urban level and considerable neglect of the areas around the existing buildings.

building and a mews adjacent to the residential terrace will reinforce the the site's permeability, creating improved physical and visual links around the centre and surrounding areas.

Located beneath a unifying roof, the leisure centre provides a clear and legible circulation system that mirrors the building's civic scale. Large-span spaces containing the sports hall and pool are arranged either side of a central spine housing gym and changing rooms. The shared entrance with the library provides a pedestrian link through the scheme, joining Adelaide Road to the interior of the public space. A completely transparent enclosure, the leisure centre will provide vibrant and animated elevations that act as illuminated beacons attracting visitors into the complex.

Social housing has been placed at the centre of the development above the leisure centre. The rooftop accommodation has balconies overlooking the central south-facing rooftop garden with panoramic views of London. Private residential apartments occupy a stepped and sloping terrace that rises from six to 16 storeys at the southern end of Winchester Road. The new community centre doubles the current provision and occupies the first two floors of the northern end of the terrace, containing a new multi-purpose hall, meeting rooms, a crèche and café. The balance of social housing is located above the community centre, creating a terrace height sensitive to the adjoining buildings. The ground floor of the Winchester Road terrace contains live-work units and private entrances to the apartments above, which will animate the street. This is in stark contrast to the existing leisure building which presents blank façades to the street. The four steps of the terrace are occupied by duplex or triplex penthouses with their own extensive terraces offering views of the new civic space.

The southern section of the terrace contains apartments and penthouses that benefit from spectacular south-facing views over London. The highest point of the whole development, the terrace tower and sloping south façade respond to the scale of the adjoining towers and generate a landmark statement.

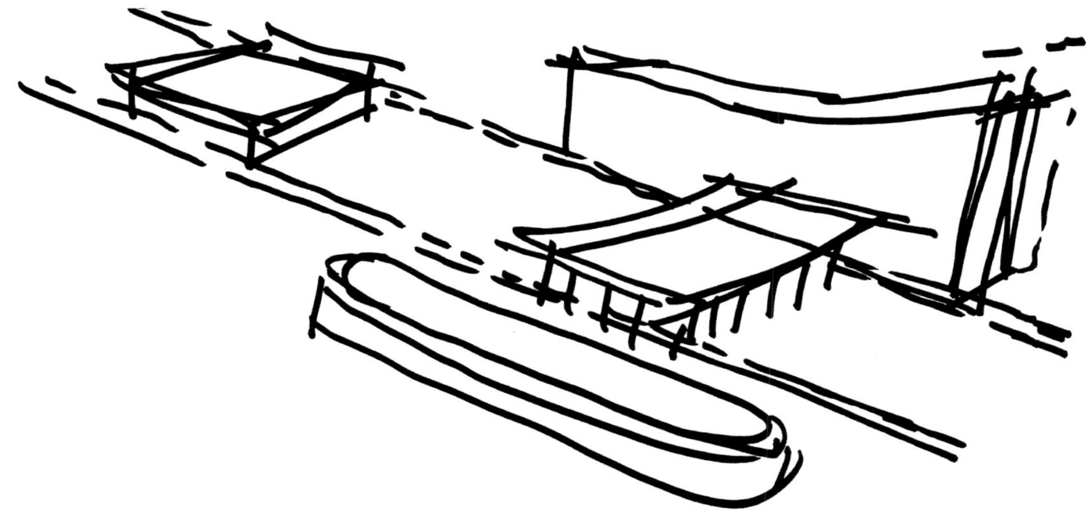

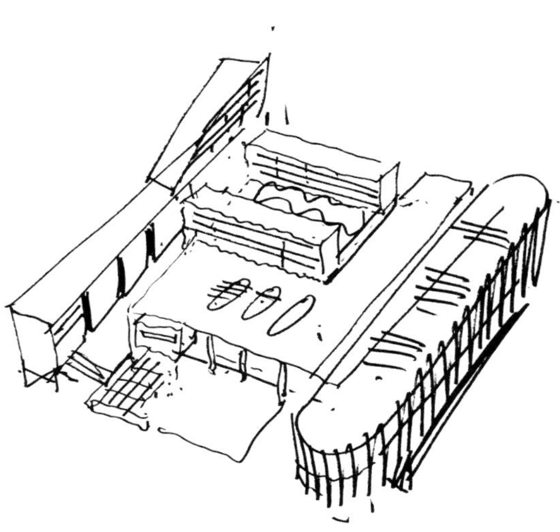

Aerial view of the proposed scheme.

Bottom left: Gustafson Porter's new park.

Bottom right: TFP's proposed residential building on Winchester Road.

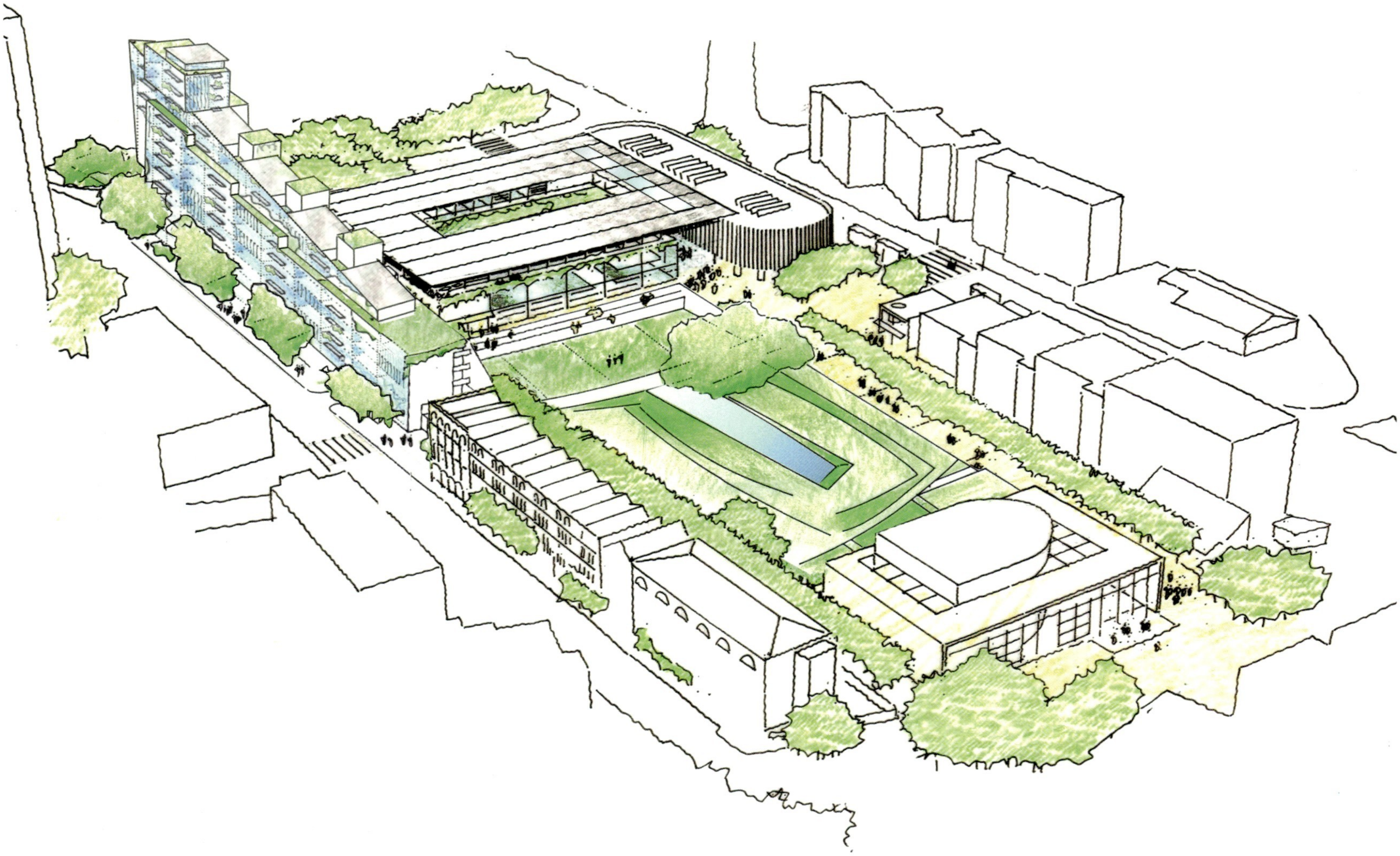

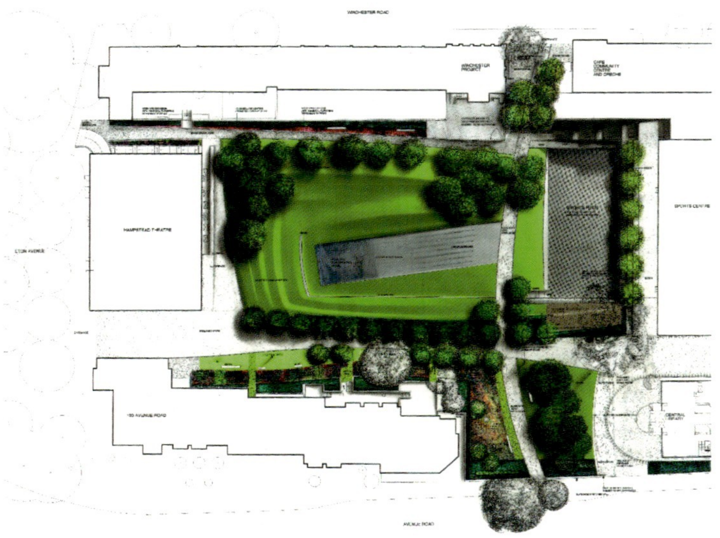

TFP's new civic building provides sports and leisure facilities, library access, shops and a doctor's surgery, while low-cost public housing is situated above.

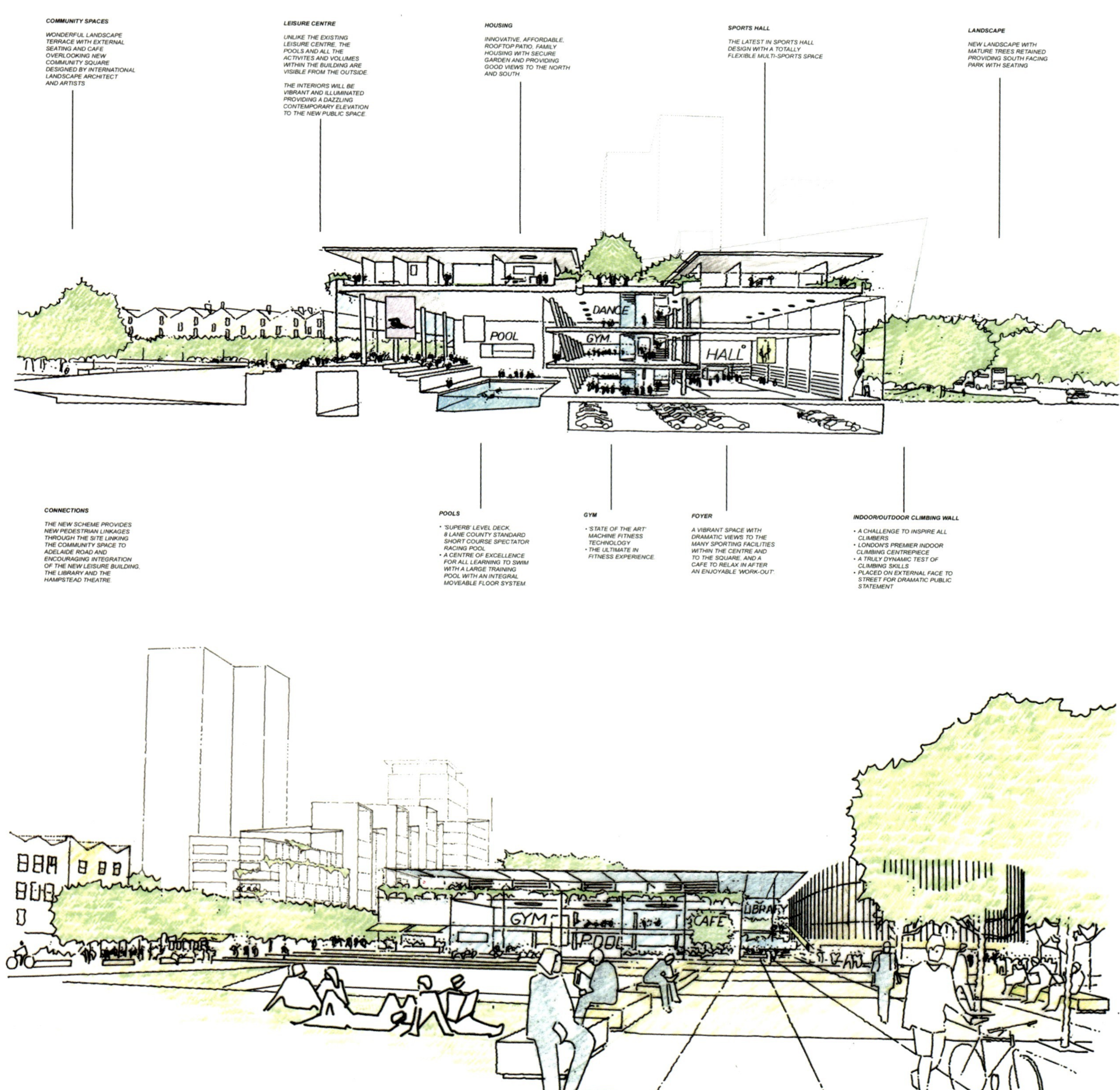

SAMSUNG EUROPE HEADQUARTERS

London's west side is characterized by historic gardens and parks. Following the serpentine course of the River Thames, these 'non-urban' domains are to be found at Boston Manor, Richmond, Chiswick, Kew, Syon, Ham, Hampton Court and Bushy. The M4 corridor cuts east–west across the landscape, bringing traffic to and from Heathrow airport and points further west.

Terry Farrell & Partners was commissioned by Samsung in 1996 to design their Europe headquarters in London. At the meeting point of the Great West Road and the elevated section of the

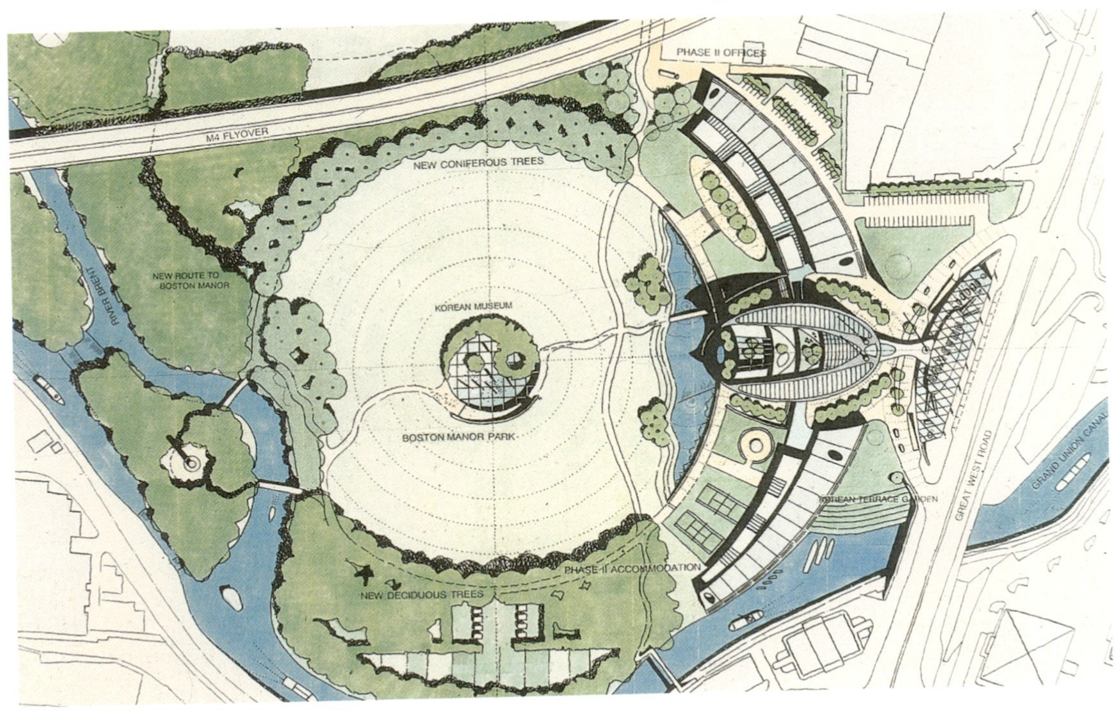

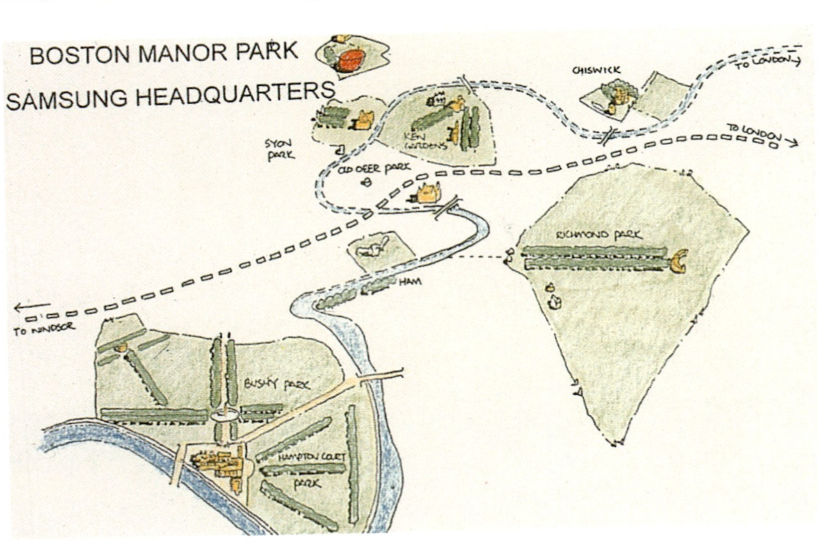

Top and bottom left: Samsung's site is linked into the outer villages of Boston Manor and Chiswick, as well as the great parks going out west, where landscape designer Geoffrey Jellicoe worked on several large plans.

Top and bottom right: Set within parkland, the headquarters building contributes to the surrounding landscaped areas.

M4 motorway, next to the historic Boston Manor Park, the site is clearly visible from an aeroplane approaching Heathrow airport. To capitalize on this, the design – a crystal in parkland – is articulated to form a distinctive gateway on the approach to London from the west. It represents Samsung's identity, its aspirations for the future, and a fusion between British and Korean culture. The architecture and landscaping strategy is inspired by traditional Korean architecture, which emphasizes the balance between a building and its natural setting.

In recognition of the site's visual prominence from major road, rail and air transport links, the building's form, a striking object in space, presents a dynamic image from all viewpoints. Consolidating the accommodation into a single tower achieves a coordinated solution for the whole area, while leaving a large part of the site free for future development, which was an important element in the Samsung brief.

Located on the central axis of Boston Manor Park, which is immediately adjacent to the site, the building comprises 43,600 square metres on 19 floors. Its innovative form – a tower, oval in plan and arranged around a central atrium that breaks open to the park – evolved from tried and tested plan forms, centralized core and flexible column-free space. Divided into three sections – base, middle and roof – the headquarters building reflects the tripartite nature of traditional Korean architecture. The base contains public spaces, reception, marketing and education facilities; the middle zone contains work spaces; and the top section contains welfare and executive functions.

The building envelope establishes a clean, simple image and a strong identity, creating a visual link between the heart of the building and the surrounding landscape. It forms a protective shell against the noise of nearby traffic and incorporates an environmental control system based on the use of solar energy. The split plan generates an axis that symbolizes links between Eastern and Western traditions. Landscaped to integrate with Boston Manor Park, the site is in keeping with the Korean convention that seeks harmony between nature and built form, as well as referencing the unified relationship between an English country house and its parkland setting. These two traditions share the qualities of the picturesque and the meeting between the formal and the informal.

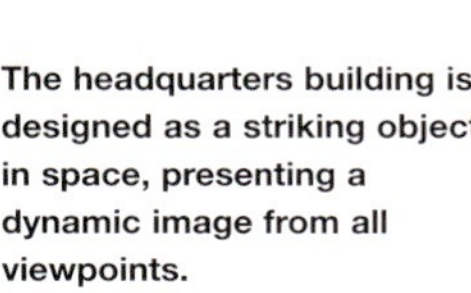

The headquarters building is designed as a striking object in space, presenting a dynamic image from all viewpoints.

The split plan generates a symbolic 'gateway' axis that links the urban frontage to the parkland setting.

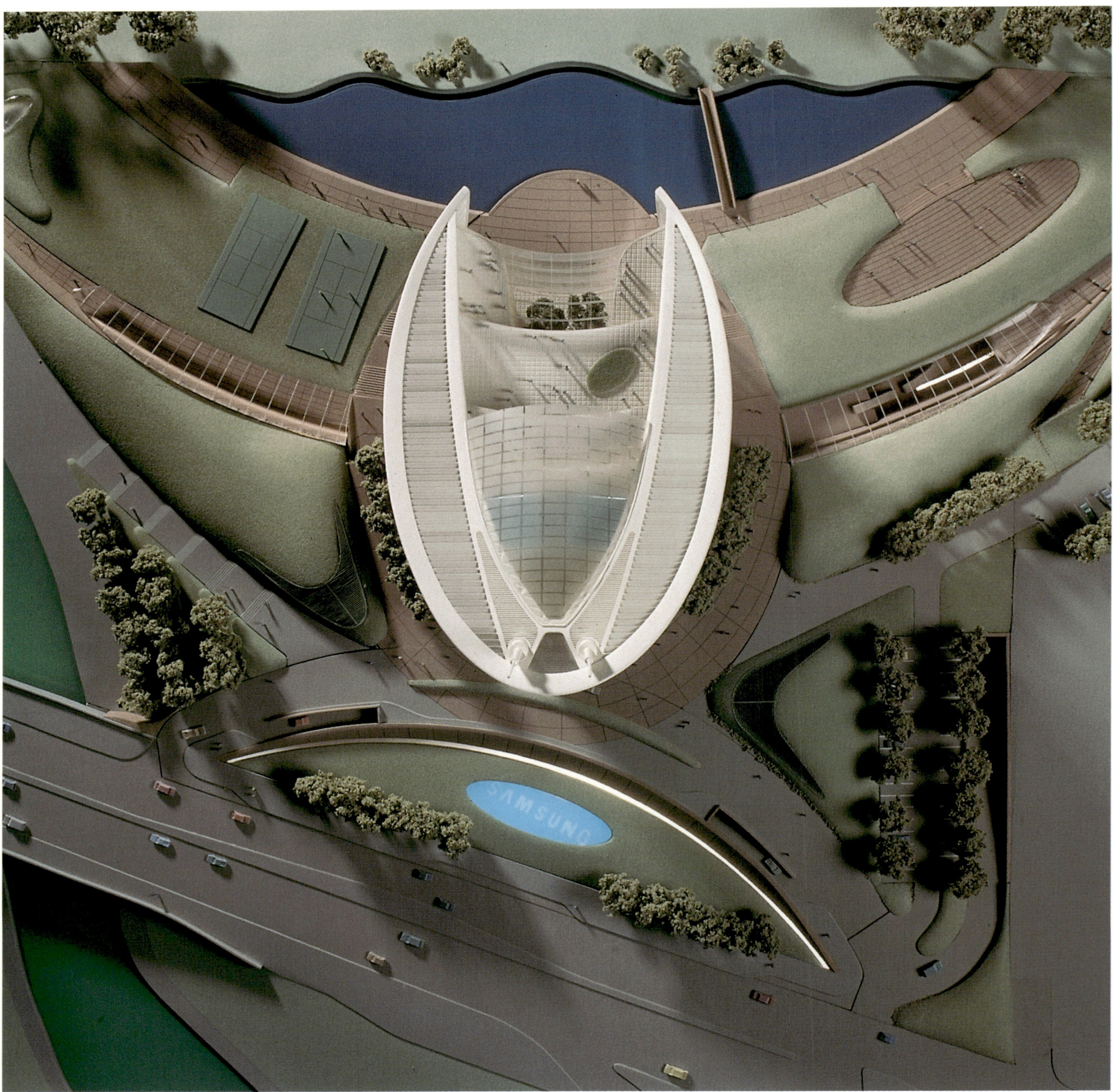

The innovative form of the 19-storey tower is an evolutionary development of tried and tested plan forms, with a centralized core and flexible column-free space.

APPENDIX

LIST OF WORKS 1991-2001

* Unbuilt scheme　　** Current project

1984–92
SOUTH BANK ARTS CENTRE MASTERPLAN*
London Borough of Lambeth

1986–91
MOOR HOUSE*
City of London, EC2

1987–92
ALBAN GATE
Lee House, 125 London Wall, London EC2
(p. 21)

1988–91
TEMPLE ISLAND
Henley-on-Thames, Berkshire
Restoration of historic building by Wyatt

1988–92
VAUXHALL CROSS
Government Headquarters Building (MI6)
Albert Embankment, London SE1
(pp. 22–23)

1989–91
TOWER HILL WINE VAULTS
Tower Hill, London EC3

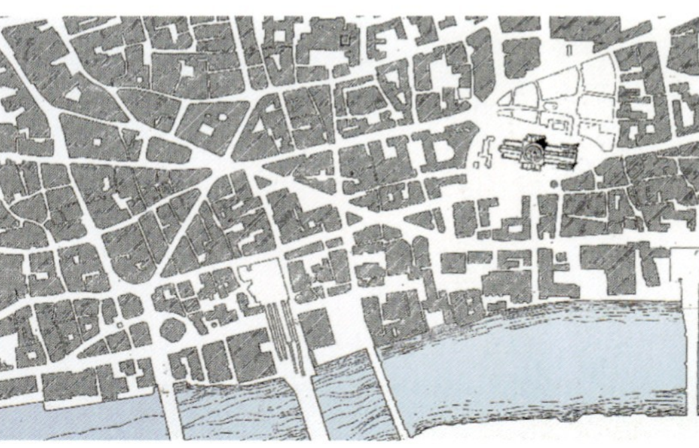

1989–92
PATERNOSTER SQUARE MASTERPLAN*
City of London, EC2
AIA Award for Urban Design, 1994

1989–92
MIXED-USE MASTERPLAN
Quarry Hill, Leeds

1989–92
CHISWICK BUSINESS PARK*
London Borough of Hounslow

1989–95
INTERNATIONAL CONFERENCE CENTRE
Morrison Street, Edinburgh
(pp. 176–185)
Silver Medal, Edinburgh Architectural Association Design Award 1995
Civic Trust Award 1996
RIBA Award 1996

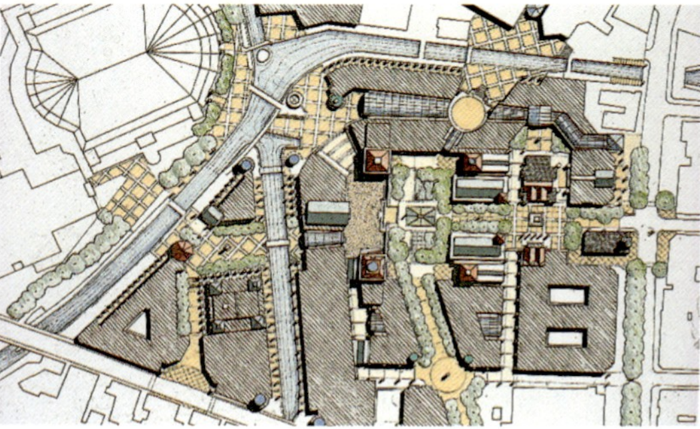

1990–92
BRINDLEYPLACE MASTERPLAN
Birmingham

1990–2001
EXCHANGE FINANCIAL DISTRICT MASTERPLAN
Edinburgh
(pp. 176–191)

1990–
SOUTH KENSINGTON STATION AND MIXED-USE DEVELOPMENT**
London SW1

1991
MEDICAL CENTRE
South Birmingham

REPORT ON THE DEVELOPMENT OF HEATHROW AIRPORT FOR THE BRITISH AIRPORTS AUTHORITY

COMMONWEALTH TRUST OFFICES AND CLUB*
London WC1

SPITALFIELDS MARKET MASTERPLAN*
London E1

WESTMINSTER HOSPITAL REDEVELOPMENT
Horseferry Road, London SW1

LLOYDS BANK HEADQUARTERS*
Pall Mall, London WC2

1991–92
LLOYDS BANK REDEVELOPMENT*
Lombard Street, EC1

MIXED-USE RENOVATION AND REDEVELOPMENT
Grey Street, Newcastle
(p. 209)

1991–93
THAMESLINK 2000 MASTERPLAN
Blackfriars, London*
(p. 253)

1991–95
THE PEAK TOWER
Hong Kong
(pp. 28, 35, 77, 78–85)

1991–98
EAST QUAYSIDE MASTERPLAN
(pp. 210–215)
Urban Design Award, Civic Trust 1998
Lord Mayor's Design Award, Landscape & Accessibility Category (Commendation) 1998
RTPI Spaces Award 1998
Civic Trust Urban Design Award 1998
BURA Best Practice Award 1999

1991–98
RAILWAY DEVELOPMENT*
Farringdon Station, London EC1

1991–
HOME OFFICE HEADQUARTERS**
London SW1
(pp. 282–289)

1992
CANON'S MARSH
Bristol

EXPO 98 MASTERPLAN*
Lisbon waterfront
(pp. 158–159)

FORT CANNING RADIO TOWER
Singapore*

1992–94
SAINSBURY'S SUPERMARKET
Harlow, Essex
Civic Trust Award 1994
RIBA Award 1995
Commendation, Civic Trust Award 1996

1992–95
PLAYER'S THEATRE
Embankment Place, Villiers Street, London WC2

1992–96
GOVERNMENT HEADQUARTERS FOR BRITISH CONSULATE AND BRITISH COUNCIL
Hong Kong
(pp. 35, 46–55)

1992–96
ROYAL PARKS STUDY
Royal Parks Review Group, London
(pp. 270–271)

1992–98
KOWLOON STATION
Hong Kong
Masterplan for transport interchange with associated buildings
(pp. 35–37, 56–77)
Best International Interchange Award, Integrated Transport Awards 2001

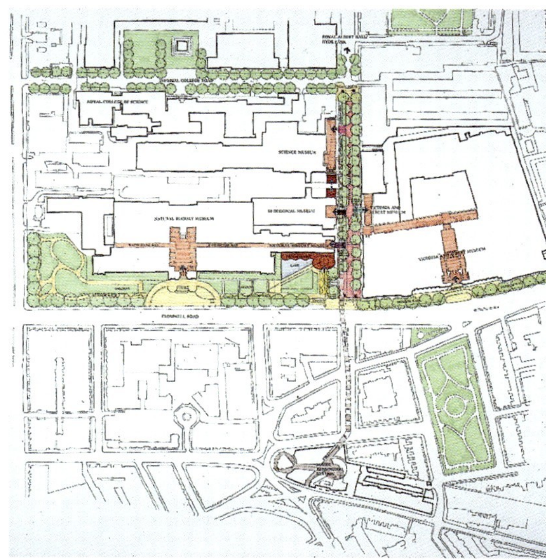

1993
ALBERTOPOLIS OUTLINE PROPOSAL
London SW1*

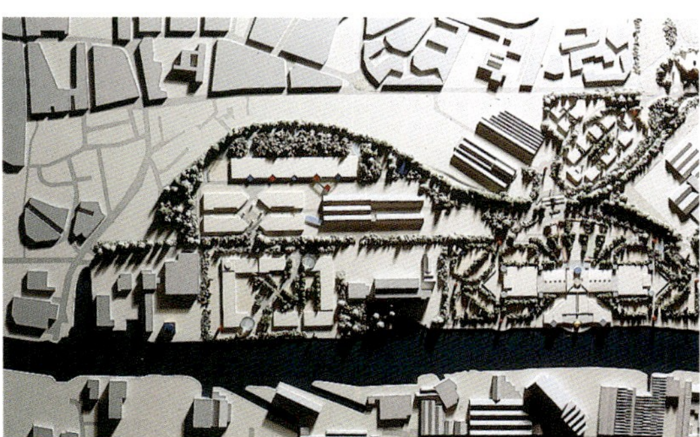

BRAEHEAD RETAIL COMPLEX
Glasgow *

AMPANG TOWER*
Kuala Lumpur

BLACKFRIARS BRIDGE*
London
(p. 253)

SMITHKLINE BEECHAM HEADQUARTERS COMPLEX*
Great Burgh, Epsom, Surrey

NEW NATIONAL GALLERY OF SCOTTISH ART AND HISTORY*
Kelvingrove Park, Glasgow

HUNGERFORD BRIDGE REDEVELOPMENT*
London
(p. 253)

EFFRA SITE*
Vauxhall, London SW8

1993–95
KOWLOON VENTILATION BUILDING
Hong Kong
(pp. 72–77)

BARREIRO FERRY STATION AND MASTERPLAN
Lisbon
(pp. 166–171)

NATIONAL HERITAGE LIBRARY AND CULTURAL CENTRE
Dubai*

VASTERAS RAILWAY STATION*
Vasteras, Sweden

1993–96
DO ROSSIO STATION MASTERPLAN
Lisbon
(pp. 162–165)

1993–2007
LONDON BRIDGE STATION REDEVELOPMENT**
London

1994
GARE DO ORIENTE*
Lisbon
(pp. 160–161)

SINCERE INSURANCE BUILDING
Hong Kong
(p. 37)

NATHAN ROAD TOWER*
Hong Kong
(p. 37)

SHEKOU MASTERPLAN*
Shenzen

'CHESTER IN CONCERT' PERFORMANCE SPACE*
Chester

1994–95
QUEEN'S ROAD MASTERPLAN*
Hong Kong

1994–96
KEELE UNIVERSITY MASTERPLAN*

1994–98
EBBSFLEET MASTERPLAN*
Kent
(p. 255)

1994–
PORT OF LISBON MASTERPLAN
Lisbon waterfront
(pp. 154–157)

1995
SUBIC BAY FREEPORT CENTRAL AREA MASTERPLAN*
Philippines

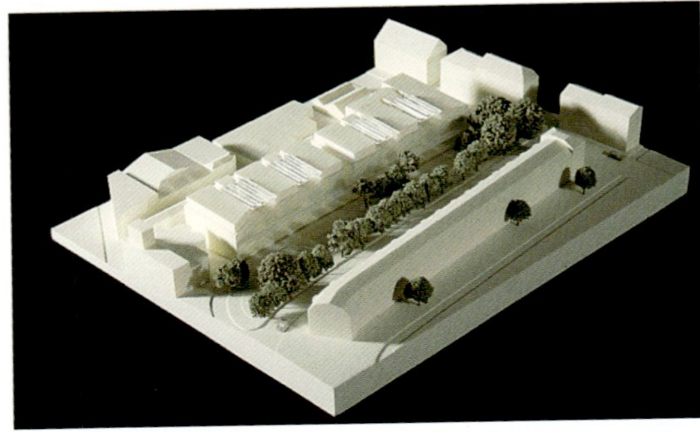

GLASGOW BUSINESS SCHOOL*
University of Glasgow

KENNEDY TOWN RAILWAY STATION*
Hong Kong

CAMBOURNE MASTERPLAN
South Cambridgeshire

'C' BUILDING*
Seoul
(pp. 116–117)

LANDMARK TOWER
Kowloon
(p. 37)

LANDMARK BUILDING*
Northumberland Cross, Northumberland

1995–96

IMPERIAL WHARF REDEVELOPMENT
London

1995–99

'Y' BUILDING*
Seoul
(pp. 112–115)

'H' BUILDINGS*
Seoul
(pp. 118–121)

1995

WEST RAIL
Hong Kong
Station scheme design and masterplanning of West Kowloon Passenger Terminal, Kam Tin, Lok Ma Chau, Tseun Wan West, Yen Chow Street and Mei Foo stations
(pp. 36, 58–59)

1996

HIGH-SPEED RAILWAY STATION
Pusan, Korea*

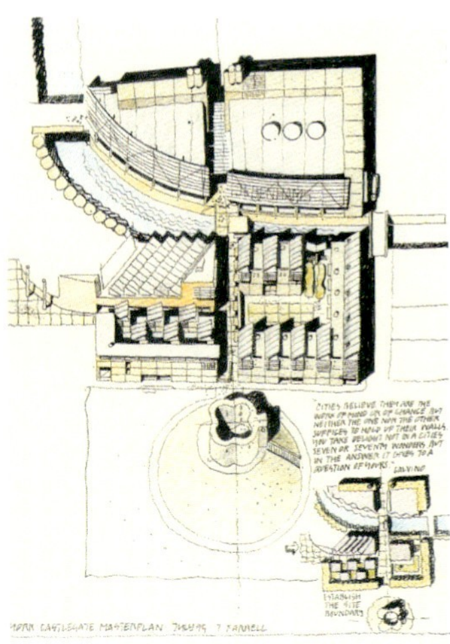

MIXED-USE REDEVELOPMENT MASTERPLAN OF HISTORIC CENTRE*
Castlegate, York

STAR FERRY TERMINAL REDEVELOPMENT*
Hong Kong

FEASIBILITY STUDY TO FIND NEW VENUE FOR ENGLISH NATIONAL OPERA LYRIC THEATRE

SAMSUNG EUROPE HEADQUARTERS*
Boston Manor Park, London
(pp. 302–305)

UNIVERSITY OF EAST LONDON MASTERPLAN*

1996–99

DEAN CENTRE ART GALLERY AND MASTERPLAN
Edinburgh
(pp. 175, 192–201)
Scottish Museum Award (Highly Commended) 1999

HEALTH CLUB AND SPA
Exchange Financial District, Edinburgh

1996–2000

BLUEWATER VALLEY MASTERPLAN
Kent
(p. 254)

INTERNATIONAL CENTRE FOR LIFE
Newcastle
Landmark Millennium Project housing a new public square and a series of buildings with facilities to explore genetic science
(pp. 216–235)
Celebrating Construction Achievement Award (North-East), 2000
Copper in Architecture Awards (Commendation) 2000

1996–2001

TRANSPORTATION CENTRE, INCHON INTERNATIONAL AIRPORT**
Seoul
(pp. 102–111)

1996–2003

PADDINGTON BASIN MASTERPLAN**
London W2
(pp. 294–297)

1996–2005

LONDON BRIDGE STATION**

1996–

LOTS ROAD**
Power Station and new housing
Chelsea, London
(pp. 272–281)

THREE QUAYS HOTEL/TOWER ENVIRONS MASTERPLAN**
London, SE1
(pp. 290–293)

1996–

STATION IMPROVEMENT PROGRAMME
Hong Kong

1997

BUCKLERSBURY HOUSE OFFICE AND RETAIL DEVELOPMENT*
London EC4

COMPUTER LABORATORY*
University of Cambridge

MTV EUROPEAN HEADQUARTERS*
London NW1
Air rights development

HUNGERFORD BRIDGE COMPETITION SCHEME*
London

SHANDONG INTERNATIONAL CONFERENCE AND EXHIBITION CENTRE
Qingdao, China

1997–2001
CRESCENT HOUSING**
Newcastle
(p. 213)

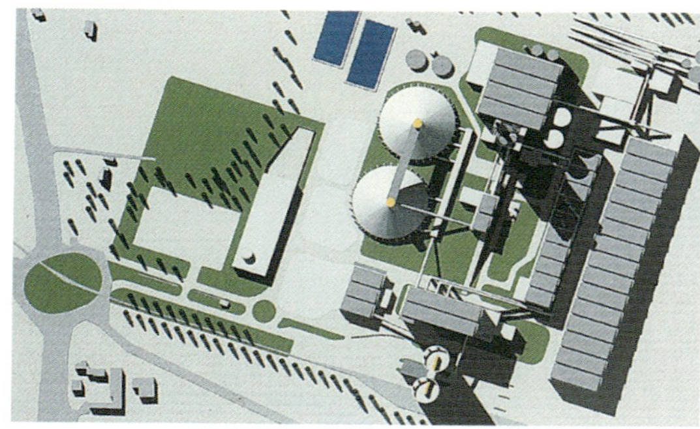

1997–2002
BLUE CIRCLE CEMENT WORKS**
Kent
(p. 255)

1997–
NATIONAL AQUARIUM**
Silvertown, London
(pp. 258–263)

1998
FERENSWAY MASTERPLAN
Hull

CAPABILITY GREEN BUSINESS PARK*
Luton

CARLTON TV HEADQUARTERS*
London W1

CHELSEA BARRACKS
London
Residential scheme for existing barracks and rehousing of barracks to new site in New Covent Garden Market

GRESHAM STREET REDEVELOPMENT
London EC2
(p. 282)

ISLAND WHARF
Hull

LIVERPOOL VISION MASTERPLAN*

MARITIME SQUARE*
Singapore
Waterfront masterplan and architecture

RESTORATION AND DEVELOPMENT OF 15–17 CHARLOTTE SQUARE
Edinburgh

PICCADILLY GARDENS*
Manchester

ARCHITECT'S STUDIO
7 Hatton Street, London NW8

SPRINGHEAD MASTERPLAN*
Ebbsfleet, Thames Gateway

1998–99
BRITISH UNIVERSITY MASTERPLAN*
Cairo

PUNGGOL STATION**
Singapore

1998–2000
NATIONAL OPERA HOUSE*
Tian'anmen Square, Beijing
(pp. 90–97)

WESTFERRY CIRCUS OFFICE DEVELOPMENT**
Canary Wharf, London E14

ELEPHANT & CASTLE MASTERPLAN*
London SE1

1998–2001
GREENWICH PROMENADE**
London SE10
(pp. 264–269)

THE DEEP**
Sammy's Point, Hull
(pp. 240–249)
Landmark Millennium Project housing a world-class aquarium exhibit, business and research centre

1998–
EUSTON STATION REDEVELOPMENT**
London

1999
BERMONDSEY SQUARE MASTERPLAN*
London

BOROUGH ROAD MASTERPLAN*
London

COURTYARD DEVELOPMENT*
Fitzwilliam Museum, Cambridge

THE MOUND*
Edinburgh
Undercroft linking National Galleries of Scotland with Royal Scottish Academy
(pp. 202–205)

OUSEBURN VILLAGE MASTERPLAN
Newcastle

RIVER HULL CORRIDOR MASTERPLAN*
(pp. 238–239)

AQUARIUM AND MASTERPLAN FOR PACIFIC NORTH-WEST**
Seattle
(pp. 140–149)

BUSINESS COMMUNITY AND MIXED URBAN DEVELOPMENT
Stonecastle, Kent

MASTERPLAN FOR DISUSED COLLIERY SITE
Westoe Hill, South Shields

WORLD SQUARES MASTERPLAN
London
(p. 270)

ROYAL INSTITUTION OF GREAT BRITAIN REDEVELOPMENT**
Albemarle Street, London W1

1999–2001

WATERFRONT REGENERATION
Margate

CAMPBELL PARK MASTERPLAN
Milton Keynes

1999–2003

BANK ONE HEADQUARTERS*
Cardiff

2000–

SOUTHERN GATEWAY**
South central Manchester
Mixed-use development in new urban quarter

BLUEWATER VALLEY MASTERPLAN**
Kent

BRUNSWICK SQUARE REDEVELOPMENT
Leeds

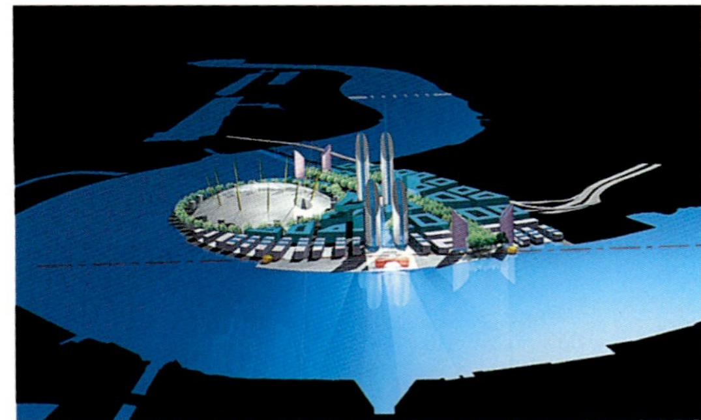

NORTH GREENWICH PENINSULA MASTERPLAN
London

CLYDE CORRIDOR MASTERPLAN**
Glasgow

CULTURAL PLAZA FOR GUANGZHOU DAILY HEADQUARTERS BUILDING**
Guangzhou
(pp. 42–45)

PARADISE STREET REDEVELOPMENT
Liverpool

FORTH TOWERS**
Edinburgh
Commercial building

PARRAMATTA RAIL LINK
Sydney**
(pp. 124–133)

PEARL ISLAND MASTERPLAN**
Shenzen
(pp. 38–41)

ROYAL DOCKS MASTERPLAN*
London
(pp. 256–257)

SWISS COTTAGE REDEVELOPMENT**
London NW3
(pp. 298–301)

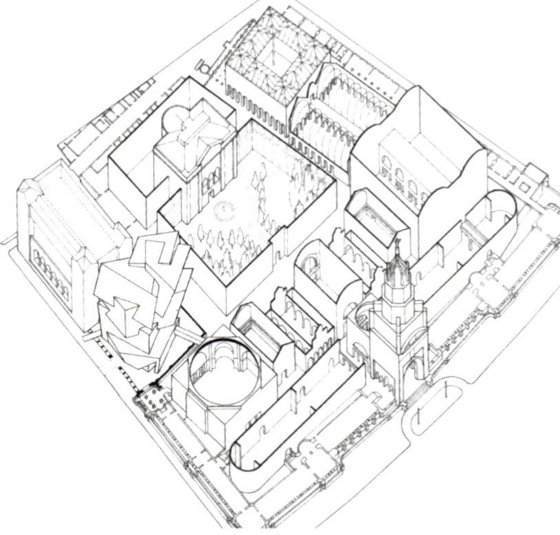

VICTORIA & ALBERT MUSEUM MASTERPLAN*
London SW1

SOUTH SEATTLE MASTERPLAN**
(pp. 138–139)

2001

ORANGE HEADQUARTERS**
Paddington, London
(pp. 294–297)

BRISTOL BREWERY MASTERPLAN**

PETERSHAM HOUSING
Richmond, London**

Design partners (left to right) Doug Streeter, Terry Farrell and Aidan Potter.